TOWARD A CANON-CONSCIOUS READING OF THE BIBLE

New Testament Monographs, 34

Series Editor
Stanley E. Porter

Toward a Canon-Conscious Reading of the Bible

Exploring the History and Hermeneutics of the Canon

Ched Spellman

SHEFFIELD PHOENIX PRESS

2014

Copyright © 2014 Sheffield Phoenix Press

Published by Sheffield Phoenix Press
Department of Biblical Studies, University of Sheffield
Sheffield S3 7QB

www.sheffieldphoenix.com

A CIP catalogue record for this book
is available from the British Library

Typeset by CA Typesetting Ltd
Printed on acid-free paper by Lightning Source

ISBN-13 978-1-909697-26-3
ISSN 1747-9606

Dedication

For my Family
¡Lo Hicimos!

CONTENTS

viii*A Canon-Conscious Reading of the Bible*

1. The Book of Moses 67
2. The Book of the Twelve 69
3. The Fourfold Gospel 71
4. The Letters of Paul 79
5. The Grouping of the Groupings 83
6. The Role of the Believing Community 84
7. Summary 86
External Evidence Implies a Canon-Consciousness
among the Believing Community 87
1. External Evidence for the Shape of the Hebrew Bible 88
2. External Evidence for the Shape of the New Testament 95
Concluding Reflections 99

Chapter 3
THE CANONICAL FEATURE OF CONTEXTUALITY 101
The Canon Guides Readers through the Biblical Material 101
Canon as a Mental Construct 101
The Effect of the Canonical Framework 103
The Canonically Generated Metanarrative 106
The Canon Generates Textual Connections (Contextuality) 108
Mere Contextuality 110
Meant Contextuality 120
The Shape of the Hebrew Bible 123
The Shape of the New Testament 128
Concluding Reflections 140

Chapter 4
INTERTEXTUALITY WITHIN THE CANONICAL CONTEXT 142
The Study of Intertextuality 142
The Study of Biblical Intertextuality 148
A Production-Oriented Approach to Intertextuality 150
Intertextual Quotations 154
Intertextual Allusions 156
Intertextual Echoes 159
Discerning Intertextual Connections 161
Intertextuality within the Canonical Context 164
The Contextual and Intertextual Function of
The Book of Revelation within the Canonical Context 172
The Book of Revelation Fittingly Concludes the
New Testament Canon 172
Structural Connections 173
Verbal and Thematic Connections 174
Jesus' Book 174
Jesus' Lineage 175

PREFACE

> But resume your course, O my story, for this
> aging monk is lingering too long over marginalia.[1]

Traversing the long and winding road that led to the final form of this book has been both humbling and rewarding. I am grateful for the support and interaction with family, friends, and colleagues I have experienced along the way. I am particularly thankful for the faithful support of my wife Leigh Anne and my two spunky daughters Hope and Kate.

In line with the function of this autographic paratext, I will only preface the content of what follows further by articulating one of my favorite intertextual tautologies: What I have written, I have written.

Ched Spellman
Cedarville, OH

---

1. Umberto Eco's narrator Adso of Melk in *The Name of the Rose* (trans. William Weaver; San Diego, CA: Harcourt, 1994), p. 25.

LIST OF ABBREVIATIONS

ABD	*Anchor Bible Dictionary*
ANF	*The Ante-Nicene Fathers: Translations of the Writings of the Fathers down to A.D. 325* (ed. Alexander Roberts and James Donaldson; rev. A. Cleveland Coxe; American Reprint of the Edinburgh Edition; 10 vols.; Grand Rapids, MI: Eerdmans, 1983).
AF	*The Apostolic Fathers: Greek Texts and English Translations* (ed. Michael W. Holmes; Grand Rapids, MI: Baker, 2007).
Baba Bathra	*The Talmud of Babylonia: An American Translation* (ed. Jacob Neusner; Tractate Baba Batra; Chapters 1–2, 22A; Atlanta, GA: Scholars Press, 1992).
BDAG	*Greek-English Lexicon of the New Testament and Other Early Christian Literature* (ed. Walter Bauer; trans. and rev. W.F. Arndt, F.W. Gingrich and F.W. Danker; Chicago, IL: University of Chicago Press, 3rd edn, 2000).
BHS	*Biblia Hebraica Stuggartensia* (ed. K. Elliger and W. Rudolph; Stuttgart: Deutsche Bibelstiftung, 1977).
BJRL	*Bulletin of the John Rylands Library*
Canon Debate	*The Canon Debate* (ed. Lee Martin McDonald and James A. Sanders; Peabody, MA: Hendrickson Publishers, 2003).
CBQ	*Catholic Biblical Quarterly*
Did	*Didache*
DSS	The Dead Sea Scrolls
DBAT	*Dielheimer Blätter zum Alten Testament*
DTIB	*Dictionary for Theological Interpretation of the Bible* (ed. Kevin J. Vanhoozer; Grand Rapids, MI: Baker, 2005).
EH	Eusebius of Caesarea, *Ecclesiastical History* (or *Church History*), in *A Select Library of the Nicene and Post-Nicene Fathers of the Christian Church* (ed. and trans. Philip Schaff and Henry Wallace; 14 vols.; Grand Rapids, MI: Hendrickson, 1994), I, pp. 73-404.
ESV	English Standard Version
EuroJTh	*European Journal of Theology*
HALOT	*The Hebrew and Aramaic Lexicon of the Old Testament* (ed. Ludwig Koehler and Walter Baumgartner; Leiden: Brill, 1990).
Hermas	*The Shepherd of Hermas*
HTR	*Harvard Theological Review*
JBL	*Journal of Biblical Literature*
JETS	*Journal of the Evangelical Theological Society*
JSJ	*Journal for the Study of Judaism in the Persian, Hellenistic and Roman Periods*
JSNT	*Journal for the Study of the New Testament*
JSOT	*Journal for the Study of the Old Testament*
JTI	*Journal of Theological Interpretation*

JTS	*Journal of Theological Studies*
Kenyon	*The Chester Beatty Biblical Papyri: Descriptions and Texts of Twelve Manuscripts on Papyrus of the Greek Bible* (ed. Frederic G. Kenyon; 16 vols.; London: Emery Walker, 1933–41).
Lampe	*A Patristic Greek Lexicon* (ed. G.W.H. Lampe; Oxford: Clarendon Press, 1961).
Liddell–Scott	*A Greek-English Lexicon* (ed. Henry G. Liddell and Robert Scott; ed. and rev. Henry S. Jones; Oxford: Clarendon Press, 9th edn, 1996).
Louw-Nida	*Greek-English Lexicon of the New Testament based on Semantic Domains* (ed. Johannes P. Louw and Eugene A. Nida; New York: United Bible Societies, 2nd edn, 1989).
LXX	The Septuagint
MT	The Masoretic Text
NA[27]	*Novum Testamentum Graece*, 27th edn
NASB	New American Standard Bible
NICNT	New International Commentary on the New Testament
NIGTC	New International Greek Testament Commentary
NIV	New International Version
NPNF	*A Select Library of the Nicene and Post-Nicene Fathers of the Christian Church.*
NovT	*Novum Testamentum*
NRSV	New Revised Standard Version
NTL	New Testament Library
NTS	*New Testament Studies*
PMLA	*Publications of the Modern Language Association of America*
PNTC	Pillar New Testament Commentary
RBL	*Review of Biblical Literature*
Skeat	Theodore C. Skeat, *The Collected Biblical Writings of T.C. Skeat* (ed. J.K. Elliott; Supplements to Novum Testamentum, 113; Leiden: Brill, 2004).
SBL	The Society of Biblical Literature
Sira	*Ben Sira*
SP	*Studia Patristica*
SWJT	*Southwestern Journal of Theology*
TDNT	*Theological Dictionary of the New Testament* (ed. Gerhard Kittel and Geoffrey W. Bromiley; trans. Geoffrey W. Bromiley; 10 vols.; Grand Rapids, MI: Eerdmans, 1965).
Thayer	*A Greek-English Lexicon of the New Testament Being Grimm's Wilke's Clavis Novi Testamenti* (trans. and rev. Joseph Henry Thayer; New York: American Book Company, 1889).
TNTC	Tyndale's New Testament Commentaries
ubs[4]	*The Greek New Testament* (ed. Barbara Aland, Kurt Aland, Johannes Karavidopoulos, Carlo M. Martini, and Bruce M. Metzger; Stuttgart: Deutsche Bibelgesellschaft, 1993).
VTS	*Supplements to Vetus Testamentum*
WBC	Word Biblical Commentary
ZAW	*Zeitschrift für die Alttestamentliche Wissenshaft*
ZNW	*Zeitschrift für die Neutestamentliche Wissenschaft*
ZTK	*Zeitschrift Theologie und Kirch*

INTRODUCTION

Questioning Canon

What is the Bible, and how does it work? In a community of faith whose identity is directly related to a collection of sacred writings, these questions are particularly relevant. The Christian churches have rightly developed a high view of the biblical canon they have received. However, there is sometimes little reflection among evangelical believers on how this book actually came into being. Evangelical Christians confess the authority of a closed canon. However, evangelical treatments of bibliology have sometimes tended to neglect the formation of that canon in their construction of a doctrine of Scripture.[1] This disposition is unfortunate because one's understanding of the story of how the Scriptures came to be has a direct impact on how God's revelation is understood and how the Bible is interpreted.

Several scholars have recently called for a reversal of this perceived oversight. For instance, Craig Allert argues that 'delving into the important history of how our primary source documents came to be collected is a foundational issue' for those affirming a high view of Scripture.[2] Stephen

---

1. E.g., in his recent book *Words of Life: Scripture as the Living and Active Word of God* (Downers Grove, IL: IVP, 2009), Timothy Ward devotes one full page to the issue of canon formation and only a sentence to describing the actual process (pp. 91-92).

2. Craig D. Allert, *A High View of Scripture? The Authority of the Bible and the Formation of the New Testament Canon* (Grand Rapids, MI: Baker, 2007), p. 36. Noting that 'it is a significant lacuna that the understanding of the formation of the Bible is rarely broached by those who offer a "high view of Scripture"', Allert argues that 'a high view of Scripture should take account of the historical process that bequeathed to us the Bible' (p. 10). The question mark in Allert's title looms large, as he contends that the history of canon formation calls into question an evangelical 'high view' of Scripture. For Allert, 'a historical understanding of the formation of the New Testament canon should inform an evangelical doctrine of Scripture' primarily because 'the content of the biblical canon, as we know it today, was not a particularly early feature of ancient Christianity: the Bible was not always "there" in Christianity. Yet, the church still continued to function in its absence' (p. 12). In Chapters 1 and 2 below, I seek to take up this task in general and interact with some of Allert's arguments specifically. For a recent polemical defense of the authority of Scripture in light of the canon debate, see James M. Hamilton, 'Still Sola Scriptura: An Evangelical View of Scripture', in *The Sacred Text* (ed. Michael Bird and Michael Pahl; Piscataway, NJ: Gorgias Press, 2010), pp. 215-40.

Chapman issues a similar charge, arguing that an evangelical understanding of Scripture must deal directly with the implications of the canon formation process.[3] The question of how and why the Christian canon 'came to be' inherently involves a history that has implications for the reception of that canon among the community that views it as authoritative. Questions of canon thus have considerable significance for the doctrine of Scripture and the interpretive task.[4]

When discussing the function and formation of the biblical canon, there are generally two areas that require careful attention. First, external historical evidence is examined. This external evidence consists of extra-biblical material that mentions, quotes from, or expounds upon biblical material. Many times, this type of external evidence is the only kind of data that is used in understanding the formation of the canon. In recent years, though, there has been a recognition of the importance of internal evidence from the biblical texts themselves. This line of inquiry asks if the biblical writers might have had a robust 'canon-consciousness'.[5] If the biblical writers

3. Stephen B. Chapman, 'Reclaiming Inspiration for the Bible', in *Canon and Biblical Interpretation* (ed. Craig Bartholomew, *et al.*; Grand Rapids, MI: Zondervan, 2006), pp. 167-206. Chapman is primarily concerned with the notion of inspiration and how the canon formation process affects its claims. He asks, 'Can a theological doctrine of Scripture successfully embrace what history says about how Scripture became Scripture? Is the biblical canon an accident of history or an inspired work of God?' (p. 168).

4. Thomas Söding begins the wide-ranging collection of essays in *The Biblical Canons* (ed. J.M. Auwers and H.J. de Jonge; Leuven: Leuven University Press, 2003) by stating, 'Der theologische Anspruch des biblischen Kanons ist enorm' ('Der Kanon des alten und neuen Testaments. Zur Frage nach seinem theologischen Anspruch', in *The Biblical Canons*, p. xlvii). One of Söding's overarching concerns in developing a 'canonical hermeneutic' is to emphasize the theological impact of the concept of revelation on the formation of the Jewish and Christian canons. Similarly, Christoph Dohmen and Manfred Oeming begin their study of the 'what' and 'why' of the biblical canon by affirming, 'Die Bildung des biblischen Kanons ist für Theologie und Kirche von enormer Bedeutung' (*Biblischer Kanon: Warum und Wozu? Eine Kanontheologie* [Freiburg: Herder, 1992], p. 11). Bruce M. Metzger laments in 1987 that 'few works in English consider both the historical development of the New Testament canon and the persistent problems that pertain to its significance' (*The Canon of the New Testament: Its Origin, Development, and Significance* [Oxford: Clarendon Press, 1987], p. v). Metzger seeks to address this lacuna by including after his survey of external evidence a major section on historical and theological problems concerning the canon (pp. 251-88).

5. Stephen G. Dempster, 'Canons on the Right and Canons on the Left: Finding a Resolution in the Canon Debate', *JETS* 52 (2009), pp. 47-78, outlines the current state of the canon debate and makes a case for the relevance of internal as well as external evidence. He also emphasizes the value of the notion of 'canon-consciousness'. According to Brevard S. Childs, *Biblical Theology of the Old and New Testaments: Theological Reflection on the Christian Bible* (Minneapolis, MN: Fortress Press, 1992), pp. 70-71, this type of canonical approach argues that 'canon was not a late, ecclesiastical

wrote their books in light of other writings that were already deemed authoritative and in that sense 'canonical', this internal evidence can be useful in
the canon formation discussion.[6] An investigation of the internal evidence
also seeks to understand the function that individual writings serve within
the canon as a whole. In the interpretive task, the first step is to understand
how a particular document ended up in the collection of biblical writings.
The next step is then to understand how that individual writing functions in
its position in the wider collection.

With this step, the discussion moves from the realm of history to the
realm of hermeneutics. Once the canon has been established historically,
one can investigate the hermeneutical role that the concept of 'canon' plays
in the interpretive task. Recognizing the possibility that biblical writers and
later church leaders likely had some form of 'canon-consciousness' lends
support for a similar pursuit among subsequent generations of biblical interpreters. If a contemporary interpreter accepts the canon as a legitimate historical reality, then he or she would benefit from intentionally appropriating
this 'canon-conscious' mindset as well.

Outline of Thesis and Development of Argument

In this book, I will seek to demonstrate that contemporary interpreters of
the Bible have legitimate grounds for utilizing the concept of canon as
a control on the interpretive task. The notion of 'control' here is a way
of asserting that the concept of canon is a significant and meaningful
factor in biblical interpretation. In other words, this concept of canon both
guides and *governs* biblical readers.[7] These reflections also aim to provide

ordering which was basically foreign to the material itself, but that canon-consciousness
lay deep within the formation of the literature'. Cf. Daniel R. Driver's extensive discussion in *Brevard Childs, Biblical Theologian* (Tübingen: Mohr Siebeck, 2010), pp. 137-
59. Chapter 2 develops this notion of canon-consciousness.

6. See the section below on intertextuality. Cf. John Sailhamer, *Introduction to Old
Testament Theology: A Canonical Approach* (Grand Rapids, MI: Zondervan, 1995), pp.
212-13, who notes that 'many written texts, especially biblical ones, were written with
the full awareness of other texts in mind. Their authors assumed the readers would be
thoroughly knowledgeable of those other texts. The New Testament books, for example, assume a comprehensive understanding of the OT. Many OT texts also assume their
readers are aware and knowledgeable of other OT texts'.

7. Cf. the work of George Aichele, *The Control of Biblical Meaning: Canon as a
Semiotic Mechanism* (Harrisburg, PA: Trinity Press International, 2001), who examines how the concept of canon functions as a 'semiotic mechanism' that suppresses and
limits readers as they interact with the biblical text. Though he notes that canon also
has a generative hermeneutical function, Aichele focuses on the ideological limitations
that the concept of canon necessarily invokes. Aichele generally views the positive features of canon that follow in this study as negative. For him, the canon is an 'oppressive

a strong foundation for the practice of canonical interpretation of both testaments.

The development of the above argument will take place in four broad stages. Chapters 1 and 2 form the first major section. In Chapter 1, methodological decisions and the key terms of the canon debate will be delineated. This chapter will function as more than a perfunctory review of the research and a statement of methodology, though it will accomplish these ends. Rather, in defining the relevant terms, crucial elements of the argument are already being introduced and defended. Important definitional discussions here include the terms 'canon', 'Scripture', and 'canon-consciousness'.[8] Historical evidence will also be considered that recognizes the existence of the canon as a historical artifact (i.e. an actual entity). Working through the historical evidence will involve outlining the process of canon formation and also summarizing the external attestation of the Old and New Testaments by extra-biblical sources. In Chapter 2, this external historical evidence will be examined for possible indications of a 'canon-consciousness' among the believing community during and after the biblical period.[9]

When defining the nature and extent of the Christian canon, several questions immediately arise. Is the biblical canon best understood in historical, theological, or hermeneutical terms? In discussions of canon, there is often a tendency to gravitate toward one of these three emphases. As mentioned above, some theological accounts of the nature of Scripture do not exhibit an awareness of the hermeneutical features of the biblical text as a collection of literary documents. Conversely, in a history of religions approach, the biblical writings are viewed in the same category as any other writing in the same period.[10] Thus, in this approach, the theological aspects of the bib-

---

ideological institution' that '*prevents* people from reading these diverse and ambiguous books or that so controls the reading of these texts that people are in effect blinded and crippled by the canonical constraints' (p. 226). He also maintains that the ideological 'control' of the canon ultimately fails due to the open nature of textuality in general: 'Canonical control fails because of "unlimited semiosis", in other words, because signifying systems always exceed any possible level of control' (p. 17). This discussion will be revisited in Chapter 4 in a section on the nature of textuality in relation to the concept of intertextuality.

8.	For a summary of these important definitions, see 'The Terms of the Debate and the Role of Presuppositions' section below in Chapter 1.

9.	Other evidence of 'canon-consciousness' among the believing community includes historical documents such as the prologue to Sirach (for the Old Testament) and the Muratorian Fragment (for the New Testament), as well as biblical texts such as Lk. 24.44 (which possibly alludes to the tripartite shape of the Hebrew Bible during New Testament times). See the discussion of this evidence in Chapter 2.

10. E.g., Allert seeks to discuss the formation of the New Testament from the perspective of a 'sympathetic *religious historian*' (*High View*, p. 13). The religious historian 'looks at the contexts of antiquity as neutrally as possible and then describes them

lical canon are generally underdeveloped. Furthermore, in some purely literary approaches, the historical and theological issues that swirl around the canon debate are bracketed out of the investigation in favor of exclusively synchronic readings.[11]

The definitional discussion of Chapters 1 and 2 will seek to demonstrate the interconnectedness of the theological, historical, and hermeneutical features of the biblical canon. To illustrate (and anticipate subsequent discussions), the provisional definition of canon as 'God's word to his people' can serve to highlight each of these aspects of the nature of 'canon'. That it is *God's* word to his people points to the 'dogmatic location' of the canon in the economy of salvation. This theological emphasis seeks to account for the way God uses Scripture in his action of revelation and redemption.[12] That it is God's *word* to his people highlights the verbal aspects of canon as a collection of literary writings (i.e. words!) that require skillful reading and interpretation. That it is God's word *to his people* points to the historical location of the canon and its gradual development among a believing community of authors and readers. Any account of 'canon' that takes one of these three areas as primary to the exclusion of the other most likely has not adequately accounted for the fundamental aspects of what a canon in general, and the biblical canon in particular, entails. All three aspects of the nature of 'canon' are important and worthy of sustained academic

as accurately as possible' (p. 13). The alternative, for him, is the pastoral apologist perspective (that 'starts from the modern perspective and imposes it upon…the evidence of antiquity') or the 'neophyte' or 'generalist' perspective (that 'comes to the topic with little to no disciplined theological or historical training with which to tackle the topic').

11. Some of these purely literary approaches will be addressed in Chapter 4's discussion of the textual feature of intertextuality.

12. For a study of Scripture along these lines, see John B. Webster, *Holy Scripture: A Dogmatic Sketch* (Cambridge: Cambridge University Press, 2003); and John B. Webster, 'A Great and Meritorious Act of the Church? The Dogmatic Location of the Canon', in *Die Einheit der Schrift und die Vielfalt des Kanons* (ed. John Barton and Michael Wolter; Berlin: W. de Gruyter, 2003), pp. 95-126. Webster's goal is 'a dogmatic ontology of Holy Scripture: an account of what Holy Scripture *is* in the saving economy of God's loving and regenerative self-communication' (*Holy Scripture*, p. 2). In *Words of Life*, Ward develops a theological account of bibliology by emphasizing that the Scriptures are an integral part of 'God's action in the world'. In this regard, see also Kevin J. Vanhoozer, *The Drama of Doctrine: A Canonical-Linguistic Approach to Christian Theology* (Louisville, KY: Westminster/John Knox Press, 2005), pp. 113-237; Kevin J. Vanhoozer, 'From Speech Acts to Scripture Acts: The Covenant of Discourse and the Discourse of the Covenant', in *First Theology: God, Scripture & Hermeneutics* (Downers Grove, IL: IVP, 2002), pp. 159-203; Peter Jensen, *The Revelation of God* (Downers Grove, IL: IVP, 2002); and Scott R. Swain, *Trinity, Revelation, and Reading: A Theological Introduction to the Bible and Its Interpretation* (London: T. & T. Clark, 2011).

treatment.[13] Moreover, the fullest definition of canon will incorporate all three elements.

However, after delineating various aspects of these distinctive approaches, I shift into a study of the hermeneutical and literary aspects of the nature of the biblical canon. The rationale for this movement is twofold. First, the scope of a single book is not wide enough to cover all three aspects adequately. Second, of the three areas, the hermeneutical aspect has not received as much attention in the broader field of canon studies and thus merits further study.

Accordingly, in Chapter 3, I will argue that the existence of a canon as a historical reality allows for the affirmation that the collection has an inevitable and significant contextual effect on its readers ('Mere Contextuality'). Reading an individual writing as part of a larger collection affects the nature and direction of the connotations and assumptions that are made by the reader (i.e. it affects the reading process). This phenomenon is a hermeneutical factor that takes place regardless of the ordering and contents of the collection being read (e.g. the Hebrew Bible versus the Septuagint ordering of the Old Testament). In this sense, the point here is a general hermeneutical insight, though it will be applied directly to the Christian canon in the next steps of the argument.[14] This hermeneutical phenomenon is also practically inevitable, as it has an impact whether or not the reader acknowledges this factor.

After establishing the existence of this contextual effect on readers of a canonical collection, internal biblical evidence will be examined for possible indications of a 'canon-consciousness' among the biblical authors. There are indications that the biblical authors wrote their works with an awareness of a pre-existing body of authoritative literature and that they saw themselves as contributing to this body of literature.[15] This type of evidence would indicate the possibility that elements of the contextual effect of canonical shaping might have been intended by the biblical authors themselves ('Meant Contextuality').

In Chapter 4, I will argue that the presence of a canon with intended contextual features sets the limits for discerning intertextual connections

---

13. Joseph Blenkinsopp argues that 'study of the canon is not a panacea for Biblical Studies nor can it explain everything. But no historical or theological explanation will be adequate which neglects it' (*Prophecy and Canon: A Contribution to the Study of Jewish Origins* [Notre Dame, IN: University of Notre Dame Press, 1977], p. 17). Blenkinsopp also contends that 'it should be obvious by now that the study of the canon is not just of historical, archeological or literary interest. On the contrary, it raises questions of rather basic significance for both synagogue and church' (p. 151).

14. A simple case in point is the way Christian readers understand the New Testament in light of the Old Testament.

15. The phrase employed here ('an awareness of a pre-existing body of authoritative literature') can be understood as a preliminary definition of 'canon-consciousness'.

among the writings within that canon. This discussion is a natural implication of the arguments of Chapters 1–3. Because the biblical writings are part of a broader collection (i.e. a canon) and this canonical context has an inevitable and possibly intended effect on readers, these aspects of the canon can function as a control on the types of intertextual connections that an interpreter will discern and view as legitimate. If the broad framework of the canon is in some way intentional, then the scope and direction of intertextual possibilities can be understood in a similarly intended manner. In other words, the canon both guides and governs a biblical interpreter's detection and interpretation of intertextual references and their fertile potential for rich biblical meaning. Moreover, the concept of canon eliminates certain views of the nature of intertextuality and also limits the exponentially large number of possible intertextual connections that might be brought to bear on biblical texts.

In Chapter 5, I will seek to demonstrate that the contextual effect of the intertextually informed shape of the canon helps identify the intended audience of the Bible as a whole.[16] The question of 'original' or intended audience is a perennial issue in the interpretation of any ancient text. Taking the shape of the biblical material into account allows biblical readers to identify and voluntarily associate with the expectations generated by an authoritative canonical collection. Strategic biblical texts identify the ideal readers of the biblical canon as those who allow their sense of this intentionally designed canon to direct their textual investigations and their response to its theological witness.

All in all, the development of the argument as a whole will include an integration of exegetical, historical, and hermeneutical analysis. The study will also seek to bring the broad areas of canon studies, historical studies, and literary studies into a fruitful interdisciplinary dialogue. Thus, the book and bibliography that follows includes interaction with substantial works that deal with canon formation, the nature of external historical evidence for canon, and the hermeneutical issues of textuality, contextuality, and intertextuality.[17]

16. This chapter relates to my thesis in particular by showing an important way *the concept of canon* is *utilized* in the interpretive task, namely, to help identify the intended readership.

17. Unless otherwise noted, all biblical texts cited in English are from the NASB, and all biblical texts cited in Greek are from the ubs[4].

Chapter 1

DEFINING THE CANON (DEBATE)

Now, what I want is, Facts. Teach these boys and girls nothing but Facts. Facts alone are wanted in life. Plant nothing else, and root everything else. You can only form the minds of reasoning animals upon Facts: nothing else will ever be of any service to them. This is the principle on which I bring up my own children, and this is the principle on which I bring up these children. Stick to the Facts, sir![1]

Melito to Onesimus his brother, greeting...since you wished to know the accurate facts about the ancient writings, how many they are in number, and what is their order, I have taken pains to do thus, for I know your zeal for the faith and interest in the word, and that in your struggle for eternal salvation you esteem these things more highly than all else in your love towards God. Accordingly... I set down the facts and sent them to you.[2]

All we want are the facts, ma'am.[3]

The Terms of the Debate and the Role of Presuppositions

An important first step in examining the process of canon formation is delineating the terms of the debate and recognizing the role of presuppositions in the assessment of historical evidence (both internal and external). Definitional clarity is especially important in the canon debate, as a large portion of the discussion hinges on the meaning of certain key terms and concepts.[4] Indeed, the decision made regarding these concepts has serious

---

1. Mr Gradgrind's opening monologue in Charles Dickens, *Hard Times: For These Times* (London: Penguin Books, 2003), p. 9. According to Mr Gradgrind (a satirized caricature of the nineteenth century English educational system), knowledge of 'facts' is 'the one thing needful' in any endeavor.

2. Melito of Sardis (c. 180 CE) to Onesimus, as recorded by Eusebius in his *Ecclesiastical History* 4.26.13-14 (Kirsopp Lake's 1926 translation).

3. Sergeant Joe Friday in Jack Webb's 1950s police drama *Dragnet*.

4. In a recent article, Stephen B. Chapman, 'The Canon Debate: What It Is and Why It Matters', *JTI* 4 (2010), pp. 273-94, also strongly affirms the urgent need for definitional clarity in the canon debate. For him, 'the dating issue is subordinate to a prior semantic question: What does "canon" mean?' (p. 273).

consequences for how an interpreter will assess the significance of the historical data. As Barton affirms, 'a lack of agreement about the use of terms bedevils many areas of study'.[5] Barton laments with considerable justification, 'It hardly matters how the word "canon" is used, if only we can agree about it; but there is no more consensus now than there was a hundred years ago—perhaps, indeed, less.'[6]

Further, it is important to recognize that providing an account of canon formation involves the task of telling an untold story.[7] Remarkably, no ancient writer or source delineates in detail the process of how the Bible came to be. As Metzger marvels, 'Although this was one of the most important developments in the thought and practice of the early Church, history is virtually silent as to how, when, and by whom it was brought about.'[8] He concludes that 'nothing is more amazing in the annals of the Christian Church than the absence of detailed accounts of so significant a process'.[9] Throughout church history, varying accounts of the history of the biblical canon, and the New Testament in particular, have been put forward for acceptance among the churches. Indeed, both the ancient and contemporary canon debates can be viewed as a struggle of dueling historiographies. The

---

5. John Barton, *Holy Writings, Sacred Text: The Canon in Early Christianity* (Louisville, KY: Westminster/John Knox Press, 1997), p. 157. Similarly, von Campenhausen writes, 'the situation is further confused by the fact that there is no one agreed definition of the concept of the canon, and that its use is often very hazy indeed' (*Formation of the Christian Bible*, p. 103).

6. Barton, *Holy Writings, Sacred Text*, p. 157. Barton also bemoans 'the sterility of the resulting discussion' that arises because 'the question is inappropriate to the material being examined' (p. 14). In other words, 'Given their diverse definitions of "canon", almost all the scholars we have discussed are in a sense right in their conclusions... but in another sense practically all the scholars are also wrong' (p. 14). Cf. Eugene Ulrich's interaction with Barton on this definitional point in 'The Notion and Definition of Canon', in *Canon Debate*, pp. 21-35. Ulrich argues that 'for future discussion to be useful and to escape from the confusion that now muddies the water, it is imperative to reach consensus on the definition of canon' (p. 33).

7. Childs, 'Canon in Recent Biblical Studies', p. 36, calls this situation the 'central problem' in studying canon formation. Holmes, 'Biblical Canon', p. 421, reflects on the 'methodological problems of properly utilizing scattered reports from different regions and times to write a single narrative'. He asks, 'How does one avoid the temptation to generalize about "the church" or "the early Christian movement" when the only evidence is a sparse collection of "snapshots" from various regions?' Cf. Sailhamer, *Meaning of the Pentateuch*, p. 209: 'According to many biblical scholars, interpretation of the "hard evidence" for both the traditional view and various recent views has reached something of an impasse. The external historical witnesses to the process of canonization of the OT are remarkably silent about important factors of their history, apart from the fact that they are often open to conflicting interpretations.'

8. Metzger, *Canon of the New Testament*, p. 1.

9. Metzger, *Canon of the New Testament*, p. 1.

story of canon formation has been used as the basis for theological trajectories as well as doctrinal directions.

Though most evangelicals will affirm that God's providential hand was at work in the process of canon formation, they must still grapple with the details of how the biblical canon was composed, collected, transmitted, and treasured by the believing community. Appealing to a vague notion of inspiration while turning a blind (or at least indifferent) eye toward the vagaries of historiographical reconstruction of how the process actually took place is simply inadequate. The issue of whether it is possible to hold to a high view of Scripture in the light of increased knowledge regarding the process of canon formation has recently become a point of contention.[10] Evangelicals must be able to support their claims about Scripture both theologically *and* historically.

To tell the story of canon formation, a historian or interpreter must reconstruct the narrative sequence from a fragmentary array of archeological, historical, and textual evidence.[11] Because there is only a limited set of sparse historical data, the presuppositions of the interpreter often become determinate factors in how this historical evidence will be appropriated.[12] There is relatively little controversy over the 'facts' involved in the history of the formation of the biblical canon as 'most of it has been known for the last two centuries'.[13] While there is little *disagreement* over these historical

---

10. See especially Allert, *High View of Scripture?* As mentioned in the introduction, one of Allert's primary assertions is that an evangelical 'high view of Scripture' is not able to account for the historical vagaries of the canon formation process. For a snapshot of this type of discussion, see the dialogue between Kenton L. Sparks, *God's Word in Human Words: An Evangelical Appropriation of Critical Biblical Scholarship* (Grand Rapids, MI: Baker, 2008); Robert W. Yarbrough, 'God's Word in Human Words: Form-Critical Reflections', in *Do Historical Matters Matter to Faith? A Critical Appraisal of Modern and Postmodern Approaches to Scripture* (ed. James K. Hoffmeier and Dennis R. Magary; Wheaton, IL: Crossway, 2012), pp. 327-44; and Robert W. Yarbrough, 'The Embattled Bible: Four More Books', *Themelios* 34 (2009), pp. 6-25.

11. Cf. Childs, 'Canon in Recent Biblical Studies', p. 36: 'The task is rather left to a critical reconstruction of the process from indirect evidence (Ben Sira, Josephus, Church Fathers, Talmud, etc.)'.

12. In his discussion of the terms 'canon' and 'Scripture', Sheppard acknowledges 'the need for more careful definitions and historical finesse' and that 'in the application of both terms to a religion, the interpreter stands within a hermeneutical circle' ('Canon', p. 68).

13. Barton, *Holy Writings, Sacred Text*, p. 1. Barton adds that 'no theory about the biblical canon has any hope of success unless it finds a place' for this historical evidence (p. 1). However, as Barton emphasizes, these 'facts' are 'plainly not sufficient' for 'there remains little agreement on their interpretation' (p. 1). For a listed outline of these standard primary sources, see Lee M. McDonald, *The Biblical Canon* (Peabody, MA: Hendrickson, 2007), pp. 431-38.

'facts', there is also little *agreement* regarding their proper interpretation. In other words, the 'inferences' one makes based on the available data will be shaped by the definition of the object one pursues. As Dempster articulates, 'What is perfectly clear is that everyone has assumptions and that the idea of neutrality in this age of postmodernity is a pipe dream. There is not only the "tyranny of canonical assumptions", but also a tyranny of non-canonical assumptions.'[14] However much historians and interpreters would like to 'just stick to the facts', the essence of historiographical reconstruction often hinges on how these facts are perceived and ordered in the complex nexus of historical factors that bear on the process being described and the time period being explored.

Even as new research and evidence emerges, an interpreter's matrix of prior assumptions informs the significance attributed to new developments.[15] This unavoidable reality makes much of the internal and external evidence that has a bearing on canon formation 'difficult to identify' and 'delicate to interpret'.[16] This situation makes the history of canon formation

14. Dempster, 'Canons', p. 68. Dempster is responding to the type of claim Robert A. Kraft makes in 'Para-mania: Besides, Before and Beyond Bible Studies', *JBL* 126 (2007), pp. 5-27. One of his major sections is entitled, 'The Tyranny of Canonical Assumptions: The *Para*Scriptural Worlds' (pp. 10-18). He defines this 'tyranny' as 'the temptation to impose on those ancients whom we study our modern ideas about what constituted "scripture" and how it was viewed' (p. 17). Cf. Gamble, 'New Testament Canon', p. 271, who observes that 'the question...is how the evidence is to be interpreted and integrated into a comprehensive explanatory scheme that attends to all the relevant considerations and properly places the emphasis'.

15. For instance, James Sanders gives an interesting autobiographical account of his response to Jack Lewis' seminal work on the council of Jamnia (e.g. J.P. Lewis, 'What Do We Mean by Jabneh?', *JBR* 32 [1964], pp. 125-32). Lewis' argumentation demonstrated that the council of Jamnia in the first century CE did not 'close' the Hebrew Bible but rather represented dialogue regarding a few key books/issues. Sanders recounts that some 'took [this evidence] to mean that the Tanak had already been canonized by the second century BCE, whereas I took it to mean that the Ketuvim were not stabilized until later' ('Issue of Closure', pp. 253-54). In Sanders' mind, the scholars of the older consensus (and those who currently disagree with him on this issue) 'had read too much Western thinking into the various references to Yavneh/Jamnia'. Thus, the same evidence confirmed for various scholars arguments on opposite ends of the interpretive spectrum. The issue did not regard Lewis' work per se, but rather what his work implied. Cf. Carola Krieg, 'Javne und der Kanon. Klärungen', in *Kanonisierung—die Hebräische Bibel im Werden* (ed. Georg Steins and Johannes Taschner; Göttingen: Neukirchener Theologie, 2010), pp. 133-52.

16. Metzger, *Canon of the New Testament*, p. 40, makes this comment about the writings of the Apostolic Fathers in particular. C.H. Roberts speaks of 'the jejune and scrappy references in [the] literary sources' with which historians must work (*Manuscript, Society and Belief in Early Christian Egypt* [London: Oxford University Press, 1979], p. 1).

'one of the most complicated parts of church history'.[17] Despite the necessarily tentative and modest nature of any conclusions drawn from fragmentary evidence, interpretive agnosticism is nevertheless not the only feasible response. The historical evidence cannot provide absolute certainty, but it does offer the possibility of adequate knowledge upon which to support or deny a given assertion about the canonical process.[18]

Recognizing the critical function of presuppositions in the interpretation of historical data, the distinction between minimalism and maximalism can also prove helpful.[19] A 'minimalist' would seek 'minimal but assured results that can be achieved on the basis of methodologically rigorous close readings of particular texts'.[20] Conversely, a 'maximalist' will seek to maintain a level of methodological rigor, but will not typically require absolute certainty in order to draw conclusions from the historical evidence (such as a quotation or verbal parallel).[21] These distinctions are relative rather than

17. Balla, *Challenges*, p. 91. Balla is summarizing the opinions of H. Lietzmann (1907) and Wilhelm Schneemelcher (1980). After noting the interdisciplinary work of recent canon study, Gamble remarks that 'clearly the day is past when the history of the canon can be narrowly construed or easily charted' ('New Testament Canon', p. 275). He ends his essay by confessing that reconstructing the history of canon formation 'is a daunting task' (p. 294).

18. In his classic work on canon, *Formation of the Christian Bible*, von Campenhausen takes a similar stance. He notes that because of the 'scanty' evidence, it is tempting to 'fill the gaps with more or less fantastic hypothesis, or to overstrain the little evidence we have by violent interpretation' (p. ix). Nevertheless, he maintains that 'given the requisite caution', it is possible 'to reconstruct the main lines of the formation of the Canon' (p. ix). 'The man who wants to know too much', von Campenhausen opines, 'loses the thread, and in the end learns nothing'. However, 'the man who turns his attention to what is actually there perceives to his astonishment that the links are by no means so obscure as had at first appeared' (p. ix). Accordingly, 'the right course is not to concentrate simply on isolated individual texts but—more in the manner of the historian than of the literary critic—to observe those lines which link up and finally form a discernable pattern' (p. ix).

19. Dempster, 'Canons', p. 48, uses these categories to discuss positions on the state of the Hebrew Bible at the beginning of the early church. Cf. Hill's discussion of the background and nature of minimalism in historical scholarship (*Who Chose the Gospels*, pp. 185-89).

20. Andrew F. Gregory, '*1 Clement* and the Writings that Later Formed the New Testament', in *The Reception of the New Testament in the Apostolic Fathers* (ed. Andrew Gregory and Christopher Tuckett; Oxford: Oxford University Press, 2005), p. 157. Cf. Kraft's overarching methodological cautions in 'Para-mania', pp. 5-27.

21. Hill notes that the minimalist position errs on 'the side of *not* claiming a knowledge of a New Testament book unless it can be demonstrated beyond reasonable doubt' (*Who Chose the Gospels*, p. 188). He concedes that 'this method assuredly has its place in scholarship, and it is always helpful to have a collection of "minimal but assured results"' (p. 188). However, 'these should simply not be confused with final, concrete, or definitive results, lest a *lack of certainty* about what an Apostolic Father *did* know slide

absolute, and somewhat fluid rather than fixed.[22] For example, a scholar giving a maximal reading of a biblical citation in a patristic text might also give a minimalist reading to a citation of an apocryphal writing in the same piece of literature. In this scenario, the interpreter is giving a maximalist reading of one type of evidence and a minimalist reading of another type of evidence. This process is not necessarily arbitrary, as there are an assortment of factors that impinge upon the decision to give either a minimalist or maximalist reading in any given case. It is a question of which type of evidence is being minimalized (or relativized) and which type of evidence is being maximalized (or emphasized).

Defining Canon

Paramount among the critical items in need of clear definition is the term 'canon'. Both the critical importance of and difficulties associated with the issues generated by this term have become well established. Most treatments of canon now begin with at least a brief discussion of the etymology and definition of 'canon'.[23] Ulrich observes in this regard that 'it is an understatement to say that confusion currently surrounds the term and permeates recent discussions of the topic'.[24] He also bemoans the 'lack of clarity and agreement regarding terminology'.[25] Holmes echoes this assessment and observes that 'issues and problems attending [canon's] definition lead to the heart of contemporary discussion'.[26]

---

imperceptibly into a *certainty* about what he *didn't* know' (pp. 188-89). Cf. Hill's methodological reflections in '"In These Very Words": Methods and Standards of Literary Borrowing in the Second Century', in *The Early Text of the New Testament* (ed. Charles E. Hill and Michael J. Kruger; Oxford: Oxford University Press, 2012), pp. 261-81.

22. Further, the categories of 'minimalist' and 'maximalist' readings do not necessarily have anything to do with being theologically liberal (the 'left') or conservative (the 'right'). They are simply a heuristic device that helps an interpreter understand the reason for divergent interpretations of the same fragmentary evidence. One can be theologically conservative yet take a minimalist approach to a certain piece of patristic evidence, for instance. Conversely, one might be a theological liberal and give a maximalist interpretation of a given citation in the external evidence. Dempster deals with this issue in 'Canons', p. 48 n. 8: 'It should be noted that these views do not necessarily correlate with conservative and liberal theological views. There are those who are maximalists who are far to the left theologically and there are minimalists who are evangelicals'.

23. E.g., see (inter alia) Bruce, *Canon of Scripture*, pp. 17-18; McDonald, *Biblical Canon*, pp. 38-69; and Ulrich, 'Notion and Definition'. Metzger also provides a supplemental appendix on the 'History of the Word Κανών' (*Canon of the New Testament*, pp. 289-93).

24. Ulrich, 'Notion and Definition', p. 21.

25. Ulrich, 'Notion and Definition', p. 22.

26. Holmes, 'Biblical Canon', p. 407.

In light of this definitional deep water, some have either questioned the viability of the discussion or simply preferred alternative terminology.[27] However, because the heart of the canon formation discussion involves reconstruction based on key concepts, at least a minimal delineation of the critical terms is necessary. Further, because the term 'canon' in particular bears multiple senses, has been utilized in sundry ways both in contemporary scholarship and throughout the history of the church, and is attached to the development of the theological doctrine of Scripture, a definitional discussion remains a fruitful (if not imperative) endeavor.

Within the semantic domain of the word κανών, there are two major nuances in the history of its usage in relation to the Scriptures.[28] Originally a 'Semitic loanword', the term κανών initially meant something like a 'straight rod', 'measuring stick', or a 'ruler'.[29] By figurative extension, the term came to imply the normative ideas of 'rule', 'standard', or 'guide'.[30] A

27. For instance, Holmes concludes that 'the disagreement regarding a formal definition of the specific term "canon" may be to some degree beside the point' ('Biblical Canon', p. 408). For him, 'the legitimate concern to define "canon" should not be permitted to overshadow the fundamental significance of the distinction between "scripture" and "canon"' (p. 408). However, when Holmes insists on the strict distinction between canon and Scripture, he himself is putting the definitional question in the forefront (and by no means beside the point in his understanding). Also, the difficulties regarding the term 'canon' are directly affected by how one understands and utilizes the term 'Scripture' in relation to canon. Holmes commendably wants to avoid overemphasis on terminology in favor of focusing more extensively on 'larger' and 'more interesting' questions. But one's definitional decisions/assumptions directly inform the nature and extent of those other areas. For instance, Holmes concludes that 'during the Christian movement's early years, there apparently did not exist a "closed" canon of Hebrew Scriptures for it to take over' (p. 409). The reason this conclusion is reached in this manner, though, is because he has *defined canon* as a closed list.

28. As Metzger notes, the term is used in Greek, Latin, and English 'in a kaleidoscopic variety of senses' (*Canon of the New Testament*, p. 289). According to his tally, there are at least eleven senses in English and nine in Latin.

29. For the term's usage in classical Greek, see especially, Liddell–Scott, s.v. 'κανών'. See also BDAG, s.v. 'κανών'. Thayer, s.v. 'κανών', includes that the original term referred to 'a rod or straight piece of rounded wood to which any thing is fastened to keep it straight' and was 'used for various purposes'. Metzger comments that 'besides being straight, for other uses the κανών had to be incapable of bending. Thus, the word refers to the beam of a balance as well as the scribe's ruler (translated by the Latin *regula*). It is from this literal sense of a *level* or a *ruler* that all the metaphorical senses are derived' (*Canon of the New Testament*, p. 289). Cf. David L. Dungan, *Constantine's Bible: Politics and the Making of the New Testament* (Minneapolis, MN: Fortress Press, 2007), pp. 11-53. Dungan argues that the notion of κανών is inextricably linked to the 'polis ideology' of the Greco–Roman culture of the time period. For him, this historical background is determinative not just for the etymology of the term κανών, but also for the developing 'concept of canon' as it was applied to the New Testament collection in the fourth century.

30. Cf. the lexical data from secular Greek compiled by H.W. Beyer in his entry on

κανών was something you measured something else with or by (e.g. 'rule of law', or 'rule of faith'). This guiding function of the term shows up in the artistic (e.g. a 'model' sculpture), architectural (e.g. a 'ruler' to measure by), and moral spheres (e.g. a 'moral compass').[31]

When the word occurs in the New Testament (only four times), it has this sense of norm or standard. In his concluding exhortation in his letter to the Galatians, Paul remarks, 'Those who will walk by this rule [τῷ κανόνι τούτῳ], peace and mercy be upon them' (Gal. 6.16).[32] This sense of the term is paralleled in the period directly following the New Testament. For example, at the turn of the first century, the author of *1 Clement* commends his readers for teaching the young women 'to abide by the rule of obedience' (τῷ κανόνι τῆς ὑποταγῆς).[33] Similarly, later in the second century, Clement of Alexandria admonishes his readers to live according to the 'rule of faith'

'κανών', in *TDNT*, III, pp. 596-97. Beyer notes that 'in secular usage the basic Semitic sense of "reed" yielded to the figurative use of κανών for a "straight rod or staff"'. After the generalization of the term, κανών becomes 'the "norm" whether the perfect form and therefore the goal to be sought on the one hand, or the infallible criterion (κριτήπιρον) by which things are to be measured on the other'. Thayer, s.v. 'κανών', collates the various elements of this 'metaphorical' usage: 'any rule or standard; a principle or law of investigating, judging, living, or acting'.

31. See Beyer's survey in 'κανών', p. 597. He notes that 'in music [during this time period] the monochord, by which all other tonal relationships are controlled, is called the κανὼν μουσικός'. Beyer draws his examples from those listed in Liddell–Scott, s.v. 'κανών'. Liddell–Scott also convey that the notion of 'straightness' or 'standard' is present in many of the usages. E.g., an unuseful 'canon' would be one that was malleable (μολίβδινος κανών), as 'a flexible *rule*' could not be 'depended on for straight measurement'. In this regard, Louw-Nida locate κανών within the same semantic domain as νόμος ('law'). Cf. Zahn, 'Permanent Value of the New Testament Canon', p. 4, who writes, 'When it becomes necessary to determine the bounds within which a certain structure shall be contained it is essential that the rule be of the proper length and that it shall not be shortened or lengthened by the arbitrary decision of the artificer.'

32. Cf. *4 Macc.* 7.21 and 2 Cor. 10.13-16. In Phil. 3.16, there is a textual variant in some later manuscripts (e.g. Siniaticus' third hand) that includes an occurrence of κανών. Most likely, κανών here is a scribal expansion on the enigmatic phrase τῷ αὐτῷ στοιχεῖν. Thus, the Textus Receptus has τῷ αὐτῷ στοιχεῖν κανόνι (i.e. 'by the same *standard*'). Cf. Bruce Metzger, *Textual Commentary on the Greek New Testament* (Stuttgart: Deutsche Bibelgesellschaft, 1994), p. 615. The lexical sense of this usage entails 'a means to determine the quality of something' (BDAG, s.v. 'κανών'). Beyer, 'κανών', pp. 598-600, analyzes these passages; however, the rare occurrences of κανών in Paul's letters do not really inform the development of the term in relation to the history of the formation of the canon.

33. *1 Clem.* 1.3. Later in the letter, Clement urges, 'Let us conform to the glorious and holy rule of our tradition' (*1 Clem.* 7.2, τῆς παραδόσεως ἡμῶν κανόνα). In *1 Clem.* 41.1, he also encourages his readers not to overstep the 'designated rule' (τὸν ὡρισμένον κανόνα) of their own ministries. For a brief discussion of the authorship and first century dating of *1 Clem.*, see Michael Holmes' treatment in *AF*, pp. 33-38.

(ὁ κανών τῆς πίστεως).³⁴ These uses of κανών represent the first and most dominant major nuance of the term in the first few centuries CE.³⁵

Eventually during the Patristic period, the term took on the sense of 'list, register, or catalogue'.³⁶ For example, when Eusebius drew up a list of various orderings of the four Gospels, he called them 'canons' (κανόνες).³⁷ In Eusebius' usage, these 'canons' were not 'some kind of rules or principles, but were systematically arranged lists of numerals that corresponded to the numbered sections in the text of the Gospels, by which one could quickly locate parallel passages'.³⁸ In relation to this sense of 'list', κανών was also used at the Council of Nicaea for the 'official list or catalogue of clergy who were attached to a given church'.³⁹ In line with this linguistic development, κανών began to be applied to the group of writings that the churches considered normative. The collection of sacred writings could now be conceived

34. Clement of Alexandria makes this comment in *Stromata, Or Miscellanies* 4.15, in *ANF* II, p. 427. His exhortation 'what you are commanded to do by the rule of faith' comes after a long string of quotations from the book of 1 Corinthians. Compare also the interesting comment in *Stromata* 6.15, in *ANF* II, p. 509: 'He says, "on the housetops", understanding them sublimely, and delivering them in a lofty strain, and according to the canon of the truth explaining the Scriptures.' After this, Clement mentions 'those who receive and observe, according to the ecclesiastical rule, the exposition of the Scriptures explained by Him'. This ecclesiastical rule is 'the concord and harmony of the law and the prophets in the covenant delivered at the coming of the Lord'. Cf. Eusebius, *EH*, III, 32.7, who mentions those who were attempting to corrupt 'the sound norm of the preaching of salvation'.

35. Accordingly, the three headings under BDAG's entry for κανών discuss the senses of 'norm', 'guide', and 'rule', but not of 'canon' as a collection of writings/Scriptures. As they note, 'The use of κανών as "list" in reference to the canonical scriptures, as well as in the sense of "(synodical-) canon", is late' (BDAG, s.v. 'κανών').

36. See especially the 'κανών' entries in Lampe, Thayer, and Liddell–Scott. Cf. Metzger, *Canon of the New Testament*, p. 291: 'Another development in the use of the word κανών (and one that bears closely upon its subsequent reference to the books of Scripture) was the application of the word to a list, index, or table—terms that carry the suggestion of something fixed and established, by which one can orient himself.'

37. See Eusebius, *EH*, III, 25.1-7. Eusebius' heading for this section is, 'The Divine Scriptures that are Accepted and Those that are Not'. His four main categories for the books are 'recognized', 'doubtful', 'rejected', and 'cited by heretics'. The editor notes that 'this chapter is the only place in which Eusebius attempts to treat the canon systematically, and in it he is speaking purely as a historian, not as a critic. He is endeavoring to give an accurate statement of the general opinion of the orthodox Church of his day in regard to the number and names of its sacred books' (*EH*, III, 25.1 n. 1). For a convenient list of Eusebius' 'canons', see McDonald, *Biblical Canon*, p. 446.

38. Metzger, *Canon of the New Testament*, p. 291. The term was also used in historiography. E.g., the phrase χρονικοὶ κανόνες referred to 'timetables to fix historical events' (Beyer, 'κανών', p. 598).

39. Metzger, *Canon of the New Testament*, p. 292. Metzger also notes that 'those members of the clergy who were thus enrolled were referred to as οἱ ἐν τῷ κανόνι'.

of as a *canon*, i.e. a list of writings that were included in that collection. In other words, the canon represented an enumeration of the collection of writings ('canon as list') that was deemed to be authoritative/scriptural by the churches ('canon as rule'). The standard or rule against which interpretations of Israel or the church's history were to be measured was the κανών of Scripture (that is, does a particular interpretation or assertion cohere with what is contained in the books on *this* list or within *this* collection?).[40]

Despite this clear shift in usage, the original sense of 'rule' or 'norm' did not entirely dissolve in the new ways the term was applied. In fact, this connotation of normativity is likely one of the central reasons the term was used to refer to the biblical material in the first place.[41] Because of the authoritative nature of the components of the biblical collection, it is natural and fitting that the collection itself would be understood in a similar manner.[42] In lexicographical terms, the rule/guide sense of κανών precedes and follows the use of κανών as collection/list.[43] The initial sense of κανών is well established long before it is applied to the collection of authoritative biblical writings and its initial sense lingers in new applications of the term.[44]

---

40. In the fourth century, Athanasius seems to utilize 'canon' in this manner. For him, the writings that the church recognized as Scripture are the ones that have the ability to expose the error in heretical writings. He quotes scriptural passages to 'expose as impious' and 'heretical' a diverse spectrum of heterodox teachings, such as the Manichaeans, Marcion, Montanists ('Phrygians'), Arians, and Melitians ('parasites' of Arius). This section of Athanasius's letter comes from a Coptic fragment and can be found in David Brakke, 'A New Fragment of Athanasius's Thirty-Ninth *Festal Letter*: Heresy, Apocrypha, and the Canon', *HTR* 103 (2010), pp. 47-66. See also the discussion below of Athanasius's *39th Festal Letter*.

41. In a general sense, Sheppard notes this connection in 'Canon', p. 66: 'The recognition of canon 1 materials, defined as traditions offering a normative vehicle or an ideal standard, occurs in most world religions and usually contributes momentum to an impulse within the history of a religion to totalize, to circumscribe, and to standardize these same normative traditions into fixed, literary forms typical of canon 2.'

42. As Metzger discerns, though, this assertion is debatable: 'Scholars today dispute whether the meaning "rule" (that is, "standard" or "norm") or the meaning "list" was uppermost in the minds of those who first applied the word to the Scriptures' (*Canon of the New Testament*, p. 293).

43. That κανών as rule/guide is well established can be seen from Lampe, s.v. 'κανών'. The 'Canon of Scripture' section is dwarfed by the 'Rule of Faith' entry as well as the entries for the other senses of the term. The same is true of words within the semantic domain of κανών such as the verbal cognates κανονικῶς and κανονίζ-ω.

44. On the development of these concepts, Bruce's reconstruction is helpful: 'While the "canon" of scripture means the *list* of books accepted as holy scripture, the other sense of "canon"—*rule* or *standard*—has rubbed off on this one, so that the "canon" of scripture is understood to be the *list* of books which are acknowledged to be, in a unique sense, the *rule* of belief and practice' (*Canon of Scripture*, p. 18). Metzger concludes his treatment of this subject by arguing that 'both the material and the formal

As Bruce observes, 'when once the limits of holy scripture came to be generally agreed upon, holy scripture itself came to be regarded as the rule of faith'.[45] Indeed, 'the term canon as a designation for the Church's Bible was suggested by the history of its meaning within the Church'.[46] In other words, there is an organic relationship between the two senses of the term and how their use developed and evolved in the believing community.

Especially as groupings began to form and an overall shape to the Hebrew Bible and the New Testament began to emerge, the notion of a canonical whole would have informed someone's thinking about the individual writings within that collection.[47] Combining these two senses, the 'biblical canon' was and can be understood as an authoritative collection of authoritative writings.[48] In this understanding, the individual documents within the canon are considered authoritative, and the collection as a whole is also considered authoritative (i.e. 'the whole counsel of God'). In this manner, there is both an active and a passive aspect of the fully orbed meaning of the notion of canon. The active sense refers to 'those books

sense eventually were seen to be appropriate, for the recognized custom of the Church in looking to a certain group of books as providing the standard for faith and life would naturally cause the books that conformed to it to be written in a list' (*Canon of the New Testament*, p. 293). Beyer, 'κανών', p. 601, concurs, arguing that 'what really counted was the concept of norm inherent in the term, i.e. its material content as the κανών τῆς ἀληθείας in the Christian sense'.

45. Bruce, *Canon of Scripture*, p. 18. Sheppard also argues that 'these ideal distinctions between canon as a norm and canon as a list or standardization of text usually overlap in the actual assessment of a particular religion' ('Canon', p. 67).

46. Wilhelm Schneemelcher, 'General Introduction', in *New Testament Apocrypha* (ed. Wilhelm Schneemelcher; Louisville, KY: Westminster/John Knox Press, 1991), p. 12. Schneemelcher also argues that in the second century and following, 'the word κανών presented itself as a designation that could express unmistakably what ecclesiastically was now obligatory' (p. 11).

47. For an examination of this process, see Chapter 2.

48. See Metzger, *Canon of the New Testament*, pp. 282-88. Metzger argues that there are only two alternatives. Either the canon is a 'collection of authoritative writings' or an 'authoritative collection'. For him, 'an authoritative collection of authoritative writings' is merely a modification of the second option. Metzger dismisses this option out of hand and without comment. However, in his nuancing of these two distinctions a few paragraphs later, he seems to allow for a version of the third option. He writes, 'In one case the Church recognizes the inherent authority of the Scriptures; in the other she creates their authority by collecting them and placing on the collection the label of canonicity' (p. 283). After making these distinctions, Metzger quickly points out the difficulty of separating the processes: 'Actually, however, the making of the empirical canon required a long period of time and involved a complex historical process that progressed, not in a straight line, but in a zig-zag development' (p. 284). Thus, the churches indeed primarily recognize the inherent authority of certain documents, but not apart from the complex process of canon formation.

that serve to mark out the norm for Christian faith and life', and the passive sense refers to 'the list of books that have been marked out by the Church as normative'.[49] The history of the concept of 'canon' is thus inextricably wrapped up in the notions of authority and normativity.

With these two nuances in place, by the fourth century the term κανών became the standard way to describe the entire collection of the Old and New Testament Scriptures. A writing that was deemed scriptural was understood to be 'canonical' (τὰ κανονικά), and something non-scriptural was 'non-canonical' (τὰ ἀκανόνιστα).[50] In the middle of the fourth century, for instance, Athanasius rejects the normative authority of the *Shepherd* by asserting that this particular writing is 'not in the canon' (μὴ ὂν ἐκ τοῦ κανόνος).[51] Here, the term canon clearly indicates the collection of authoritative scriptural writings. By the time of Athanasius's important *39th Festal Letter* of 367 CE, the list of Old and New Testament books are described as the 'canonical books' (κανονιζόμενα...Βιβλία) in contradistinction to the 'apocryphal' books (ἀπόκρυφα). After listing the biblical books, Athanasius writes, 'But the former, my brethren, are included in the Canon, the latter being [merely] read.'[52] Athanasius's comment is one of the first instances of the verbal form of κανονίζω ('to canonize' or 'make canonical') being used in relation to a writing being included in or excluded from the 'canon of

49. Metzger, *Canon of the New Testament*, p. 283. Metzger uses the Latin notions of *norma normans* ('the rule that prescribes') and *norma normata* ('the rule that is prescribed') to delineate further the active and passive aspects of κανών.

50. The terms ἐκκλησιαζόμενος and κανονιζόμενος were also used in order to distinguish what was normative (i.e. 'canonical') from what was either not sanctioned or simply spurious. The Council of Laodicea in Phrygia (363 CE) makes a distinction between canonical and non-canonical books. The former were to be read in the churches as Scripture and the latter were not (*Can. 59*; see Metzger, *Canon of the New Testament*, pp. 210, 292).

51. Athanasius, *Decrees of the Synod of Nicaea* (no. 18, as cited by Lampe, s.v. 'κανών').

52. The classical English translation of the section of Athanasius's *39th Festal Letter* that treats the canon question is found in *NPNF*, IV, pp. 551-53. David Brakke provides a full translation and interpretation of a recently discovered Coptic fragment of this letter (the 'Moscow fragment') in 'New Fragment of Athanasius's Thirty-Ninth *Festal Letter*', pp. 47-66. Brakke comments that Athanasius's letter 'remains one of the most significant documents in the history of the Christian Bible' (p. 47). He also notes that 'most studies of the formation of the Christian canon, including very recent ones, only examine [the] Greek fragment and so discuss only the contents of the lists [of biblical books]' (p. 47). The Coptic translations provide a fuller picture of Athanasius's understanding of both canonical boundaries and also the nature of orthodoxy and heresy. Brakke's main contention is that 'Athanasius promoted a biblical canon not only—as I argued earlier—to support one form of Christian piety, social formation, and authority in opposition to others, but also to refute the specific teachings of persons and groups that he deemed "impious" and "heretics"' (p. 48).

Scripture'.[53] At this point, the term κανών refers to a collection of authoritative documents within a community. Thus, someone writing in 400 CE could use the phrase 'Canon of the New Testament' (κανών τῆς καινῆς διαθήκης) without qualification or expansion.[54]

John Chrysostom is one of the first figures to refer to the canonical collection of the Old and New Testaments as the 'Bible' (Βίβλος).[55] The term βίβλος is the word often translated as 'scroll' in the New Testament.[56] The word can denote the physical entity that the words were written on, but it can also denote the idea of a 'work'. In this regard, a βίβλος could mean either a 'brief written message' in general (e.g. a certificate of divorce in Mt. 19.7) or a 'long written composition'. A 'book' or βίβλος, then, could be written on a tablet, a scroll, or in codex form.[57] Once the full collection of writings could fit within the bounds of a single codex, that codex could collectively be referred to as a 'book' (βίβλος). Using a term that emphasizes the collective or unified nature of the work may have also had a theological

---

53. See, for instance, the data collated by Lampe, s.v. ʿκανώνʾ.

54. This phrase occurs in an apologia titled *Apocriticus of Macarius Magnes* (4.10) around 400 CE. See Metzger, *Canon of the New Testament*, p. 292.

55. Bruce claims that 'Chrysostom's usage is the origin of our word "Bible"' (*Canon of Scripture*, p. 214). He cites Chrysostom's *Homilies on Matthew*, 47.3. Cf. Chrystostom's comment in *NPNF*, X, p. 29: 'For we ought not as soon as we retire from the Communion, to plunge into business unsuited to the Communion, but as soon as ever we get home, to take our Bible into our hands, and call our wife and children to join us in putting together what we have heard, and then, not before, engage in the business of life.' In a homily on Acts 8.26-27, Chrysostom uses both the plural and singular forms of βίβλος. Noting that the Ethiopian eunuch read the Scripture in public on his chariot, Chrysostom chides, 'Not so you: none takes the Bible in hand: nay, everything rather than the Bible' (*NPNF*, XI, p. 127). He continues by colorfully declaring that they might as well 'tie up the Bibles' if they will not listen to their content. Note the similar usage in Chrysostom's discussion of the ordering of the biblical books (*NPNF*, XI, p. 336). Cf. as well *NPNF*, XIV, pp. 113-14, 190. For two recent studies of Chrysostom's use of Scripture, see Robert C. Hill, 'St John Chrysostom: Preacher on the Old Testament', *Greek Orthodox Theological Review* 46 (2001), pp. 267-86; and Lauri Thurén, 'John Chrysostom as a Rhetorical Critic: The Hermeneutics of an Early Father', *Biblical Interpretation* 9 (2001), pp. 180-218.

56. Cf. Bruce, *Books and Parchments*, pp. 9-14.

57. Cf. BDAG, s.v. ʿβίβλοςʾ. Etymologically, the word derives from βύβλος, the word for Egyptian papyrus. The bark of this papyrus was used in the production of writing materials. Louw-Nida indicate that the terms βίβλος and βιβλίον are within the same semantic domain and both derive etymologically from βύβλος. These terms can refer to either an individual scroll or the more complex concept of 'book'. For instance, in Lk. 4.17, Jesus picks up the book of Isaiah (βιβλίον) and unrolls the scroll (βιβλίον). Further, the 'books' mentioned in Acts 19.19 likely 'consisted of sheets of parchment or of papyrus sewn together in the form of long scrolls or bound in the form of a book' (Louw-Nida, s.v. ʿβίβλοςʾ).

motivation (i.e. this book is *the* book). Both 'canon' and 'Bible' seem to allow for these particular connotations, making them fitting terminological choices for these important writings.

Consequently, around the fourth century κανών and βίβλος were virtually interchangeable and could both refer to the entire collection of sacred writings (Scripture).[58] For instance, in the early fifth century, Isidore of Pelusium could urge his readers, 'Let us examine the canon of truth, I mean the divine Scriptures.'[59] As the term 'Bible' continued to be used of the canon of Scripture, it increasingly took on a singular sense.[60] This interrelated rendering of the meaning of 'canon' and 'Bible' has endured in contemporary usage.[61]

Broad and Narrow Understandings of Canon

Drawing on this etymological discussion, proponents of particular understandings of canon emphasize differing senses of the term. Scholars 'continue

58. Cf. Ulrich, 'Notion and Definition', p. 30, who argues that 'Bible' in the singular 'denotes a written form of the full collection of canonical books. Whereas the canon is the normative list of the books, the Bible is the material copy of that fixed collection of books, conceived of as a single anthology, and usually presented as such.'

59. *Epist.* 4.114 (τὸν κανόνα τῆς ἀληθείας, τὰς θείας φημὶ γραφάς κατοπτεύσωμεν). Here the 'canon of truth' is in an appositional position to 'the divine Scriptures'. For this text and reference, see Metzger, *Canon of the New Testament*, p. 293 n. 12.

60. Peter J. Williams, 'The Bible, The Septuagint, and The Apocrypha: A Consideration of Their Singularity', in *Studies on the Text and Versions of the Hebrew Bible in Honour of Robert Gordon* (ed. Geoffrey Khan and Diana Lipton; Leiden: Brill, 2012), pp. 169-72, traces the shift away from the original plurality of the term 'Bible'. He argues that it should not be forgotten that the term originally invoked the plural idea of 'collection' and that 'we need to be aware that the tendency towards using a singular word for Bible or related terms has a long complex history' (p. 172).

61. Ulrich, 'Notion and Definition', pp. 27-28, surveys several contemporary definitions along these lines. See also Bruce, *Canon of Scripture*, p. 17: 'When we speak of the canon of scripture, the word "canon" has a simple meaning. It means the list of books contained in scripture, the list of books recognized as worthy to be included in the sacred writings of a worshiping community.' Carson and Moo, *Introduction*, p. 726, also note that 'the "canon" has come to refer to the closed collection of documents that constitute authoritative Scripture'. Cf. Blenkinsopp, *Prophecy and Canon*, p. 3: 'We may dispense with etymologies and original meanings and begin by saying that a canon is generally taken to be a collection of writings deemed to have a normative function within a particular community.' These scholars echo the traditional formulation of Zahn in 'The Permanent Value of the New Testament Canon for the Church', p. 3: 'In considering the Biblical canon we think of the Bible itself as a collection of writings recognized by the church not only as credible sources of the divine revelation, but also as the standard and measure of all churchly doctrine.' Notice that Zahn's definition dually highlights the 'canon as list' as well as the 'canon as rule' senses of the term 'canon'. Contra Dungan, *Constantine's Bible*, pp. 1-10, who posits this type of usage as an example of comprehensive historical ignorance of the canon formation process.

to disagree whether the weight of the later Christian references to the term *canon* for scripture turns primarily on the term's denotation of either a binding "norm" or an ecclesiastically approved "list" of inspired books'.[62] Accordingly, there are typically two main understandings of the notion of canon in contemporary scholarly dialogue. The two 'options' delineated here resonate in some ways with Gerald Sheppard's rubric of Canon 1 and Canon 2.[63] Canon 1 denotes the initial understanding of canon as a rule, guide, or norm. Canon 2 denotes the subsequent sense of list, 'standardization', and 'enumeration'.[64] Sheppard notes that the term canon 'inherently vacillates between [these] two distinct poles, in both secular and religious usage'.[65] Sheppard summarizes, 'the former dimension emphasizes internal signs of an elevated status'. Conversely, 'the latter puts stress on the precise boundary, limits, or measure of what, from some preunderstood standard, belongs within or falls outside of a specific "canon"'.[66]

These two understandings of what 'canon' entails can be categorized generally under the heading of a 'broad understanding of canon' and a 'narrow understanding of canon'.[67] Depending on which of these definitional options

---

62. Sheppard, 'Canon', p. 64. As will be discussed in this section, the major contemporary disagreements on canon formation can typically be traced back to this definitional issue.

63. See Sheppard, 'Canon', pp. 62-69. For a survey of the scholars defending both of these interpretive positions, see Dempster, 'Canons', pp. 47-78.

64. Sheppard, 'Canon', p. 64.

65. Sheppard, 'Canon', p. 64. He also notes that 'this "ideal" distinction only demarcates poles in a continuum of options, since the essential nature and status of a normative tradition or a "scripture" within a religion inevitably emerges through its own unique, dialectical interplay between these polarities' (p. 64).

66. Sheppard, 'Canon', p. 64.

67. Cf. Driver, *Brevard Childs*, p. 22: 'Possibly the single greatest difference [between the two streams of canon scholarship] hinges on narrow and broad definitions of canon.' In this regard, Barton summarizes, 'We may clearly identify a scholarly tradition which speaks of texts as "canonical" if they are widely received as possessing authority, and another which reserves the term for those texts which, after a process of sifting and evaluation, have been approved and stand on a limited list' (*Holy Writings, Sacred Texts*, p. 12). Attempting methodological balance, Barton also argues that the historical evidence does not allow for a firm commitment to either of these options: 'Whether we summarize all this by saying that "the canon" is an early or a late development is largely a matter of choice. What is important is that we recognize *both* truths, and do not try to escape from one by holding fast to the other' (p. 31). Echoing Barton's caution, Kruger concludes that 'there is more common ground between competing canonical models than is often realized' (*Canon Revisited*, p. 292). Confusion and distortion arises 'when a single aspect of canon is absolutized at the expense of others' (p. 293). Kruger reiterates this conclusion in 'The Definition of the Term "Canon": Exclusive or Multi-Dimensional?', *Tyndale Bulletin* 63 (2012), pp. 1-20. Kruger contends that 'insisting that only a single definition rightly captures the depth and breadth of canon may end

is taken, there follows a series of important implications regarding various aspects of the body of relevant historical evidence. The dating of the canon formation process in particular is affected by how one defines key terms.[68] Some of the most important points of discussion in the secondary literature germane to the canon debate include: (1) the distinction between 'canon' and 'Scripture', (2) the nature of canonical closure, (3) the pivotal century for the formation of the canon, (4) the primary catalysts for the canonization process, and (5) the function of the Hebrew Bible in the formation of the Christian canon as a whole. Most of these areas overlap and do not lend themselves to neat distinction; though, they are each substantive topics in their own right. Of these five areas, the distinction between 'canon' and 'Scripture' is the most crucial. Indeed, many of the differences of opinion in the other four areas directly relate to the decision made in this first area.

The Distinction between Canon and Scripture

As discussed above, the two main understandings of canon are the products of two streams of competing historiographies of the canon formation process.[69] One of the crucial steps that led to the current consensus in canon studies regarding the basic outline of the process of canon formation is the strict distinction between 'canon' and 'Scripture'.[70] Reviewing the *Wirkungsgeschichte* of the strict and absolute distinction between these two terms elucidates the present state of scholarship on canon formation.[71] In particular,

up bringing more distortion than clarification' (p. 20). He concludes, 'If canon is a multi-dimensional phenomenon, then perhaps it is best defined in a multi-dimensional fashion' (p. 20). Cf. Brevard S. Childs, *Introduction to the Old Testament as Scripture* (Philadelphia, PA: Fortress Press, 1979), pp. 57-58: 'The difficulty of the subject and its complex historical usage should caution against too quickly claiming the exclusive right for any one definition. It is important that the use of the term does justice to all the dimensions of the issue without prematurely resolving problems merely by definition.'

68. Chapman, 'Canon Debate', pp. 273-74, argues that 'the dating dimension of the debate is largely secondary and derivative, arising from a prior semantic disagreement'. He further suggests that this definitional disagreement 'reveals more fundamental differences in the conceptual presuppositions held by scholars active in canon-oriented research' (p. 274).

69. For a brief but thorough survey of the literature on New Testament canon formation published prior to and during the twentieth century, see Metzger, *Canon of the New Testament*, pp. 11-36.

70. E.g., Holmes argues that Sundberg's worked out distinction between canon and Scripture was 'path setting in this respect' and is a 'fundamental feature of recent research' ('Biblical Canon', p. 407). His survey article on the canon debate begins with a section contrasting canon and Scripture.

71. Brevard S. Childs, 'The Canon in Recent Biblical Studies: Reflections on an Era', in *Canon and Biblical Interpretation* (ed. Craig G. Bartholomew, *et al.*; Grand Rapids, MI: Zondervan, 2006), pp. 33-57 (34), notes that the debate between Zahn and Harnack

the work of Theodor Zahn, Adolf von Harnack, and Albert C. Sundberg represents the progression of these developments.[72] As the distinction between canon and Scripture becomes more rigid in the history of scholarship, the germane time period for canon formation moves later and later in the history of the church. Consequently, the nature of canonical closure and the perceived motivations and catalysts for canon are significantly affected as well. How one parses this distinction proves determinative for how one wades through the constellation of historical concerns surrounding the canon debate.

Theodor Zahn. At the turn of the twentieth century, German scholar Theodor Zahn (1838–1933) produced a number of major studies on the formation of the New Testament canon.[73] One of his areas of emphasis was the citations and citation formulas of patristic writers when they referred to the texts of the emerging body of New Testament literature. Zahn surveys the writings of the patristic period and highlights their use and employment of New Testament texts. For Zahn, whenever a patristic figure quotes a writing that eventually becomes part of the New Testament canon, one could suppose that that figure not only knew some version of the particular writing he was quoting, but also understood it to be an authoritative and normative work. In this investigation, references to congregational practices were viewed as particularly significant.[74] Zahn also argues that the judg-

(see below) was the hallmark of a previous era's canon debate. Childs observes that Ernst Käsemann's book *Das Neue Testament als Kanon* (Göttingen: Vandenhoeck & Ruprecht, 1970) 'pointed backward and marked the end of [this] earlier German debate'.

72. Harry Y. Gamble, 'The New Testament Canon: Recent Research and the *Status Quaestionis*', in *Canon Debate*, pp. 267-94, begins his survey of recent canon research by outlining the interaction of Zahn, Harnack, and Sundberg. Barton (*Holy Writings, Sacred Texts*, pp. 1-34) and Allert (*High View of Scripture*, pp. 40-47) also highlight the importance of these three figures for the history of canon formation.

73. Zahn's major work on the formation of the New Testament canon comprises the ten volumes of *Forschungen zur Geschichte des Neutestamentlichen Kanons und der Altkirchlichen Literatur* (Leipzig: A. Deichert, 1881–1929). For a condensed 'outline' of this larger project, see *Grundriss der Geschichte des Neutestamentlichen Kanons* (Leipzig: A. Deichert, 1904). Zahn's entry on 'Canon of Scripture' in *New Schaff-Herzog Encyclopedia of Religious Knowledge* (ed. S.M. Jackson; New York: Funk and Wagnalls, 1908), II, pp. 398-400, surveys the history of the canon and represents a summary product of his methodological decisions. Peter Balla seeks to recover Zahn's contribution to the canon debate in *Challenges to New Testament Theology: An Attempt to Justify the Enterprise* (Tübingen: Mohr Siebeck, 1997), esp. Chapter 3 (pp. 86-146). For Balla, Zahn's 'analyses of the evidence in relation to canon are…unduly neglected' (p. 87). Balla aims to supplement deficiencies and lacuna in Zahn's work with the contribution of new evidence and the development of scholarship since the nineteenth century.

74. See Zahn, 'Permanent Value of the New Testament', p. 6: 'In considering these differences and waverings we are not concerned, as has been at times superficially suggested, with the personal judgments of individual greater or lesser teachers. We must

ment concerning the content of the New Testament 'has not been given to the individual Christian as an indispensable means of salvation, but to the congregation as a firm rod for its pilgrimage through the ages'.[75]

Zahn assigned a high level of significance to the many citations of the New Testament made in the century following the New Testament period. Thus, for him, the pivotal century in the process of canon formation was the first century, the period when the texts of the New Testament begin to surface in extra-biblical ecclesial writings. By the time of Marcion and Montanism in the second century, the churches had 'a New Testament already commonly so called'.[76] Zahn can also speak of the 'common edition of the "Prophets and Apostles"' in this same time period.[77] For him, 'it is evident that the church possessed a New Testament in addition to the Old Testament about the year 200'.[78] Further, for Zahn, 'During the third century the New Testament underwent no essential change.'[79] As Barton summarizes, 'the essential point in Zahn's reconstruction is that the New Testament was a spontaneous creation of the first generations of Christians, not something forced on the Church by internal or external pressures'.[80]

Adolf von Harnack. One of Zahn's primary dialogue partners was Adolf von Harnack (1851–1930). Harnack was a German theologian and church historian, and his work includes writings on history, theology, and biblical

deal directly with the congregational usage and the universal valuation of the books according to the great centers of early Christianity as they differ in provinces, nationalities and languages.'

75. Zahn, 'Permanent Value of the New Testament', p. 24.

76. See Zahn, 'Canon of Scripture', p. 393: 'The Church had a New Testament already commonly so called, over against the Montanistic contention of a new period of prophecy already opened which was to lead the way to a wider development.' He concludes that 'the Church regarded the age of revelation as closed with the death of the last surviving apostle and the canon of the New Testament as completed, though discussion still went on as to the inclusion of some books therein' (p. 393). Zahn speaks of Marcion 'receiving' a collection from the church that he in turn radically alters.

77. Zahn, 'Canon of Scripture', p. 395. Zahn also argues that 'the foundation of the canon of the most important schools of Gnostics, 140-170, is that of the Church of 200' (p. 396).

78. Zahn, 'Permanent Value of the New Testament Canon', pp. 4-5. Recognizing that early church leaders (e.g. Clement or Tertullian) did not necessarily refer to the collection as 'The New Testament', Zahn maintains that 'there was in existence a collection of writings from the early period of the church, which was read in the service of the congregation as the now scriptural Word of God and of the Lord Jesus Christ, and was made the basis of the sermon, besides being applied as the primary source and highest norm in all theological disputations and churchly transactions' (p. 5).

79. Zahn, 'Canon of Scripture', p. 397.

80. Barton, *Holy Writings, Sacred Text*, p. 3.

studies.[81] While he is perhaps best known as a theologian in the tradition of 'classical liberalism', he also devoted a significant portion of his scholarly career to the history of the New Testament canon.[82] His historiographical account of canon formation in *The Origin of the New Testament* helped shaped the discussion about the canon in the late nineteenth century.[83]

In this work on the New Testament canon, Harnack interacts with Zahn's first-century thesis and seeks to refute it by demonstrating a flaw in Zahn's methodology and questioning the relevance of the data he assembles.[84] For Harnack, reckoning with mere citations of New Testa-

81. Wilhelm Pauck, *Harnack and Troeltsch: Two Historical Theologians* (Oxford: Oxford University Press, 1968), p. 14, characterizes Harnack as a 'historical theologian'. Cf. F.F. Bruce, 'Harnack, Adolf', in *New Dictionary of Theology* (ed. Sinclair Ferguson and David Wright; Downers Grove, IL: IVP, 1988), pp. 286-87.

82. Bruce refers to Harnack as 'the spokesman of liberal Protestantism' ('Harnack, Adolph', p. 286). One of the reasons for this appellation is Harnack's view that the goal of Christian communities should be the pursuit of a 'core of Christianity'. In this view, theologians and interpreters should seek to discern the essential elements of the Christian message and base the Christian life on that basic set of values. An example of this mindset can be found in Harnack's important set of lectures that he later published as *What Is Christianity? Lectures Delivered in the University of Berlin during the Winter-Term, 1899-1900* (London: Williams and Norgate, 1901). Cf. Martin Rumscheidt, *Adolf von Harnack: Liberal Theology at Its Height* (San Francisco, CA: Harper & Row, 1989), pp. 9-41.

83. Adolf von Harnack, *The Origin of the New Testament and the Most Important Consequences of the New Creation* (trans. J.R. Wilkinson; London: Williams & Norgate, 1925). In his account of the creation of the New Testament, Harnack aims to 'forward and complete' the work of other canonical histories. He views his method of treating both motives for and consequences of the New Testament canon as a unique contribution to the discussion 'that hitherto has been seldom taken into account' (p. v). Harnack asks the sometimes neglected question, 'How did the Church arrive at a second authoritative Canon in addition to the Old Testament?' (p. 4). For Harnack, the best way to answer this query is by closely examining the motives that prompted the early church community to create or produce the New Testament. Accordingly, the first part of *Origin of the New Testament* is entitled 'The Needs and Motive Forces that Led to the Creation of the New Testament'. Harnack sees these issues as raising five 'chief problems'. He first addresses the 'motives' question (§1), and then in the following sections, he seeks to answer why the New Testament contains epistles in addition to Gospels (§2), why there are only four Gospels (§3), why there is only one Apocalypse (§4), and if the New Testament was created 'consciously' (§5). Though he does point out many benefits of the canon, Harnack is quick to return to the stifling, restrictive, and oppressive consequences of its creation (e.g. §9-11). This overall assessment of the canon resonates with some of the elements of Harnack's larger liberal theological agenda and intellectual context.

84. See especially Harnack's appendix entitled, 'A Short Statement and Criticism of the Results of Zahn's Investigations into the Origin of the New Testament', in *Origin of the New Testament*, pp. 218-29. Cf. Gamble, 'New Testament Canon', p. 268: '[Harnack] did not challenge Zahn's data but his interpretation of it, claiming that Zahn failed to provide a *history* of canon, not only because he located its existence at so early a time

ment documents is inadequate grounds for the assertion that those authors held those particular writings to be normative ('canonical') writings. He points out that Zahn has only demonstrated that these works were read in public worship and quoted by church leaders. For Harnack, this does not *necessarily* entail that these works were 'canonical' in the sense that they were to be used exclusively. He even notes that Zahn's work 'ought not to bear the title *History of the Canon of the New Testament*, but *History of the Public and Private Use of the Works that were Afterwards United in the New Testament*'.[85] Harnack states strongly that 'the right to be read publicly and the right to be included in the Canon are jumbled together by Zahn as if they were identical'.[86]

He continues by arguing that 'public lection was certainly a most important preliminary condition for the canonizing of a book...but it was by no means the sole condition'.[87] According to Harnack, the 'unjustifiable identification of public lection and Canon' is neither sufficient nor decisive for understanding the formation of the canon. In order to remedy this flawed approach, Harnack adjusts Zahn's method by focusing on the references to New Testament texts that were not only cited, but cited specifically as Scripture (e.g. 'It is written'). If a text was cited as Scripture and read as authoritative alongside of Old Testament texts, *then* it could be considered 'canonical' in a formal sense. Essentially, Harnack makes a distinction between an author citing a text on one hand, and an author citing a text *as Scripture* on the other.[88] Harnack would rather take as '*punctum saliens* not the public lection of the separate works, but the setting of a new collection of sacred writings on a level with the Old Testament'.[89]

---

and did not bring it into any connection with the theological controversies of the second century, but also because he rested too much on public reading, as though public reading and canonical standing were the same thing.' Consequently, Harnack finds Zahn's evidence to be 'irrelevant for the real issue' (p. 268).

85. Harnack, *Origin of the New Testament*, p. 219.

86. Harnack, *Origin of the New Testament*, p. 219. Harnack goes on to note that Zahn himself 'admits that the conception of what should be regularly read at public worship "had not been clearly defined". It is indeed, quite true, that every work that was "Canonical" (in the sense of the Old Testament) was also read publicly, but the converse statement is simply inadmissible' (p. 219).

87. Harnack, *Origin of the New Testament*, p. 219.

88. Barton argues that 'the present majority view of the Christian Bible owes more, perhaps, to this distinction, painstakingly applied by a long line of distinguished scholars, than to any other single discovery' (*Holy Writings, Sacred Texts*, p. 5).

89. Harnack, *Origin of the New Testament*, p. 228. Cf. von Campenhausen, *Formation of the Christian Bible*, p. 103: 'One can, in my view, speak of "canon" only where of set purpose such a document or group of documents is given a special, normative position, by virtue of which it takes its place alongside the existing Old Testament "scriptures".'

Because the first instances of this type of citation are not found in the patristic period until the second century CE, Harnack figures that it is not until then that one can demonstrate that the churches viewed particular writings as Scripture. Thus, according to Harnack, the pivotal century for canon formation is the second century rather than the first. Consequently, the external factors that served as catalysts for the formation and solidification of the canon were second century heresies such as Marcionism and Montanism.[90] Because of the methodological divergence of Zahn and Harnack's approaches to interpreting patristic citations, the debate at this point ended in 'a frustrating stalemate'.[91] Harnack's reconstruction of the history of canon formation, though, gained widespread support and functioned as the consensus view.[92]

Albert C. Sundberg, Jr. In the mid-twentieth century, Albert C. Sundberg, Jr re-evaluated the Zahn-Harnack debate and sought to take it one step further.[93] Sundberg critiques Harnack's methodology and criteria for determining when the New Testament literature was deemed 'canonical'. In so doing, Sundberg self-consciously seeks to revise the consensus he understands to have been

---

90. Harnack's work on Marcion has been extremely influential in the historiography of the patristic period. See his *Marcion: Das Evangelium vom fremden Gott* (Leipzig: Hinrichs, 1924). In recent scholarship, Harnack's understanding of the role of Marcion (and the other second century heresies) in the canonization of the New Testament has come under critical scrutiny. For example, David Balás argues that 'the Marcion known to most present day students is Adolf von Harnack's Marcion', and that it 'seems quite certain that [Harnack's] work was strongly shaped by his personal theological judgments and interests' ('Marcion Revisited: A "Post-Harnack" Perspective', in *Texts and Testaments* [ed. W. Eugene March; San Antonio, TX: Trinity University Press, 1980], p. 95). Balás concludes that 'Harnack's Marcion is in need of a serious revision'. See also in this regard B. Aland, 'Marcion: Versuch einer neuen Interpretation', *ZTK* 70 (1973), pp. 420-47; and Barton, 'Marcion Revisited', in *Canon Debate*, pp. 341-54.

91. Childs, 'Canon in Recent Biblical Studies', p. 35.

92. Von Campenhausen's book, *Formation of the Christian Bible*, is a comprehensive work based on Harnack's historical and methodological argumentation. Gamble notes that von Campenhausen's work is 'the most comprehensive and influential elaboration' of Harnack's view ('New Testament Canon', p. 268). Trobisch echoes this valuation, noting that this volume 'still represents a milestone in the history of research and serves as a reference work for all later studies' (*First Edition of the New Testament*, p. 109 n. 11).

93. Sundberg's seminal work in this area is the revised form of his Harvard dissertation published as *The Old Testament of the Early Church* (Cambridge, MA: Harvard University Press, 1964). In this study, Sundberg seeks to deconstruct the notion of a viable 'Alexandrian canon' that was consciously adopted for use among the early church. Cf. A.C. Sundberg, 'The "Old Testament": A Christian Canon', *CBQ* 30 (1968), pp. 143-55.

established by Harnack's work on the New Testament.[94] He makes the critical distinction between 'canon' and 'Scripture' and then re-evaluates the data analyzed by both Zahn and Harnack.[95] For Sundberg, 'In order to write a coherent and accurate history of the New Testament canon it becomes necessary to distinguish between the terms "scripture" and "canon" as *termini technici* in the history of the canon'.[96] The church did not receive 'an Old Testament canon' from Judaism but rather 'scripture on the way to canonization'.[97] Therefore, Sundberg argues, Harnack's critique of Zahn does not go far enough because even the concept of 'Scripture' is not settled by the second century CE.

Sundberg defines canon narrowly in terms of closure. The canon is a 'closed collection of "scripture", to which nothing is to be added, from which nothing is to be subtracted'.[98] For Sundberg, 'list' and 'canon' stand in conceptual apposition: 'the formation of the New Testament list, the New Testament canon'.[99] The term 'scripture', by contrast, is a loose and inclusive category that simply refers to writings that could be 'appealed to for religious authority', but are not necessarily normative or exclusive. The fact that a person calls a particular writing 'Scripture', then, does not really indicate whether or not they view it as 'canonical'. Because this literature was 'cited as authoritative, it is proper to call it "scripture"', but because 'it was not a closed collection, it is not proper to call it "canon"'.[100] Sundberg concludes that 'a clear technical differentiation between "scripture" and "canon" becomes essential to a clear and accurate history of the New Testament canon'.[101]

94. See especially the introduction to 'Towards a Revised History of the New Testament Canon', in *Studia Evangelica 4* (ed. F.L. Cross; Berlin: Akademie Verlag, 1968), pp. 452-61. This brief article adumbrates the rest of Sundberg's work on canon and the ensuing consensus built around his argumentation and reconstruction of canon history, making it a highly significant primary source for the development of canon studies in the twentieth century. In this regard, see von Campenhausen's initial reaction to Sundberg's criticism in *Formation of the Christian Bible*, p. 327 n. 4: 'The objection to this procedure raised by A.C. Sundberg...derives in part from a somewhat different conception of what is meant by "canonical", and has failed to convince me.' He also adds that 'in other respects [Sundberg's] sketch has repeated points of contact with the theses of the present work' (p. 327 n. 4).

95. Gamble characterizes Sundberg's view as 'a more phenomenological approach' ('New Testament Canon', p. 269).

96. Sundberg, 'Revised History', p. 453.

97. Sundberg, 'Revised History', p. 453. He reiterates later that 'the Jewish literature received by Christianity was not a closed collection; it was not a canon'. Here Sundberg draws on the thesis he develops in *Old Testament of the Early Church*.

98. Sundberg, 'Revised History', p. 454.

99. Sundberg, 'Revised History', p. 460.

100. Sundberg, 'Revised History', p. 453.

101. Sundberg, 'Revised History', pp. 453-54.

Further, because 'lists' and 'tables' of biblical books do not appear until the fourth century CE and beyond, Sundberg moves the pivotal century of canon formation to this later period in the history of the church.[102] Consequently, the external factors at play during the time period of canon formation are the ecclesiastical debates and councils of the fourth century. What comes to be understood as canonical is a result of the external decisions made by authoritative individuals and groups of leaders at church councils. In this scenario, political and ideological factors play a significant role. Sundberg's conclusion to his pioneering article encapsulates and anticipates the core tenants of the contemporary consensus on the history of the canon formation process:

> The recognition that canonization proper is the definition of a New Testament list to which nothing can be added, nothing subtracted, moves canonization from the tacit implication that somehow canonization adheres to apostles, apostolic men, and the hearers of apostolic men and leaves the formation of a closed New Testament list as unequivocally the decision of the church.[103]

An important point to recognize is that the evidence does not change in each of these three historical assessments. Zahn, Harnack, and Sundberg all agree on the nature of the historical data (i.e. 'the facts'). What shifted were the definitions given to key terms and the subsequent effect those definitions had on the presuppositions of the investigator. As Holmes articulates, 'For all their definitional differences, however, none of the three really disagrees about the basic facts or evidence.'[104] Sundberg's extensive argumentation in this area has had a decisive influence on subsequent studies of the history of canon formation.[105] Scholars such as John Barton, James Sanders,

---

102. See Sundberg, 'Revised History', pp. 460-61: 'Such a revised outline for the history of the New Testament canon will have the effect of moving the decisive period of canonical history from the second century to the end of the second century onward into the fourth and the beginning of the fifth centuries.' Cf. Gamble, 'New Testament Canon', p. 269: 'This terminological rigor means...the period of canon formation proper can be located only with the appearance of such lists'.

103. Sundberg, 'Revised History', p. 461.

104. Holmes, 'Biblical Canon', p. 408. Barton also highlights this methodological observation (see *Holy Writings, Sacred Texts*, pp. 1-34). He comments that the Zahn-Harnack-Sundberg spectrum is about 'the definitions of terms, rather than about matters of substance' (p. 11). For Barton, 'it should be obvious that much in the progressively later dating of "canonization" from Zahn through Harnack to Sundberg is generated simply by an ever-increasing narrowness of definition for the term "canon"' (pp. 11-12).

105. Childs notes that 'the initial effect of this terminological distinction was that Sundberg's book marked the beginning of a new phase in the study of the canon within the English-speaking world, and shifted the discussion primarily to the historical problems related to the process that ended in the canonization of the Jewish and Christian Bibles ('Canon in Recent Biblical Studies', p. 36).

Lee M. McDonald, and Craig Allert follow Sundberg's strict distinction between canon and Scripture and analyze the external evidence accordingly. Barton and McDonald in particular have been influential in establishing the Sundberg distinction. For example, in his conclusion to *Holy Writings, Sacred Scripture*, Barton writes, 'I have tried to defend a usage which Sundberg was, to my knowledge, the first to introduce, in which a distinction is drawn between the "Scripture" which results from the growth of writings perceived as holy, and the "canon" which represents official decisions to exclude from Scripture works deemed unsuitable.'[106] In Barton's view, 'this distinction can greatly clarify our thinking about both the Old and New Testament'.[107]

Further, virtually all of the contributors to the important book *The Canon Debate*, edited by James A. Sanders and Lee M. McDonald, adopt the Sundberg distinction and represent the current scholarly consensus. For instance, at the conclusion of his essay on Eusebius, Everett R. Kalin writes, 'It is quite likely that Albert C. Sundberg Jr's perspective on New Testament canon history is preferable to the commonly accepted view.'[108] On the next page, Geoffrey M. Hahneman begins his essay on the Muratorian Fragment by clearly stating that 'Albert Sundberg's important distinction between "scripture" and "canon" remains essential in understanding the formation of the Christian Bible in the midst of the fourth century.'[109] Moreover, Sanders and McDonald's introduction and Ulrich's lead essay on the 'Notion and Definition' of canon argue strongly for the Sundberg distinction as well.[110] In his essay toward the end of the volume on the criteria for canonicity, McDonald reflects, 'I believe that it is best to follow the advice of Albert Sundberg Jr and Eugene Ulrich and employ the term 'canon' to refer to a delimited collection of Christian literature that makes up our current biblical canon.'[111] Though alternative views are examined and argued for in

---

106. Barton, *Holy Writings, Sacred Text*, pp. 157-58.

107. Barton, *Holy Writings, Sacred Text*, p. 158. Barton's sustained and substantial work on the canon question throughout his career can now be accessed in John Barton, *The Old Testament: Canon, Literature and Theology: Collected Essays of John Barton* (Burlington, VT: Ashgate, 2007). Cf. John Barton, 'Canonical Approaches Ancient and Modern', in *The Biblical Canons* (ed. J.M. Auwers and H.J. de Jonge; Leuven: Leuven University Press, 2003), pp. 199-209.

108. Everett R. Kalin, 'The New Testament Canon of Eusebius', in *Canon Debate*, pp. 386-404 (404).

109. Geoffrey Mark Hahneman, 'The Muratorian Fragment and the Origins of the New Testament Canon', in *Canon Debate*, pp. 405-15 (405).

110. McDonald and Sanders, 'Introduction', in *Canon Debate*, pp. 3-20; Ulrich, 'Notion and Definition', pp. 21-35.

111. McDonald, 'Identifying Scripture and Canon in the Early Church: The Criteria Question', in *Canon Debate*, pp. 416-39 (423 n. 21). Further, the first major part of McDonald's substantive and influential volume on canon formation begins with a

various places throughout the volume, Sundberg thus gets the first, middle, and last word in this particular 'debate'.[112]

Conversely, those who have pushed back on the strictness of this distinction include Brevard S. Childs, Christopher R. Seitz, Stephen Chapman, and Stephen Dempster. In a survey of the canon debate in recent years, Childs notes the significance of this distinction for the way scholars discuss the canon and related issues in English/American and German contexts.[113] Because English-speaking scholarship largely follows Sundberg's distinctions, there is typically a contrast between the way 'canon' is treated in the two streams of scholarship. In Germany, the distinction between canon and Scripture was never accepted or developed as fully, and so German discussions of canon tend not to separate the concept of canon from the theological issues of authority and normativity in their treatment of the process of canon formation.[114] In summary, Childs observes that because the Sundberg distinction was not adopted in the German debate, 'the focus did not fall

section working out the distinction between 'Scripture and Canon' (see *Biblical Canon*, pp. 3-70). For a recent critical interaction with McDonald's crucial methodological decisions, see Timothy J. Stone, 'The Biblical Canon According to Lee McDonald: An Evaluation', *EuroJTh* 18 (2009), pp. 55-64.

112. Though the majority of the essays are on the opposite end of the spectrum, the essays by Balla and Ferguson represent a contrasting perspective. See Peter Balla, 'Evidence for an Early Christian Canon (Second and Third Century)', in *Canon Debate*, pp. 372-85; and Everett Ferguson, 'Factors Leading to the Selection and Closure of the New Testament Canon: A Survey of Some Recent Studies', in *Canon Debate*, pp. 295-320. Balla argues for an early closure to the New Testament canon, and Ferguson supports the legitimacy of internal (rather than exclusively external) motivations for the formation of the New Testament. Cf. Dempster's comment on the perspectival disparity of this volume in 'Canons', p. 47 n. 4: 'There were strong efforts to make the debate representative (see p. 17), but the omissions noted read like a *Who's Who* for one perspective in the field of canonical studies: Bruce Metzger, Roger Beckwith, Earle Ellis, Brevard Childs, and the late Gerald Sheppard.'

113. See Childs, 'Canon in Recent Biblical Studies', pp. 33-57.

114. For an example of scholarship working from this type of approach to canon, see the essays in *Der Bibelkanon in der Bibelauslegung: Methodenreflexionen und Beispielexegesen* (ed. Egbert Ballhorn and Georg Steins; Stuttgart: Kohlhammer, 2007). In his review of this book, Daniel R. Driver reflects, 'It is a truly remarkable feature of the volume under review that nowhere is the Frankemölle/McDonald/Sanders line upheld. Rather, with Steins, each writer who touches on the matter (and several do) takes for granted that the formation of biblical literature testifies to a growing consciousness of canon, even while recognizing that many texts have been caught up in the canonizing process without regard for a putative original intent. At the same time, the diversity of canons past and present is still frequently affirmed, even celebrated' (*RBL* [2008], http://www.bookreviews.org/pdf/6401_6893.pdf). Melanie Köhlmoos also interacts with this volume at length in 'Kanon und Methode: Zu einer Zwischenbilanz der "Kanonischen Auslegung"', *Theologische Rundschau* 74 (2009), pp. 135-46.

exclusively on the historical forces at work in the process which dominated the English-speaking debate'.[115] Rather, 'within the larger traditional category of Sacred Scripture, a distinction was made between the canonical *process* and the *end product* of canonization'.[116]

A Narrow Understanding of Canon

Once the strict distinction between 'canon' and 'Scripture' solidifies, the resulting consensus naturally encourages a narrow understanding of canon.[117] Though there is obviously significant diversity on a wide range of issues among those who adopt a narrow understanding of canon, the main contours of this position (and the alternative position discussed below) are nevertheless generally consistent. This approach adopts the '*exclusive* sense' of the term canon, where 'canon' refers specifically (and exclusively) to the list of sacred writings ('canon as list').[118] Here canon means 'a closed official list, incapable of alteration, that consciously both includes and excludes'.[119] Consequently, the concept of canon is understood primarily in terms of closure.[120] When the list of writings is finally complete with no further revision, the existence of a 'canon' becomes a possibility.

115. Childs, 'Canon in Recent Biblical Studies', p. 45.

116. Childs, 'Canon in Recent Biblical Studies', p. 45. Emphasis added. Cf. Chapman's overview of this debate in *The Law and the Prophets: A Study in Old Testament Canon Formation* (Tübingen: Mohr Siebeck, 2000), pp. 106-10.

117. Childs, 'Canon in Recent Biblical Studies', pp. 42-43, argues that this narrow understanding of canon (the Sundberg distinction) along with its constellation of resultant interpretive decisions has become an established consensus in English-speaking scholarship. Cf. Driver, *Brevard Childs*, p. 21: 'For many it is also axiomatic that canon must be sharply distinguished from scripture, in part because most communities that cherish a canon stand at some remove from the communities that produced the scriptures in it.'

118. Chapman, 'Canon Debate', p. 278. Cf. Holmes, 'Biblical Canon', p. 407: 'Canonicity is a matter of list-making, not scriptural status.'

119. Holmes, 'Biblical Canon', p. 407. Ulrich provides a paradigmatic articulation of this approach. For him, canon 'denotes the final, fixed, and closed list of the books of scripture that are officially and permanently accepted as supremely authoritative by a faith tradition, in conscious contradistinction from those books that are not accepted' ('Notion and Definition', p. 31).

120. Jonathan Z. Smith, 'Canons, Catalogues and Classics', in *Canonization and Decanonization* (ed. A. van der Kooij and K. van der Toorn; Leiden: Brill, 1998), pp. 295-311, argues that 'closure remains the sole discriminator of canon in contradistinction to list or catalogue' (p. 313). In 'Sacred Persistence: Toward a Redescription of Canon', in *Imagining Religion: From Babylon to Jonestown* (Chicago: Chicago University Press, 1982), Smith states that 'canon is a subtype of the genre *list*' (p. 44). Cf. James A. Sanders, 'The Issue of Closure in the Canonical Process', in *Canon Debate*, pp. 252-63. For Sanders, canonical closure/canonicity is 'something officially or authoritatively imposed upon certain literature' (p. 252).

The crucial phase of the canon formation process is when the community sets the number, order, and content of its authoritative collection. In this approach, external factors such as persecution, political expediency, and heretical alternatives are highlighted.[121] Thus, the church, through the use of 'criteria of canonicity', sets the boundaries of the large repository of writings in current circulation and available to them. The canon formation process is seen as a type of delimiting task, where canonization creates the authority. Further, for a list to be truly authoritative, it would need universal recognition. In other words, 'canonization is an act of authority by which a limited number of texts are imposed upon a particular community as binding for all members, for all times'.[122]

The notion of 'selection' here is more appropriate than the notion of 'recognition', as the 'exclusive sense of canon entails selectivity and conscious

121. See Hahneman's summary of these germane external factors in 'Muratorian Fragment', pp. 414-15. The two primary motivations Hahneman lists are persecution and political pressure. McDonald also posits these aspects (i.e. persecution under Diocletian and political pressure from Constantine) as crucial motivations for canonization (see 'Identifying Scripture and Canon', pp. 417-18; *Biblical Canon*, pp. 310-22; and *Origin of the Bible*, pp. 192-231). Similarly, Dungan states unequivocally, 'In terms of the history of Christianity, a canon of scripture, properly so called, did not appear until church officials, acting under the guidance of the highest levels of the Roman government, met together on several specific occasions to create a rigid boundary around the approved texts, forever separating them from the larger "cloud of sacred texts"' (*Constantine's Bible*, p. 3). Dungan elaborates on his reconstructed portrait of political maneuvering by reflecting, 'Once the bishops and priests began to receive salaries from the state, once church councils could be called and their business personally directed by the emperor, once huge new buildings were built at the emperor's personal expense and given to the Catholic Christians for Sunday worship, once the emperor had personally ordained Sunday as the universal day of rest, it was just a matter of time before canon law became inextricably intertwined in the process of deciding which writings of the Lord's disciples should be read at Sunday worship (the Holy Scripture) and what was the proper interpretation of the doctrines contained in them (the Creed)' (pp. 9-10).

122. Karel van der Toorn, *Scribal Culture and the Making of the Hebrew Bible* (Cambridge, MA: Harvard University Press, 2007), pp. 7-8. Van der Toorn also argues that 'the biblical canon is typically a list of works, as their combination into one volume (the one Bible) does not occur until the birth of the codex' (p. 8). For him, 'this list is closed. It is comparable to the catalogue of a library or the curriculum of a school but is nonetheless a category in its own right' (p. 8). A central element of Van der Toorn's argument is that neither authors nor books (understood as physical compositional entities) existed during most of Israel's history. In this regard, his first chapter is entitled, 'Books That Are Not Books' (p. 9). Cf. Georg Steins, 'Zwei Konzepte—ein Kanon. Neue Theorien zur Entstehung und Eigenart der Hebräischen Bibel', in *Kanonisierung—die Hebräische Bibel im Werden* (ed. Georg Steins and Johannes Taschner; Göttingen: Neukirchener Theologie, 2010), pp. 8-45. Steins compares and contrasts the two very different 'konzepte' of canon developed by van der Toorn ('The Idea of a Canonical Era', pp. 26-32) and Chapman ('The Core Canon of the Law and the Prophets', pp. 22-26).

decision'.[123] The existence of a canon 'represents a conscious, retrospective, official judgment'.[124] Accordingly, the absence of a deliberated list of 'canonical' books in a historical period entails the absence of an authoritative canon in that period. The use of the term canon before the end of the fourth century is therefore an anachronism.[125] For this option, an 'open canon' is a contradiction in terms.[126] Indeed, an open canon is no 'canon' at all.[127] This option also usually argues that the Hebrew Bible was still in flux in New Testament times and beyond.[128] The early church did not receive and respect a fixed or stable collection of Hebrew Scriptures. In this approach, the formation of the New Testament canon along with the Christian canon occurs late in the life of the church (i.e. fourth century) and involves the adjudication of institutional authorities.[129] In this model, there

123. Chapman, 'Canon Debate', p. 278.

124. Ulrich, 'Notion and Definition', p. 32. Ulrich describes this selection process in philosophical terms as 'reflective judgment'. A corollary of this reflective judgment is that 'an essential part of the process toward the canon was the judging and sifting to determine which books were supremely authoritative and which not' (p. 32).

125. Cf. Hahneman, 'Muratorian Fragment', p. 406: 'To speak of a Christian "canon" of scriptures is an anachronism before the second half of the fourth century because it is only after that time that Christian writers begin to employ the word...for a list of books counted as accepted scriptures'. Likewise, Kraft argues that 'there was no "Bible" as we know it—that is, a set of sacred writings organized into a single physical object, the codex book—until well into the fourth century of the common era' ('Paramania', p. 10).

126. Cf. Gamble, 'New Testament Canon', p. 269: 'Since, according to Sundberg, a canon is by definition fixed and closed, it obscures categories and misconstrues issues to speak of an "open canon", a "core canon", or a "developing canon".'

127. Ulrich argues that 'as long as the list was open, there was a collection of authoritative books, a collection of scriptures, but there was not yet an authoritative collection of books, a canon' ('Notion and Definition', p. 32). In summary, Ulrich argues that 'the requirement of reflective judgment and an exclusively closed list of books...are essential elements in the concept of canon'.

128. Sundberg argues strongly that 'the Jewish canon was not finally closed until about CE 90 and it was not until after CE 70 that a need to define the "Writings" collection was felt... That is to say, the Christian church did not receive a canon of scripture but scripture on the way to a definite canon in Judaism' ('Revised History', p. 453). Dempster characterizes the 'minimalist position' as one that argues that 'the completed canon was not a fact at least by the early second century AD' ('Canons', p. 49).

129. A paradigmatic articulation of this position in the history of New Testament theology is given by William Wrede (1859–1906) in 'The Task and Methods of "New Testament Theology"', in *The Nature of New Testament Theology* (ed. and trans. Robert Morgan; London: SCM Press, 1973). Wrede avers confidently that 'no New Testament writing was born with the predicate "canonical" attached'. Rather, 'the statement that a writing is canonical signifies in the first place only that *it was pronounced* canonical *afterwards* by authorities of the second-to-fourth-century church, in some cases only after all kinds of hesitation and disagreement' (pp. 70-71, emphasis added). For Wrede,

is a somewhat arbitrary connection between the internal nature of the texts themselves and the external forces of the communities that transmit and preserve them.[130]

A Broad Understanding of Canon
Representing the current historiographical minority report, the alternative option is to employ a broad understanding of canon.[131] This option 'insists on an overlap between Scripture and canon'.[132] Further, the term 'canon' or 'canonical' can cover a range of interrelated concepts such as normative authority, stable boundaries, and usefulness for the churches.[133] The canon is understood to be a stable collection of authoritative writings, though not necessarily a completely closed collection during the period of its formation. Within the writings themselves, there are significant associations in place, such that, even before the writings reach a final, consolidated state, there are strong connections that bind certain works and corpora together in

this scenario demands that scholars view the New Testament in the purview of a broad history-of-religions paradigm. Any privileging of the boundaries of the New Testament are arbitrary and driven by theological concerns. In contemporary scholarship, Heikki Räisänen has sought to continue and develop Wrede's brand of biblical theology with an emphasis on the distinction between the historical and theological task. For instance, see *Beyond New Testament Theology: A Story and a Programme* (London: SCM Press, 2000). Balla seeks to respond to the Wrede/Räisänen charge on historical grounds in *Challenges*.

130. Cf. Gamble, 'New Testament Canon', p. 271: 'An emphasis on the sharp distinctions furnished by lists tends to represent canonization more as a process of *exclusion* than of *inclusion*, thus emphasizing polemical and apologetic motives. This view also stresses the role of ecclesiastical authorities—bishops, synods, and councils—and downplays the importance of second-century controversies with heterodox movements' (emphasis added).

131. As Driver notes, 'Adoption of a broad semantic range for canon has made Childs and those who follow him outliers in recent discussions' (*Brevard Childs*, p. 24). Driver highlights the wide divergence between Childs's *Pauline Corpus* and Allert's *High View of Scripture*. In Driver's own opinion, 'the broad use of canon which has bemused so many of Childs' readers is at once theologically advantageous and historically defensible' (p. 24).

132. Chapman, 'Canon Debate', p. 278.

133. E.g., von Campenhausen writes, 'I have not taken the concept of the canonical in too narrow a sense. *It has to correspond to the actual history of the Canon.* It is purely arbitrary to make liturgical use, or formal definition, or the concept of inspiration, or, worse still, official ecclesiastical confirmation the only criterion, according to one's taste, of what is canonical'. Rather, for him, 'the fundamental idea—*in keeping with the meaning of the word*—is the status of a standard or norm which some writing or collection of writings has acquired for faith and life' (*Formation of the Christian Bible*, p. x; emphasis added).

a consistent and coherent fashion.[134] Canon formation is seen as a process of recognition, where canonization happens *because* of the authority and mutual interdependence of the biblical material. Thus, long before the final form of the entire canon closes, there is a growing but stable body of literature that functions with theological and conceptual authority in the believing community.[135] In this sense, there is an 'open canon' that functions with genuine authority that precedes the final consolidation or even final shaping of that collection.[136] Balla argues in this regard that 'there is a closer link between the authoritative character of a writing and the final "canonisation" of that writing than most scholars assume'.[137]

This option usually argues that the Hebrew Bible was a relatively stable, coherent unit in New Testament times, though not necessarily consolidated.[138]

---

134. Cf. Seitz, *Goodly Fellowship*, p. 45: 'Order and association precede lists, and they are accomplishments of a deeply theological nature to begin with.'

135. Chapman notes that this approach 'contends that, historically, the term *canon* has designated a norm as well as a list, that a canon is likely to function as a norm before being formalized, and that this formalization is better understood as the recognition of an already-authoritative literary collection than as the conferral of authority' ('Canon Debate', p. 278). Drawing on Zahn, Balla also argues that 'there is still room for looking for traces of a canonical process in the earlier periods, a process which led later to the formation of the canon as a list of books' (*Challenges*, p. 95).

136. Interacting with Sundberg's strict distinction between canon and scripture, Childs argues that 'to conceive of canon mainly as a dogmatic decision regarding its scope is to overestimate one feature within the process which is by no means constitutive of canon. It is still semantically meaningful to speak of an "open canon"' (*Introduction to the Old Testament as Scripture*, p. 58). Cf. Sanders' concise comment in 'Canon: Hebrew Bible', in *ABD* I, p. 843: 'Canon *as function* antedates canon *as shape*.' Peter R. Ackroyd calls this the 'canonical principle' (*Continuity* [Oxford: Blackwell, 1962], p. 15).

137. Balla, *Challenges*, p. 117. Cf. Ian Provan, 'Canons to the Left of Him: Brevard Childs, His Critics, and the Future of Old Testament Theology', *SJT* 50 (1997), p. 10: 'The question I am asking is whether the idea of scripture does not itself imply the idea of limitation, of canon, even if it is not yet conceived that the limits have been reached. I believe that it does so imply.' Interacting with Childs, Provan also notes that 'closure is only one element in the process of canon, and not constitutive of it... Scripture and canon cannot be sharply distinguished' (p. 10). Similarly, Chapman reflects, 'It is difficult to know how such "authoritative scripture" could have been *completely* unlimited' (*Law and Prophets*, p. 108).

138. Dempster notes that the maximalist position 'essentially argues that the Hebrew/ OT was a "done deal" by the time of the early church and the early church was born "with a canon in its hands"' ('Canons', p. 48). Chapman, too, argues, 'even though the boundaries of Israel's literary collection still may have been porous or open, application of the term *canon* is justified according to these scholars because the essential contours of the later formalized canon and a certain characteristic dynamic between the community and its Scripture were already palpably in place' ('Canon Debate', p. 279). After noting the presence of fluidity, von Campenhausen argues that 'what was settled was the

The presence of a Hebrew Bible during New Testament times and the patristic period provides an analogy and impetus for the concept of a New Testament canon. In other words, the existence of an authoritative collection early in the life of the church makes it possible that a canon-conscious mindset was present in some form during this time period. Further, the formation of the New Testament along with the Christian canon as a whole occurs early in the life of the church (i.e. second century).[139] In this model, there is an organic connection between the internal nature of the texts themselves and the external forces of the communities that transmit and preserve them. The thrust of canon formation is carried along by the effect of the texts themselves and not solely as a result of external forces. Accordingly, the churches recognize that the canon has, in this sense, 'imposed itself' on the believing community.[140]

The Process of Canon Formation

The basic outline of the process of canon formation is another area where definitions are important. Most historiographical accounts of canon formation include at least three stages, even if they are not mentioned directly.[141]

idea of a normative collection of scared writings, the concept of "canon" as such. It has already been in existence for a long time, and nowhere met with resistance' (*Formation of the Christian Bible*, p. 2). Beckwith makes a stronger claim for an early closed Old Testament: 'Despite the later fluidity of order which both Jewish and Christian tradition reflect, the earliest evidence is of a single, agreed order, and since this order is referred to by Jesus, it provides a measure of confirmation that the closing of the canon had already taken place by Jesus's time' (*Old Testament Canon*, p. 222).

139. Cf. Zahn, 'Permanent Value of the New Testament Canon', p. 5: 'This sounds as if [the New Testament] had already become a collection of original writings, strictly outlined, minutely determined, and therefore adopted as the standard of churchly teaching and action.' Zahn also quickly notes, though, that there continued to be disagreements about the content of this collection. Similarly, Harnack argues that, from the second century onward, the church had 'given form to the new collection of sacred writings and had *in idea* created a closed Canon' (*Origin of the New Testament*, pp. 113-14). He concludes that 'at the end of the second century the new collection of sacred writings attached to the Gospels was organized and crystallized under the influence of a grand and simple conception' (p. 114).

140. Trobisch observes that 'often the cryptic German formula of "der sich selbst durchsetzende Kanon" (the canon imposed itself) is used to describe this position' (*First Edition of the New Testament*, p. 110 n. 16). Trobisch surveys discussion of this position, including von Campenhausen who notes that 'the Canon (thought of in terms of its content) imposed itself, and was in any case not a product of the Church on which it was binding' (*Formation*, p. 331 n. 13). Harnack notes that 'this New Testament, clear and intelligible in its structure, and in regard to its content differing little from its immediate forerunners, gradually established itself in the Churches' (p. 109). For Harnack, 'this is an astounding fact, yet so it happened' (p. 114).

141. John Sailhamer, 'Biblical Theology and the Composition of the Hebrew Bible', in

First, there is the initial composition of the biblical material. Second, there is a period of gradual canonization where these initial compositions are gathered into groupings and associated with other documents. Third, sometime after these two stages, there is a move to consolidate and formalize the order and content of the biblical material. This last stage is sometimes understood as the 'closing of the canon'.

In the following analysis, the first two stages of this process are the primary focus. However, the observations made regarding these initial phases have implications for the nature of the consolidation phase. Accordingly, if it can be plausibly demonstrated that a form of canon-consciousness was at play during the composition and canonization phases, then less is at stake in identifying the exact moment in time when the canon closed for good. For the conceptual and theological authority of the biblical writings making up that canon would have already been established long before.[142]

In light of the preceding discussion, a preliminary and working definition of canon can include the notion of 'a literary collection of writings deemed authoritative by a certain community'. The Christian canon, then, is the collection of writings Christians understand to be authoritative. The term

Biblical Theology: Retrospect and Prospect (Downers Grove, IL: IVP, 2002), pp. 25-37, articulates these three phases of the canon formation process. He calls this description a 'text model'. Many scholars begin with canonization/consolidation and view the process in gradually progressing historical phases. For instance, see Gamble, 'New Testament Canon', pp. 272-73; Barton, *Holy Writings, Sacred Text*, pp. 14-27; Allert, *High View of Scripture*, pp. 48-52; and Holmes, 'Biblical Canon', pp. 415-17. Cf. Ulrich's parsing of the 'canonical process' in 'Notion and Definition', p. 30. Barton understands the canon formation process to involve two broad phases of 'growth' (*der kanonische prozeß*) and then also 'delimitation' or 'selection' (*kanonisierung*) (see, e.g., *Holy Writings, Sacred Text*, pp. 133-34). On this distinction, Barton interacts with Dohmen and Oeming, *Biblischer Kanon*, pp. 91-113. Dohmen and Oeming seek to describe the movement 'vom kanonischen prozeß zum Kanon' and distinguish the two notions (p. 91). E.g., they write, 'Die lebendige Glaubensgeschichte, die sich in der jahrhundertelangen Fortschreibung (dem *kanonischen Prozeß*) der Heiligen Schrift niedergeschlagen hat, kommt nicht zum Abschluß oder erstarrt geradezu durch die *Kanonisierung*, sondern wird unter neuen Bedingungen, nämlich denen der 'Schriftauslegung', aufgenommen und weitergeführt. Ist die Heilige Schrift 'Seele der Theology', dann wird in der Theologie und durch sie die lebendige Glaubensgeschichte der Bibel weitergeführt' (p. 110).

142. Reflecting on the nature of this type of antecedent authority, Seitz argues that 'the desire to claim that there is no authority to the OT unless the literary limits are closed in some straightforward way leads to the necessity to claim that this (now quite crucial aspect) happens later, when the NT is achieving its canonical status. This makes "closure" more significant than it is; it tends then to misrepresent stability and authority in an "open" canon; and it leaves vacated any sense that the Scriptures address the church and provide the very canon of truth operative in the period in question, which is crucial to an account of the OT as Christian Scripture' (*Character of Christian Scripture*, p. 201). For a contrasting view of the phenomenon of 'closure', see Sanders, 'Issue of Closure in the Canonical Process', pp. 252-66.

'Scripture' simply denotes any individual writing that is deemed valuable and normative in some way (i.e. 'holy writings').[143] These definitions overlap, but distinguishing between them allows one to speak with more meaning and nuance (e.g. in the designation 'canon of Scripture').

The phrase 'believing community' is used throughout this study to indicate the remnant of believing Israel in Old Testament times centered around the prophetic witness, the believers' church in New Testament times centered around the apostolic witness, and also the early church that represents a continuation of this same community during the patristic period. This group of individuals that flows from the prophets and apostles is the community primarily responsible for the preservation and transmission of the biblical canon.[144]

Reshaping the Boundaries of the Canon Discussion

For many, the vagaries of the historical, terminological, and theological issues involved in the canon debate are enough to disabuse them of ever entering the fray.[145] However, as long as individuals and communities (both academic and ecclesial) continue to engage in the canonical material, there will always be fodder for the field of canon studies. In light of this reality and the preceding discussion, one might point to five broad areas that have become increasingly relevant to the canon discussion. There is something of a burgeoning consensus in the field that these areas represent fruitful lines of enquiry. Tentative conclusions here can help redirect the tenor and direction of further work in canon studies. These concluding reflections also lay the groundwork for the rest of this study.

a. Answering the Charge of Anachronism
In historical research, the charge of anachronism is serious business. Importing categories or terminology into an era prior to the period when those categories or terminology were developed is to do an injustice to the primary

---

143. Barton describes the main characteristics of a 'scriptural' writing as 'the importance or non-triviality of the text; its relevance to every reader; its internal consistency; and its excess of meaning' (*Holy Writings, Sacred Text*, p. 134).

144. Cf. John H. Sailhamer, 'The Messiah and the Hebrew Bible', *JETS* 44 (2001), pp. 5-23, who argues that 'the Hebrew Bible was not written as the national literature of Israel', but rather 'as the expression of the deep-seated messianic hope of a small group of faithful prophets and their followers' (p. 23).

145. Cf. Ernest Best, 'Scripture, Tradition, and the Canon of the New Testament', *BJRL* 61 (1979), pp. 258-89: 'No matter where we look there are problems and it may therefore be simpler at this stage to cut our losses and simply dispense with the concept of canon' (p. 275). As early as 1780, Johann G. Eichorn laments, 'it would have been desirable if one had never even used the term canon' (as quoted in Childs, *Introduction to the Old Testament as Scripture*, p. 36).

sources from the earlier period. In the canon debate, the charge of anachronism is a commonly wielded weapon. Those who maintain the Sundberg-distinction argue that to speak of a 'canon' before the fourth century is an 'anachronism of the worst kind'.[146] Indeed, if the Sundberg-distinction is unassailable, then the proponents of a broad understanding of 'canon' cannot easily escape the force of the accusation. However, as the preceding discussion has sought to demonstrate, there are legitimate and historically verifiable grounds for questioning the strict distinction between canon and Scripture.

Though it is problematic to import a fourth century understanding of the term 'canon' into a discussion of the second century, it is perhaps equally problematic to impose a strict distinction between the notions of canon and Scripture. A relevant question to ask is whether the term 'canon' was *ever* used solely as a descriptor of 'list' devoid of notions of normativity and authority. In its history of usage, the term canon has the two senses of Canon 1 ('canon as norm') and Canon 2 ('canon as list') and could have been employed as a descriptor for the biblical collection for precisely this reason. In other words, the ambiguity of the term 'canon', far from being a reason to avoid using it, was likely one of the primary reasons it was employed in the first place. There is a natural, organically developing dialectic between the notions of 'rule' and 'list' in the way the term 'canon' was used in the early church. If the usage of the first four centuries demonstrates the presence of this ambiguity, then it would actually be anachronistic to argue for a strict distinction between 'canon as rule' and 'canon as list', calling the former Scripture and the latter canon. In other words, the Sundberg-distinction could itself be considered a type of anachronism.[147] Further, in

---

146. Barton, *Holy Writings, Sacred Text*, p. 11. Barton makes this comment in relation to the ways some scholars speak of Theophilus' 'canon' in *ad Autolycum*. He states bluntly that 'modern scholars plainly equivocate when they use the term' canon (p. 12). One of Barton's central methodological concerns is to avoid this type of equivocation: 'We need to be on our guard against the danger of anachronism in thinking that either concept ['canon' or 'scripture'] was clearly in the minds of early rabbinic or patristic writers. Any discussion which starts by assuming that there was always something called "the canon", and that the question is only when and how it came to be delineated, is doomed to anachronism from the outset' (*Holy Writings, Sacred Text*, p. 158). Cf. the similar sentiment in Allert (*A High View of Scripture?*, pp. 44-49, 151-52), McDonald (*Biblical Canon*, p. 190), and Hahneman ('Muratorian Fragment', pp. 405-406).

147. Chapman argues that this view (i.e. the strict distinction between canon and scripture made by Sundberg and McDonald) is 'hard pressed to defend such an understanding in the ancient period' (*Law and Prophets*, p. 108). 'Why insist', Chapman wonders, 'on a definition of "canon" as a phenomenon which does not seem ever to have existed?' (p. 108). See also Stone, 'Biblical Canon According to Lee McDonald', pp. 57-58. After outlining the role of the Temple in helping to provide the conceptual *space* for an authoritative collection of writings, Stone comments, 'To make lists of the holy books while

contemporary usage, the term 'canon' seems to have an enduring usefulness *because of* rather than *in spite of* its multifaceted meaning potential.[148]

b. *The Recognition of a 'Core Canon' Consensus*

One subtly striking element of many studies of canon formation is their
implicit agreement on the notion of a 'core canon' early in the life of the
believing community. Though there are significant disagreements about
what the implications are of early recognition of a core set of authoritative documents, there is widespread agreement that this phenomenon took
place.[149] For instance, the assertion that the four Gospels and the Pauline

---

the temple remained standing would be superfluous and such a demand by McDonald may (ironically) betray an anachronistic appeal to the *formulation* of canons *as* lists
in the second to fourth century CE in the church. Within Judaism, however, catalogues
of canonical books never occur in the period under investigation' (p. 57). Cf. Kruger,
Canon Revisited, p. 37: 'The challenge for Sundberg's definition, then, is that it never
fully corresponds to any historical reality. To insist that we have a canon only when there
is an officially closed list with no exceptions is to insist on a canon that never existed.
Ironically, then, it is the exclusive definition of *canon* that appears to be, at least at some
points, "anachronistic".'

148. See the survey of the 'broad' and 'narrow' understanding of canon sections developed above. In this vein, Dempster argues that 'scholars are not guilty of historical
anachronism when the term "canon" is being used for an earlier period. The final stage
represents a culmination of a process rather than something radically new. An open
canon is closed. There are earlier and later stages of the canon' ('Canons', p. 51). Dempster also interacts with Ulrich's pointed charge of anachronism (p. 51 n. 22). After noting
that 'an anxiety shared by many who incline toward narrower usage is that broader usage
imports anachronistic dogma by applying the term too early' (*Brevard Childs*, p. 23),
Driver counters that 'an early application of the term canon is not automatically anachronistic, so long as the way the concept is defined fits the situation it describes' (p. 23
n. 78). At this point, Driver draws on Georg Steins' interaction with the charge of anachronism in 'Kanon und Anamnese: Auf dem Weg zu einer Neuen Biblischen Theologie',
in *Der Bibelkanon in der Bibelauslegung*, pp. 110-29 (115). Christoph Dohmen outlines
complementary argumentation in *Die Bibel und ihre Auslegung* (Munich: C.H. Beck,
2006), pp. 20-23. Cf. Kruger, 'Definition of Canon', p. 19: 'In the end, this term can be
employed with a substantial amount of flexibility; and this flexibility is a reminder of the
depth and richness of this thing we call "canon".'

149. Barton comments in this regard that 'in the first stage, which was complete astonishingly early, the great central core of the present New Testament was already being
treated as the main authoritative source for Christians' (*Holy Writings, Sacred Text*, p.
18). He also observes that early in the life of the church 'much of the core already had as
high a status as it would ever have' (p. 19). In sum, 'the Church entered the second century with a core New Testament already enjoying "scriptural" status, and never found
any reason to change it' (p. 26). In his development of the notion of 'core canon', Barton
draws on Franz Stuhlhofer's statistical analysis of patristic citation patterns in *Der
Gebrauch der Bibel von Jesus bis Euseb: Eine statistiche Untersuchung zur Kanonsgeschichte* (Wuppertal: R. Brockhaus, 1988).

corpus were understood as authentic and authoritative collections early in the life of the churches is generally uncontroversial.[150] The contemporary consensus regarding this historical consensus is an important point of agreement in the canon debate.[151]

c. *The Relevance of Manuscript Evidence*
Another important recent development is the wealth of manuscript evidence now available to historians of the biblical canon. Discovery of ancient manuscripts and artifacts is ongoing. The growing number of extant manuscripts that have been discovered in the last century has enhanced historiographical reconstructions of the history of canon formation.[152] As Hurtado notes, 'Christian manuscripts from the second and third centuries witness strongly to the rich and diverse fund of texts produced, read, copied, and circulated among Christians.'[153] Further, there has been a concomitant recognition that

---

150. For instance, in *The Spirit and the Letter: Studies in the Biblical Canon* (London: SPCK, 1997), Barton states clearly that 'astonishingly early, the great central core of the present New Testament was already being treated as the main authoritative source for Christians. There is little to suggest that there were any serious controversies about the Synoptics, John, or the major Pauline Epistles' (p. 18). Discussing the perception of New Testament literature, Gamble also observes that Paul's letters and the Gospels 'had been valued so long and so widely that their orthodoxy could only be taken for granted: it would have been nonsensical for the church to have inquired, for example, into the orthodoxy of Paul!' (*The New Testament Canon: Its Making and Meaning* [Philadelphia, PA: Fortress Press, 1985], p. 70). Cf. James D.G. Dunn, 'How the New Testament Began', in *From Biblical Criticism to Biblical Faith* (ed. William H. Brackney and Craig A. Evans; Macon, GA: Mercer University Press, 2007), p. 137: 'The *de facto* canon of Jesus and Paul, gospel and epistle, was already functioning with effect within the first thirty years of Christianity's existence.'

151. See the important survey and discussion of the nature of this 'core canon' consensus in Chapman, 'Canon Debate', pp. 279-87. Particularly illuminating is the similar terminology employed by scholars from across the spectrum of the canon debate (see p. 286 n. 56).

152. Regarding New Testament manuscript evidence, see Trobisch, *The First Edition of the New Testament*, pp. 3-7. Trobisch notes that much work on the canon relies on the 'indirect evidence' of citations of biblical material in extrabiblical writing. Conversely, Trobisch focuses on manuscript evidence and the internal 'redactional frame' of the 'first published edition' of the New Testament itself. For him, because of recent manuscript discoveries, interpreters should not limit themselves solely to external indirect evidence when investigating the canon formation process.

153. Larry W. Hurtado, *The Earliest Christian Artifacts: Manuscripts and Christian Origins* (Grand Rapids, MI: Eerdmans, 2006), p. 4. He also argues that 'though nearly all are only portions, and in many cases mere fragments, of the full manuscripts, enough survives to tell us that collectively early Christians produced, copied, and read a noteworthy range of writings' (p. 4). Further, 'with all due allowance for the limitations in the likely extent of literacy in this period, the impression given is that early Christianity

these manuscripts have a story to tell and have a tangible bearing on questions of canon formation.[154]

For instance, the manuscript fragments of many of the New Testament documents indicate that they were circulated within codex-bound collections very early in their existence. The nature of the extant manuscript evidence lends legitimacy to the task of examining the function of individual writings within collection units (e.g. Romans within the Pauline corpus) and also the function of those discrete units within the larger biblical collection (e.g. the Pauline corpus within the New Testament).[155]

d. *The Relevance of Internal Evidence*

Alongside the recognition of the value of manuscript evidence is the recovery of internal evidence as significant data in the reconstruction of the history of the biblical canon. Many traditional treatments of canon formation deal solely with external historical evidence and rely on extrabiblical references to biblical books or the canonical collection. For instance, a study of the New Testament canon might restrict its discussion to biblical references in sources from the apostolic and patristic era. This type of external

represented a religious movement in which texts played a large role' (p. 24). Important too is his brief mention of the nature of literacy in the ancient world in general and the early church in particular (p. 24 n. 59). In this regard, see the significant discussion (which Hurtado draws upon) by Harry Y. Gamble in *Books and Readers in the Early Church: A History of Early Christian Texts* (New Haven, CT: Yale University Press, 1995), pp. 1-41.

154. See Hurtado, *The Earliest Christian Artifacts*; Gamble, *Books and Readers*; and Trobisch, *First Edition of the New Testament*. Hurtado in particular argues strongly for the relevance of manuscript evidence to the reconstruction of early Christian origins. In *Earliest Christian Artifacts*, he urges scholars to 'take earliest Christian manuscripts seriously as historical artifacts, paying attention to their physical and visual characteristics as well as the texts that they contain' (p. 5). He also states clearly that 'it is precisely the failure to realize that manuscripts *are* artifacts that I seek to correct in this book' (p. 1 n. 1). See also his essay 'The "Meta-Data" of Earliest Christian Manuscripts', in *Identity and Interaction in the Ancient Mediterranean. Jews, Christians and Others: Essays in Honour of Stephen G. Wilson* (ed. Zeba A. Crook and Philip A. Harland; Sheffield: Sheffield Phoenix Press, 2007), pp. 149-63; and 'Manuscripts and the Sociology of Early Christian Reading', in *The Early Text of the New Testament* (ed. Charles E. Hill and Michael J. Kruger; Oxford: Oxford University Press, 2012), pp. 49-62. Similarly, Kruger comments that the artifactual features of manuscripts 'hold tremendous potential in helping us understand the origins and development of the New Testament canon' (*Canon Revisited*, p. 234). For Peter Brandt's understanding of the 'gesamtbild' of the 'bibelhandschriften' of the Greek tradition, see *Endgestalten des Kanons: Das Arrangement der Schriften Israels in der Jüdischen und Christlichen Bibel* (Berlin: Philo, 2001), pp. 172-91.

155. The role of manuscript evidence and this type of argumentation will be addressed particularly in Chapters 2–3.

historical evidence is significant and crucial to any historiographical analysis of canon formation. However, there is a growing consensus that internal evidence from the biblical texts themselves can also shed light on the canon formation process.[156]

e. *The Value of Canon-Consciousness*

A corollary of the increased awareness of the relevance of internal evidence for the history of canon formation is the recognized value of the notion of 'canon-consciousness'. The internal evidence often embodies a certain perspective on the collection within which it is found. This recognition of a wider collection and of a higher authority is central to the notion of canon-consciousness. Chapter 2 will discuss the nature of this concept in particular and seek to demonstrate its relevance to the history of canon formation.

---

156. For a survey of recent developments in this area, see Dempster, 'Canons', pp. 68-77. Sailhamer notes that 'some have suggested that we must go back to the drawing board and view afresh the internal evidence from the OT texts to see whether there is in them any literary and canonical shaping that might suggest a theological motive' (*Meaning of the Pentateuch*, p. 209). Cf. H.G.L. Peels, 'The Blood "from Abel to Zechariah" (Matthew 23,35; Luke 11,50f.) and the Canon of the Old Testament', *ZAW* 113 (2001), p. 600: 'Alongside the study of the external witnesses of the history of the canon, to which up until now a great deal of energy has been devoted, interest in the internal evidence pertaining to the history of the canon has grown in recent years. Perhaps up until now there has been far too little of it.'

Chapter 2

THE NATURE OF CANON-CONSCIOUSNESS

The Nature of Canon-Consciousness

The second element of the phrase 'canon-consciousness' refers to the contention that 'canon' was a genuine category of thought during the composition and canonization of the biblical material. For instance, would a biblical writer have been able to construe the notion of canon in a conscious way? Would the early church communities have even thought to view the various New Testament documents in light of some larger whole? Depending on which option is taken in defining canon, the notion of 'canon-consciousness' will be either a convenient descriptor or a misconstrued anachronism. For, if the canon is understood as a closed list only ('narrow understanding'; Canon 2), then no one before the later centuries would have been able to have it 'in mind'. In this respect, McDonald and Sanders query, 'With such a long delay in the church's use of the term "canon" to describe a closed body of Christian scriptures, one may well ask why there was an emergence of "canon consciousness" in the church of the fourth century CE and little evidence of it before?'[1]

---

1. McDonald and Sanders, 'Introduction', in *Canon Debate*, p. 13. Some of the scholars who mention canon-consciousness bring it up in order to deny that the concept existed before later centuries. For instance, McDonald unambiguously states, 'The earliest Christian church was not canon conscious. The NT has *no hint* of a discussion of a closed biblical canon' (*Biblical Canon*, p. 214; emphasis added). He also argues that 'it seems more reasonable to assume an imprecise understanding in both Judaism and early Christianity about the scope of their biblical canons at the end of the first century CE. Canon consciousness appears to have emerged first in Judaism in the late first century, but this emergence is not a fully developed biblical canon like we see later in more developed Judaism and in fourth-century Christianity' (p. 160; cf. pp. 249, 332, 423). Similarly, Allert contends, 'We must, therefore, be wary of the implicit assumption that the early church consciously and explicitly thought about a closed written collection of Christian writings—that the church had a canon consciousness' (*High View of Scripture*, p. 68). Tellingly (in light of Chapter 1's discussion), Allert notes that 'foundational in this respect is the important distinction between the terms "canon" and "Scripture"' (p. 68). Allert also clarifies that the criteria for canonicity are 'not a reference to an explicit canon consciousness (in Sundberg's sense) in

Conversely, if the concept of canon is understood more broadly ('broad understanding'; Canon 1), then 'canon-consciousness' can provide an accurate description of the mindset of the biblical writers and of the early church.[2] In this approach, the notion of a stable, authoritative body of literature was in fact a legitimate category of thought during the process of canon formation.[3] This 'other historical assessment' sees a 'consciousness of canon emerging far earlier, coincident in meaningful ways with the distinct concept of scripture'.[4] Because the term 'canon' includes the sense of authoritative rule or guide, it can be helpful when used to identify and discuss literature that eventually comes to be labeled 'canonical' in the formal sense.

These definitional discussions regarding the term 'canon' also relate to the proper understanding of the catalysts for canon. Were these catalysts primarily external and phenomenological, or were they primarily internal or theological? Was the canon 'pulled' along by external forces, or was it 'pushed' by internal elements?[5] The former option is exemplified in Sundberg's comment that 'the formation of a closed New Testament list [is] unequivocally the decision of the church'.[6] In this approach, the catalysts for canon come from outside of the literature itself. An alternative, though,

the first few centuries of this "reflection"' (p. 52). See also the discussion below on the legitimacy of understanding a four-gospel *canon* to be an implication of a four-gospel *codex*.

2. Dempster, 'Canons', p. 50, notes that 'the church simply used a word, which indicated a standard or model, to signify a collection of literature'. Cf. the discussion regarding the charge of anachronism in Chapter 1.

3. After a survey of the relevant internal and external evidence, I give my position regarding these definitional issues at the conclusion of this chapter.

4. Driver, *Brevard Childs*, p. 22.

5. This way of distinguishing between the internal and external factors comes from David G. Meade, 'Ancient Near Eastern Apocalypticism and the Origins of the New Testament Canon of Scripture', in *The Bible as a Human Witness to Divine Revelation* (ed. Randall Heskett and Brian Irwin; London: T. & T. Clark, 2010), p. 304: 'A central question that arises out of the morass of controversy is the question of the direction from which the canonical process of the New Testament proceeds. In other words, is the formation of the New Testament "pushed" from elements inherent within itself or its Jewish origins or is it "pulled" into being by forces of the church and society largely external to the texts themselves?' In formulating this question, Meade draws on Childs, *New Testament as Canon*, p. 19: 'An important and highly debatable issue turns on determining the direction from which the New Testament canonical process proceeded. Did the canonization of the New Testament develop in analogy to an Old Testament process which had largely reached its goal of stabilization before the New Testament period, or rather did the major canonical force stem from the side of the Christian church (Gese, Stuhlmacher, Sundberg), which resulted in the definition of the Jewish Scriptures as an Old Testament within a larger Christian Bible?'

6. Sundberg, 'Revised History', p. 461.

to this view of the external motivation for canon is to affirm that there was a force at work that was internal to the writings being collected. This alternative asks whether there is something about the growth of the scriptural collection that is more organic to the literature itself. Was there a force at work for the authors and collectors of these writings that compelled them to associate certain writings with one another? Was there a canon-consciousness among the biblical authors and the believing community? These questions again highlight the importance of definitions and are the concern of the following sections.[7]

The Importance of Canon as a Mental Construct
The notion of a 'concept of canon' involves understanding the nature and authority of the larger whole of the canonical collection conceptually. In other words, the developing macrostructural framework of the intertextually informed canonical collection serves as a 'mental construct' that can guide an author or a reader's sense of the Bible as a whole. In this 'mind'-set, an individual (author or reader) is aware or conscious of a broader theological and literary context. The makeup of this mindset includes an awareness of togetherness (*Zusammen-Denken*) and a consciousness of a broader canonical context (*Kanonbewußtsein*).[8] Acknowledging the viability of this possibility lends legitimacy to the notion that an individual might be able to conceptualize a distinct reading context. Even without a definitive list, someone could still conceive of an interrelated body of literature as a distinct and coherent entity. In relation to the formation of the biblical canon, the notion of canon-consciousness entails an awareness of Canon 1 ('authority') and Canon 2 ('interrelatedness'). In the historical process of composition and canonization, in other words, there is an awareness both of the authority of certain traditions (either oral or written) and also a sense

7. As Driver puts the matter, 'Is there, as some have seen, a *Kanonbewußtsein* deep in the formation of the literature itself? That depends on what a person means by canon' (*Brevard Childs*, p. 29).
8. Magne Sæbø speaks of the *Zusammen-Denken* at work during the development of the Hebrew Bible in 'Vom "Zusammen-Denken" zum Kanon. Aspekte der traditions-geschichtlichen Endstadien des Alten Testaments', in *Zum Problem des biblischen Kanons* (Neukirchen–Vluyn: Neukirchener Verlag, 1988), pp. 115-33. See Balla's discussion of Sæbø's work (*Challenges*, pp. 102-104). On the notion of *Kanonbewußtsein*, see the section on Childs below. Peter Höffken uses this concept in his study of the nature of Josephus's awareness of the Hebrew Bible in 'Zum Kanonbewusstsein des Josephus Flavius in *Contra Apionem* und in den *Antiquitates*', *JSJ* 32 (2001), pp. 159-77. Cf. Blenkinsopp, *Prophecy and Canon*, p. 9, who speaks of 'first, the importance of the location of a text within an ongoing tradition; and second, that canon implies the attempt to impose a definitive shape and meaning on the tradition as it comes to expression in texts'.

of the interrelated nature of those traditions.[9] In this regard, Balla writes, 'Although there were disputes over the question of what books should belong to the collection of Holy Scripture, there was also a consciousness that there existed a circle of sacred writings which *was* Holy Scripture.'[10]

The nature of publishing technologies of a given historical time period also impinges upon the concepts of canon that are possible among a given group of people or a society at large.[11] As technological paradigms shift, the shockwaves of those changes affect the array of elements that constitute

---

9. The notion of 'inner-biblical exegesis' developed by Michael Fishbane highlights the way authoritative traditions were shaped and transmitted by a believing community. See Michael Fishbane, *Biblical Interpretation in Ancient Israel* (Oxford: Oxford University Press, 1985); Michael Fishbane, 'Revelation and Tradition: Aspects of Inner-Biblical Exegesis', *JBL* 99 (1980), pp. 343-61; and Michael Fishbane, 'Inner Biblical Exegesis: Types and Strategies of Interpretation in Ancient Israel', in *The Garments of Torah: Essays in Biblical Hermeneutics* (ed. Michael Fishbane; Bloomington, IN: Indiana University Press, 1992), pp. 3-18. Fishbane discusses how the Torah was utilized and shaped during the biblical period (pre-exilic and post-exilic) and also reflects on the complex process of the *traditum* (the content of the tradition) and the *traditio* (the result of the transmission process). For Fishbane, 'the predominant authority of revelation over tradition in the diverse genres and expression of inner-biblical exegesis reflects an incipient canonical consciousness. Texts believed to be divinely revealed had a fixed and controlling legitimacy about them in relation to all new developments' ('Revelation and Tradition', p. 343). During the canonical process, according to Fishbane, 'older deposits of revelation had already achieved an authoritative status—thus suggesting a canonical consciousness of sorts, insofar as such authoritative texts would constitute a precanonical canon' (pp. 359-60). In this model, 'each solidification of the *traditum* was the canon in process of its formation; and each stage of canon-formation was a new achievment in *Gemeindebildung*, in the formation of an integrated book-centered culture' (*Biblical Interpretation in Ancient Israel*, p. 6).

10. Balla, *Challenges*, p. 104. Balla makes this comment about the New Testament, but he applies it as well to the formation of the canon as a whole. He argues that 'a process similar to that of what [Sæbø] describes as "Zusammen-Denken" was going on in the process of the writing of the New Testament: an activity of handling traditions which were regarded as "sacred"' (p. 104). He also argues that 'the New Testament authors intended to put another canon alongside that of the Old Testament. In other words, they wrote with a canonical awareness; they wrote, what we may term as, a "second canon"' (p. 101).

11. Gamble states strongly that 'the failure to consider the extent to which the physical medium of the written word contributes to its meaning—how its outward aspects inform the way a text is approached and read—perpetuates a largely abstract, often unhistorical, and even anachronistic conception of early Christian literature and its transmission' (*Books and Readers*, p. 42). In this sense, for Gamble, 'the physical object is also a social artifact', and 'all aspects of the production, distribution, and use of texts presuppose social functions and forces' (p. 43). See also Roberts, *Manuscript, Society and Belief*, pp. 49-73. Cf. Kraft's methodological cautions in this regard ('Para-mania', pp. 10-12).

what a collection of writings might be understood as. These paradigm shifts in the way written materials are composed and disseminated have a significant impact on how those writings are perceived. Thus, areas of study such as codicology, archeology, paleography, and papyrology, for instance, have bearing on the canon formation discussion in general and the issue of 'canon-consciousness' in particular. Manuscript discoveries and investigation impact any reconstruction that seeks to elucidate the use and circulation of those texts.[12] The movement from the tablet to the scroll to the codex form has wide ranging effects on both the process of manuscript transmission as well as the nature of biblical composition.[13]

Before the development of the codex book form, for instance, a canon-conscious 'mental construct' was crucial for the conceptual cohesion of the Hebrew Bible and the New Testament in the mind of the reader.[14] During the Old Testament period, biblical books were written and transmitted on scrolls. Because it was impractical for a single roll to contain the full contents of most biblical writings, any notion of the biblical text as a whole was by necessity conceptual.[15] As the Hebrew Bible formed, the groupings of

12. See the section on 'The Relevance of Manuscript Evidence' in Chapter 1. Cf. Gamble, 'New Testament Canon', p. 274: 'What manuscripts and their textual traditions reveal about the actual use of texts and about early attitudes toward them are suddenly primary considerations for the history of the canon.' After noting the implications of the discovery of P[45] for interpreting Irenaeus' defense of a four-fold Gospel canon, Frederic Kenyon writes, 'In this respect purely bibliographical facts have their bearing upon Biblical criticism' (Kenyon, *General Introduction*, p. 13).

13. Cf. Colin H. Roberts and T.C. Skeat, *The Birth of the Codex* (London: Oxford University Press, 1983), p. 1: 'The most momentous development in the history of the book until the invention of printing was the replacement of the roll by the codex.'

14. Though he does not use the expression 'canon-consciousness', Sailhamer provides a helpful complementary discussion related to how one might read 'canonically' before the canon was a physical reality (see *Meaning of the Pentateuch*, pp. 208-212). He argues that 'a mental construct was just as important, or more so, than the actual physical shape of the OT canon' (p. 211). For Sailhamer, this mental construct is like the picture on the box of a jigsaw puzzle that enables one to conceive of an individual piece in light of the larger image. He states strongly, 'Given the mental force of such a construct, a physical copy of the OT canon would have been unnecessary' (p. 212).

15. Sailhamer notes that 'any talk of a specific shape of the OT canon at that time would necessitate approaching it not in terms of its physical reality, but as a mental construct' (*Meaning of the Pentateuch*, p. 211). In this setting, an individual reading only a fragment of a text 'could have understood it from within the larger context of this mental construct' (p. 211). See also Stephen G. Dempster, *Dominion and Dynasty: A Theology of the Hebrew Bible* (Downers Grove, IL: IVP, 2003), p. 31: 'The diversity of books is seen to reflect a conceptual unity of the words of a divine author, even though the publication of one complete volume of all such words, a Book in the modern sense, was technologically impossible.' Gamble also discusses 'the presence of the "idea" or "concept" of a theoretically determinate body of writings, even if a

Law, Prophets, and Writings became an overarching framework by which to order the biblical material.[16] Thus, when readers picked up a portion of a biblical scroll, they had to locate the portion that they were holding conceptually in relation to the other writings held sacred.

In this setting, only a canon-conscious reader would be able to make sense of the larger whole when reading a portion or fragment of a biblical book. Without a larger framework in place, this situation could have seriously hampered one's ability to understand the broader canonical context. However, even a rough mental construct could function as the 'conceptual glue' that would allow for a holistic reading. This 'conceptual glue' allows a reader to maintain a 'wide-angle lens view' that keeps in sight the multifaceted mosaic of meaning that the biblical authors have stitched together through their editorial work. The 'conceptual glue', then, connects the reader to the 'canonical glue'.[17] The wide-ranging literary texts, contexts, meanings, and messages found within the biblical literature are bound together by a reader's sense of the 'big picture' of the canonical context.[18]

Though this conceptual framework applies especially to the Hebrew Bible, as the codex form developed only as the New Testament was forming, the same practice would have applied in the writing and reading of any New Testament document. For example, the conceptual background for the Gospels is the entirety of the Hebrew Bible. That the Gospel writers had this mindset can be seen in their constant and pervasive use of the Hebrew Bible in their narratives. The first sentence of the New Testament canon is inscrutable apart from at least the Pentateuch and the Former Prophets ('Son of David, Son of Abraham', Mt. 1.1). Acknowledging the possibility that biblical authors had some sense of the whole of the Scriptures 'in mind' helps explain how the concept of canon could function in a meaningful way before the rise of book forms that were capable of holding the full content of the biblical collection. Indeed, recognizing a canon-consciousness among the biblical writers demystifies this phenomenon and rescues one's

---

fixed list of them had yet to be finally determined' ('New Testament Canon', p. 271). Cf. Ulrich, 'Notion and Definition', p. 25: 'With scrolls, the table of contents of the scriptures was a *mental notion*, but it became a *physical object* when a codex contained those books included in that table of contents and not others.'

16. On the shape of the Hebrew Bible as Law, Prophets, and Writings, see below.

17. Peels, 'From Abel to Zechariah', p. 601, uses the term 'redactional glue' to describe the textual editorial seams that tie the biblical material together. He asks, 'Does the canon of the Old Testament itself deliver signals of an intended closure? Was there a purposeful final redaction not only of the individual books but also of the books of the Old Testament as a whole? Is it possible to trace the "redactional glue" between the different sections of the canon?' Sailhamer uses the phrase 'canonical glue' in a similar fashion (*Meaning of the Pentateuch*, pp. 253, 465).

18. See especially the discussion of contextuality in Chapter 3.

reconstruction of the canon formation process from the realm of the arbitrary.[19] This discussion also highlights that the biblical *authors* were also careful biblical *readers*.

Around the first century ce, the birth of the codex represents a seismic paradigm shift in the way written material was produced, transmitted, and understood by the typical reader.[20] By at least the fourth century, the entire biblical canon was able to fit on one physical codex, bound together with contextual relationships ordered and solidified. Readers of the canon striving to read individual writings in light of each other were greatly aided by this technological innovation. Though the specific content of the canon varies in different faith communities, it is easier to conceive of the Scriptures as a whole when they are bound together in a single codex. The rise of Gutenberg's printing press during the Reformation era standardized the book form and allowed for the unprecedented dissemination of published material.[21] This remarkable invention created the text-based culture that has endured for over half a millennium.[22] These important connections between

19. An alternative to viewing this process as intentional is to understand it as a virtually arbitrary process involving pure happenstance and circumstantial expediency. See, for instance, the comments of Lee M. McDonald, 'Wherein Lies Authority? A Discussion of Books, Texts, and Translations', in *Exploring the Origins of the Bible: Canon Formation in Historical, Literary, and Theological Perspective* (ed. Craig A. Evans and Emanuel Tov; Grand Rapids, MI: Baker, 2008), p. 205: 'Some students of the Bible assume that the ancient writers were consciously aware of writing sacred Scripture, but almost without exception, this was not the case.' He also denies canon-consciousness in the early church, because when it began 'the technology for producing codicies (or books) was not yet sufficiently advanced to contain in one volume all of the books of the current Bible' (p. 205).

20. For the now classic work on the development of the codex form, see Roberts and Skeat, *Birth of the Codex*. Skeat updates in light of new manuscript discoveries their explanation of the early and unanimous Christian preference for the codex in 'The Origin of the Christian Codex', *Zeitschrift für Papyrologie und Epigraphik* 102 (1994), pp. 263-68. Cf. also (inter alia) Trobisch, *First Edition of the New Testament*, pp. 69-77; Hurtado, *Earliest Christian Artifacts*, pp. 43-94; and Robert A. Kraft, 'The Codex and Canon Consciousness', in *The Canon Debate*, pp. 229-34.

21. For an analysis of the impact the transition from 'script to print' had on society in the late fifteenth century, see Elizabeth L. Eisenstein, *The Printing Press as an Agent of Change* (Cambridge: Cambridge University Press, 1980). Eisenstein characterizes the establishment of a print culture as 'the unacknowledged revolution'. Cf. Paul D. Wegner, *The Journey from Texts to Translations: The Origin and Development of the Bible* (Grand Rapids, MI: Baker, 1999), pp. 243-72.

22. Neil Postman observes that 'until the mid-nineteenth century, no significant technologies were introduced that altered the *form*, *volume*, or *speed* of information. As a consequence, Western culture had more than two hundred years to accustom itself to the new information conditions created by the press' (*Technopoly: The Surrender of Culture to Technology* [New York: Vintage Books, 1993], p. 65). On the effect of New

publishing technology and canon studies will be examined throughout the discussions of internal and external evidence.

Canon-Consciousness in the Secondary Literature
An important pioneer of the notion of canon-consciousness is Brevard S. Childs. As he notes in his survey of the canon debate, 'The term "canon consciousness" was occasionally used by a few biblical interpreters, but largely the assumption that it was an active theological force at work in shaping the structure and content of the biblical corpus was denied.'[23] For Childs, the result of this trend is that these scholars 'attributed little or no exegetical significance to canon', and 'the idea of a canonical intent reflected in the biblical structure was largely disregarded'.[24]

Childs develops his understanding of canon in his *Biblical Theology of the Old and New Testament*.[25] In a chapter that seeks to describe 'the hermeneutical implications of the Christian canon', Childs lays out his broad understanding of canon and the specific function of the notion that canon-consciousness plays in that understanding.[26] In his previous *Introduction*s to the Old and New Testaments, Childs argued that 'the lengthy process of the development of the literature leading up to the final stage of canonization involved a profoundly hermeneutical activity on the part of the tradents'.[27]

Media's paradigm shift from 'text' to 'hyper-text' on the biblical canon and its readers, see Ched Spellman, 'The Canon After Google: Implications of a Digitized and Destabilized Codex', *Princeton Theological Review* 16 (2010), pp. 39-42.

23. Childs, 'Canon in Recent Biblical Studies', p. 39.

24. Childs, 'Canon in Recent Biblical Studies', p. 40. A recent example of this position is Gerald Bray's pointed critique of Childs's program in 'Biblical Theology and From Where It Came', *SWJT* 55 (2013), pp. 193-208. Bray strongly concludes, 'It seems that the canon established itself by use over time and was not consciously assembled by anyone with a particular theological aim in view, which makes it hard to establish what its underlying theological principles might be and therefore almost impossible to construct an objectively verifiable Biblical Theology on the basis of it' (pp. 207-208).

25. In important ways, *Biblical Theology* is the *magnum opus* of Childs's career, representing the culmination of his biblical-theological reflection on canon and the character of biblical theology that began with the publication of *Biblical Theology in Crisis* (Philadelphia, PA: Westminster/John Knox Press, 1970).

26. See Childs, *Biblical Theology*, pp. 70-79. This chapter and the notion of canon-consciousness in particular is perhaps the hermeneutical key to unlocking Childs's own understanding of his 'canonical approach'. Moreover, many of Childs's critics that view his approach as incoherent or contradictory neglect this crucial component (see n. 34 below).

27. Childs, *Biblical Theology*, p. 70. See Brevard S. Childs, *Introduction to the Old Testament as Scripture* (Philadelphia, PA: Fortress Press, 1979); and Brevard S. Childs, *The New Testament as Canon: An Introduction* (Philadelphia, PA: Fortress Press, 1984). Childs sees this position as a direct contrast to James Barr's formulation

Because the traditions were being passed down as authoritative, 'they were transmitted in such a way as to maintain a normative function for subsequent generations of believers within a community of faith'.[28] For Childs, then, the concept of canon (Canon 1) was at work during the compositional activity that accompanied the passing along of the biblical traditions.[29]

After sketching the process in this manner, Childs provides a definition of canon that spans the spectrum from the early stages of composition to the final stages of consolidation:

> In my description of this process I used the term 'canonical' as a cipher to encompass the various and diverse factors involved in the formation of the literature. The term was, above all, useful in denoting the reception and acknowledgement of certain religious traditions as authoritative writings within a faith community. The term also included the process by which the collection arose which led up to its final stage of literary and textual stabilization, that is, canonization proper.[30]

Childs notes regarding his understanding of canon that 'emphasis was placed on the process to demonstrate that *the concept of canon* was not a late, ecclesiastical ordering which was basically foreign to the material itself, but that *canon-consciousness lay deep within the formation of the literature*'.[31] In construing canon in these terms, Childs seeks 'to focus

in *Holy Scripture: Canon, Authority, Criticism* (Oxford: Oxford University Press), e.g. p. 67.

28. Childs, *Biblical Theology*, p. 70. Childs characterizes his approach as 'an attempt to hear the biblical text in the terms compatible with the collection and transmission of the literature as scripture' (*Introduction to the Old Testament as Scripture*, p. 16). He argues further that 'the heart of the canonical process lay in transmitting and ordering the authoritative tradition in a form which was compatible to function as scripture for a generation which had not participated in the original events of revelation. The ordering of the tradition for this new function involved a profoundly hermeneutical activity, the effects of which are now built into the structure of the canonical text' (p. 60).

29. Childs writes, 'This process of rendering the material theologically involved countless different compositional techniques by means of which the tradition was actualized' (*Biblical Theology*, p. 70). Cf. Childs, *Introduction to the Old Testament as Scripture*, p. 41: 'It is constitutive of Israel's history that the literature formed the identity of the religious community which in turn shaped the literature. This fundamental dialectic which lies at the heart of the canonical process is lost when the critical Introduction assumes that a historically referential reading of the Old Testament is the key to its interpretation.'

30. Childs, *Biblical Theology*, p. 70. See Driver's survey of the criticism Childs receives for his broad definition of canon (particularly from Barr and Georg Steins) in *Brevard Childs*, pp. 144-47.

31. Childs, *Biblical Theology*, p. 70. Emphasis added. Cf. Childs, *Introduction to the Old Testament as Scripture*, pp. 59-60. The notion of *Kanonbewußtsein* (i.e.

attention on the theological forces at work in its composition rather than seeking the process largely controlled by general laws of folklore, by socio-political factors, or by scribal conventions'.[32]

Childs recognizes that his parsing of canon includes 'a theological extension of its primary meaning'.[33] The effect of this extension is to recover one

'canon-consciousness') originates in Isaac L. Seeligman's work on the Jewish practice of Midrash in 'Voraussetzungen des Midrashexegese', *VTS* 1 (1953), pp. 150-81. Childs makes use of the idea of *Kanonbewußtsein* in his articulation of the notion of a 'canon-consciousness' that lay 'deep within the formation of the literature'. For instance, in an essay on the canonical shape of the Psalter, Childs outlines the development of this concept: 'Hertzberg once employed the term *Nachgeschichte* to describe the process by which an Old Testament text—not simply a tradition—continued to reverberate throughout the rest of the Bible. The concept was later picked up and brilliantly developed by Seeligmann who quite correctly joined the process of inner biblical exegesis with a *Kanonbewusstsein*. Indeed, perhaps one of the most fruitful avenues by which to explore the problem of canon is by closely investigating how in fact Old Testament texts began to function normatively within the various parts of the Jewish community' ('Reflections on the Modern Study of the Psalms', in *Magnalia Dei: The Mighty Acts of God* [ed. Frank Moore Cross, et al.; New York: Doubleday, 1976], p. 382). Similarly, in *Introduction to the Old Testament Scripture*, Childs remarks that 'Seeligmann has described a process of interpretation within scripture which he correctly derived from a consciousness of canon (*Kanonbewusstsein*). This process involved the skillful use of literary techniques, word-plays, and proto-midrashic exegesis which emerged during the final stages of the formation of the canon and continued to be developed and to flower during the post-biblical period' (p. 60). Childs notes further that 'although such exegetical activity grew out of a concept of the canon as an established body of sacred writings, it is a derivative phenomenon which does not represent the constitutive force lying behind the actual canonical process' (p. 60). Instead, 'the decisive force at work in the formation of the canon emerged in the transmission of a divine word in such a form as to lay authoritative claim upon the successive generations' (p. 60). This notion of canon-consciousness (*Kanonbewußtsein*) in particular seems to inform Seitz's argument that 'order and association precede lists, and they are accomplishments of a deeply theological nature to begin with' (*Goodly Fellowship*, p. 45). For Seitz's appreciation and defense of Childs's approach, see 'Canonical Approach and Theological Interpretation', pp. 58-110; and *Character of Christian Scripture*, pp. 27-92.

32. Childs, *Biblical Theology*, pp. 70-71. In this point, Childs directly contrasts Sundberg *et al.* (see Chapter 1). Cf. Childs, *Introduction to the Old Testament as Scripture*, pp. 58-59: 'Essential to understanding the growth of the canon is to see the interaction between a developing corpus of authoritative literature and the community which treasured it. The authoritative Word gave the community its form and content in obedience to the divine imperative, yet conversely the reception of the authoritative tradition by its hearers gave shape to the same writings through a historical and theological process of selecting, collecting, and ordering.'

33. The quotations in this paragraph come from Childs, *Biblical Theology*, p. 71. As early as 1970, Childs has this type of multifaceted notion in mind when he refers to 'canon'. For instance, in *Biblical Theology in Crisis*, Childs argues that 'in its original

of the primary functions of canon, namely, to present the biblical material for future generations. He writes, 'The modern theological function of
canon lies in its affirmation that the authoritative norm lies in the literature itself as it has been treasured, transmitted and transformed...and not
in "objectively" reconstructed stages of the process.' His summary statement on the function of canon emphasizes this aspect: 'The term canon
points to the received, collected, and interpreted material of the church and
thus establishes the theological context in which the tradition continues
to function authoritatively for today'. This broad understanding of canon
and the notion of an organic canon-consciousness in particular are central to Childs's brand of biblical theology and his execution of a canonical
approach.[34]

---

sense, canon does not simply perform the formal function of separating the books
that are authoritative from others that are not, but is the rule that delineates the area in
which the church hears the word of God. The fundamental theological issue at stake is
not the extent of the canon, which has remained in some flux within Christianity, but
the claim for a normative body of tradition contained in a set of books' (p. 99).

34. Much of the criticism Childs receives flows from a neglect of this central definition of canon and his use of the notion of canon-consciousness. Especially those following James Barr's argumentation accuse Childs of definitional incoherence at this point.
For an example of Barr's direct and pointed critique of Childs's approach, see James
Barr, *The Concept of Biblical Theology: An Old Testament Perspective* (London: SCM
Press, 1999), pp. 378-438. Barr thinks that the produce of Childs's canonical approach
does not represent any advance on previous approaches and laments Childs's 'infinite
repetition of the word *canon*' (p. 379). Barr argues, in fact, that Childs's approach is
incoherent at its core and speaks of 'Childs' Biblical Theologies' in the plural (p. 395).
In the end, for Barr, 'even for those most devoted to a conception of a canonically-
based biblical theology his work must be a disappointment, for it contains numerous
compromises with those same methods and ideas which he himself has so vigorously
condemned' (p. 438). This type of critique led Barr in a review of *Introduction to
the Old Testament as Scripture* to characterize Childs's approach as methodologically
'bipolar'. See Driver, *Brevard Childs*, pp. 144-47, for a recent defense of Childs's
approach against this type of criticism. For Driver, the 'bipolar' Childs 'lives in an
ungainly body of secondary literature' and is 'largely a work of fiction, a Franken-
stein hatched in an unhappy dream that lingers in daylight much longer than it should'
(p. 58). Driver hopes 'to give some impression of the approach's aims, what problems
it identifies, and how *on its own* terms these problems are solved or mitigated' (p. 4,
emphasis added). In this sense, the burden of Driver's volume is to answer thoroughly
the question, 'What happens if Childs's work proves to have a logic of its own, even
if it is a logic one finally chooses not to enter?' (p. 59). McDonald directly interacts
with Childs in *Biblical Canon*, pp. 465-74. While ultimately critiquing the foundation
of Childs's approach, Barton ('Canonical Approaches Ancient and Modern', pp. 199-
209) helps clarify several misunderstandings of the way Childs treats the canon question. Cf. Gerald T. Sheppard, 'Canon Criticism: The Proposal of Brevard Childs and an
Assessment for Evangelical Hermeneutics', *Studia Biblica et Theologica* 4 (1974), pp.
3-17; Provan, 'Canons to the Left of Him', pp. 1-38; and Kent D. Clarke, 'Canonical

Noting the overlap between the two senses of canon, Gerald Sheppard describes this phenomenon by arguing that 'in the Tanakh [*sic*] and the New Testament one can detect evidence of "canon conscious redactions", whereby assumptions about the normativeness (Canon 1) of the traditions and of their being read together in a specific collection (Canon 2) coincide'.[35] For Sheppard, taking these types of textual connections into account 'sheds light on the complex problem of how the biblical texts were read together in the post-exilic period' and beyond.[36] He also clarifies that by 'canon conscious redactions', he means 'strictly the attempts by editors to relate one canonical book or a part of a book to some other canonical book or collection of books'.[37]

The superscriptions in the book of Psalms serves as an example of a possible 'canon conscious redaction'. Sheppard writes, 'Historicized titles added to the psalms assigned to David link these prayers contextually to the narrative about David in 1 and 2 Samuel.'[38] He also notes that the epilogue

Criticism: An Integrated Reading of Biblical Texts for the Community of Faith', in *Approaches to New Testament Study* (ed. Stanley E. Porter and David Tombs; Sheffield: Sheffield Academic Press, 1995), pp. 170-221. Clarke compares and contrasts the work of Childs and James Sanders (pp. 179-96), noting that one of the key differences between them is Childs's emphasis on the canonical *product* and Sanders' emphasis on the canonical *process*.

35. Sheppard, 'Canon', pp. 67-68. See Chapter 1's discussion of Sheppard's distinction between Canon 1 and Canon 2. Cf. Gerald T. Sheppard, 'Canonization: Hearing the Voice of the Same God through Historically Dissimilar Traditions', *Ex Auditu* 1 (1985), pp. 106-14.

36. Sheppard, 'Canonization', p. 107.

37. Sheppard, 'Canonization', p. 107.

38. Sheppard, 'Canon', p. 68. He also adds that 'the psalm titles are but one of several redactions which bring the collections of ancient hymns into context with other originally independent traditions' ('Canonization', p. 107). 'One sees in this linkage between psalms and other parts of Scripture', Sheppard notes, 'a change in function, by which the prayers of ordinary people become the Word of God to the later community of faith' (pp. 107-108). Cf. Gerald T. Sheppard, 'Theology and the Book of the Psalms', *Interpretation* 46 (1992), pp. 143-55. For a discussion of the superscriptions from a canonical perspective along these lines, see Bruce K. Waltke, 'A Canonical Process Approach to the Psalms', in *Tradition and Testament* (ed. John S. Feinberg and Paul D. Feinberg; Chicago: Moody Press, 1981), pp. 3-18; and Childs, 'Reflections on the Modern Study of the Psalms', pp. 377-88. Childs remarks that 'although the titles are relatively late, they represent an important reflection on how this secondary setting became normative for the canonical tradition' (pp. 383-84). The effect of linking the psalms to the David narratives (through the superscriptions) is that 'through the mouth of David, the representative man, [the psalms] become a personal word from God to their own situation. The titles, far from tying these poems to the ancient past, serve to contemporize and individualize them for every generation of suffering and persecuted Israel' (p. 384).

to the book of Ecclesiastes (Eccl. 12.9-14) 'summarizes the essence of the book in a manner that puts the "wisdom", or Solomonic, books in full continuity with the Torah'.[39] In sum, Sheppard utilizes the notion of canon-consciousness in order to examine 'the semantic import of the selection and editing of traditions in the formation of both the Hebrew Bible and the New Testament'.[40]

Old Testament scholar Stephen Dempster has also highlighted the strategic function that the notion of canon-consciousness can play in discussions of the formation and shape of the biblical canon.[41] In a summary article on the canon debate, Dempster posits that recognizing the 'canonical

39. Sheppard, 'Canon', p. 68. In 'Canonization', Sheppard summarizes, 'The epilogue to Qoheleth is a canon conscious redaction because it, along with the prologue (cf. 1.12), sets Qoheleth in a broader context of Solomonic "wisdom" and identified this "wisdom" with the Torah, just as Ben Sira had done in the second century BCE' (p. 108). Cf. Gerald T. Sheppard, 'The Epilogue to Qoheleth as Theological Commentary', *CBQ* 39 (1977), pp. 182-89. On the function of the concept of 'wisdom' and the wisdom literature within the canon, see Gerald T. Sheppard, *Wisdom as a Hermeneutical Construct: A Study in the Sapientializing of the Old Testament* (Berlin: W. de Gruyter, 1980), pp. 120-60. Sheppard characterizes this work as a study that 'examines the canonical understanding of "wisdom" and "wisdom books" in prerabbinic Judaism and explores similar examples of late "canon conscious redactions" within the Hebrew Bible itself' ('Canon', p. 68). He begins by investigating the wisdom theme in Ben Sira and Baruch, and then he examines 'evidence of a similar phenomenon in the OT' (p. 120).

40. Sheppard, 'Canon', pp. 68-69. See also Sheppard, 'Canonization', pp. 21-33. For a series of studies sympathetic to Sheppard's discussion of canon, see the essays in *The Bible as Human Witness: Hearing the Word of God through Historically Dissimilar Traditions* (ed. Randall Heskett and Brian Irwin; London: T. & T. Clark, 2010).

41. Dempster's work on canon has focused on both the formation and the function of the Hebrew Bible. See Stephen G. Dempster, 'An "Extraordinary Fact": Torah and Temple and the Contours of the Hebrew Canon, Part 1', *Tyndale Bulletin* 48 (1997), pp. 23-56; Stephen G. Dempster, 'An "Extraordinary Fact": Torah and Temple and the Contours of the Hebrew Canon, Part 2', *Tyndale Bulletin* 48 (1997), pp. 191-218; Stephen G. Dempster, 'From Many Texts to One: The Formation of the Hebrew Bible', in *The World of the Aramaeans I: Biblical Studies in Honour of Paul-Eugène Dion* (ed. P.M. Michèle Daviau, *et al.*; Sheffield: Sheffield Academic Press, 2001), pp. 19-56; Stephen G. Dempster, 'Geography and Genealogy, Dominion and Dynasty: A Theology of the Hebrew Bible', in *Biblical Theology: Retrospect and Prospect* (ed. Scott J. Hafemann; Downers Grove, IL: IVP, 2002), pp. 66-82; Stephen G. Dempster, 'The Prophets, the Canon and a Canonical Approach: No Empty Word', in *Canon and Biblical Interpretation* (ed. Craig G. Bartholomew, *et al.*; Grand Rapids, MI: Zondervan, 2006), pp. 293-329; and Stephen G. Dempster, 'Canon and Old Testament Interpretation', in *Hearing The Old Testament: Listening for God's Address* (ed. Craig G. Bartholomew and David J.H. Beldman; Grand Rapids, MI: Eerdmans, 2012), pp. 154-79. Dempster's canonical approach to Old Testament theology can be seen in *Dominion and Dynasty*.

consciousness' on the part of the biblical authors can guide interpreters in their reconstruction of the canon formation process.[42] This type of study involves looking for indications of closure within the biblical texts themselves. He points to the 'significant group of scholars' that acknowledge 'such editorial glue in the form of canon-conscious redactions'.[43] For these scholars, internal evidence is pointedly relevant to canon studies, and the notion of canon-consciousness is an important feature of that textual evidence.

In relation to definitions of canon, Dempster notes that 'the significance of these redactions is that they show examples of Canon 1 and Canon 2 in operation, in which a collection of *authoritative literature* is spliced together to form part of a coherent unity in which it now becomes part of an *authoritative collection* in which the books are now read together'.[44] These canon-conscious redactions and compositions associate books and sections of the canon with other books and sections of the canon.[45] The result of this strategic compositional activity by the biblical authors and editors is a biblical canon that is intelligently designed. Reflecting on this canon-conscious activity, Dempster asserts that 'the canon is not an arbitrary collection of books nor an anthology of national literature, but it has contours and shape, with theological significance'.[46] For Dempster, these types of connections

42. Dempster, 'Canons', pp. 68-76.

43. Dempster, 'Canons', p. 70. Dempster includes in this group Joseph Blenkinsopp, O.H. Steck, John Sailhamer and Stephen Chapman (see the works of these scholars in the bibliography). Cf. the previous discussion of 'canonical glue', and also the scholars mentioned in the 'Broad Understanding of Canon' section of Chapter 1.

44. Dempster, 'Canons', p. 71. See also the previous discussion regarding the etymology of κανών (especially Metzger's categories of 'collection of authoritative writings' versus 'authoritative collection of writings'). Dempster's understanding of the nature of canon combines these two senses (of Canon 1 and Canon 2). For him, 'until the Old Testament was complete, then, it would have been an "open canon" (proto-canon)' ('Canon and Old Testament Interpretation', pp. 157-58). Further, 'the attempt to explain an open canon as simply an arbitrary collection of sacred documents ("scripture") or valued religious literature as opposed to "canon" fails to understand the nature of its content' (p. 158). Cf. the definitional discussions of Chapter 1.

45. Dempster gives the example of the book of Chronicles which 'functions to signal canonical closure' ('Canons', p. 75). He also highlights the thematic unity found between the sections of the Law (Deut. 34), Prophets (Josh. 1/Mal. 4), and Writings (Pss. 1–2/Chron.). See 'An "Extraordinary Fact": Part I', pp. 23-56, and 'An "Extraordinary Fact": Part II', pp. 191-218. Dempster observes that these interconnections are part of 'an exceedingly rich intertextuality in which there are many linguistic and conceptual echoes throughout Scripture. Later biblical books consciously echo and imitate events, concepts, and language in earlier books' (*Dominion and Dynasty*, pp. 31-32). Cf. this type of discussion in Chapter 3 (e.g. the 'Shape of the Hebrew Bible' section) and Chapter 4 (e.g. the 'Intertextuality within the Canonical Context' section).

46. Dempster, 'Canons', p. 77.

serve as 'explicit signals of textual coherence' and point in the direction of 'a canon-consciousness of the biblical authors/editors, that is, an awareness that the individual books of the Bible belonged to a larger whole'.[47]

One of the key contributions that these scholars make is the way they have fore-fronted the notion of canon-consciousness as a viable category in biblical studies. Also important is that they have demonstrated the relevance of the shape of the biblical literature itself in a description of the history of its formation and the nature of its function. Moreover, the canon-conscious compositional activity highlighted by these figures has a considerable impact on the definitional discussion regarding the concept of canon. In other words, if there is a genuine overlap of the two senses of 'canon' during the compositional and canonization phases of canon formation, then a rigidly 'narrow understanding of canon' seems less tenable.

Accordingly, in the following section, I examine evidence for affirming that the biblical authors and the believing community possessed a form of canon-consciousness. This type of evidence should inform the way in which the term canon is defined and also the way in which the history of canon formation is reconstructed. The argument of these sections is that the internal and external evidence implies that a form of canon-consciousness was present during the composition and canonization of the literary material that ultimately comprises the biblical canon.

Internal Evidence Implies a Canon-Consciousness among the Biblical Writers
In determining whether or not the biblical writers and the believing community possessed a canon-consciousness mindset, internal and external historical evidence must be considered.[48] The phrase 'internal evidence' refers to material within the biblical writings themselves. The question here is whether there are indications within the biblical texts that point to an ongoing 'canon-consciousness' at work in the forming of the canonical

---

47. Dempster, *Dominion and Dynasty*, p. 30.
48. Balla, *Challenges*, pp. 86-87, helpfully distinguishes between internal and external evidence. 'On the one hand', he says, 'I have to examine arguments in relation to the reconstruction of the history of the development of the New Testament canon. This we may call the study of "external" evidence. On the other hand, I have to examine the questions: What did the early Christian authors think of the authority of their writings? What did they think of the relationship of their own writings to other early Christian writings?... The arguments brought forward from the writings may be referred to as the examination of "internal" evidence'. Trobisch distinguishes between three categories of historical evidence: indirect evidence (e.g. Patristic literature), direct evidence (the extant manuscripts), and the 'redactional frame of the New Testament itself' (*First Edition of the New Testament*, p. 3). In these terms, the direct and indirect historical evidence is considered under the 'Canonization' heading below, and the 'redactional frame' of the canon is considered in Chapter 3.

documents. How did the biblical authors perceive both the authority of their own writings and the authority of the writings on which they draw and on which they meditate? Do they seem to be aware of a broader literary context in which those writings and their own function? In any study of canon, the full implications of the writings themselves must be taken into account. Further, both the composition and canonization phase of the historical process of canon formation should be investigated.

Canon-Conscious Indications during Composition
The idea of a canon-consciousness during the composition stage involves the notion that in their works, biblical authors write in light of texts that are already deemed stable and authoritative. Signs of canon-consciousness will include indications that an author is aware of a collection of writings that he views as authoritative and normative for himself and for the audience to which he writes. Evidence of canon-consciousness during this phase will also include any indications that an author directly associates his composition with that broader (authoritative) literary context or understands his work to serve a particular function within that broader context.[49]

The seeds of canon-consciousness among the biblical authors and among the biblical community appear early in Israel's history. Beginning with the Ten Commandments or the 'Ten Words' that the Lord gives to Moses on Mount Sinai, the precedent of a set of written words that are to be set apart and viewed as sacred and authoritative is well-established. As Dempster argues, 'The roots of the concept of canon go back to Sinai, with the giving of the Ten Words *written* on two tablets, and then the original *oral* proclamation of the *book* of the Covenant.'[50]

In the composition of the books of the Hebrew Bible, the first grouping known as the Law or the Pentateuch is foundational for later writers.[51] The

49. This element of canon-consciousness in particular will be pursued under the 'Meant Contextuality' heading in Chapter 3.

50. Dempster, 'Canons', p. 57. He contends also that 'the concept of an authoritative collection of literature can be traced right back to the beginnings of Israelite history with the Ten Words, which were to be distinguished by being placed in a sacred receptacle located in a sacred chamber within a sacred tabernacle in ancient Israel' (p. 57). Dempster summarizes, 'The idea of canon began here and it is intimately related to covenant and communion… Unique content and conspicuous setting demarcate these writings and ensure their privileged authoritative status among a people with whom God has chosen to dwell. Their written form serves to ensure their relevance transcends their historical context' ('Canon and Old Testament Interpretation', p. 166). Hamilton also makes this point in 'Still Sola Scriptura', pp. 221-23, noting that 'we find evidence in the narratives that a growing amount of material was, like the Book of the Covenant in Exod. 24.7, seen to be God's word, authoritative, and canonical in that it was set apart from other writings' (p. 221).

51. Cf. von Campenhausen, *Formation of the Christian Bible*, p. 2: 'It was on this

prophets intentionally draw on the narratives and themes of the Pentateuch as they make statements about the nature of God and his promises. Subsequent writers strongly exhort the people to 'meditate day and night' on the Law of Moses.[52] These comments assume a stable and authoritative 'book' of Moses and occur at strategic points in the Hebrew Bible as a whole. That later writers intentionally appropriate Pentateuchal images, texts, and themes demonstrates that the Law *as a literary unit* functioned as an authoritative (or at least important) work. In this sense, a form of 'the book of Moses' was considered to be 'canonical'.[53] That is, the Law was considered to be stable enough as a text (not just as a norming principle) to be referenced in subsequent written works. The title given to it implies its status as a compositional entity/unity (i.e. the book of Moses). The manner in which it is cited further implies its authority in the eyes of the prophetic writers making use of it as a literary source (i.e. it is to be *meditated on* constantly with care and diligence).[54]

The result of biblical writers consciously linking their books to a previously established work in this manner is the generation of strong 'associa-

foundation [of the Pentateuch] that the total structure of the canon was built.' He also argues that 'the prophets were primarily understood as tradents and interpreters of the Tora [*sic*], and that canonical respect was accorded to their writings on this basis' (p. 2).

52. See Josh. 1.8; Mal. 4.4; Cf. Pss. 1; 19; 119. These texts will be treated more closely and characterized as 'strategic' in Chapter 5's discussion of the 'ideal reader' of the biblical canon. Cf. Chapman, *Law and Prophets*, p. 112: 'In Deut. 34.10-12 and Mal. 3.22-24 [4.4-6] the biblical canon possesses two "canon-conscious" endings. They conclude the two constitutive portions of the biblical canon in the pre-Christian, pre-rabbinic era, and therefore indicate the way in which "Law" and "Prophets" were construed together in antiquity as a scriptural "intertext" or "canon"'. For Chapman, these texts 'refer consciously to the emergent biblical canon' (p. 112).

53. Cf. Blenkinsopp, *Prophecy and Canon*, p. 116: 'That Torah was already in existence as a norm of faith before the prophetic corpus was put together suggest that the latter could itself become authoritative only by association with the former. If [the Prophets corpus] is then seen as a sort of supplement to Torah, it would seem natural to conclude that the essential function of the prophet was to transmit and interpret Torah.' For a recent evangelical treatment of the dating of the Pentateuch and the relationship between the final form of the Pentateuch and the references to the 'Law of Moses' throughout the Old Testament, see T. Desmond Alexander, *From Paradise to the Promised Land: An Introduction to the Pentateuch* (Grand Rapids, MI: Baker, 3rd edn, 2012), pp. 85-109; and Sailhamer, *Meaning of the Pentateuch*, pp. 180-218. Sailhamer argues that 'an evangelical compositional approach to biblical authorship identifies Moses as the author of the Pentateuch and seeks to uncover his strategy in "making a book"' (p. 200). For a historical overview of Pentateuchal research on this issue, see R.N. Whybray, *The Making of the Pentateuch: A Methodological Study* (Sheffield: JSOT Press, 1987); and E.W. Nicholson, *The Pentateuch in the Twentieth Century: The Legacy of Julius Wellhausen* (Oxford: Clarendon Press, 1998).

54. Cf. the section on 'The Book of Moses' below.

tions' between individual books and corpora.[55] Through the compositional shape they give to their writings and the deliberate inner-biblical/intertextual references they make to other writings, the authors of the prophetic and poetic material of the Prophets and Writings sections of the Hebrew Bible associate their compositions with a growing body of literature. In this way, the former prophets are associated with the Law, the latter prophets connect with the former, and the Twelve are associated with the three major prophets of Isaiah, Jeremiah, and Ezekiel. As a combined whole, these writings form a kind of conceptual grammar of 'Law-Prophets'. As Christopher Seitz argues, 'The Law and the Prophets...is a grammar—that is, this literary conjunction is the means (rule and syntax) by which the language of Israel's scriptures makes its voice most fundamentally heard.'[56]

This fundamental unit of Law-Prophets becomes formative for the rest of the Hebrew Bible and also for the New Testament. The group of books in the Writings, the third section of the Hebrew Bible, also draws heavily upon the Law and the Prophets. For instance, the Psalter is concerned with the messianic promise to David found in the Former Prophets (2 Samuel 7), and the book of Chronicles can be understood to function essentially as a commentary on the entire Hebrew Bible.[57] At the macrostructural level, these associations give the Hebrew Bible a marked degree of conceptual and theological coherence.[58]

---

55. Seitz introduces and develops the idea of 'association' in the formation of the Hebrew Bible in *The Goodly Fellowship of the Prophets: The Achievement of Association in Canon Formation* (Grand Rapids, MI: Baker, 2009). He calls these associative moves a 'unique achievement' (p. 32).

56. Seitz, *Goodly Fellowship*, p. 33. For a thorough analysis of the way these associations actually work, see Chapman, *Law and Prophets*. Chapman outlines the arguments for the 'pre-eminence of Torah' over the Prophets corpus in the formation of the Hebrew Bible (pp. 241-74). Chapman himself argues that 'there existed a theological "grammar" of "Law and Prophets" which functioned authoritatively earlier than the scriptural collections later known by those titles' (p. 241). For Chapman, the main exegetical points of the standard model of Old Testament canon formation actually provide complementary support for his argument for the 'pre-eminence' of a Law-Prophets foundational unit (pp. 241-42). Seitz draws freely from Chapman's study.

57. For one example of this interpretation of the Psalter, see Dempster, *Dominion and Dynasty*, pp. 194-202. His heading for the section on the Psalter reads, 'The Psalms: David, David and David'. Regarding the book of Chronicles, cross-reference the comment of John Sailhamer, *First and Second Chronicles* (Chicago: Moody Press, 1983), p. 9: 'It is possible that the writer's purpose was not simply to retell these events but to explain and expound on their meaning in Israel's history... First and Second Chronicles may then be a commentary on the historical books' (p. 9). Koorevar argues that the book of Chronicles is an 'intended conclusion' to the Hebrew Bible as a whole (see further discussion in Chapter 3 on the canonical function of Chronicles).

58. On the formation and function of the shape of the Tanak as 'Law, Prophets, Writings', see Stephen G. Dempster, 'Torah, Torah, Torah: The Emergence of the Tripartite

The notion of canon-consciousness includes both an awareness of an established body or group of writings and also an acknowledgment of the authority or normativity of those writings and of that collection.[59] That the biblical writers refer to some of these writings as Scripture confirms the presence of this canon-conscious mindset. In other words, there is recognition within certain parts of Scripture of other authoritative portions of written revelation. These references point out the possibility of 'seeds' of canon-consciousness among the biblical authors in relation to the authoritative nature of certain writings in contradistinction to others. This recognition can be seen in the Old Testament's use of the Old Testament, the New Testament's use of the Old Testament, and the New Testament's use of the New Testament.

As noted above, the references to the Law of Moses as an authoritative document illustrate this point. From the beginning, this 'book' of the covenant is set apart in the life of Israel.[60] In the books of the Prophets and the Writings section of the Hebrew Bible, this stance toward the Law is maintained. This canonical understanding of the 'book of Moses' is carried on in the Gospel accounts along with recognition of the authority of the Hebrew Bible as a whole.[61] At the end of his Gospel, Luke refers to the Old Testament as 'the Scriptures' (24.32), as 'Moses and all the Prophets' (24.27), and as 'the Law of Moses and the Prophets, and the Psalms' (24.44). Luke's usage here demonstrates the presence of a stable body of authoritative literature and exemplifies the diverse ways in which this collection could be labeled.[62]

New Testament authors can also refer to other New Testament documents as authoritative Scripture. For instance, in his second epistle, Peter associates the letters of 'our beloved brother Paul' with 'the rest of the Scriptures' (2 Pet. 3.16). Moreover, in his first epistle to Timothy, Paul discusses the recompense of an elder by quoting a passage from Deuteronomy (25.4) and also the words of Jesus found in the Gospel of Luke (10.7). Paul

Canon', in *Exploring the Origins of the Bible* (ed. Craig Evans and Emanuel Tov; Grand Rapids, MI: Baker, 2008), pp. 87-128; and Blenkinsopp, *Prophecy and Canon*, pp. 124-26. For a contrasting perspective, see Eugene Ulrich, 'The Non-Attestation of a Tripartite Canon in 4QMMT', *CBQ* 65 (2003), pp. 202-14; and Julio C. Trebolle Barrera, 'Origins of a Tripartite Old Testament Canon', in *Canon Debate*, pp. 128-45.

59. As seen in the discussions of this chapter, the function of the Law (Torah, the first five books of the Hebrew Bible) serves as an example of both of these elements. There is a recognition of the Law as a literary unit (Canon 2) and also as an absolute theological authority (Canon 1).

60. The Book of the Law is literally 'set apart' when it is placed alongside the ark of the covenant and entrusted to the Levites in Deut. 31.23-26.

61. E.g. Mk 12.26. Cf. Heb. 9.19.

62. See also the discussion of this passage in the 'External Evidence' section.

understands both of these references to be what the 'Scripture says' (1 Tim. 5.18). Significantly, Paul here attributes this quotation to Scripture rather than to the historical figure of Jesus.[63] This emphasis on the written word implies that Paul has a notion of authoritative writings that includes at least material from Luke's Gospel.[64] Thus, when Paul writes in 2 Tim. 3.16 that 'all Scripture' is breathed out by God, there is conceptual room for him to conceive of apostolic writings alongside those of the authoritative Hebrew Bible.[65]

Within the New Testament itself, writings from two of the four main groupings (Gospels and Paul) are explicitly deemed authoritative Scripture by an apostle. There thus appears to be a conscious reliance on (or at least awareness of) the presence of authoritative documents even in the composition stage of many of the biblical writings. In short, the strategic canon-consciousness comments of the biblical authors demonstrate the interrelationship of the two major senses of canon (i.e. Canon 1 and Canon 2) and show that the broader canonical context was not only a *valid* category of thought, but also a *vital* one.

Canon-Conscious Indications during Canonization

The counterpart to a canon-consciousness at work in the composition phase is the presence of this type of awareness during the canonization phase. One of the ways this process works is that the writings that have been compositionally associated with one another begin to be grouped together

---

63. On this point, I. Howard Marshall argues that 'a written source is surely required, and one that would have been authoritative' (*A Critical and Exegetical Commentary on the Pastoral Epistles* [Edinburgh: T. & T. Clark, 1999], p. 616).

64. In Paul's quotation, verbal parallels are most clear in relation to Lk. 10.7, but Mt. 10.10 also expresses the same concept. Paul cites the same idea in 1 Cor. 9.14, but there he attributes the statement directly to Jesus ('the Lord'). Cf. John P. Meier, 'The Inspiration of Scripture: But What Counts as Scripture?', *Mid-Stream* 38 (1999), pp. 71-78. After noting that 'the second citation is hardly an afterthought loosely appended to the first', Meier opines, 'the only interpretation that avoids contorted intellectual acrobatics or special pleading is the plain, obvious one. The Pastor is citing Luke's Gospel alongside Deuteronomy as normative Scripture for ordering the church's ministry' (p. 77). He adds that 'once again, we have a work that will wind up at the margins of the NT canon hinting at the beginnings of the NT canon—and this time at the end of the 1st century' (p. 77). Although Meade believes 1 Tim. to be pseudonymous, he argues that the way Deut. 25.4 is connected to a saying of Jesus from Lk. 10.7 is 'evidence of a "canon consciousness" of new tradition/revelation' ('Ancient Near Eastern Apocalypticism', p. 316).

65. Though the danger of glib anachronism is real, this observation implies that 2 Tim. 3.16 is not a necessarily illegitimate *locus classicus* for the assertion that the entire Christian canon is 'God-breathed'. Contra Allert, *High View of Scripture*, pp. 149-56.

conceptually and materially. The association typically begins conceptually and eventually moves to a material association when the codex form makes publications of large books possible. The shape of groupings in part can represent the formalizing of associations present within the writings themselves.[66] As the Scriptures are written in light of each other, the reading community begins to recognize and respect these connections. Accordingly, the earliest extant manuscript evidence demonstrates that as the biblical books were being written, they were quickly collected and circulated in groupings.[67] The presence of writings grouped together likely indicates at least a minimal cognitive judgment that these writings are related conceptually and should thus be related materially. As Hurtado argues, 'the physical linkage of texts in one manuscript probably reflects a view of them as sharing some common or related subject matter or significance for readers'.[68]

As these relatively stable groupings form and endure, a broader context of 'canon' begins to actualize. This type of association takes place regardless of how loose the connections are, as there will be flexibility among various communities and individuals. However, as this process develops and matures, more and more communities and individuals begin to share a common order of reading. The smaller groupings and larger sections begin to be read in consistent ways. In this sense, the larger canonical context can be understood as a 'collection of collections' that takes on an increasingly discernable shape.[69] The content of the concept of canon

66. Though, even under a maximal reading of the evidence, there is still room for the distinct possibility (emphasized heavily by the current consensus of canon scholars) that the internal orderings of the various corpora are merely arbitrary or ordered according solely to a provincial consideration (e.g. the length of the Pauline epistles).

67. See Trobisch, *First Edition of the New Testament*, pp. 8-44. Trobisch mounts evidence for what he calls a 'final redaction' of the New Testament and argues that virtually all of the extant New Testament manuscripts are parts of collections. His overall conclusion is that 'the evidence provided by the extant manuscripts indicates that the history of the New Testament is the history of an edition' (p. 8). One of his reasons for this conclusion is that, in his view, 'the extant manuscripts demonstrate little variation' (p. 34). For a sampling of critical interaction with Trobisch's central claims, see Gamble, 'New Testament Canon', pp. 290-91; Holmes, 'Biblical Canon', p. 421 n. 3; Gerd Theissen, *The New Testament: A Literary History* (trans. Linda M. Maloney; Minneapolis, MN: Fortress Press, 2012), pp. 222-24; and Larry W. Hurtado, Review of *Die Endredaktion des Neuen Testaments: Eine Untersuchung zur Entstehung der Christlichen Bibel*, in *JTS* 50 (1999), pp. 288-91.

68. Hurtado, *Earliest Christian Artifacts*, p. 35. He also argues that 'it must have been a deliberate choice to place particular texts together, and that means that it probably reflects some view of the texts in question' (p. 35). For Hurtado, this 'practice of combining more than one text in the same manuscript' is an 'artifactual feature' that historians of the New Testament canon should not neglect (p. 35).

69. Gamble underlines the importance of the 'history of the smaller collections'

consists of these groupings and their organic relationship to one another. In other words, the presence of trends in the way biblical documents are grouped together in the manuscript evidence demonstrates that they were in some way seen in light of one another. This scenario increases the likelihood that those writing and collecting these writings shared a canon-conscious mindset.

1. *The Book of Moses*. Recent research on the question of canon has suggested that considerations of association and grouping were present as the biblical writings were beginning to circulate. For example, the five books of the Pentateuch were initially intended to be understood as one work. Though the five-fold division of Genesis, Exodus, Leviticus, Numbers, and Deuteronomy represents an early tradition, the literary shape of the Pentateuch as a whole is well established and accords with the original compositional strategy of its author. The author of the Pentateuch, in particular, serves as a paradigmatic example of a biblical writer who is concerned about the ordering of the material that he uses to compose a complex and wide-ranging literary and compositional entity.[70]

As noted above, the 'Law of Moses' functioned from its inception as a foundational unit both in the life of Israel and in the minds of subsequent biblical writers.[71] As Rendtorff observes, 'most of the other books would not be fully understandable without knowledge of the Pentateuch, to which they frequently refer, directly or indirectly'.[72] Moreover, 'references to the Pentateuch within the OT itself show that from the earliest times it was

and argues that 'the history of the canon is not a single and undifferentiated process in which individual documents were separately in play, nor is it to be understood as a selection of some documents from a larger pool' ('New Testament Canon', p. 275). Gamble surveys the formation of the Gospels, the letters of Paul, and the catholic epistles (pp. 275-90).

70. Cf. Sailhamer, *Meaning of the Pentateuch*, pp. 207-18 (a section entitled 'How Then Did Moses "Make" The Pentateuch?'). Rendtorff notes that 'the Pentateuch is the part of the Hebrew Bible that reached its final canonical form earliest. This shows the great significance that is attached to the collection and compositional shaping of the traditions contained in it' (*Canonical Hebrew Bible*, p. 89).

71. Cf. Johan Lust, 'Septuagint and Canon', in *The Biblical Canons* (ed. J.M. Auwers and H.J. de Jonge; Leuven: Leuven University Press, 2003), p. 40: 'The Hebrew canon is construed around the notion of revelation and the Word of the Lord. God's word was revealed to mankind in the Books of Moses or the Torah. This Law is the core of the revelation and the most venerable and authoritative part of the Bible. After Moses, other prophets in the history of religion proclaimed and reworded this Law in new situations.'

72. Rendtorff, *Canonical Hebrew Bible*, p. 89. Rendtorff ends his chapter on the theology of the Pentateuch with a section entitled, 'The Pentateuch as the Founding Document of Israel' (pp. 89-93).

considered a single book'.[73] For example, after the dedication of the wall of Jerusalem in Nehemiah 12, the author records that 'on that day they read aloud from the book of Moses in the hearing of the people' (Neh. 13.1).[74] In Mark's Gospel narrative, Jesus prefaces a quotation from Exod. 3.16 by saying, 'Have you not read in the book of Moses?' (12.26).[75] Furthermore, in virtually every extant list or manuscript of the Hebrew Bible/Old Testament, the ordering of the initial volumes consists of the five components of the Pentateuch (Genesis, Exodus, Leviticus, Numbers, Deuteronomy).[76]

---

73. John H. Sailhamer, *The Pentateuch as Narrative* (Grand Rapids, MI: Zondervan, 1992), p. 1. Sailhamer surveys the evidence for viewing the Pentateuch as a single book (i.e. 'the book of Moses') and also for understanding it as five separate works (i.e. the LXX ordering of Genesis, Exodus, Leviticus, Numbers, Deuteronomy). He acknowledges that 'in any event, it is safe to conclude that the five-part division is early and no doubt reflects a custom of writing large works on multiple scrolls'. However, he also argues that 'it is equally certain' that this particular 'division was not original. The original was written as a single book' (p. 2). One of the earliest references to the shape of the Hebrew Bible refers to the Pentateuch as a single literary entity: 'Not only from this book, but even the Law itself, the Prophecies, and the rest of the books differ not a little when read in the original' (the prologue to Ben Sira, NRSV). Cf. the discussion of Ben Sira and its prologue below.

74. The phrase 'book of Moses' also occurs in 2 Chron. 25.4; 35.12; and Ezra 6.18. Occurrences of the phrase 'book of the Law' or 'book of the Law of Moses' are relevant as well. E.g., this nomenclature occurs at strategic junctures in the book of Joshua. See Josh. 1.8 ('This book of the law shall not depart from your mouth'); 8.31 ('as it is written in the book of the law of Moses'); 8.34 ('they read all the words of the law… according to all that is written in the book of the law'); 23.6 ('to keep and do all that is written in the book of the law of Moses'); 24.26 ('And Joshua wrote these words in the book of the law of God'), etc. Cf. Alexander, *From Paradise to Promised Land*, pp. 95-98, who notes the significance of these types of text but also argues for a restricted referent for the term 'Law'. For instance, Alexander posits that 'in light of Deuteronomy, there can be no doubt, although this is not always appreciated, that the Book of the Law mentioned at the start of Joshua is *not* the Pentateuch as we know it. Rather, the expression 'Book of the Law' denotes the contents of Deuteronomy 5–26 (or perhaps 5–30)' (p. 96). Alexander also, though, acknowledges that in subsequent Israelite history (e.g. among the writing prophets), there is a gradual inclusion of material from Genesis–Numbers under the rubric of 'Law of the Lord' (pp. 96-98).

75. Cf. Lk. 2.22; 24.44; Jn 1.45; 7.19, 23; Acts 13.39; 15.5; 28.23; 1 Cor. 9.9; Heb. 9.19; 10.28.

76. E.g., note the initial position and striking uniformity of these five books among the lists and manuscripts produced by the early church in Sundberg, *Old Testament of the Early Church*, pp. 58-59; and Beckwith, *Old Testament Canon of the New Testament Church*, pp. 181-234. See also the consistent ordering of the fourth century Greek uncial codex manuscripts in Appendix 1. Cf. Tov, *Textual Criticism of the Hebrew Bible*, p. 126: 'Only rarely does the reconstructed *Vorlage*+ of a [LXX] book reflect *textual* features that characterize a book as a whole. However, the *Vorlage* of [LXX-Torah] is characterized by a large number of harmonizing pluses'. He also notes that

2. *The Book of the Twelve*. The Minor Prophets were also circulated as one
multi-book unit soon after their individual compositions (i.e. The Book
of the Twelve).[77] In the case of the Twelve, then, 'ample evidence' demonstrates that soon after initial composition these prophetic books 'were
combined literarily into a single work'.[78] Several pieces of external evidence demonstrate this perceived literary unity. For instance, Ben Sira
refers to the Minor Prophets as a single literary entity. He writes, 'May
the bones of the Twelve Prophets send forth new life from where they lie,
for they comforted the people of Jacob and delivered them with confident
hope' (Sir. 49.10).[79] Similarly, in his speech before the Jewish leaders in

'in general, the translators of [LXX-Torah] represent their Hebrew source faithfully'
(p. 126 n. 227). Similarly, Alexander observes that 'the books of Genesis to Deuteronomy are linked in such a way that while they may be viewed as separate entities, it is
clear that they have been made dependent on one another, with the later books presup-
posing a knowledge of the earlier ones and the earlier books being incomplete without
the addition of the later ones' (*From Paradise to Promised Land*, p. xvi).

77. See Michael B. Shepherd, *The Twelve Prophets in the New Testament* (New
York: Peter Lang, 2011), pp. 2-3. Shepherd lists seven lines of 'historical evidence for
the unity of the Twelve'. See also his discussion of the 'variant editions of the Twelve'
(pp. 69-78). Shepherd favors the ordering of the Masoretic Text, arguing that 'the
arrangement of the Septuagint of the Twelve is most likely a case of secondary editorial maneuvering rather than an original piece of composition' (p. 75). Cf. Michael
B. Shepherd, 'Compositional Analysis of the Twelve', *ZAW* 120 (2008), pp. 184-93.
For a contrasting perspective, see Barry Alan Jones, *The Formation of the Book of the
Twelve: A Study in Text and Canon* (Atlanta, GA: Scholars Press, 1995), who posits the
Septuagint ordering as the most primitive. Bo H. Lim also argues for the value of this
ordering in 'Which Version of the Twelve Prophets Should Christians Read? A Case
for Reading the LXX Twelve Prophets', *JTI* 7 (2013), pp. 21-36. Lim concludes that
'the LXX Twelve ought to be read for its theological contribution because it, like the MT
Twelve, possesses its own thematic logic, catch-words between books, and history of
reception that acknowledges its unity' (p. 36).

78. Chapman, *Law and Prophets*, p. 138. Shepherd points out ('Compositional
Analysis', p. 184 n. 1) that as early as 1904, D. Karl Marti could remark, 'Dass die
Sammlung der Prophetenschriften, welche im Zwölfprophetenbuch vereinigt sind,
schon in relativ alter Zeit als eine zusammengehörige Einheit betrachtet wurde, lässt
sich aus verschiedenen Anzeichen erschliessen' (*Das Dodekapropheton* [Tübigen:
Mohr Siebeck, 1904], p. xiii).

79. Chapman observes that Ben Sira here 'refers to all twelve as a *literary collection*
in its overview of biblical history and literature' (*Law and Prophets*, p. 138). He also
notes that 'the evidence from Qumran provides further support for this notion, since several of the fragments from the Minor Prophets contain text from more than one book,
and perhaps always in the masoretic order', though 'a complete copy of the entire book
of The Twelve has not been found' (p. 138). These scroll fragments date to the middle of
the second century BCE. Cf. J. Nogalski, *Literary Precursors to the Book of the Twelve*
(Berlin: De Gruyter, 1993). Nogalski notes that *4 Ezra* 14.45, Josephus (*Apion* 1.37-42),
and the Talmud (*Baba Bathra* 14b) presuppose the Twelve as a literary unit (see pp. 1-3).

Acts 7, Stephen quotes a prophetic text from Amos 5.25.[80] Luke records
that Stephen introduces the quotation with the formula, 'As it is written in
the book of the prophets' (Acts 7.42). Stephen seems to refer to a single
prophetic text ('It was not to me...') as a constituent part of a larger literary collection ('the book of the prophets').[81]

Furthermore, the later Greek Nahal Hever Minor Prophets Scroll contains fragments of the twelve Minor Prophets in one scroll and is evidence
of the close physical association of these prophetic books.[82] The fact that
these twelve diverse writings are found together in the manuscript evidence
so early in their conception lends legitimacy to the complementary studies
of themes and motifs that span the collection as a whole.[83] In other words,

80. The quoted text of Amos 5.25 in Acts 7.42 reads, 'It was not to me that you
offered victims and sacrifices forty years in the wilderness, was it, O House of Israel?'

81. Cf. also Paul's sermon in Acts 13, where he exhorts his listeners to 'take heed, so
that the thing spoken of *in the Prophets* may not come upon you: "Behold, you scoff-
ers, and marvel, and perish; For I am accomplishing a work in your days, a work which
you will never believe, though someone would describe it to you"' (Acts 13.40-41).
Paul refers here to the 'Prophets' as a collection, and then quotes from one of the parts
of that prophetic collection (i.e. Hab. 1.5).

82. The Nahal Hever Minor Prophets Scroll is also known as 8HevXIIgr. For a discussion of this manuscript (along with the text and a set of fascimiles), see Emanuel Tov,
*The Greek Minor Prophets Scroll from Nahal Hever (HevXIIgr) (The Seiyal Collec-
tion I)* (Oxford: Clarendon Press, 1995). Citing a series of DSS manuscripts (4QXII[b,g],
MurXII and 8HevXIIgr), Tov states clearly, 'The Minor Prophets were regarded as
one book' (*Textual Criticism of the Hebrew Bible*, p. 194). A strong piece of straightforward evidence for the consistent association of the Twelve can also be seen in the
LXX sequence of these prophetic books in the fourth century Greek uncial codex manuscripts (Appendix 1). Chapman notes too that 'the Babylonian Talmud (*Baba Bathra*
13b) even makes an exception for The Twelve when it comes to the spacing between
biblical books: fewer lines (3) than the normal practice (4) are required of scribes when
separating each of the books within the book of The Twelve' (*Law and Prophets*,
p. 139). Shepherd adds that 'the Masoretic Text (medieval), which marks the mid-point
of every biblical book, does not mark the mid-point of each of the books of the Twelve.
Rather, it marks Mic. 3.12 as the mid-point of the whole book of the Twelve' (*Twelve
Prophets in the New Testament*, p. 3). Cf. Nogalski, *Precursors*, p. 3. These manuscript
features represent artifactual indications (and confirmation) of the literary unity of the
Twelve.

83. See, e.g., the essays in *Reading and Hearing the Book of the Twelve* (ed. James
Nogalski and Marvin A. Sweeney; Atlanta, GA: SBL, 2000); *Thematic Threads in
the Book of the Twelve* (ed. Paul L. Redditt and Aaron Schart; Berlin: W. de Gruyter,
2003); and Paul House, *The Unity of the Twelve* (Sheffield: Almond, 1990). Redditt
and Schart summarize the recently emerged scholarly consensus, noting that 'at the
end of the last century it became acceptable in scholarly biblical exegesis to view
the Book of the Twelve Prophets as a literary unity. Several book length studies and
numerous essays have demonstrated that any interpretation that takes the canonical

one of the hermeneutical effects of the physical unity of these twelve prophetic books is that it encourages readers to discern the compositional unity
of the book of the Twelve.[84]

3. *The Fourfold Gospel.* Similarly, the Gospels were circulated together
early in their existence. Though each Gospel likely had a unique compositional history and circumstantial provenance, they quickly became part of a
four-fold witness.[85] Greek manuscript discoveries in Egypt in the last century have provided important evidence for the text and circulation of the
New Testament writings. Aland argues in this regard that these manuscripts
'attest the significance of the New Testament as a most influential constant
in the self-consciousness of the communities. They are witnesses to the
awareness of a distinctive canon of Scripture'.[86] In relation to the Gospels,

text seriously has to understand the intention of the final composition of the twelve
writings' ('Foreword', in *Thematic Threads in the Book of the Twelve*, p. v). Seitz,
in particular, has maintained a sustained interest in the hermeneutical function of the
book of the Twelve within the context of the Hebrew Bible (e.g., see *Prophecy and
Hermeneutics*, pp. 189-246; *Goodly Fellowship*, pp. 23-29, 82-95; and *Character of
Christian Scripture*, pp. 162-66).

    84. For an example of this type of interaction with the book of the Twelve, see Shep-
herd, *Twelve Prophets in the New Testament*. Shepherd seeks to demonstrate that the
compositional shape of the Twelve informs the reception of the Minor Prophets in the
writings of the New Testament. He asks, 'What if quotations from the Twelve presuppose an awareness of their place within the larger composition of Hosea through Malachi? What if it is necessary to redefine the original or immediate context of any one
part of the Twelve to include the compositional strategy and theological message of
the book as a whole?' (p. 1). For Shepherd, the book of the Twelve 'consists of sources
from different times and places, which have been put together or shaped in a theologically unified way' (pp. 1-2). Consequently, 'to stop short of the final form of the
Twelve is to stop short of a real historical moment of authorship and composition'
(p. 2). Cf. Shepherd's summary statement in 'Compositional Analysis', p. 185: 'What
emerges from a compositional analysis is an intentional strategy that can be traced
along the seams where the pieces have been put together. To follow this strategy is to
follow the theological message of the Twelve Prophets.' He also notes that 'the historical dimensions of the text have not been treated adequately until the text has been
interpreted as a whole' (p. 192).

    85. Cf. Patzia, *Making of the New Testament*, p. 93: 'What we do know is that the
Gospels became part of the canon as a collection, not individually.'

    86. Barbara Aland, 'The Significance of the Chester Beatty Papyri in Early Church
History', in *The Earliest Gospels: The Origins and Transmission of the Earliest Chris-
tian Gospels—The Contribution of the Chester Beatty Gospel Codex P45* (ed. Charles
Horton; London: T. & T. Clark, 2004), p. 120. She adds, 'They show that alternative
sequences of the New Testament writings were possible (P[45]: Matthew, John, Luke,
Mark, Acts, and P[46]: Romans, Hebrews, 1 and 2 Corinthians, Ephesians, Galatians,
Philippians, Colossians, 1 Thessalonians), but that the collection of these writings was
essentially closed' (p. 120).

the P[45] codex of the Chester Beatty collection of papyrus manuscripts demonstrates the connection that was seen between the four Gospels themselves and in contradistinction to other 'gospel' literature.[87] In the case of P[45], portions of each of the four Gospels are found followed by the book of Acts. Badly damaged throughout, no page of the codex is fully intact. However, there are two fragments where the upper margin is preserved enough to recover the pagination and reconstruct the general dimensions and content of the original manuscript.[88] What is clear is that P[45] consisted of the four Gospels in sequence and in codex form.

While significant for text-critical purposes, P[45] also has significant bearing on the historical question of canon formation.[89] In this manuscript, the four

87. As Hurtado notes, 'At least for those Christians whose views are represented in the extant manuscripts, those Gospel texts that were copied together were regarded as in some way complementary and sufficiently compatible with one another to be so linked. Along the same line of reasoning, those Gospel writings that did not get linked with other texts were probably regarded as in some way sufficiently different in significance and/or usefulness that they did not belong in the same manuscript' (*Earliest Christian Artifacts*, p. 37). As Kruger observes, 'Apparently early Christians were willing to link some Gospels together in a single manuscript and not others' (*Canon Revisited*, p. 242). One of the best ways to access the manuscripts in the Chester Beatty collection is still the sixteen volume facsimile edition edited by Frederic G. Kenyon and published shortly after the manuscripts were discovered in the early 1930s. For P[45], see Kenyon, ii, *Text* and Kenyon, ii, *Plates*. Cf. *The Text of the Earliest New Testament Greek Manuscripts* (ed. Phillip W. Comfort and David P. Barrett; Wheaton: Tyndale House, 2001). For an updating of Kenyon's original assessment of the codicological aspects of P[45], see T.C. Skeat, 'A Codicological Analysis of the Chester Beatty Papyrus Codex of the Gospels and Acts (P45)', *Hermathena* 155 (1993), pp. 27-43 (=*Skeat*, pp. 141-57). See also the wide-ranging essays on the significance of P[45] for textual criticism of the New Testament and the history of early Christianity in *The Earliest Gospels*. For an overview and exposition of the early circulation of non-canonical gospels, see Christopher Tuckett, 'Forty Other Gospels', in *The Written Gospel* (ed. Markus Bockmuehl and Donald A. Hagner; Cambridge: Cambridge University Press, 2005), pp. 238-53. Tuckett provides a taxonomy of these gospels that includes narrative gospels, sayings gospels, infancy gospels, resurrection discourses/dialogues, and harmonies (pp. 243-49).

88. At the top of the page containing Acts 14.15-23 (fol. 27ᵛ) and the one containing Acts 17.9-17 (fol. 30ʳ), the pagination reads 193 and 199, respectively (see Kenyon, ii, *Texts*, pp. 47, 50; cf. also the relevant folio locations in Kenyon, ii, *Plates*). Leaves 11-12 (Lk. 10.6–11.46) and 13-14 (Lk. 11.50–13.24) also preserve 'conjoint leaves' that aid in reconstructing the original page layout. These indications allow Kenyon to deduce that 'the codex originally consisted of approximately 220 leaves [*sic*], measuring about 10x8 in., with columns of writing about 7½ in. high and 6¼ inches in width, and containing usually 39 lines of text' (Kenyon, ii, *Text*, p. vi). Alternatively, Skeat (building on Kenyon's work) calculates that the codex would have 'consisted of 56 quires of 4 pages = 224 pages, one page at the beginning and one at the end being blank and unnumbered' ('Codicological Analysis', *Skeat*, p. 156).

89. On the whole (and after its own scribal idiosyncrasies are taken into account),

canonical Gospels are physically bound together and materially juxtaposed. Unless the grouping of P[45] is completely arbitrary (a dubious assumption), then this four-fold Gospel *codex* sheds significant light on the four-fold Gospel *canon*.[90] In any case, this manuscript reflects 'both regard for, and

the text of P[45] confirms the general reliability of the textual tradition represented in the fourth century Greek uncial codices such as Sinaiticus (א 01), Alexandrinus (A 02), Vaticanus (B 03), and Ephraem Rescripti (C 04). In this regard, Kenyon notes that P[45] 'covers such a substantial portion of the Gospels that it is legitimate to draw general conclusions from it, and these show us in the early part of the third century a text of the Gospels and Acts identical in all essentials with that which we have hitherto known on the evidence of later authorities' (Kenyon, ii, *Texts*, pp. xix-x). Cf. J.K. Elliott's analysis in 'Singular Readings in the Gospel Text of P[45]', in *Earliest Gospels*, pp. 122-31; and Larry W. Hurtado, 'P[45] and the Textual History of the Gospel of Mark', in *Earliest Gospels*, pp. 132-48. On the significance of the Egyptian papyrus manuscripts for the study of scribal habits (and textual criticism in general), see James R. Royse, *Scribal Habits in Early Greek New Testament Papyri* (Leiden: Brill, 2008), pp. 17-37. Royse surveys the scholarly consensus that pre-fourth century manuscripts provide a window into a time before the standardization of the textual transmission of the New Testament texts.

90. On the relationship between the codex form and the 'canon', note the contrasting perspectives of Stanton and Head. Graham N. Stanton, 'The Fourfold Gospel', *NTS* 43 (1997), pp. 317-46; Peter M. Head, 'Graham Stanton and the Four-Gospel Codex: Reconsidering the Manuscript Evidence', in *Jesus, Matthew's Gospel and Early Christianity* (ed. Daniel Gurtner, *et al.*; London: T. & T. Clark, 2011), pp. 93-101. Cf. the remarks of T.C. Skeat in 'Irenaeus and the Four-Gospel Canon', *NovT* 34 (1992), pp. 194-99 (=*Skeat*, pp. 73-78). After discussing Irenaeus' unambiguous delineation of the four Gospels, Skeat concludes, 'In short, I would now go so far as to suggest that the Four-Gospel Canon and the Four Gospel codex are inextricably linked, and that each presupposes the other' (p. 78). Skeat reiterates this connection in 'Origin of the Christian Codex', *Skeat*, pp. 79-87. Noting that other 'gospels' were in circulation during the time when the four Gospels were selected, Skeat argues that 'inevitably the selection of the Four and their physical unity in the Codex gave them, right from the start, an authority and prestige which no competitor could hope to rival. The Four-Gospel Canon and the Four-Gospel Codex are thus inseparable' (pp. 86-87). Skeat later saw the establishment of P[4]+P[64+67] as part of one Gospel codex from the second century as support for his conjecture that the codex form was inextricably linked to an early impetus for canon (see below). Agreeing with Skeat, Stanton argues that 'the four-Gospel codex strongly encouraged acceptance of the fourfold Gospel, and vice versa' ('Fourfold Gospel', p. 340). Similarly, J.K. Elliott argues that 'canon and codex go hand in hand in the sense that the adoption of a fixed canon could be more easily controlled and promulgated when the codex was the means of gathering together originally separate compositions' ('Manuscripts, the Codex, and the Canon', *JSNT* 63 [1996], pp. 105-23 [111]). Conversely, Head suggests that 'the two things which Stanton wanted to join together—the technological hardware of the four-Gospel codex and the theological conviction about the canonicity of the four Gospels—should rather be separated' ('Graham Stanton and the Four-Gospel Codex', p. 100). Head concludes by arguing that 'there is thus a need, in my view, to set asunder that which Professor

interpretation of, the five texts that it contains, giving us a valuable artifact of at least one early Christian appropriation and construal of these texts'.[91] Furthermore, the existence and artifactual features of the manuscript itself attest to the presence of a community that valued *just these texts* enough to procure a well-crafted edition of them.[92] The relative cost to the community is difficult to determine, but 'in any event the codex represented a sizable investment'.[93]

Another intriguing piece of early artifactual evidence worth noting in this regard is the set of papyrus fragments known as P[4], P[64] + P[67]. The four leaves of P[4] contain portions from the beginning of Luke's Gospel.[94] The combined fragments of P[64] + P[67] contain material from the beginning and end of Matthew's Gospel.[95] Though they show only a limited amount of

---

Stanton joined together—the four-Gospel canon and the four-Gospel codex; and to seek for some means of conceptualizing the growing canon consciousness separately from the specifically four-Gospel-codex theory' (pp. 100-101).

91. Hurtado, *Earliest Christian Artifacts*, p. 38. Hurtado also notes generally that P[45] demonstrates that 'by the late second century some Christians were beginning to put two or more Gospels together in one manuscript' (pp. 36-37).

92. Significantly, the manuscript evidence contains no contemporary record of non-canonical gospels (or other literature similar to the New Testament writings) being bound together and circulated as a group. Cf. Elliott, 'Manuscripts, the Codex, and the Canon', p. 107: 'Collecting the four chosen Gospels into one codex had the effect of according a special status to those four, but possibly more significant, helped to limit the number of Gospels to these four and no more!... The Gospels that were rejected from that fourfold collection were never bound together with any or all of those four. There are no manuscripts that contain say Matthew, Luke and Peter, or John, Mark and Thomas.' For Elliott, the reason Christians preferred the codex could have been 'to safeguard the four Gospels from either addition or subtraction. This is in effect the operation of a "canon"' (p. 107).

93. Aland, 'Significance of the Chester Beatty Papyri', p. 114. By way of comparison, Aland notes that 'since P[45] comes from the first half of the third century we are on fairly firm ground: the community paid for their codex a little more than a scribe's monthly income, but a little less than a cattleman would have earned' (p. 115 n. 32). Skeat calculates that the total cost for producing the P[45] manuscript would have run around 43-44 drachmas ('Codicological Analysis', *Skeat*, pp. 156-57). Cf. Skeat, 'The Length of the Standard Papyrus Roll and the Cost-Advantage of the Codex', *Zeitschrift für Papyrologie und Epigraphik* 45 (1982), pp. 169-76 (=*Skeat*, pp. 65-70). One of Skeat's important methodological cautions in this discussion is that calculation of economic practices of book production in the ancient world are extremely difficult (and tenuous) due to the paucity of germane historical data.

94. The actual texts accessible on the P[4] fragment are (roughly) Lk. 1.58-59; 1.62–2.1; 2.6-7; 3.8–4.2; 4.29-35; 5.3-8; and 5.30–6.16.

95. The text accessible on P[64+67] includes (roughly) Mt. 3.9, 15; 5.20-22, 25-28; 26.7-8, 10, 14-15, 22-23, and 31-33. See T.C. Skeat's survey of the content of these fragments in 'The Oldest Manuscript of the Four Gospels?', *NTS* 43 (1997), pp. 1-2, 16-19. Cf. also Tommy Wasserman's summary table in 'A Comparative Textual Analysis of P[4] and P[64+67]', *Textual Criticism* 15 (2010), p. 6.

text, these small fragments have considerable potential significance for the history of New Testament manuscript production and canon formation. In 1997, T.C. Skeat argued that these fragments were portions of a four-Gospel codex from the second century and thus represented 'the oldest manuscript of the four Gospels'.[96] Skeat makes the case for this conclusion by seeking to establish three points: that all three fragments come from the hand of the same scribe, that Matthew would not have been followed by Luke in a bound manuscript, and that the original manuscript was a single-quire codex.[97] Based on his reconstruction of the text and structure of the codex itself, Skeat concludes that 'in any case, it is clear that the codex has a very good claim to be regarded as the oldest known codex of the four Gospels, and to that extent the answer to the question asked in the title to this article must be: "Yes"'.[98] Further, for Skeat, this manuscript represents 'proof of a four-Gospel codex the ancestors of which must go back well into the second century'.[99]

Though Skeat bases his conclusion on years of study and minute development of technical detail, some have called his analysis and reconstruction into question. Peter Head, in particular, demonstrates how much weight Skeat assigns to a number of crucial presuppositions and assumptions.[100] For Head, even granting the shared scribal identity of all three fragments, there is simply not enough indisputable evidence to suggest that the manuscript

96. See Skeat, 'Oldest Manuscript', pp. 1-34. Prior to Skeat's article, papyrologist C.H. Roberts had asserted (but not defended) that these fragments came from one four-gospel codex (see *Manuscript, Society and Belief,* p. 13: 'There can in my opinion be no doubt that all these fragments come from the same codex which was reused as packing for the binding of the late third century codex of Philo'). Skeat's argument was quickly echoed and commended by Stanton in 'The Fourfold Gospel'. Stanton was actually involved in Skeat's research (Skeat acknowledges the 'help and encouragement' he received from Stanton in 'Oldest Manuscript', p. 33).

97. Cf. Peter M. Head, 'Is P[4], P[64] and P[67] the Oldest Manuscript of the Four Gospels? A Response to T.C. Skeat' *NTS* 51 (2005), pp. 450-57. In his critical response, Head emphasizes these three elements of Skeat's argumentation.

98. Skeat, 'Oldest Manuscript', p. 30.

99. Skeat, 'Oldest Manuscript', p. 32.

100. See Head, 'A Response to T.C. Skeat', pp. 450-57. Head's article is often taken as a starting point for those critiquing Skeat's claims. Head argues that 'Skeat's theory that P[4] + P[64] + P[67] represents a four-gospel codex is not so much an historical datum that can be drawn upon in support of a theory about the origins of the four-gospel canon-codex, as a product of that theory impressed upon limited evidence which will not bear the weight' (p. 455). Similarly, see Scott Charlesworth, 'T.C. Skeat, P[64+67] and P[4], and the Problem of Fibre Orientation in Codicological Reconstruction', *NTS* 53 (2007), pp. 582-604. Charlesworth demonstrated that the 'fibre orientation' of the respective fragments preclude the notion that they originally formed elements of a single-quire codex (Head also deconstructed the reconstructive word-count calculations Skeat used to make this particular argument).

fragments in question were originally constituent parts of a single-quire codex that contained all four canonical Gospels.[101]

   These points of contention are difficult to dismiss and have enhanced the scholarly discussion of this particular set of papyrus manuscripts.[102] However, because of the nature of the evidence, the assumptions necessary to make these critiques are susceptible to question as well. For instance, Tommy Wasserman posits that Skeat's original text-critical assertion that the same hand likely penned each of the fragments holds up under closer scrutiny.[103] Further, Hill argues that multiple parts of a text did not have to reside in a single (single-quire) codex in order for them to have been viewed as material elements of a single work.[104] Each of the

   101. These factors form the climax of Head's argumentation: 'Our conclusion must be that, far from establishing his theory "beyond reasonable doubt", the difficulties outlined here are sufficient to call into question Skeat's case in both of its particulars, even allowing for the proposed identification of P[4], P[64], and P[67] as surviving remnants of the same original codex. There is simply insufficient evidence to conclude that the manuscript was originally a single-quire codex, and there is no evidence that the original codex (of whatever format) contained anything beyond the Gospels of Matthew and Luke' ('A Response to T.C. Skeat', p. 457).

   102. As an example of the pre-Head/Charlesworth assessment of the fragments, in their brief 2005 survey Metzger and Ehrman characterize P[4], P[64], and P[67] as a single-quire codex that contained all four Gospels. They also state that these fragments 'represent the oldest four-Gospel manuscript known to exist and push the practice of organized text division back into the second century' (*Text of the New Testament*, p. 53). At the least, Head and Charlesworth have shown that the case is not without problems (and that the fragments certainly did not originate from a single-quire codex).

   103. See Wasserman, 'A Comparative Textual Analysis of P[4] and P[64+67]', pp. 1-26. Limiting his discussion of this issue to the realm of textual criticism, Wasserman points out that Skeat's original text-critical analysis was based on comparison of deviations from the *Textus Receptus*. Wasserman broadens the scope of the comparative work (i.e. uses NA[27] as a base) and affirms the scribal identity of the fragments. He assigns all three fragments a 'strict' textual quality and transmission character and concludes that 'this textual analysis further confirms the palaeographic evidence that we have to do with the same scribe, who took great care to copy the respective exemplars' (p. 26). He also notes that the reconstructed codex size 'typical of the earliest NT codices' (i.e. 13 × 18 cm) 'correlates well' with his text-critical analysis of the fragments, 'pointing towards a controlled production' (p. 26). For an explanation of the technical terms used in his conclusion, see his methodological sketch on pp. 4-5, and in his essay, 'The Early Text of Matthew', in *The Early Text of the New Testament* (ed. Charles E. Hill and Michael J. Kruger; Oxford: Oxford University Press, 2012), pp. 84-85. His summary statement for P[4, 64+67] is that 'in any case, the fragments are most probably copied by the same scribe, and the textual character is also very similar' (p. 95).

   104. See Charles E. Hill, 'Intersections of Jewish and Christian Scribal Culture: The Original Codex Containing P[4], P[64], and P[67], and its Implications', in *Among Jews, Gentiles, and Christians in Antiquity and the Middle Ages* (ed. R. Hvalvik and J. Kaufman;

fragments demonstrates a striking set of similar features.[105] One of these shared features is that they each exhibit the marks of originally belonging to a multiple-quire codex.[106] In fact, the combined codicological and paleographical elements of the fragments contribute to the substantive case that can be made for the conclusion that P[4], P[64], and P[67] come from the same scribe, were part of the same multiple-quire codex, and thus represent one of the earliest (late second century) extant copies of a multiple (perhaps four!) Gospel codex.[107] Moreover, these fragments could be considered part of a four-fold Gospel corpus even if they formed parts of individual codices.[108]

Trondheim: Tapir Academic Press, 2011), pp. 75-91. This is the published form of a paper Hill delivered at SBL in 2010 entitled 'Skeat's Thesis, Not Dead Yet? On the Making of P[4], P[64], and P[67]'.

105. Hill, 'Intersections', pp. 78-85.

106. Charlesworth had argued (against Skeat) that 'when the differences in ekthetic projection and colour are added to issues arising from provenance, fibre direction, and copying', it is clear 'that Luke came from another codex entirely' ('Problem of Fibre Orientation', pp. 598-99). He states further that 'the objective facts of the fibre orientation of the surviving fragments declare that P[64+67] and P[4] come from different multiple-quire codices', and that the differences he outlines 'confirm the results of codicological analysis and mandate the conclusion that P[64+67] and P[4], though written by the same scribe, are not from the same single- or indeed multiple-quire codex' (p. 604). Hill systematically considers the five areas that Charlesworth forefronts and seeks to demonstrate that they are not 'fatal to the single-codex theory' ('Intersections', p. 78). Hill concludes that 'Skeat was wrong about the quire makeup', but his 'notion that these fragments were from an elegant codex which once contained all four Gospels has not been disproved, it is simply incapable of proof or disproof at the present time. So it remains not dead yet' ('Skeat's Thesis, Not Dead Yet?').

107. See Hill's summary of the 'significant commonalities which *enhance* the case that they all came from the same codex' ('Intersections', pp. 84-85). These common features include the same orthography, multiple-quire construction, alternating fiber pattern, page size, (rare) two-column format, column dimensions, system of paragraph divisions, and 'the same restricted number of *nomina sacra*' (pp. 84-85). In sum, Hill affirms the 'original codicological unity of P[4], P[64], and P[67]', arguing that 'these fragments all originally belonged to the same codex, a multi-Gospel codex containing at least Matthew and Luke and possibly other Gospels' (p. 76). He concludes in particular that 'in all probability' the 'fragments of Matthew and Luke were from the same codex. All the scribal and codicological features one would look for to identify two fragments as coming from the same codex seem to align and there is nothing which prevents their identification' (p. 88).

108. Hill entertains this notion in his conclusion: 'If Matthew of P[64+67] and Luke of P[4] were not part of the same codex, they were meticulously constructed to look like companions, two in a set. They would have shared everything, codicologically speaking, except the same cover. In this case, it perhaps makes little difference whether they were actually bound together; their virtually identical format may have signified much the same thing as binding them together does' ('Intersections', p. 88).

The interchange between these scholars is instructive in that it exposes the fragmentary nature of much of the evidence for the formation of the New Testament, demonstrates the importance of working methodological assumptions, and confirms the central role and level of reconstruction that is necessary in order to make sense of the historical data and the vagaries that inform an assessment of its significance. What the $P^{4+64+67}$ fragments do demonstrate in this case is the existence of an early grouping of multiple canonical Gospels that circulated among the believing community. A feature related to this early circulation is that these codex manuscripts were also designed for liturgical use and easy public reading.[109] In any case, the more stable conclusions that can be drawn from P^{45} at least represent an analogy to the type of evidence that $P^{4+64+67}$ can provide regarding the canon formation process.[110]

109. See Hill, *Who Chose the Gospels*, pp. 118-19: 'It seems agreed, however, that the books of Matthew and Luke represented in $P^{4, 64, 67}$ were copied by the same scribe, whether bound together with Mark and John or not. And it seems that this scribe was commissioned to copy books that would function as one church's Scripture.' Noting that the codex was 'handsomely and painstakingly executed', Hill also argues that 'it is very unlikely that in $P^{4, 64, 67}$ we have stumbled upon something which was the first of its kind' (p. 119). For him, 'we are looking at a codex which was not simply executed for the private reading of an individual Christian, but was a "pulpit edition" made to be read out to the congregation during a service of worship' (p. 119). Cf. Hill, 'Intersections', p. 90: 'Scribal features indicate that this codex [$P^4 + P^{64+67}$] and its text were very carefully prepared in a controlled setting, most likely for reading aloud to a congregation of believers.' Charlesworth observes also that P^{64+67} 'is the elegant product of a careful scribe' ('Problem of Fibre Orientation', p. 585). See also Scott Charlesworth, 'Public and Private—Second- and Third-Century Gospel Manuscripts', in *Jewish and Christian Scripture as Artifact and Canon* (ed. Craig A. Evans and H. Daniel Zacharias; London: T. & T. Clark, 2009), pp. 148-75; and Juan Hernández, Jr, 'The Early Text of Luke', in *The Early Text of the New Testament*, pp. 124-26. Hernández observes that 'the traces of early Christian piety emerge prominently in P^4' (p. 124). He also speaks of 'unmistakable marks' of 'early Christian readership' that appear on the leaves of the manuscript (p. 125).

110. The P^{75} manuscript from the Bodmer papyrus collection can also be included in this evidence for a multiple Gospel manuscript. P^{75} is a single-quire papyrus codex containing portions of the Gospel of Luke and the Gospel of John. An important feature of the manuscript is that it shows the end of Luke and the beginning of John on the same folio. Thus, at the very least, one can say that it contained these two Gospels in sequence and is thus evidence of a multiple Gospel codex (from the late second century). Accordingly, Skeat argues that 'it seems to me quite possible that the Bodmer codex of Luke and John, P75, is in fact the second half of a four-Gospel codex, since it consisted, when complete, of a single-quire codex of 72 leaves' ('Origin of the Christian Codex', p. 80). Stanton ('Fourfold Gospel', pp. 326-27) and Bruce (*Canon of Scripture*, p. 129) also endorse this conclusion. Head issues a number of cautionary comments in 'Graham Stanton and the Four-Gospel Codex', pp. 97-98. Head notes that 'this is of course, not impossible, but there is, it needs to be noted, absolutely no

Further, the manuscript evidence represented by the early papyrus codex manuscripts (e.g. P⁴⁵, P⁷⁵, and P⁴⁺⁶⁴⁺⁶⁷) also suggests that patristic mentions of Gospel groupings such as Justin Martyr's reference to the 'memoirs of the Apostles' (ἀπομνημονεύματα τῶν ἀποστόλων, *1 Apol.* 66.3; 67.3) and Irenaeus' later defense of a clearly defined 'four-fold Gospel' collection (εὐαγγέλιον τετράμορφον, *Adv. Haer.* 3.1.1; 3.11.8) are not purely innovative but rather descriptive of a previously established grouping.[111] In other words, the fragmentary manuscripts that exhibit signs of being part of an established collection represent a substantial independent witness that corroborates later testimony on behalf of an early four-fold Gospel collection that functioned with authority and possessed tangible boundaries.

4. *The Letters of Paul.* The various letters of Paul also began circulating as a discernable collection early in the life of the churches.[112] Within the New

evidence in support of this view' (p. 97). For a brief survey of P⁷⁵'s significance, see Comfort, *Encountering the Manuscripts*, pp. 72-73; and Metzger and Ehrman, *Text of the New Testament*, pp. 58-60. Metzger and Ehrman note that the 'textual significance of this witness is hard to overestimate, presenting as it does a form of text very similar to that of Vaticanus' (p. 59). Cf. Sarah A. Edwards's text-critical and codicological analysis in 'P75 Under the Magnifying Glass', *NovT* 18 (1976), pp. 190-212.

111. For the Greek text of Irenaeus' defense of the 'four-fold Gospel' and an exposition of its significance, see Skeat, 'Irenaeus and the Four-Gospel Canon', *Skeat*, pp. 73-78. Jordan D. May, 'The Four Pillars: The Fourfold Gospel Before the Time of Irenaeus', *Trinity Journal* 30 (2009), pp. 67-79, argues that Irenaeus did not 'establish' but rather 'inherited' the four-fold Gospel corpus. Hill notes that Irenaeus' argumentation 'relies on these Gospels already having an underlying plausibility to his readers' (*Who Chose the Gospels*, p. 38). In other words, 'Irenaeus writes as if the church had been nurtured by these four Gospels from the time of the apostles' (p. 41). For a survey of Irenaeus' relevance to canon formation in general, see von Campenhausen, *Formation of the Christian Bible*, pp. 176-201. On Justin's use of the New Testament writings (and the Gospels in particular), see Charles E. Hill, 'Justin and the New Testament Writings', *Studia Patristica* 30 (1997), pp. 42-48. See also the group of essays in *Justin Martyr and His Worlds* (ed. Sara Parvis and Paul Foster; Minneapolis, MN: Fortress Press, 2007) (esp. the section, 'Justin Martyr and His Bible'), pp. 53-114. Cf. Metzger, *Canon of the New Testament*, pp. 143-48; and Bruce, *Canon*, pp. 124-29. On the possible origins and Justin's use of the concept of 'memoirs' (ἀπομνημονεύματα), see Richard Heard, 'The ΑΠΟΜΝΗΜΟΝΕΥΜΑΤΑ in Papias, Justin, and Irenaeus', *NTS* 1 (1954), pp. 122-33; and more recently, Joseph Verheyden, 'Justin's Text of the Gospels: Another Look at the Citations in 1 Apol. 15.1-8', in *The Early Text of the New Testament* (ed. Charles E. Hill and Michael J. Kruger; Oxford: Oxford University Press, 2012), pp. 313-35.

112. Regarding this aspect of the Pauline corpus, see Childs, *Church's Guide for Reading Paul*, pp. 3-7. Childs asserts that 'the earliest manuscript evidence that we have of Paul's letters...is of a Pauline collection, that is, of an edited corpus' and 'not of independent letters' (pp. 3-4). Similarly, von Campenhausen argues that 'it is clear that [Paul's] Letters were collected at an early stage, and were soon well known everywhere' (*Formation of the Christian Bible*, p. 143). He adds in this context, 'more

Testament, the existence of a literary collection of Pauline correspondence is explicitly mentioned by Peter and anticipated by Paul himself. Peter alludes to a collection when he notes that there were false teachers in some churches twisting the words of 'our beloved brother Paul' found 'in all his letters' (2 Pet. 3.16, ἐν πάσαις ἐπιστολαῖς).[113] Peter seems to mention an individual letter ('Paul...wrote to you') in light of a larger collection of letters ('as also in all his letters'). Moreover, on multiple occasions, Paul actually exhorts the recipients of a given letter to circulate it among the churches in the area.[114] Thus, even in the composition of individual letters to particular congregations on specific occasions, Paul envisions a broad audience for his literary compositions. Implied in this scenario, and confirmed by the nature of publishing of the time period, is the awareness that Paul's letters to the various churches would be preserved, highly valued, and associated with one another.[115] The individuals responsible for consolidating this collection of Paul's letters likely followed the guidelines found in Paul's own compositions.[116]

---

precise than this we cannot be' (p. 143 n. 186). Cf. Trobisch, *Paul's Letter Collection*, p. 9: 'We do not find an edition of a single letter of Paul in a manuscript. When we read Paul's letter to the Romans, we read it as part of a collection.'

113. Though he argues that 2 Peter is pseudonymous, von Campenhausen concedes that the text of 2 Pet. 3.15-16 itself claims normative authority for Paul's letters: 'For "Peter", therefore, the Pauline letters are already reckoned among the "scriptures"' (*Formation of the Christian Bible*, p. 178 n. 155). Cf. Polycarp's similar statement about the 'twisting' of the words 'of the Lord' (Polycarp, *Phil.* 7.1-2, *AF*, p. 289).

114. E.g., 2 Cor. 10.9-10; 2 Thess. 3.17; and Col. 4.16. Compare also Paul's commentary on his own literary activity in 1 Cor. 7.17; 2 Cor. 3.1; 10.9-10; 2 Thess. 2.2; 3.17.

115. Cf. *1 Clement*'s mention of Paul's letter to the Corinthians: 'Take up the epistle of the blessed Paul the apostle. What did he first write to you in the beginning of the gospel?' (*1 Clem.* 47.1-2). Clement's reference to Paul's letter demonstrates that Paul's letters were kept (and probably copied) by the original recipient church to be reread and also that these preserved/collected letters were known to others elsewhere (i.e. Clement is writing from Rome and refers to a letter preserved by the church in Corinth). In this regard, Jenson argues that 'Paul did not have to reckon with a single exposure' but could 'count on his letters being studied and argued about and restudied and so on' (*Canon and Creed*, p. 35). Contra Patzia, *Making of the New Testament*, p. 110: 'At the time of writing, Paul had no idea that his letters would be collected or become authoritative and canonical for the universal church as they are today.'

116. Porter notes in his survey that one of the points of agreement among the theories of the origin of Paul's collection is the notion of 'personal involvement' by an individual (or group of individuals) in a specific location (see 'Pauline Canon', p. 122). Recognizing the impact of Trobisch's formulations, Porter concludes that 'there is reasonable evidence to see the origin of the Pauline corpus during the latter part of Paul's life or shortly after his death, almost assuredly instigated by a close follower if not by Paul himself, and close examination of the early manuscripts with Paul's letters

Accordingly, the earliest extant manuscript evidence for any of Paul's letters exhibits the marks of originating from a Pauline collection dated to around the late second century.[117] At least for the scribe who produced the papyrus codex P[46] and the client/community that procured it, Paul's individual letters were understood to be components of 'Paul's Letters'.[118] The nature of publication in the early church period informs discussions of the circulation and provenance of manuscripts. Accordingly, in order for a work the size of P[46] to be produced, there would have to have been a 'market' for it that would justify the labor and expense it would take to produce such a manuscript.[119] There would also need to be multiple parties involved in the

seems to endorse this hypothesis' (pp. 126-27). Cf. Gamble, *Books and Readers*, p. 98: 'These observations show that the early copying and circulation of Paul's letters was not mere happenstance, and that, at least in the cases of Galatians and Romans, it was already taking place in Paul's lifetime.' Gamble adds that 'the authority of Paul was perpetuated, the scope of his influence extended, and the substance of his teaching elaborated in new circumstances through these specifically literary means' (p. 98). For a contrasting perspective (denying Paul's role in the collection process), see Andreas Lindemann, 'Die Sammlung der Paulusbriefe im 1. Und 2. Jahrhundert', in *The Biblical Canons* (ed. J.M. Auwers and H.J. de Jonge; Leuven: Leuven University Press, 2003), pp. 321-52.

117. There are around 800 extant copies of Paul's letters, most from Byzantine manuscripts. See Trobisch, *Paul's Letter Collection*, pp. 1-27. Cf. Porter, 'Pauline Canon', pp. 96-97: 'What is known is that by the mid-second century, at or by the time of the formation of Marcion's canon, there was some form of consolidated group of Pauline letters.' Porter surveys the main theories regarding the formation of the Pauline Corpus and critically interacts with Trobisch's work on Paul's letters. Generally sympathetic with Zahn and Harnack, both Metzger (*Canon of the New Testament*, p. 259) and Bruce (*Canon of Scripture*, p. 130) agree that Paul's letters circulated as a collection very early (c. 2nd century CE). Patzia adds that 'with the possible exception of Clement of Rome (who may have had his own partial collection), all subsequent collectors, including Marcion, worked from an early *corpus Paulinum*' (*Making of the New Testament*, p. 140). For a contrasting perspective, see Harry Y. Gamble, 'The Redaction of the Pauline Letters and the Formation of the Pauline Corpus', *JBL* 94 (1975), pp. 403-18. Gamble argues that the notion of a prototypical Pauline collection (he also calls it a 'single first edition', p. 406, and an 'original edition', p. 414) 'cannot be convincingly maintained in the face of available evidence' (p. 405). Gamble, though, is arguing against a particular construal of an 'original edition', one in which the individual letters *never* had an original provenance (see p. 414). This conception, for Gamble, is 'untenable' and 'has not been particularly fruitful' (p. 415).

118. For access to P[46], see Kenyon, p. iii, *Text*, and Kenyon, iii, *Plates*.

119. Aland discusses the nature of the 'commissioning community' of the Greek papyrus manuscripts such as P[45], P[46], and P[47] in 'Significance of the Chester Beatty Papyri', pp. 117-21. She notes that as the New Testament literature became increasingly familiar (through publications like the papyrus manuscripts), there was a growing 'text consciousness' among the believing community, and as a result their 'quotations were no longer pure paraphrases or adaptions of the original text' but rather became

production of an extensive codex like P[46]. This manuscript therefore represents a significant piece of artifactual evidence in the process of collection and association involved in the formation of the Pauline corpus and the New Testament as a whole.[120] Hurtado affirms these basic points and writes, 'As indisputably shown in P[46], and very possibly also in some or all of the other proposed remnants of Pauline codices...at a very early point (certainly by sometime in the second century and perhaps even in the late first century) Pauline letters were physically treated as a collection by copying them in a single codex.'[121] Hurtado concludes further that 'in this development we have a material indication that the Christians behind it clearly regarded the Pauline Epistles very highly. Indeed, the copying of multiple Pauline epistles in one codex would have had the effect of marking off all of them as enjoying a high regard, the smaller and less weighty epistles as well as the larger ones.'[122]

It must also be noted that alongside the evidence of an early collection, there are nevertheless many fragments containing only (sometimes miniscule) portions of an individual Pauline letter.[123] For instance, the manuscript P[30] contains only portions of the Thessalonian correspondence, and P[92] contains only Ephesians and 2 Thessalonians.[124] However, taking the nature of the entire spectrum of manuscript evidence into account, one can plausibly presume that these manuscript fragments represent constituent elements of larger collections (since there is no clear evidence to the contrary). Moreover, there is no indisputable evidence of an individual letter that circulated independently for any significant length of time.[125]

'extensive literal citations from what was recognized as a New Testament' (p. 117). In sum, 'the papyri are a witness to the beginnings of a text consciousness in the community in the sense of the New Testament to be cited and subject to exegesis' (p. 120). She also notes the considerable liberty that writers in the patristic period took even when quoting large blocks of New Testament text.

120. Cf. Jenson, *Canon and Creed*, p. 13: 'If a Christian publisher of the later second century—and there surely may have been such enterprises—brought out a collection of Gospels, Pauline letters, and other writings, it will have been because these were the texts that Christian congregations, and individual Christians with the money to buy expensive hand-produced books, already wanted to have at hand.'

121. Hurtado, *Earliest Christian Artifacts*, p. 39.

122. Hurtado, *Earliest Christian Artifacts*, p. 39.

123. E.g., the following manuscripts are fragments of individual letters: P[10, 11, 14-16, 26, 27, 31-32, 34, 40, 49, 51, 65, 68, 87, 94].

124. For a survey of the content of these manuscripts, see Comfort, *Encountering the Manuscripts*, pp. 64, 74; and Comfort and Barrett, *Text of the Earliest New Testament Greek Manuscripts*, pp. 128-33.

125. On this way of assessing the fragments of Paul's letters represented in these manuscripts, see Porter, 'Pauline Canon', pp. 119-20; Hurtado, *Earliest Christian Artifacts*, pp. 38-39; and Philip W. Comfort, 'New Reconstructions and Identifications of

A prominent example of the way Paul's readers received and preserved his correspondence is found in the letter of Polycarp (bishop of Smyrna, c. 110 CE) to the Philippians.[126] In the course of his letter, Polycarp mentions that he writes at the invitation of the Philippians, not at his own initiative on the basis of his own authority.[127] The reason for this humility is, Polycarp confesses, because 'neither I nor anyone like me can keep pace with the wisdom of the blessed and glorious Paul'.[128] He then mentions Paul's literary activity and directs the Philippians in the way they should respond to it: 'When he was with you in the presence of the people of that time, he accurately and reliably taught the word concerning the truth. And when he was absent *he wrote you letters*' (ὑμῖν ἔγραψεν ἐπιστολάς).[129] Polycarp continues by telling his readers, '*If you study them carefully*, you will be able to build yourself up in the faith that has been given to you.'[130] Polycarp's comments are an example of the high authority vested in Paul's person ('the blessed and glorious Paul'), his written correspondence ('he accurately and reliably taught...and...wrote you letters'), and his continuing literary influence ('study them carefully'). There is also recognition here of at least some type of gathered collection of Pauline correspondence (the plural 'letters', and the comment 'if you study *them*').

5. *The Grouping of the Groupings.* In terms of the New Testament as a whole, there is some diversity in the arrangement of the four main corpora of the New Testament (Gospels, Praxapostolos/General epistles, Pauline corpus, Revelation), but within the different groupings, there is significant consistency of content. The ordering within these groupings may have initially been formed according to 'literary convention', but as the

New Testament Papyri', *NovT* 41 (1999), pp. 214-30. James R. Royse, 'The Early Text of Paul (and Hebrews)', in *The Early Text of the New Testament* (ed. Charles E. Hill and Michael J. Kruger; Oxford: Oxford University Press, 2012), pp. 200-201, considers the possibility that the smaller papyrus fragments (see n. 123 above) could have originally been part of a larger Pauline corpus. He also sounds a note of caution in this regard: 'We are free to speculate that those manuscripts are the tiny remnants of once extensive manuscripts of the entire corpus, but it is also perfectly possible that they originally contained only one book' (p. 200). Cf. Royse, *Scribal Habits*, pp. 199-205.

126. Holmes notes that the dating of Polycarp's epistle to the Philippians is tied to the dating and provenance of Ignatius' letters (*AF*, pp. 275-76). Ignatius' letters are (following Lightfoot's argumentation) dated around 110 CE. See J.B. Lightfoot, *The Apostolic Fathers*, II/2, pp. 435-72. Cf. Holmes, *AF*, p. 170.

127. Polycarp writes, 'I am writing you these comments about righteousness, brothers, not on my own initiative but because you invited me to do so' (Polycarp, *Phil.* 3.1).

128. Polycarp, *Phil.* 3.2 (*AF*, p. 283). Compare the Muratorian Fragment's characterization of Paul as 'the blessed apostle Paul himself' (lines 47-48).

129. Polycarp, *Phil.* 3.2 (*AF*, p. 285). Emphasis added.

130. Polycarp, *Phil.* 3.2 (*AF*, p. 285). Emphasis added.

community receives them, the arrangement of the books takes on a 'canonical function'.[131] Eventually, as was the case with the Hebrew Bible, the New Testament groupings were arranged with a level of consistency that allowed a rough order of reading to be established. To give two broad examples, the Gospels were naturally to be read first as they contain the 'beginning of the Gospel of Jesus Christ' (Mark 1.1), and the Book of Revelation was logically to be read at the 'end' as it is preoccupied with what will take place at the 'end of days'. An early indication of this type of reading order can be seen provisionally in the Muratorion Fragment.[132] Accordingly, when the individual groupings of the New Testament begin circulating together, they follow this broad conceptual arrangement.[133]

During the consolidation phase, the collected groupings and this reading arrangement of the New Testament solidifies and the canon closes for various communities. Alongside this development, the New Testament was associated and attached to the Hebrew Bible. Thus, the four major Greek uncial codex manuscripts of the fourth century (Sinaiticus ℵ 01, Alexandrinus A 02, Vaticanus B 03, and Ephraem Rescripti C 04) include a version of the Hebrew Bible along with the New Testament.[134] Moreover, the four major examples of stable groupings of biblical writings in the manuscript evidence (the book of Moses, the book of the Twelve, the fourfold Gospel, and the letters of Paul) serve as historical and artifactual support for the overall thrust of this study. That is, once one comes to grips with the bare fact of a canonical collection of interrelated writings, the logical (and perhaps intended!) response is to read them in light of one another.

6. *The Role of the Believing Community*. At the least, the presence of a received canon in the history of the church demonstrates that a community of individuals existed that consciously preserved and shaped the writings they viewed as authoritative Scripture. In other words, the churches not only received and treasured the biblical writings, they also handed them down to later generations in a way that would preserve their compositional

131. Childs, *Church's Guide for Reading Paul*, p. 7, makes this point regarding the place of the book of Romans in the Pauline corpus. Romans is not only the longest letter of Paul, but also the most expansive theologically, rendering it an excellent introduction to the rest of Paul's letters. The salient point here is that this introductory function of Romans is a feature of its canonical form. This phenomenon (from 'literary' to 'canonical' considerations) is the focus of Chapter 3.

132. See the discussion of the importance and difficulties associated with this document below.

133. See Trobisch, *First Edition of the New Testament*, pp. 24-29.

134. See Appendix 1. Also observe that in different communities, consolidation takes different forms. This accounts for the various orders and inclusion of individual books that occur in some communities but not in others.

shape and extend their literary legacy. In fact, the concept of canon implies that these authoritative writings were collected and shaped for the purpose of preserving them for future generations of readers. In an acute sense, 'We are not prophets or apostles', but the point of a canonical collection (a 'canon') is to compensate for this reality.[135] Though communities of believers can no longer be guided by the actual hands of the prophets and apostles, they can be guided by their handiwork.

A community guided by the message of the prophets and apostles gathered the prophetic and apostolic writings into collections and groupings. Members from this community, in turn, designed the shape of the canon for a larger audience.[136] Accordingly, the Christian canon shows signs of the editorial shaping of the prophetic/apostolic community as they gathered the writings into a coherent whole.[137] Transposed into this canonical context, the biblical writings now have as their intended readership 'all Christians'.[138] The par-

---

135. Childs uses the phrase, 'We are neither prophets nor apostles', in *Biblical Theology*, p. 381: 'We are neither prophets nor Apostles. The function of the church's canon is to recognize this distinction. The Christian church does not have the same unmediated access to God's revelation as did the Apostles, but rather God's revelation is mediated through their authoritative witness, namely through scripture.' See also Childs, *Biblical Theology in Crisis*, pp. 99-114. Seitz exposits and develops this idea at length in *Character of Christian Scripture*, pp. 93-114. Cf. Seitz, 'Canonical Approach and Theological Interpretation', p. 99: 'A canonical approach insists the inspired witness is building a bridge to us which is sure and which has our seasons in mind. We are not prophets or apostles, but the canon appreciates this reality with all its witnessing majesty, as we are brought fully into the range of the Holy Spirit's work by virtue of the canon's shape and character as witness.'

136. Cf. Sailhamer's compositional understanding of the canonization stage of the canon formation process in 'Biblical Theology and the Composition of the Hebrew Bible', p. 31: 'Individuals are a part of communities and speak for communities, but in the last analysis, the work of composition and canonization was the work of individuals.' Sailhamer views canonization as a series of 'creative moments of formation that arise within multiple canonical contexts' (pp. 30-31). An almost direct contrast to this position on authorship and canonization can be found in van der Toorn, *Scribal Culture* (e.g. pp. 27-50).

137. This shaping occurs in both Testaments and in the Christian canon as a whole. A few often-cited examples include the end of Deuteronomy (34.10-12), the end of Malachi (4.4), the end of the Gospel of John (21.24-25), and the bookends of the book of Revelation (1.1-3, 22.18-19).

138. Cf. Richard Bauckham, 'For Whom Were Gospels Written?', in *The Gospels for All Christians* (Grand Rapids, MI: Eerdmans, 1998), pp. 9-48. Bauckham demonstrates that the Gospel writers expected their works to 'circulate widely among the churches' and envisioned their audience as 'any church (or any church in which Greek was understood) to which [their] work might find its way' (p. 11). The fact that these Gospels were put into a collection and became part of a canon would only aid in the execution of this intended authorial purpose. The question of the canon's 'intended audience' is discussed further in Chapter 5.

ticularity of the laws, prophecies, narratives, and epistles are not emptied of their occasional nature, but rather are placed within a canonical context that enables them to be understood and appropriated by a readership wider than the original historical audience of the original document.[139] The melodies of occasional writings now resonate in a patchwork of an orchestrated harmony.[140] Inclusion into an authoritative collection influences the way a biblical document is received by its readers and shapes the way it is related to other writings.[141] In this way, the 'canon' is the church's guide for reading all of the Scripture it contains.[142]

7. *Summary.* To sum up this section, there is ample internal indication that the biblical authors had at least an initial concept of a stable body of authoritative writings in mind as they composed and shaped their own writings. This compositional strategy in turn influenced the way these individual books were gathered into groupings. The achievement of association evidenced in the biblical corpora demonstrates an awareness of canonical considerations by the authors producing and the community preserving and shaping these documents.[143] Moreover, if one adopts a broad understanding

139. For instance, Childs argues that within the Pauline corpus there is an 'intentional inclusion of a wider audience beyond the letter's original recipient' (*Church's Guide for Reading Paul*, p. 6). He writes elsewhere that the canonical shape of the New Testament books involves 'the effect which the collection had in unleashing a new potential within the literature for each new generation of hearers' (*New Testament as Canon*, pp. 32-33).

140. Of course, depending on one's understanding of the content and cadence of the biblical material, the 'orchestrated harmony' will either be a symphony of cohesive tones or a cacophony of contrived counter-melodies. For instance, after his account of the 'creation' of the New Testament in *Origin of the New Testament*, Harnack delineates the 'consequences of the creation of the New Testament' (p. 115). These consequences were largely positive and had a preserving effect that the early church benefited from greatly. In these ways, the church was able to maintain and promulgate the Gospel and its implications (pp. 116-63). However, for Harnack, most of these positive blessings also have more sinister corollaries. He posits, among other things, that the exclusive authority of the New Testament canon led to an 'increase in the patchiness and incoherence of doctrine' (pp. 159-60). For him, 'the narcotic of Scriptural authority paralysed the intellect in its restless search for truth' (p. 160). The distorting effect of a normative set of documents led Harnack to describe 'men's minds' of the post-apostolic period as 'ever haunted by the spectre of the Canon' (p. 152).

141. This effect is part of the nature of collections in general and also a characteristic of 'published letters' in antiquity. See Gamble, *Books and Readers in the Early Church*, pp. 82-143.

142. The phrase 'church's guide for reading' comes from Childs, *Church's Guide for Reading Paul*.

143. After a discussion of manuscripts and publishing technology in the early church, Kruger argues that these factors 'confirm, once again, that early Christians had a canon

of canon, then this internal evidence will translate into a compelling case
for the presence and importance of a robust canon-consciousness during the
entire process of canon formation.

*External Evidence Implies a Canon-Consciousness among the Believing
Community*
If one accepts the definitions of the terms discussed above and analysis of
the internal evidence, then the external evidence confirms that the biblical writers and a significant portion of the believing community possessed
a form of canon-consciousness. The phrase 'external evidence' refers to
extra-biblical material that mentions or expounds upon biblical material.
Any history of the biblical canon must closely and carefully take this external historical evidence into account.

In relation to both the Old and New Testament, there are a number of external documents that mention either books or groupings of books that eventually become parts of the final form of the canon. The fact that these external
documents sometimes do not discuss the biblical groupings in detail does not
mean that those groupings were not actually viewed as a whole. Rather, often
the stable, authoritative status of these writings is assumed or presupposed.[144]
Thus, when an extra-biblical writer mentions a biblical book or grouping,
there is at least a legitimate possibility that the document mentioned was
widely recognized as canonical, in the sense described above.

The fragmentary and scattered nature of the external evidence makes
reconstruction a delicate process and should temper any claims of absolute
confidence or certainty. In order to outline a coherent narrative, the histo-
rian/interpreter must piece together a plausible scenario based on the evidence at hand. In spite of the modest nature of any possible conclusion, the
evidence that is available can serve as guideposts for the historian's sojourn
through the historical data. These guiding lights should not be deemed
unnecessarily dim solely because they are few and far between. The light
they emit is illuminating nonetheless. This digression regarding the value
of isolated external evidence is important because sometimes this evidence
is set aside in reconstruction simply because it is isolated.

---

consciousness from a very early point as they read, copied, collected, and distributed
those documents they viewed as central to their religious life and worship. They busied
themselves not just with oral proclamation but also, and perhaps primarily, with the
written text. At their core, they were people of the book' (*Canon Revisited*, p. 259).

144. This summary assertion will be demonstrated in the discussion of each individual historical example in this section. This type of 'assumption' is also obviously
debatable. A maximalist might take a reference to a biblical grouping as a possible
indication that the content of that grouping was in view for that writer. Conversely, a
minimalist might point out that there is no way of knowing, one way or the other (and
thus it is better not to make a positive reconstruction without direct evidence).

1. *External Evidence for the Shape of the Hebrew Bible.* Regarding the overall shape of the Hebrew Bible, an important work is the book of Ben Sira, a Jewish writer in the Second Temple period.[145] Written in a wisdom literature genre similar to the book of Proverbs, Ben Sira's work is rife with quotations and allusions to texts from the Law, Prophets, and Writings.[146] As Dempster notes, 'the work of Ben Sira is steeped in books which are later found to be part of the divisions of the Law, the Prophets, and the Writings and not many others'.[147] One example of this practice is the way Ben Sira populates his 'eulogy of the fathers' with biblical figures from the narratives of canonical books (Sir. 44.1–49.16). He exhorts his readers, 'Let us now sing the praises of famous men, our ancestors in their generations' (Sir. 44.1).[148] The figures noted span from Enoch to Nehemiah and the presentation follows the biblical order (from Genesis to Nehemiah). In this historical survey, it appears that Ben Sira gives a 'canon-conscious reading' of these 'fathers'.[149] Not only the names listed, but also the overall portraits

145. The author identifies himself at the end of his work: 'Instruction in understanding and knowledge I have written in this book, Jesus son of Eleazar son of Sirach of Jerusalem, whose mind poured forth wisdom' (Sir. 50.27). Because of his invitation to 'draw near to me, you who are uneducated, and lodge in the house of instruction' (Sir. 51.23), most scholars believe Ben Sira was a teacher in a school for 'prospective scribes and sages, perhaps in association with the Jerusalem temple complex' (Daniel J. Harrington, 'Introduction to Sirach'). Cf. Paul McKechnie, 'The Career of Joshua Ben Sira', *JTS* 51 (2000), pp. 3-26, who challenges the traditional social reconstruction and argues that Ben Sira was 'a Jerusalem-born resident of Alexandria and probably a Ptolemaic courtier' (p. 26).

146. There are many thorough surveys of Ben Sira's content, as its relevance to the canon formation question has long been recognized. For a brief survey of the scholarship demonstrating Ben Sira's use of texts from the Law, Prophets, and Writings, see Douglas E. Fox, 'Ben Sira on OT Canon Again: The Date of Daniel', *WTJ* 49 (1987), pp. 335-41. In a traditional maximalist account of Ben Sira's use of Scripture, Solomon Schechter and C. Taylor argue that Ben Sira, 'though not entirely devoid of original ideas, was, as is well known, a conscious imitator both as to form and as to matter, his chief model being the book of Proverbs' (*The Wisdom of Ben Sira* [London: C.J. Clay & Sons, 1899], p. 12). They conclude that 'the impression produced by the perusal of Ben Sira's original on the student who is at all familiar with the Hebrew Scriptures is that of reading the work of a post-canonical author, who already knew his Bible and was constantly quoting it' (p. 26). For them, 'There can be no reasonable doubt that [the biblical allusions] were either suggested to Ben Sira by, or directly copied from the Scriptures' (p. 25). Most other scholars are more cautious in their calculations.

147. Dempster, 'Canons', p. 59.

148. Dempster observes that 'the heroes are not really introduced formally, as Ben Sira assumes they are virtually household names to his audience' ('Canons', p. 59).

149. Regarding this phrase and interpretation of Ben Sira's list of historical figures, see Alon Goshen-Gottstein, 'Ben Sira's Praise of the Fathers: A Canon-Conscious Reading', in *Ben Sira's God: Proceedings of the International Ben Sira Conference* (Berlin: W. de Gruyter, 2002), pp. 235-67.

and characterization of these figures resonates with the biblical texts from which they are drawn.[150] In other words, Ben Sira seems to draw not only on the *events* of Israel's history, but also on the *interpretation* of those events found in the narratives of Israel's Scripture.[151]

In a few places, the writer of Ben Sira also seems to be aware of the larger divisions and smaller groupings of the Hebrew Bible. For instance, he distinguishes between the Law and the Prophets (or at least between Moses and Joshua), labeling Joshua as 'the successor of Moses in the prophetic office' (Sir. 46.1).[152] Following his discussion of Joshua and Caleb, he views 'the judges also, with their respective names' as a unit before moving on to the prophet Samuel (Sir. 46.11-12). At one point, he explicitly mentions the 'Twelve Prophets' (Sir. 49.10), suggesting that he views the Minor Prophets in light of a single literary entity (The Book of the Twelve) rather than merely individual historical figures.[153]

In the second century BCE, Ben Sira's grandson translated the work into Greek and added a brief preface.[154] He begins his introduction by writing,

---

150. To give one example, the discussion of Abraham (44.19-21), Isaac (44.22), and Jacob (44.23) focuses on the enduring covenant God makes with them based on faith through which 'the nations would be blessed through his offspring' (44.32). The detailed account of 'the zeal of Phineas' is another striking example (44.23-24; cf. Num. 25.1-13 and Ps. 106.30).

151. There is at least one clear reference to a written text rather than a bare historical tradition in the description of Elijah. Ben Sira writes of Elijah that 'at the appointed time, *it is written*, you are destined to calm the wrath of God before it breaks out in fury, to turn the hearts of parents to their children, and to restore the tribes of Jacob' (Sir. 48.10, emphasis added). This written text is Mal. 4.5-6, which concludes the 'Twelve Prophets' (which are mentioned as a unit in Sir. 49.10).

152. On the status of the Law, Childs argues that Ben Sira's 'knowledge and use of all the legal portions can only presuppose the canonical status of the entire Pentateuch' (*Introduction to the Old Testament as Scripture*, p. 64).

153. After mentioning Jeremiah and Ezekiel, the text reads, 'May the bones of the Twelve Prophets send forth new life from where they lie, for they comforted the people of Jacob and delivered them with confident hope' (49.10). As noted above, Ben Sira directly draws on the conclusion to this corpus (Mal. 4.5-6).

154. In his preface, the grandson overviews the content of his grandfather's work and explains the provenance of the current translation. He came to Egypt in 'the thirty-eighth year of the reign of Euergetes [i.e. Ptolemy VII, Euergetes II, in 132 BCE] and stayed for some time'. During his stay, he received education and decided to translate the book. After much effort ('I applied my skill day and night'), the grandson completed and published the book 'for those living abroad who wished to gain learning and are disposed to live according to the law'. For a discussion of the grandson's (sometimes neglected) translational technique, see Benjamin G. Wright, 'Why a Prologue? Ben Sira's Grandson and his Greek Translation', in *Emanuel* (Leiden: Brill, 2003), pp. 633-644. Wright notes that the influence of the LXX ('Law and the Prophets, and the other books') might help explain the nature of the Greek translation (pp. 643-44).

'Many important truths have been handed down to us through the law, prophets, and the later authors.'[155] He adds later that his grandfather wrote his *Book of Wisdom* after a diligent study of 'the Law and the Prophets, and the other books of our ancestors' (ἐις τε τὴν τοῦ νόμου καὶ τῶν προφητῶν καὶ τῶν ἄλλων πατρίν βιβλίω ανάγνωσιν).[156] He mentions the three elements again when discussing the difficulties of translation.[157] In this brief foreword, Ben Sira's grandson refers to the Hebrew Bible three times as a body of literature made up of these three parts.[158] Further, each of these parts can be viewed as literary units.[159] Thus, two hundred years before the time of the New Testament, Ben Sira's grandson knows the Hebrew Bible as an entity that has at least three major divisions and a relatively stable overall shape.[160]

The evidence from Ben Sira's writing resonates with the overall shape of the 'Scriptures' likely utilized by Jesus and the apostles. Luke 11 and

155. This translation comes from the NRSV. The Greek text reads, πολλῶν καὶ μεγάλων ημιν διὰ τοῦ νόμου καὶ τῶν προφητῶν καὶ τῶν ἄλλων τῶν κατ' αυτοὺς ηχολουθηχότων δεδομένων.

156. The grandson adds that Ben Sira 'had acquired considerable proficiency in them' and was 'led to write something pertaining to instruction and wisdom'. He wrote so that 'by becoming familiar also with his book those who love learning might make even greater progress in living according to the law'. The grandson's interpretation of his grandfather's motive implies that Ben Sira sees his work as distinct from the content of the 'Law and the Prophets, and the other books'.

157. The grandson writes, 'For what was originally expressed in Hebrew does not have exactly the same sense when translated into another language. Not only this book, but even the Law itself, the Prophecies, and the rest of the books [αυτὸς ο νόμος καὶ αι προφητεῖαι καὶ τὰ λοιπὰ Τῶν βιβλίων] differ not a little when read in the original.'

158. Cf. Dempster, 'Torah, Torah, Torah', pp. 107-14. E. Earle Ellis, *The Old Testament in Early Christianity: Canon and Interpretation in the Light of Modern Research* (Grand Rapids, MI: Baker, 1992), pp. 39-40, makes the important observation that the grandson's statement 'mentions each of the three divisions with the same degree of preciseness and, to be meaningful to the reader, it must refer to definite, identifiable books'. He also argues that it 'could be interpreted otherwise only if one were already convinced that the tripartite canon could not have existed as a subsistent entity at this time' (p. 40). After surveying the relevant scholarship, Beckwith, *Old Testament Canon*, p. 111, agrees against the consensus that the prologue points to a tripartite Hebrew canon.

159. Harry M. Orlinsky, 'Some Terms in the Prologue to Ben Sira and the Hebrew Canon', *JBL* 110 (1991), pp. 483-90, surveys the many translations that render the third element as personal (writers/authors) rather than literary entities. Orlinsky argues that the better rendering is 'other books' based on philological and contextual considerations.

160. Significant also is that Ben Sira's grandson knows this tripartite shape in Greek as well as Hebrew. In this regard, Sailhamer comments, 'An important implication of the prologue to Sirach is that even the OT in Greek was read in a threefold form' (*Meaning of the Pentateuch*, p. 170).

24 provide important indications of the shape of the Hebrew Bible during the life of Jesus and the apostolic community.[161] In this case, the New Testament writings (typically understood as 'internal evidence') are 'external evidence' for the shape and content of the canon of the Hebrew Bible.[162] In Lk. 11.34-54, Jesus rebukes a group of Pharisees and lawyers.[163] Jesus appeals to Israel's history to condemn their 'fathers' who killed and persecuted the 'prophets and apostles' that the 'wisdom of God' had sent (Lk. 11.49). Jesus asserts that the 'blood of all the prophets, shed since the foundation of the world' is to be required of 'this generation' (11.50). Jesus describes this generation by the phrase, 'from the blood of Abel to the blood of Zechariah' (ἀπὸ αἵματος Αβελ ἕως αἵματος Ζαχαρίου, 11.51).

The temporal spectrum that Jesus presents is not only *historical* but also *textual*. Zechariah is not the last historical prophet to be martyred in the recorded history of Israel, but he is the last prophet killed in the book of Chronicles (2 Chron. 24.20-24).[164] By juxtaposing Abel, the first murdered individual recorded in the Pentateuch (Gen. 4.8-10), with Zechariah, the last murdered individual recorded in the book of Chronicles, Jesus seems to be referencing the shape of the narrative that is generated by the framework of the Tanak.[165] In this sense, Jesus brings the entirety of the Hebrew

<hr>

161. Bruce, *Canon of Scripture*, pp. 30-32, acknowledges the relevance of these texts to the shape of the Hebrew Bible in the first century. McDonald concedes that these texts 'give evidence for an emerging tripartite biblical canon in the first century BCE and first century CE', but also seeks to downplay their significance for the shape of the Hebrew Bible (*Biblical Canon*, pp. 96-100).

162. Cf. Orlinsky, 'Some Terms in the Prologue to Ben Sira', pp. 488-89.

163. See also the parallel passage in Mt. 23.34-36. In Matthew, Jesus' description of both Abel and Zechariah is expanded. Matthew records, 'from the blood of righteous Abel to the blood of Zechariah, the son of Berechiah, whom you murdered between the temple and the altar' (Mt. 23.35).

164. Chronologically, Zechariah is not the last prophet to be murdered in Israel's history. For instance, during the reign of 'King Jehoiakim', the prophet Uriah is hunted down and killed (Jer. 26.20-23). I. Howard Marshall, *The Gospel of Luke: A Commentary on the Greek Text* (Grand Rapids, MI: Eerdmans, 1978), p. 506, notes that 'if the Books of Chronicles stood last in the OT canon of the time, then the reference is to the last murder of a prophet in the Scriptures. There is no doubt that Luke has rightly understood his source in this sense.' Marshall also grapples with the difficulties presented by Matthew's identification of Zechariah as 'the son of Berechiah' (Mt. 23.35).

165. Joseph A. Fitzmyer comments in *The Gospel According to Luke (X–XXIV)* (Garden City, NY: Doubleday, 1985), p. 946: 'Jesus' words take on a critical edge: Unless this generation breaks with the past, it will answer for all the injustice done to God's chosen ones from Abel to Zechariah—from the first to the last person murdered in the first and last books of the Hebrew canon of the OT.' Fitzmyer also cautions against uncritically relating this text to the history of formation of the canon (p. 951). Cf. Beckwith, *Old Testament Canon*, p. 215: 'All the martyrdoms from Abel to Zechariah are therefore equivalent to all the martyrdoms from one end of the Jewish

Bible to bear on the individuals he is condemning in Luke 11.[166] Ben Sira had given a canon-conscious reading of Israel's past in order to 'praise' the fathers, and here Jesus gives a canon-conscious articulation of the darker side of Israel's history.

The discourse between Jesus and two of his disciples on the road to Emmaus that Luke records in Luke 24 is also significant for the status of the Hebrew Bible during the New Testament period. After chiding the disciples as 'foolish' and 'slow of heart to believe in all that the prophets have spoken', Jesus asks, 'Was it not necessary for the Christ to suffer these things and to enter into his glory?' (Lk. 24.25-26). Luke then recounts that 'beginning with Moses and with all the prophets', Jesus 'explained to them the things concerning himself in all the Scriptures' (Lk. 24.27). Later in the chapter, Jesus appears to the rest of the disciples and 'opens their minds to understand the Scriptures' (Lk. 24.45). These 'Scriptures' are identified by Jesus when he tells them 'that all things which are written about Me in the Law of Moses and the Prophets and the Psalms must be fulfilled' (Lk. 24.44). This discourse that Luke presents implies an awareness of the Scriptures as an entity that can be described collectively ('all the Scriptures'), in bipartite (Moses and the Prophets), or in tripartite fashion (Law of Moses,

---

Bible to the other.' Beckwith conludes from this observation that Matthew and Luke are 'thus confirming that the traditional order of books, which began with Genesis and ended with Chronicles, goes back in all essentials to the first century. Nor [are they] the inventor of this order. [Their] allusive way of indicating the whole canon would be intelligible only if the order were already widely received' (p. 220). On the 'blood of Abel', see also Heb. 11.1; 12.24, and *1 En.* 22.

166. Peels observes that 'virtually all exegetes believe that Mt. 23.35 and Lk 11.51 mirror the structure and scope of the Old Testament canon of that time' ('From Abel to Zechariah', p. 586). He lists commentators from both perspectives (p. 586 n. 8) and acknowledges that 'according to the prevailing exegesis, the phrase "from Abel to Zechariah" implies that in the New Testament era the canon extended from Genesis through Chronicles and had the same structure and boundaries we encounter later in the enumeration given in BB 14b-15a' (p. 587). Peels offers the opposite conclusion in his study. He critically interacts with Beckwith's defense of a stable tripartite Hebrew Bible in the time of Jesus (e.g. *Old Testament Canon*, pp. 211-22) and concludes that 'a further analysis of Jesus' words in the texts cited shows...that the import of the phrase "from Abel to Zechariah" is not temporal-chronological but rather descriptive and qualificatory in character' (p. 601). Accordingly, for Peels, 'these New Testament texts [cannot] be used as proof for an early closing of the canon' (p. 601). Though Peels' cautions are important, it seems that if an interpreter is simply looking for early indications of the overall shape of the Hebrew Bible, then these texts (Matthew 23/ Luke 11) are still relevant even if they lack the luster of being the 'crown witnesses' (p. 601) of an argument for a 'fixed and closed' Old Testament canon at the time of Jesus. Further, Beckwith does highlight this 'one important piece of implicit evidence in the gospels', but he also acknowledges that 'it would not be possible to interpret this piece of evidence without the help of later sources' (*Old Testament Canon*, p. 181).

Prophets, and Psalms). In each case, the reference is to a distinct body of writings. Though it is not absolutely certain that the tripartite expression in Lk. 24.44 refers to the Law, Prophets, and Writings sections of the Tanak viewed as a whole, the complementary evidence from Ben Sira increases the probability that it does. The overall shape of the Bible that Jesus was familiar with thus seems to include these three broad groupings.[167]

This historical external evidence points to an early awareness of the concept of canon (Law, Prophets, and Writings) in the Jewish community and also provides extra-biblical verification of the biblical writers' understanding of the shape of the Hebrew Bible. Two other important instances where the Hebrew Bible is mentioned in a comparable way include the documents found at Qumran and the comments made by the early church historian Josephus, who asserts that the Jewish community had a stable (and ancient) twenty-two book collection of Scripture.[168]

In relation to the chronology of canon formation, the presence of a stable Hebrew Bible would have had a far-reaching theological *and* material influence on the development of a New Testament canon.[169] Because there was an authoritative Hebrew Bible, the early church would not have been unaware of the concept of a canon.[170] The historical evidence surveyed above suggests

---

167. Cf. Sailhamer, *Meaning of the Pentateuch*, p. 170: 'Along with other possible forms, the Tanak existed in its threefold form for a considerable period of time and for a significantly large portion of Judaism. According to Lk. 24.44, the Tanak was the "final shape" of the Bible of Jesus.' Fitzmyer provides a contrasting perspective: 'Does the tripartite division of the Hebrew Scriptures found in this verse reflect an awareness of a "canon" of Scripture? This has often been suggested, but the psalms scarcely stand for all the *Ketubim*' (*Gospel According to Luke*, p. 1583).

168. See Dempster, 'Torah, Torah, Torah', pp. 114-19, for an exposition and analysis of both of these important sources. McDonald provides a thorough examination of the evidence for the origins of the Hebrew Bible from a contrasting perspective in *Biblical Canon*, pp. 73-169. Cf. Stone's interaction with McDonald's analysis in 'Biblical Canon According to Lee McDonald', pp. 60-61. For Stone, both Josephus and *4 Ezra* 'testify to a fixed canon made up of the same books at the end of the first century CE. From this one should not conclude that there was a fixed canon only at the end of the first century; rather, both witnesses, when explicitly addressing canonical concerns reveal that the canon has been fixed for some time within mainstream Judaism' (p. 61).

169. Cf. Seitz, *Goodly Fellowship*, p. 103: 'In its formal and material givenness, the Law and the Prophets pattern has influenced the formal and material development of the NT as canon.' Brandt outlines possible 'structural analogies' (*strukturanalogie*) between the Old Testament and New Testament (*Endgestalten des Kanons*, pp. 358-82). He engages the 'weighty problem' (*gewichtiges problem*) of 'einer Abhängigkeit zwischen dem Arrangement des AT und dem des NT' (pp. 358-59). He also clarifies that, for him, the idea of a parallel structure between the Testaments 'kann nur teilweise geschichtlich rückgebunden werden' (p. 360). In his discussion, Brandt interacts (inter alia) with Trobisch, Beckwith, Erich Zenger, and David Noel Freedman.

170. Following Sundberg, Allert denies the existence of a stable tripartite Hebrew

that the early church likely knew the Hebrew Bible 'in its entirety' and 'as an entirety'.[171] The process of New Testament canon formation, then, involved understanding new apostolic writings in relation to an already accepted authoritative set of Scriptures.[172] This expectation of a coming canonical collection was also part of a pattern of revelation and inscripturation that was already established within the Hebrew Bible.[173] That authoritative apostolic

Bible and draws the exact opposite conclusion: 'If the church did not inherit the idea of a delimited list of authoritative writings from Judaism, there is no clear reason to think that this would be *on the minds* of Christians for their own (uniquely Christian) writings' (*High View of Scripture*, p. 48; emphasis added).

171. Sailhamer makes this comment about the Bible of Jesus (*Meaning of the Pentateuch*, p. 210). He argues later that 'the Tanak was, for the most part, the only Bible that Jesus and the early church acknowledged as Scripture (cf. 2 Tim. 3.15). The early first-century church…did not yet have the completed NT, but they did have the OT, and it was their NT' (p. 606).

172. Von Campenhausen highlights this reality in *Formation of the Christian Bible*, pp. 65-66. Cf. Childs, *Introduction to the Old Testament as Christian Scripture*, pp. 41-42: 'In the early church the question was not whether the Jewish scriptures were still canonical, but whether the claims of Jesus Christ could be sustained on the basis of scripture.' Childs summarizes, 'The early Christian church inherited the Jewish scriptures along with its understanding of canon. It was simply assumed that these writings functioned authoritatively in the life of the church, even though the extent of the canon and the nature of its authority continued to be debated' (p. 41).

173. Recently, Hill has used this line of thinking to support the idea that a written New Testament canon was a fitting and natural extension of the period of fresh revelation brought about by Christ and his gospel message (see 'New Testament Canon', pp. 105-106). He develops this notion further in 'God's Speech in These Last Days: The New Testament Canon as an Eschatological Phenomenon', in *Resurrection and Eschatology* (ed. Lane G. Tipton and Jeffrey C. Waddington; Phillipsburg, NJ: P&R, 2008), pp. 203-54. Cf. also Kruger's complementary discussion of the 'anticipation of a new redemptive message' in *Canon Revisited*, pp. 160-74. Kruger reasons, 'If early Christians came to believe that the actions of Jesus were the fulfillment of this long-awaited redemption of God, and if they were immersed in the Old Testament writings and the redemption-revelation pattern that it contained, then it is only natural that they would expect a new revelation deposit to accompany that redemption' (p. 171). Harnack argues that one of the motivations for the New Testament canon involves the need for a foundational document for the New Covenant period of revelation. He argues that 'the conception of the "New Covenant" necessarily suggested the need of something of *the nature of a document;* for what is a covenant without its document?' (*Origin of the New Testament*, p. 13). In Pauline terms, Harnack reasons, 'if the written Law is abolished then the written Grace and Truth must appear in its place' (p. 13). Drawing on extrabiblical parallels from the ancient Near East, Meade argues that 'apocalypticism' provides the 'ideological basis and impetus for the emergence of new (later to be called New Testament) Scripture' ('Ancient Near Eastern Apocalypticism', p. 307). The apocalyptic impulse is crucial to the New Testament, according to Meade, because 'it provides the ideological basis for the *extension* of Scripture' (p. 308).

writings would eventually form into an authoritative collection of writings would not have been a totally foreign concept to authors and a community already in possession of a similar body of literature.

Of course, this awareness does not necessarily mean that the authors of the New Testament literature understood themselves to be 'replacing' or 'improving upon' a now defunct set of Scriptures.[174] On the contrary, they unanimously affirm the authority of the Old Testament and the importance of its discrete witness (e.g. 2 Tim. 3.16). However, they did understand that the new revelatory events that had occurred with the coming of Jesus (the Christ) were to be recorded and interpreted for the sake of future generations of believers (e.g. Lk. 1.1-4; Jn 20.30-31; Acts 1.1-3; and 1 Cor. 15.3-4).[175] Again, this pattern of revelation, inscripturation, and instruction is present already throughout the Old Testament (e.g. Deuteronomy 6; Psalm 78; and Psalm 102).

2. *External Evidence for the Shape of the New Testament.* Concerning the New Testament, the Muratorian Fragment represents a similar type of evidence that Ben Sira does for the Hebrew Bible. Because its contents describe the shape of the New Testament and appear to be from an early date in the history of the church, the Muratorian Fragment 'has often served as the pivot-point in the history of the canon'.[176] Around 1740, Lodovico Muratori discovered a codex from the seventh century. One part of this codex is a fragment of a document written in Latin that appears to be a translation of a Greek original that comments on the content of the New Testament.[177] This partial document was named after its discoverer and is commonly referred to

---

174. Cf. von Campenhausen, *Formation of the Christian Bible*, p. 146: 'It is not by chance that the whole idea of a new canon to complement the ancient "scripture" is missing from the sources; and we have no right to supply it.' Smith summarizes a perspective typical of the biblical studies guild: 'The presumption of a historical distance, and consequent difference of purpose, between the composition of the NT writings and their incorporation into the canon of Scripture is representative of our discipline' ('When Did the Gospels Become Scripture?', p. 3). Regarding the Gospels, Smith's own measured conclusion is that 'the intention to write scripture should not be excluded from a consideration of the purpose as well as the result of the composition of the Gospels. Perhaps in purpose as well as effect the Gospels tell us something about what scripture is' (p. 19).

175. Cf. Peter Balla's discussion in 'Evidence for an Early Christian Canon (Second and Third Century)', in *Canon Debate*, pp. 372-85.

176. Gamble, 'New Testament Canon', p. 269.

177. The translational Latin of the fragment is poorly composed. Metzger observes that the fragment is 'written in barbarous Latin and with erratic orthography'. He also surmises that the codex that contains the fragment was 'a commonplace book of some monk, who copied a miscellaneous assortment of texts from various sources' (*Canon of the New Testament*, p. 191).

as the Muratorian Fragment. Because the second century CE historical context of the fragment rests on internal indications, there is significant debate regarding its dating and provenance.[178] Regardless of the dating of the fragment (i.e. second or fourth century CE), its relevance to the canon formation discussion should not be dismissed.

The primary reason the content of the Muratorian Fragment is significant is that it adumbrates the shape of the New Testament canon. The outline of books given there begins with a description of a Gospel corpus. The beginning of the document is lost, but when Luke is mentioned, it is described as the 'third book of the Gospel' (lines 2-3). That Luke was the author, a 'well-known physician', and a companion of Paul on his missionary journeys is assumed to be 'according to [the general] belief' (lines 4-6). The fragment continues by stating that 'the fourth of the Gospels is that of John, [one] of the disciples' (line 9). After the factors influencing John's composition of his Gospel, the author notes that 'though various elements may be taught in the individual books of the Gospels, nevertheless this makes no difference to the faith of believers, since by the one sovereign Spirit all things have been declared in all' (lines 17-20). The fragment is thus clearly aware of a four-fold Gospel collection. The author also seems to have reflected on the implications of having four 'individual books' making up one Gospel collection.

After the narrative framework of the Gospels (and John's sequence in particular), the fragment notes, 'Moreover, the acts of all the apostles were

---

178. Regarding this discussion, Gamble notes that 'the evidence is largely circumstantial and the arguments are delicately balanced' ('New Testament Canon', p. 270). In 1968, von Campenhausen comments (reflecting on the situation as early as 1926) that 'the literature on the Muratorianum long ago became quite unmanageable, and there is little hope that the forest of hypotheses will ever be cleared' (*Formation of the Christian Bible*, p. 243). The previous second century consensus was challenged by Sundberg in 'Revised History', pp. 458-59; and 'Canon Muratori: A Fourth Century List', *HTR* 66 (1973), pp. 1-41; and more recently by G.M. Hahneman in *The Muratorian Fragment and the Development of the Canon* (Oxford: Clarendon Press, 1992); and 'Muratorian Fragment and the Origins of the New Testament Canon', in *Canon Debate*, pp. 405-15. Both date the origin of the fragment well into the fourth century. See Metzger, *Canon of the New Testament*, pp. 305-307, for the text of the fragment and an argument for a second century dating. Two important responses to the fourth century dating of the fragment are Everett Ferguson, 'Canon Muratori: Date and Provenance', *SP* 17 (1982), pp. 677-83; and Charles E. Hill, 'The Debate over the Muratorian Fragment and the Development of the Canon', *WJT* 57 (1995), pp. 437-52. Likewise, Joseph Verheyden, 'The Canon Muratori: A Matter of Dispute', in *The Biblical Canons* (Leuven: Leuven University Press, 2003), pp. 487-556, interacts directly with Sundberg and Hahneman and avers that none of their arguments for a fourth century date are convincing.

written in one book' (lines 34-35).[179] Following the mention of Acts, the fragment continues by mentioning Paul's letters: 'As for the Epistles of Paul, they themselves make clear to those desiring to understand, which ones [they are], from what place, or for what reason they were sent' (lines 40-41). The seven letters to the churches are listed, described, and compared to the seven letters of the Apocalypse.[180] The letters to Philemon, Titus, and Timothy are then mentioned as letters that are 'held sacred in the esteem of the Church catholic for the regulation of ecclesiastical discipline' (lines 62-63).

After describing Paul's letters, the fragment notes and rejects the letter to the Laodiceans, and the letter to the Alexandrians, which are both said to be 'forged in Paul's name to [further] the heresy of Marcion' along with 'several others which cannot be received into the catholic church' (lines 65-67).[181] Next the Epistle of Jude and two letters 'bearing the name of' John are said to be 'counted (or used) in the catholic [Church]' (line 69). The 'book of Wisdom' that was 'written by the friends of Solomon in his honour' rounds out the books listed as part of the New Testament canon (line 70).[182] The fragment mentions both the Apocalypses of John and Peter, but mentions that the Apocalypse of Peter is not allowed to be read in the church by some.[183] Though the fragment mentions the book of Revelation here among other disputed literature, at this point the author has already assumed the legitimacy and apostolic authorship of John's Apocalypse twice in previous lines.[184] The fragment concludes with a neutral assessment of the *Shepherd* (it should be read, but not as authoritative) and a negative assessment of the writings of the Gnostic and Marcionite writers.[185]

---

179. The author adds, 'For "most excellent Theophilus" Luke compiled the individual events that took place in his presence—as he plainly shows by omitting the martyrdom of Peter as well as the departure of Paul from the city [of Rome] when he journeyed to Spain' (lines 35-41).

180. The fragment oddly names John as Paul's predecessor (lines 49-50). The author writes, 'For John also in the Apocalypse, though he writes to seven churches, nevertheless speaks to all' (lines 57-60).

181. The fragment remarks, 'for it is not fitting that gall be mixed with honey' (line 67).

182. Cf. Metzger, *Canon of the New Testament*, p. 198, who observes, 'Why this intertestamental book should be included in a list of Christian gospels and epistles is a puzzle that has never been satisfactorily solved.'

183. The fragment reads, 'We receive only the apocalypses of John and Peter, though some of us are not willing that the latter be read in church' (lines 72-73).

184. See lines 49-51, 57-60.

185. Cf. lines 81-85: 'But we accept nothing whatever of Arsinous or Valentinus or Miltiades, who also composed a new book of psalms for Marcion, together with Basilides, the Asian founder of the Cataphrygians.'

The list is fragmentary and incomplete, but the overall shape of what will become the New Testament canon is present.[186] Though there is an absence of books that are eventually included in the New Testament (1 and 2 Peter, James, and Hebrews), and prominence given to a few books that are eventually not considered canonical (Apocalypse of Peter, the *Shepherd*), the 'core' of the New Testament is represented here as a stable body of sacred writings. Moreover, because the fragment discusses the books in terms of acceptance and rejection by the churches, it demonstrates that there was an early awareness of the boundaries of an authoritative body of biblical literature. What is to be read publically in the churches was a significant question. Because the author does not deem the *Shepherd* as authoritative and apostolic, he urges that, though indeed it should be read, 'it cannot be read publicly to the people in the church either among the prophets, whose number is complete, or among the apostles, for it is after [their] time' (lines 77-81). In this sense, the Muratorian Fragment can be viewed as plausible evidence of a notable canon-consciousness early in the life of the church.[187]

In addition, when figures in the early church refer to the Scriptures, they consistently speak in terms of 'recognition' rather than 'selection'.[188] A

186. Cf. von Campenhausen, *Formation of the Christian Bible*, p. 246: 'The corpus of works for church reading recognized by the Muratorianum contains, taken as a whole, little that our own day finds surprising.' He concludes that the Muratorian Fragment is 'a valuable document' because 'it displays for the first time *the concept of a collection* of New Testament scriptures, which has deliberately been closed, and the individual books of which are regarded as "accepted" and ecclesiastically "sanctified", that is to say, that...they have been "incorporated" into the valid corpus' (pp. 261-62; emphasis added).

187. Cf. Hill, 'New Testament Canon', p. 115: 'An early date for the Muratorian Fragment...is not required for the historian to recognize that a concern for the boundaries of the NT Scriptures existed at a time when Barton, Hahneman, McDonald and others believe it did not.'

188. Hill demonstrates that the Muratorian Fragment, Irenaeus, and Serapion of Antioch 'speak of "receiving", "recognizing", or "confessing" certain books and not "selecting" or "choosing" them'. He also provides a selection of quotations with documentation. Cf. Bruce Metzger, *The New Testament, Its Background, Growth and Content* (Nashville, TN: Abingdon, 2003), p. 318: 'Neither individuals nor councils created the canon; instead they came to recognize and acknowledge the self-authenticating quality of these writings, which imposed themselves as canonical upon the church.' Acknowledging that 'in the period under review official decisions by the Church are not involved', von Campenhausen classically argues that 'the Church knew that she had been called into life by this [apostolic] testimony, and had not herself created the Scriptures. She could merely accept, affirm, and confirm them. Hence one could also say, with equal or even greater justification, that the Canon (thought of in terms of its content) imposed itself, and was in any case not a product of the Church on which it was binding' (*Formation of the Christian Bible*, p. 331 n. 13). Similarly, at the end of their survey of canon formation, Carson and Moo argue that 'because the canon

prime example is the abovementioned Muratorian Fragment. The fragmentist speaks of 'receiving', 'accepting', and affirming books that are 'held sacred'.[189] Even the tone of the fragment itself is descriptive rather than prescriptive. The fragmentist is explaining things he seems to view as non-controversial for the most part.[190] This preferred terminology also implies a consciousness of a conceivable body of writings that was authoritative for the believing community.

Concluding Reflections

In sum, the cumulative effect of this internal and external evidence points toward an ongoing canon-consciousness among the believing community and also suggests a canon-consciousness among the biblical writers. As mentioned above, there is compelling evidence that indicates that the core of a three-part Hebrew Bible made up of Law, Prophets, and Writings was relatively stable at the time of the New Testament. The New Testament canon also appears to have formed and stabilized early in the history of the church. In this understanding, the Greek uncial codex manuscript traditions of the fourth and fifth century represent the presence of a previously accepted body of literature making up the Old and New Testament. In other words, the early church inherited a discernable collection of authoritative writings (a 'canon') and never existed without one.[191] They possessed the

is made up of books whose authority ultimately springs from God's gracious self-revelation, it is better to speak of recognizing the canon than of establishing it' (*Introduction to the New Testament*, p. 742).

189. See Metzger, *Canon of the New Testament*, p. 199: 'The terminology employed in referring to those books that are regarded as canonical is *recipere* ("to recognize, or receive", lines 66, 72, 82); other verbs that are also used are *habere* ("to accept", line 69) and *sanctificatae sunt* ("are held sacred", line 63).'

190. Metzger also makes this observation in *Canon of the New Testament*, p. 200.

191. The issue of when the church 'had' a canon again highlights the importance of definitions. For instance, patristic scholar Maurice F. Wiles argues, 'There was never a time when the Church was without written Scriptures. From the beginning she had the Old Testament and it was for her the oracles of God' ('Origen as Biblical Scholar', in *The Cambridge History of the Bible: From the Beginnings to Jerome* [ed. Peter R. Ackroyd and C.F. Evans; Cambridge: Cambridge University Press, 1993], pp. 454-89 [454]). Childs argues in this regard that 'the early church was never at any period of its history without a canon of authoritative writings', because they 'simply assumed the authority of Israel's Scriptures' (*New Testament as Canon*, p. 31). Conversely, Sundberg states unequivocally, 'The church did not inherit a canon of Scripture from Judaism. The church was forced to determine her OT for herself' ('A Christian Canon', p. 152). Allert also avers that 'the Bible was not always "there" in early Christianity. Yet, the church still continued to function in its absence' (*High View of Scripture*, p. 12). Cf. the treatment of definitions in Chapter 1 and the discussion of the significance of the Old Testament for the shape of the Christian canon as a whole in Chapter 3.

Hebrew Scriptures from the beginning, and the New Testament canon was never far behind.

In the previous discussion, I have not attempted to argue for a specific content or particular ordering of the biblical canon. Rather, the primary focus has been on the formation and function of the concept of canon. The concept of canon, in turn, informs (inter alia) examination of the shape of the canonical collection, the phenomenon of canonical 'closure', and also the various orderings of the biblical material in different traditions. Rather than specifying the particular content of the canon or arguing for the superiority of one ordering among the many, I modestly posit that a form of canon-consciousness was at work during the composition and canonization phases of the formation of the biblical canon. Further, my goal is to account for the historical fact that the canon has indeed formed (which is obvious), and that reading portions of it as part of a canonical collection has significant hermeneutical implications for readers (which is sometimes neglected).

Chapters 1 and 2 serve as Part I of the current study. In this major section, I discuss and develop the historical factors that are relevant to the canon question. In Chapter 1, I seek to bring clarity to this definitional issue. Anyone examining the actual etymology and usage of the term 'canon' in the early church will quickly realize that overly strict or simplistic definitions will not suffice. The usage of this term includes historical, theological, and hermeneutical connotations. The 'canon of Scripture' entails the idea of authority and normativity (Canon 1, 'canon as rule') as well as the notion of tangible boundaries and coherent shaping (Canon 2, 'canon as list'). Because of this multiplex function of the term and concept, the 'narrow understanding of canon' is not the most appropriate way to conceive of the formation and function of the biblical literature.

Two of the strongest reasons to adopt a broader understanding of the notion of canon are (1) because it is more appropriate to the historical usage of the relevant terms and concepts, and (2) because it can then describe and account for the phenomenon of canon-consciousness that was at work during the composition and canonization phases of the formation of the biblical collection prior to final consolidation in various communities. In Chapter 2, I have outlined the type of evidence that demonstrates the presence of a canon-conscious mindset among both the biblical authors who were writing the texts of Scripture and also the believing community that was copying, preserving, and treasuring those texts as they passed them on to later generations. These two chapters serve as the foundation on which the next major section of this study builds (Chapters 3-5).

Chapter 3

THE CANONICAL FEATURE OF CONTEXTUALITY

The Canon Guides Readers through the Biblical Material

After establishing the *fact* of canon in history, this investigation now shifts into describing the *effect* that the historical artifact of canon has on the community that reads it and submits to the theological and hermeneutical guidance it has to offer. This shift moves from examining how the canon *formed* into examining how the canon *functions*.[1] Moreover, this hermeneutical study seeks to take into account the results of the preceding historical study.

One of the most intuitive ways that the canon functions as a control on interpretation is how it guides readers through the biblical material. The notion of canon-consciousness applies here to the reader of the biblical text. Just as an awareness of canon was a factor for biblical *writers*, it can also serve an interpretive function for biblical *readers*. As discussed in Chapters 1 and 2, the biblical authors demonstrated an awareness of a broader canonical context as they composed their writings. The believing community, in turn, recognized and respected the nature of this mindset by generally associating and ordering the biblical material as part of a broader collection. The result of this canon-conscious composition and canonization was a canonical collection that was shaped for future generations. In this chapter, the interpretive value of this canonical context will be explored. Subsequent readers of the canon (historical and contemporary) have the option of sharing the canon-conscious mindset of the biblical writers and the believing community. A canon-conscious reading of Scripture is one that follows the guidelines generated by the canonical context.

Canon as a Mental Construct

As noted in Chapter 2, this notion of canon-consciousness implies that the concept of canon is also a type of mental construct. During the formation

---

1.   Robert Wall uses the terms 'canonical *process*' and 'canonical *product*' to delineate these two types of investigation. Nevertheless, he still employs the 'canonical formation' and 'canonical function' terminology as the main headings of his analysis (e.g., see Robert W. Wall, 'The Function of the Pastoral Letters within the Pauline Canon of the New Testament: A Canonical Approach', in *Pauline Canon* [ed. Stanley Porter; Leiden: Brill, 2004], pp. 29, 35).

of the biblical literature (especially the Old Testament period), any notion of the biblical text as a whole was by necessity conceptual. Though there was not a physical entity (e.g. a large codex) that contained all of the scriptural writings, an individual reading only a fragment of a text 'could have understood it from within the larger context of this mental construct'.[2] Thus, when readers picked up a portion of a biblical text, they could locate it conceptually in relation to the other books held sacred. Even as the codex form was developing, a mental construct would still be necessary in order to relate physical groupings with one another.[3] Similarly, the presence of this type of mental construct in the mind of a contemporary reader generates a hermeneutical grid that inevitably informs the reading process. For contemporary readers of the biblical canon, even a rough mental construct can function as the 'conceptual glue' that would allow for a holistic reading. This 'conceptual glue' allows a reader to maintain a 'wide-angle lens view' that keeps in sight the multifaceted mosaic of meaning that the biblical authors have stitched together through their editorial work. The 'conceptual glue', then, connects the reader to the 'canonical glue'.[4] The wide-ranging literary texts, contexts, meanings, and messages found within the biblical literature are bound together by a reader's sense of the 'big picture' of the canonical context.

The notion of a mental construct is part of the 'context' experienced by biblical readers. A canonical approach seeks to highlight the fecundity of this canonical context. The canon not only delineates the boundaries of the biblical writings but also serves as a 'bounded space' in which literary and theological meaning can be discovered. In an attempt to fill out the nature and effect of this type of conceptual context, Paul Fiddes explores the metaphors of space and place in relation to the canon. There is a 'space' opened up by the reading and inner-dialogue of canonical texts that creates opportunities for a divine encounter, a 'place' to hear the Word of God.[5] Fid-

---

2. Sailhamer, *Meaning of the Pentateuch*, p. 211.

3. Cf. Hurtado's discussion of the nature of a 'virtual collection' of Paul's written correspondence before the development of a codex form that could contain them all (*Earliest Christian Artifacts*, pp. 38-39). For the point being made here, the notion of a 'virtual collection' conceptually precedes the formal actualization of that collection in a fixed entity (e.g. a codex containing Paul's gathered letters like P[46]). Especially given the publishing technology of a manuscript culture, a haphazard juxtaposition is unlikely. In other words, it would have been financially prohibitive to publish something devoid of careful prior reflection on the content of the publication.

4. See the implications of the notion of 'canon as a mental construct' for the canon formation process in Chapter 2. One of the reasons there is overlap in these discussions is the basic insight that the biblical *authors* were also biblical *readers*.

5. See Paul Fiddes, 'The Canon as Space and Place', in *Die Einheit der Schrift und die Vielfalt des Kanons* (Berlin: W. de Gruyter, 2003), pp. 127-50. Cf. Chapman, *Law*

des's metaphors highlight the connection between the possibilities of both the hermeneutical and theological meaning that can be generated within a canonical context. Similarly, Vanhoozer asserts that the canon is 'the norm that delineates the *area* in which the church hears the word of God'.[6] These observations provide additional theological motivation for recognizing the role and function of the canon in the life of the church.

The Effect of the Canonical Framework

In markedly hermeneutical terms, the effect of the canonical framework is similar to the literary concept of 'framing in discourse'. Framing relates to the 'observation that the wording used to introduce and narrate a story offers clues to the audience regarding how to interpret a narrative'.[7] It also involves 'cues given by a narrator which guide an audience in interpreting the narrative' and can function as 'a hermeneutical tool to help the audience understand what they hear or read'.[8] The present study seeks to suggest that the overall shape of the various canonical corpora 'frames' the biblical content.[9]

The result of this framing is a canonical setting that evokes certain expectations and deeply affects the reading process from start to finish. The type of

---

and Prophets, p. 109: 'The notion of limitation as such is secondary to the more primary sense of "canon" as a *range* of scriptural witnesses, ordered in such a way that it invites and compels the continual examination of the self and the reexamination of the scriptures.'

6. Kevin J. Vanhoozer, *The Drama of Doctrine: A Canonical-Linguistic Approach to Christian Theology* (Louisville, KY: Westminster/John Knox Press, 2005), p. 146. Emphasis added.

7. See Kenneth Litwak, *Echoes of Scripture in Luke–Acts: Telling the History of God's People Intertextually* (London: T. & T. Clark, 2005), p. 56.

8. Litwak, *Echoes of Scripture in Luke–Acts*, p. 56. Cf. Marie Maclean, 'Pretexts and Paratexts: The Art of the Peripheral', *New Literary History* 22 (1991), pp. 273-74: 'The frame may act as a means of leading the eye into the picture, and the reader into the text, thus presenting itself as the key to a solipsistic world; or it may deliberately lead the eye out, and encourage the reader to concentrate on the context rather than the text. Sometimes indeed the frame defines the text, by appropriateness or complementarity; at others it defines the context, like an elaborately carved art nouveau setting to a simple mirror.' Maclean is here speaking of the 'frame' in the terms of paratextuality (see below discussion).

9. See also Deborah Tannen, 'What is a Frame? Surface Evidence for Underlying Expectations', in *Framing in Discourse* (Oxford: Oxford University Press, 1993), pp. 14-56; and Gale L. MacLachlan and Ian Reid, *Framing and Interpretation* (Carlton: Melborne University Press, 1994). This basic 'framing' function of a canonical context is developed in the section below on contextuality. As Chapman reasons, 'Because the goal of the canonical process was to transmit a framework for interpretation (or "grammar") along with the sacred writings themselves, the received form of the text contains literary features which act as hermeneutical guides for present-day readers' (*Law and Prophets*, p. 108).

expectation that a canonical context evokes finds a possible parallel in what E.D. Hirsch calls 'genre expectations'.[10] Hirsch notes that 'the details of meaning that an interpreter understands are powerfully determined and constituted by his meaning expectations'.[11] The 'genre idea' deals with notions like, 'In this type of utterance, we expect these types of traits.'[12] Canon affects these types of expectations. Indeed, the canonical framework influences the 'structures of expectations' that 'make interpretation possible'.[13]

The canonical context essentially sets up 'guideposts' for readers to follow as they make preliminary assumptions about the nature of the text as a whole. For Hirsch, 'an interpreter's preliminary generic conception of a text is constitutive of everything that he subsequently understands'.[14] In this scenario, Hirsch contends that 'without helpful orientations like titles and attributions, readers are likely to gain widely different generic conceptions of a text, and these conceptions will be constitutive of their subsequent understanding'.[15] A reader's interpretive guesses will be impoverished 'in the absence of guideposts'.[16] Moreover, the reader's 'notion of the type of meaning he confronts will powerfully influence his understanding of details'.[17]

Readers of the canon encounter individual documents as parts of a developed whole. The concept of canon, then, forms the basis of 'understanding' in the church's reading of Scripture.[18] Readers understand and encounter

---

10. See E.D. Hirsch, *Validity in Interpretation* (New Haven, CT: Yale University Press, 1967). Hirsch employs a nuanced understanding of the notion of 'genre' that enables him to tie the 'generic expectations' directly to an author's intention. Structuralist literary theorist Gérard Genette analyzes the multifaceted nature of genre under the rubric of 'architext' in *The Architext: An Introduction* (trans. Jane E. Lewin; Berkeley, CA: University of California Press, 1992). Cf. Gérard Genette, *Palimpsests: Literature in the Second Degree* (trans. Channa Newman and Claude Doubinsky; Lincoln, NE: University of Nebraska Press, 1997), p. 5: 'Generic perception is known to guide and determine to a considerable degree the readers' expectations, and thus their reception of a work.' On Genette's approach, see below.

11. Hirsch, *Validity*, p. 72.

12. Hirsch, *Validity*, p. 73.

13. For these phrases, consult Tannen, 'What is a Frame', pp. 16, 21.

14. Hirsch, *Validity*, p. 74.

15. Hirsch, *Validity*, p. 75.

16. Hirsch, *Validity*, p. 75.

17. Hirsch, *Validity*, p. 75.

18. After noting the importance of the Spirit, tradition, and the church, Vanhoozer asserts that 'it is the *text*, read in a certain canonical way and in a canonical context, that occasions understanding' (*Drama of Doctrine*, p. 118). This comment comes in a discussion of what went on in the Acts 8 account of Phillip and the Ethiopian. Vanhoozer writes, 'Philip represents a special kind of external aid, namely, the strategy of reading the Scriptures in their broader apostolic and canonical context' (p. 119). In other words, 'Philip represents *canonical consciousness:* the new awareness that the testimony to the God of Israel and the testimony to Jesus Christ belong and make sense together' (p. 119).

meaning within the framework of this bounded space, this hermeneutically significant set of literary boundaries. In other words, the canon functions as the *Sitz im Leben* of the church's grappling with God's Word to his people and the necessary context for 'whole Bible' interpretation.[19] To state the obvious and sometimes neglected point, reading canonically would be impossible without a canonical context.[20] Once a reader experiences an individual text in the setting of a larger collection, that broader textual context then plays a significant and unavoidable role in the reading of that individual text.

The existence of the canonical concept puts pressure on readers of the Bible to relate the individual parts (e.g. narratives, poems, epistles) to an integrated whole. C. Kavin Rowe's use of the idea of 'biblical pressure' provides some fodder for those interested in the effect of reading the biblical texts within the framework of an authoritative canon.[21] A significant part of Rowe's argument regarding the development of doctrine is that the

---

19. See Brevard S. Childs, *Introduction to the Old Testament*, p. 78: 'Israel defined itself in terms of a book! The canon formed the decisive *Sitz im Leben* for the Jewish community's life, thus blurring the sociological evidence most sought after by the modern historian.' Childs argues further that 'when critical exegesis is made to rest on the recovery of these very sociological distinctions which have been obscured, it runs directly in the face of the canon's intention'. Cf. Driver's comparison and contrast of Childs and Old Testament form critic Hermann Gunkel in *Brevard Childs*, pp. 105-136. Driver argues that Childs 'consciously *inverts*' Gunkel's method, 'contradicting the usual form critical account in form critical terms'. In this sense, 'the canon itself became the setting for the life of the people, the community of faith'. According to Driver, Childs seeks to answer the question, 'Does canonical scripture transcend the circumstances of its creation and provide the *Sitz* for a community's life of faith and practice?' (p. 105). Cf. the similar terminology in Bockmuehl, *Seeing the Word*, p. 114.

20. In her 'zwischenbilanz' of recent research on 'kanonischen auslegung' in the German academic context, Köhlmoos, 'Kanon und Methode', pp. 135-46, notes that canonical interpreters sometimes neglect a direct discussion of the material questions regarding canon and the canon formation process. Accordingly, she queries toward the end of her review, 'Kanonisch ohne Kanon?' By delineating and discussing canon formation in Chapters 1–2, I have sought to connect these two distinct but integrally related fields of inquiry.

21. See C. Kavin Rowe, 'Biblical Pressure and Trinitarian Hermeneutics', *Pro Ecclesia* 11 (2002), pp. 295-312. Cf. Childs's use of Rowe's development of the notion of 'biblical pressure' in *Church's Guide for Reading Paul*, pp. 44-45. Cf. Brevard S. Childs, 'The One Gospel in Four Witnesses', in *The Rule of Faith: Scripture, Canon, and Creed in a Critical Age* (ed. Ephraim Radner and George Sumner; Harrisburg, PA: Morehouse, 1998), p. 53: 'The initial point to make is that the canonicity of the four Gospels was not an ecclesiastical decision dictated from above, but rather the Church leaders affirmed later what had already been established in the use of these Gospels by individual congregations. In the hearing, preaching, and liturgical use of this material, these writings *exerted an authoritative coercion* on those receiving their word' (emphasis added).

canon as a whole exerts pressure on readers to think about God in Trinitarian terms. In turn, the development of Trinitarian discussion is a phenomenon that is generated by the formation of a canon that includes the Old Testament and New Testament as two vital parts of a consistent and coherent storyline. For example, Rowe states, 'It is safe to say that the doctrine of the Trinity would never have arisen on the basis of the Old or the New Testament taken in isolation. The problematic emerges precisely because the writers of the New Testament presupposed the authority of the Old Testament and made explicit use of the theological grammar that undergirds the Old Testament's language about the one God.'[22] By directly associating their writings with those of the Old Testament, the New Testament writers generate a framework that pressures readers to view the person and work of Jesus within a two-Testament understanding of who God is and how he works in the world.[23]

The Canonically Generated Metanarrative

A further way that the canon shapes the expectations of its readers is the way that it frames the biblical metanarrative and situates the prophetic and apostolic discourse in that larger story. The term 'metanarrative' entered intellectual discourse by way of Jean-Francois Lyotard's often-quoted characterization of postmodernity as 'incredulity toward metanarrative'.[24] Though Lyotard has a technical understanding of what a metanarrative is, biblical scholars have used the term 'to refer to the overall story told by the Christian Scriptures, which is not totalizing or oppressive, and which makes possible the "redemptive-historical" level of biblical interpretation'.[25]

---

22. Rowe, 'Biblical Pressure', p. 299. On the Trinitarian logic of the New Testament's language about God, see also Jensen, *Canon and Creed*, pp. 43-50. Jensen argues that the developed doctrine of the Trinity in the Patristic period is a 'conceptualized appropriation of the...logic of the New Testament's way of speaking about God. Christians speak and so live in a spiritual space shaped by specific coordinates: Father of this Son/ Son of this Father/liberating Spirit of their love' (pp. 47-48). Consequently, 'the pattern of the [Apostolic/Nicene] creed and the grammar of the New Testament's specific God-discourse are identical' (p. 48).

23. Cf. Childs, *Biblical Theology in Crisis*, p. 112: 'The acknowledgement of a canon is a confession that both Testaments are testifying to the same God at work.'

24. See *The Postmodern Condition: A Report on Knowledge* (Minneapolis, MN: University of Minnesota Press, 1984), p. xxiv.

25. Albert Wolters, 'Metanarrative', in *Dictionary for Theological Interpretation of the Bible* (ed. Kevin J. Vanhoozer; Grand Rapids, MI: Baker, 2005), pp. 506-507. Wolters briefly notes the positive and negative connotations of the word. See also Wolters' related entry on 'Worldview' in the same volume (pp. 854-56). Cf. Brown, *Scripture as Communication*, p. 44: 'A hermeneutical contribution of postmodernism is its emphasis on the pervasiveness and power of story in describing how humans perceive and understand their world.' Brown also notes the connection between meta-narrative and

The stories recounted in the biblical canon encourage a certain world-view, one in which the readers are implicated and a part of the 'real world' those narratives generate.[26] In *The Eclipse of Biblical Narrative*, Hans W. Frei argues that this type of mindset was predominant before the rise of the modern period.[27] According to Frei's analysis, precritical interpreters held that the Bible contained 'all those stories which together went into the making of a single storied or historical sequence'.[28] For them, 'the real world' was formed 'by the sequence told by the biblical stories'.[29] By using

worldview. She reflects, 'Since I will work to bring coherence to my various beliefs and experiences by seeing them through a storied lens, this assumed meta-narrative is another way of referring to my worldview.' For a recent engagement with and critique of a 'Worldview-Story' approach to biblical theology, see Edward W. Klink III and Darian R. Lockett, *Understanding Biblical Theology: A Comparison of Theory and Practice* (Grand Rapids, MI: Zondervan, 2012), pp. 93-122. In this vein, see also Andreas Köstenberger, 'The Present and Future of Biblical Theology', *Themelios* 37 (2012), pp. 445-64. Köstenberger briefly interacts with approaches to biblical theology that emphasize 'that there is an overarching metanarrative that unifies the Scriptures' (p. 455).

26. Meir Sternberg, *The Poetics of Biblical Narrative: Ideological Literature and the Drama of Reading* (Bloomington, IN: Indiana University Press, 1985), p. 1, articulates the nature of biblical narrative as 'a functional structure, a means to a communicative end, a transaction between the narrator and the audience on whom he wishes to produce a certain effect by way of certain strategies'. Reflecting on this engaging feature of narrative, Thiselton observes that 'narrative components thus constitute not bare events in a sequence, but active contributions to the flow and movement of the plot. They both serve to build a whole, and also conversely they derive their significance from their place *within* this coherent whole. This "whole" now becomes the narrative-world of the reader. But when the reader is seized by this "re-figured" world, the narrative-effects…become *revelatory and transformative*' (*New Horizons*, p. 355). More pointedly, Michael B. Shepherd, *The Textual World of the Bible* (New York: Peter Lang, 2013), p. 1, writes that 'the Bible is the real world' and that 'the biblical authors are in the business of world making, and they insist that theirs is the only real world'. Cf. Paul Ricoeur, *Time and Narrative* (vol. 1; Chicago: University of Chicago Press, 1984), p. 34: 'The effects of fiction, revelation, and transformation are essentially the effects of reading.'

27. Hans W. Frei, *The Eclipse of Biblical Narrative: A Study in Eighteenth and Nineteenth Century Hermeneutics* (New Haven, CT: Yale University Press, 1974). On this point, see also the chapter below on the 'ideal readers' of the biblical canon.

28. Frei, *Eclipse*, p. 1. Cf. Joel B. Green, 'Practicing The Gospel in a Post-Critical World: The Promise of Theological Exegesis', *JETS* 47 (2004), pp. 392-93: 'The particular narratives related in the biblical books, together with the non-narrative portions of Scripture, participate in a more extensive, overarching narrative (or meta-narrative)'.

29. Frei, *Eclipse*, p. 1. In this regard, Brown, *Scripture as Communication*, p. 46, observes that the 'biblical authors both assume and contribute to the meta-narrative of Scripture because they are convinced that they are participants in the biblical story'. For readers, 'we may speak of entering the world of the text as a way of allowing its normative story to shape us'. Developing what he calls the 'foolproof composition' of biblical narrative, Sternberg reflects, 'Follow the biblical narrator ever so uncritically, and by no

figural interpretation, these interpreters made sense of the biblical stories 'by weaving them together into a common narrative referring to a single history and its patterns of meaning'.[30] The biblical reader, in turn, was 'to see his disposition, his actions and passions, the shape of his own life as well as that of his era's events as figures of that storied world'.[31] This feature of biblical narrative can also be understood as an effect of canon on the reader who encounters those world-projecting narratives in the context of a collection of authoritative writings.[32] The structure of the storied world of biblical narrative rests upon the foundation of the context undergirded by the canon.

In sum, the canon sets the historical, textual, and conceptual framework for reading both Testaments. Readers encounter the biblical material within the bounds of a particular context that bears a particular shape. Through the aforementioned features, the canon guides its readers to think in certain ways about its content.

The Canon Generates Textual Connections (Contextuality)

Though the canon serves the purpose of limiting possible intertextual connections (see Chapter 4), it also generates new textual connections that would not have actualized otherwise. The concept of canon has the dual effect on the interpretive task of both limiting and generating. Acknowledging this delimiting and generative effect of the canonical context, Vanhoozer affirms that the canon 'encourages a play of meaning, as it were, but only within carefully prescribed boundaries'.[33] Any account of the hermeneutical impact that the canon has on its readers needs to take into account both types of meaning-full effects.

The concept of canon in general allows for a study of 'contextuality' that notes the generation of meaning produced by juxtaposing *just these works* in *just this fashion*. Sailhamer defines biblical 'con-textuality' as 'the notion

great exertion you will be making tolerable sense of the world you are in, the action that unfolds, the protagonists on stage, and the point of it all' (*Poetics of Biblical Narrative*, p. 51). In the search for the meaning of the narrative, in this sense, 'the reader cannot go far wrong even if he does little more than follow the statements made and the incidents enacted on the narrative surface' (p. 51).

30. Frei, *Eclipse*, p. 2.

31. Frei, *Eclipse*, p. 3. Cf. Sternberg's critical interaction with Frei's central claims about narrative and history in *Poetics of Biblical Narrative*, pp. 81-83.

32. Referring to the final form of the Tanak (rather than earlier stages of its prehistory), Shepherd comments that 'it is this rendering of the present arrangement of the Scriptures that establishes the framework of the real world into which the reader must fit' (*Textual World of the Bible*, p. 2).

33. Vanhoozer, *Meaning in this Text*, p. 134.

of the effect on meaning of the relative position of a biblical book within a prescribed order of reading'.[34] Though not many scholars use the phrase 'contextuality' in this manner, others use related terms to discuss the same concept. Greg Goswell speaks of contextuality as a 'para-textual' element of Scripture.[35] Pierre Bayard acknowledges the effect of contextuality in general reading by highlighting the significance of 'location'.[36] Hendrik J. Koorevaar engages this topic in terms of a work's broad 'macrostructure'.[37] David Trobisch investigates the 'redactional frame' of the 'canonical edition' of the New Testament.[38] These notions are in some ways complementary and each seek to take into account a given work's broader textual context and spatial relationship to other literary entities.

The term contextuality has the benefit of emphasizing the notion of *context*. The study of contextuality is the study of a writing's textual/literary context.[39] Where an individual writing is positioned in relation to other

34. Sailhamer, *Introduction*, p. 213. Cf. Childs's concern 'to deal seriously with the effect which the shape of the canonical collection has on the individual parts. At times the larger corpus exerts a major influence by establishing a different context from that of a single composition' (*New Testament as Canon*, p. 52).

35. On Goswell's approach in this area, see below.

36. Pierre Bayard, *How to Talk about Books You Haven't Read* (London: Granta Books, 2007), p. 11. Goswell mentions and sources Bayard's concept of location.

37. E.g., see Hendrik J. Koorevaar, 'The Torah Model as Original Macrostructure of the Hebrew Canon: A Critical Evaluation', *ZAW* 122 (2010), pp. 65-80. Koorevar interacts with and critiques the methods of Sailhamer and Goswell. He is skeptical both of the notion that 'text' and 'paratext' can be kept in isolation (Goswell) as well as the notion that the Law functions in a canonically foundational way (Sailhamer). See the interaction between these scholars below.

38. Trobisch, *First Edition of the New Testament*, p. 3. Trobisch argues that 'when editors publish material they guide readers to interpret it in a specific way by setting certain signals within a redactional frame' (p. 45). The notion of intentionality is important and will be dealt with in the sections below.

39. Childs describes context as 'the environment of that which is being interpreted' (*Biblical Theology in Crisis*, p. 97). More specifically, 'as a literary term, context denotes the parts of a composition that constitute the texture of the narrative' (p. 97). In this sense, 'to interpret a sentence "out of context" is to disregard its place in its larger literary design' (p. 97). See also the variety of senses that 'context' bears in biblical studies noted by Joel B. Green in 'Context', in *DTIB*, pp. 130-33. He deals specifically with context as sociohistorical setting, context as 'cotext' (i.e. literary context), and context as readerly situation. Moisés Silva discusses 'context' from a linguistic viewpoint in *Biblical Words and Their Meaning: An Introduction to Lexical Semantics* (Grand Rapids, MI: Zondervan, 1994), pp. 138-48. Silva stresses the importance of accounting for the linguistic nexus generated by a word's 'syntagmatic relation' to its verbal and literary surroundings (from word level to discourse level). Cf. Sheppard, 'Canon Criticism', p. 13: 'To the degree that historical-grammatical or historical-critical exegesis is successful in reviving a "lost" historical context, it effectively de-canonizes the literature by putting it in some other context than the canonical.'

writings in a collection (either materially or conceptually) has significant hermeneutical ramifications. In this sense, the broad 'context' of a given writing involves all of the writings within its textual proximity.[40] This type of study seeks to uncover the 'semantic effect of a book's relative position' within the biblical canon.[41] In this sense, 'context' is now 'context within the literary shape of the final form of the canon'.[42] Contextuality is in play any time a physical or conceptual reading sequence has been established.

Mere Contextuality
The level of analysis that observes these contextual effects without dealing with the issue of intention might be described as 'mere contextuality'. Mere contextuality is the effect that arises in the mind of the reader when writings are seen in relation to other writings. This level of analysis focuses on the connections produced by a broader literary context. Moreover, studies in mere contextuality are not concerned necessarily with how individual writings come to be included in a collection, associated with certain groupings, or juxtaposed in a specific manner. Instead, the focus is deliberately on the result of that placement/location. The concern is more on the meaning generated by the juxtaposition rather than the origin of the ordering. In sum, here the goal is to demonstrate and observe the meaningful effect that an order of reading has on the biblical books.

An important element of Sailhamer's compositional approach to hermeneutics involves the general study of contextuality within the biblical canon. He notes that the 'concept of con-textuality does not necessitate an *intentional* linkage of books within the structure of the OT Canon. Contextuality, as such, merely recognizes the obvious fact that context influences meaning.'[43] For Sailhamer, 'con-textuality only raises the question of the effect of context on meaning, not of the intent that lies behind it'.[44]

40. Cf. Greg Goswell, 'The Order of the Books of the New Testament', *JETS* 53 (2010), p. 225: 'Readerly habit views enjambment as a clue that significant relations are to be discerned between a particular book and its neighbors in the library of canonical books.'

41. Sailhamer, *Introduction*, p. 213. Cf. Blenkinsopp, *Prophecy and Canon*, p. 11: 'Redaction study also must take account of the canon as context. The reason is, of course, that canon implies a positive attempt to give form, structure and meaning to traditional material by placing it in a particular context.'

42. Seitz, *Prophecy and Hermeneutics*, p. 179. Seitz makes this comment in light of recent developments within scholarship that view the twelve Minor Prophets in light of the larger literary context of the book of the Twelve. Cf. Georg Steins, 'Der Kanon ist der erste Kontext: Oder, Zurück an den Anfang!', *Bibel und Kirche* 62 (2007), pp. 116-21.

43. Sailhamer, *Introduction*, p. 215. Emphasis added. Sailhamer notes that issues of intention 'are important questions, but they go beyond the limits of the concept'.

44. Sailhamer, *Introduction*, p. 215.

Accordingly, 'the question of intentionality is addressed by means of the study of OT composition and redaction'.[45] He also observes that contextuality is 'the aspect of canonical shape that is least traceable to a distinct authorial or compositional intention'.[46]

To illustrate his understanding of contextuality, Sailhamer discusses the 'montage effect' that occurs in film. Originally developed by cinematographer Sergei Eisenstein, the notion of 'montage in cinematography' seeks to describe 'the effect of meaning which one achieves by juxtaposing two related or unrelated pieces of film'.[47] According to Eisenstein, typical film viewers 'are accustomed to make, almost automatically, a definite and obvious deductive generalization when any separate objects are placed before us side by side'.[48] The film can consistently have this effect because 'compe-

45. Sailhamer, *Introduction*, p. 215.

46. Sailhamer, *Introduction*, p. 249. In this respect, 'of the three approaches to the theological shape of the OT Canon, the notion of con-textuality, or montage, is the most problematic' (p. 249).

47. Sailhamer, *Introduction*, p. 214. The main work Sailhamer utilizes is Sergei Eisenstein, *The Film Sense* (trans. Jay Leyda; New York: Harcourt Brace, 1942). See also Sergei Eisenstein, 'Methods of Montage', in *Film Form: Essays in Film Theory* (ed. and trans. Jay Leyda; San Diego, CA: Harcourt, 1969), pp. 72-83; and Sergei Eisenstein, 'A Dialectic Approach to Film Form', in *Film Form*, pp. 45-63. For Eisenstein, 'montage is an idea that arises from the collision of independent shots—shots even opposite to one another' ('Dialectic Approach', p. 49). Arthur Knight, *The Liveliest Art: A Panoramic History of the Movies* (London: Macmillan, 1957), p. 79, observes that as a result of the popularity of some of Eisenstein's films (e.g. *October: Ten Days that Shook the World*), 'the word montage came to identify not cutting in general, but specifically the rapid, shock cutting that Eisenstein employed in his films. Its use survives to this day in the specially created "montage sequences" inserted into Hollywood films to suggest, in a blur of double exposures, the rise to fame of an opera singer or, in brief model shots, the destruction of an airplane, a city or a planet.' Cf. Jean Mitry, *The Aesthetics and Psychology of the Cinema* (trans. Christopher King; Bloomington, IN: Indiana University Press, 1997), pp. 89-167 (a section entitled 'Rhythm and Montage').

48. Eisenstein, *Film Sense*, p. 4. The 'montage effect' is similar to the Kuleshov Effect, named after Soviet film director Lev Kuleshov. Kuleshov analyzed the effect that editing sequences had on film viewers. In a famous short film experiment, Kuleshov interspersed the same footage of a man's face devoid of expression between a series of random images (e.g. a hot bowl of soup, a woman lying in a coffin, and a young girl playing with a stuffed animal). The juxtaposition of these images had the effect of projecting a series of differing emotional responses among viewers. While the man's expressions appeared to change in response to each new image, the footage was in fact exactly the same (though there is debate regarding the details of this experiment). For a brief overview of this effect, see Maria T. Pramaggiore and Tom Wallis, *Film: A Critical Introduction* (Boston, MA: Allyn & Bacon, 2011), pp. 191-93, 217-21. Pramaggiore and Wallis observe that Kuleshov's analysis 'illustrated that the meaning of a shot was determined not only by the material content of the shot, but also by its association with the preceding and succeeding shots' (p. 192). Both Eisenstein and Kuleshov are key

tent viewers (or readers) always seek to understand the parts in light of the whole'.[49] 'Juxtaposition of parts', then, 'implies a whole, so that even where such a whole does not actually exist, a whole is supplied by the viewer (or reader)'.[50]

For Sailhamer, this inevitable meaning-making drive in viewers or readers is at the heart of what contextuality entails. He argues that 'the semantic purpose of montage in film (and biblical texts) is to represent themes and images that are larger than the limitation of the medium itself—that is, larger than an individual "shot-piece" (a discreet piece or frame of film)'.[51] When two shots are juxtaposed on screen, 'the viewer is forced to identify elements of both shots that are characteristic of a single theme or an image of a theme'.[52] For Sailhamer, the ordering of biblical books involves the same type of process. As he writes, 'a canonical order insures that the books of the OT are read in a predetermined context'.[53] There are in fact multiple ways that the canon has been ordered and 'each of these contexts has its own particular semantic effect (montage) on the meaning of the individual biblical books'.[54]

pioneers and advocates of Soviet montage theory (see the first two chapters of David C. Gillespie, *Early Soviet Cinema: Innovation, Ideology and Propaganda* [London: Wallflower Press, 2000], pp. 22-56). Contemporary cinematography scholars usually temper the original enthusiasm of Kuleshov and his students regarding the success of this 'effect'. For instance, Adrienne L. McLean comments, 'While *some* meaning can be produced through editing, a considerable amount of contextualization is required before spectators provide the "crucial interpretive linkages" that the Kuleshov effect theoretically comprises' ('Kuleshov Effect', in *Critical Dictionary of Film and Television Theory* [ed. Roberta E. Pearson and Philip Simpson; London: Routledge, 2001], pp. 254-55). For the present study, the relevant insight of both the montage effect and the Kuleshov Effect is that juxtaposing discrete elements in a work of art (i.e. literature/film) has significant impact on the meaning that viewers/readers perceive.

49. Sailhamer, *Introduction*, p. 214.
50. Sailhamer, *Introduction*, p. 214.
51. Sailhamer, *Introduction*, p. 214. Pramaggiore and Wallis argue that 'one of the basic theoretical principles of [film] editing is that the meaning produced by joining two shots together transcends the visual information contained in each individual shot. In other words, the meaning of a sequence of shots is more than the sum of its parts' (*Film*, p. 192). They also note that 'as the Soviet practitioners understood, editing synthesizes the cinematography and *mise en scène* of individual shots into a series of images that, when taken as a whole, transcend the limitations of any one of the images in isolation' (p. 220).
52. Sailhamer, *Introduction*, p. 214.
53. Sailhamer, *Introduction*, p. 214.
54. Sailhamer, *Introduction*, p. 214. He notes in this regard that 'in the history of the OT Canon there are, in fact, several such canonical contexts, e.g. the order of the English Bible, the Greek Septuagint, or the Hebrew texts, for which, in fact, there are several contending orders'.

Greg Goswell provides a study in the mere contextuality of the biblical canon in three recent journal articles.[55] In terms of hermeneutics, Goswell's work here is helpful in drawing out the contextual implications that the concept of canon entails. Goswell takes pains to clarify that he is only making observations about the various extant orders and is not attempting to demonstrate a canonical intentionality on any level. He writes, 'I am not concerned with genetics but with the effect on the reader of the present arrangement of biblical books, however that arrangement may have been produced.'[56] In this approach, 'it is not necessary to decide upon any particular order of books, favouring it over other contending orders, for differing orders highlight different features of the books thus categorized, so that each order in its own way may be valid and useful to the reader'.[57] He adds in his examination of the New Testament that this type of study is not 'a historical investigation into the formation of the canon of the NT, but an exploration of the hermeneutical implications of the order of the biblical books, with book order viewed as an aspect of the paratext of Christian Scripture'.[58]

Goswell focuses on the interaction between the shape of the collection/ material and the perception of the reader. He begins his analysis by arguing that 'the Bible as a literary work is made up of text and paratext'.[59] A 'paratext', in Goswell's understanding, is 'everything in a text other than the words, that is to say, those elements that are adjoined to the text but are not part of the text itself if the "text" is limited strictly to the words'.[60] The paratextual features of Scripture include 'the order of the biblical books,

55. See Greg Goswell, 'The Order of Books in the Hebrew Bible', *JETS* 51 (2008), pp. 673-88; Greg Goswell, 'The Order of Books in the Greek Old Testament', *JETS* 52 (2009), pp. 449-66; and Goswell, 'Order of New Testament', pp. 225-41.

56. Goswell, 'Order of Hebrew Bible', p. 674.

57. Goswell, 'Order of Hebrew Bible', p. 674. He clarifies what he is *not* doing in his study by saying that 'this is not a history of the formation of the canon of Scripture' (p. 673). Acknowledging the value of those studies, he puts the 'research and conclusions' of those studies 'to a different use than that of plotting the historical genesis of the collection of books that now makes up the Hebrew Bible' (p. 673). He justifies this methodological decision by affirming that 'it is not necessary to decide upon any particular order of books, favouring it over other contending orders, for differing orders highlight different features of the books thus categorized' (p. 674). Accordingly, 'each order in its own way may be valid and useful to the reader' (p. 674).

58. Goswell, 'Order of New Testament', p. 225. Similarly, in his study of LXX ordering, Goswell states that 'it is not necessary to make a judgment about how deliberate the proces of ordering was, for the focus of this study is *the effect* on the reader of a given order, not its historical production' ('Order of Greek Old Testament', p. 449).

59. Goswell, 'Order of the Hebrew Bible', p. 673. Cf. the discussion of Genette's understanding of paratextuality below.

60. Goswell, 'Order of Hebrew Bible', p. 673.

the names assigned to the different books, and the differing schemes of textual division within the books'.[61] Because these paratextual elements are 'adjoined to the text, they have an influence on reading and interpretation'.[62]

For the purpose of his study, Goswell assumes 'that text and paratext (though conceptually differentiated) are for all practical purposes inseparable and have an important interrelationship that influences the reading process'.[63] The paratextual feature Goswell focuses on is the ordering of the biblical writings in different textual traditions.[64] His foundational contention is that the way biblical books are ordered has a hermeneutically significant impact on the perceptions and expectations of biblical readers.[65] Indeed, for Goswell, 'consciously or unconsciously, the reader's evaluation of a book is affected by the company it keeps in the collected library of Scripture'.[66] In this type of analysis, 'the placement or location of a biblical book relative to other books influences a reader's view of the book'.[67] Goswell defines 'location' as 'physical propinquity in the anthology of Scripture'.[68] In sum, the bulk of Goswell's analysis seeks to describe the

61. Goswell, 'Order of Hebrew Bible', p. 673.

62. Goswell, 'Order of Hebrew Bible', p. 673.

63. Goswell, 'Order of Hebrew Bible', p. 673.

64. The three textual traditions he analyzes are the Hebrew Bible (Tanak: Law, Prophets, and Writings), the Greek Old Testament (LXX ordering), and the Greek New Testament. Though he avoids discussion of the history of canon formation, Goswell does acknowledge the historical problems associated with these traditions. His goal is *merely* to 'tease out hermeneutical implications of the canonical orders settled upon by different communities of faith' ('Order of the Hebrew Bible', p. 674).

65. Goswell posits that 'where a biblical book is placed relative to other books influences, initially at least, a reader's view of the book, raising expectations regarding the contents of the book. A reader naturally assumes that material that is juxtaposed is in some way related in meaning. It is this habit that forms the basis for the following survey and analysis' ('Order of the Hebrew Bible', p. 673).

66. Goswell, 'Order of Hebrew Bible', p. 688. He states strongly, 'In almost every case, the location of a biblical book relative to other canonical books, whether in terms of grouping in which it is placed, or the book(s) that follow or precede it, has hermeneutical significance for the reader who seeks meaning in the text' (p. 688). Goswell restates this assertion in the conclusion to his study of the New Testament and stresses 'the importance of a deliberate examination of this aspect of the paratext of Scripture' ('Order of the New Testament', p. 241).

67. Goswell, 'Order of New Testament', p. 225. Goswell adds that 'the assumption is that a book is more closely related to books next to it or nearby, and less closely related to books placed far from it' (p. 225). Cf. his explanation in 'Order of Greek Old Testament', p. 464: 'The reader naturally assumes that the placement of books in close physical proximity implies that they are related in some way. Propinquity is taken as an indication that there is a significant connection between the books so conjoined. This readerly habit has formed the basis of this survey and analysis of the biblical order.'

68. Goswell, 'Order of New Testament', p. 225.

effect on biblical readers of the mere contextuality of the ordered material in the Old and New Testament.

The way Goswell describes the hermeneutical effect of contextuality has a parallel in literary theory to the concept of paratextuality.[69] Literary theorist (and structuralist) Gérard Genette has developed the notion of paratextuality at length.[70] Genette explains that a 'paratext' marks 'those elements which lie on the threshold of the text and which help to direct and control the reception of a text by its readers'.[71] A paratextual element is something that exists alongside of ('para') a text. In Genette's terms, 'the paratext consists...of all those things which we are never certain belong to the text of a work but which contribute to present—or 'presentify'—the text by making it into a book'.[72]

Elements such as title construction, cover design, front matter (prefaces, table of contents, etc.), promotional blurbs on the back cover, the size of the book, or even its typography all serve as 'paratextual elements which are designed to assist the reader in establishing what kind of text they are being presented with and how to read it'.[73] One of Genette's central insights

69. Goswell does not draw directly on Genette's theoretical development of paratextuality (he cites Genette in 'Order of Hebrew Bible', p. 673 n. 1), though he consistently describes the ordering of the biblical material as a 'paratextual feature' (e.g. 'Order of Hebrew Bible', pp. 673, 677, 679, 683, 688; 'Order of Greek Old Testament', p. 449; and 'Order of New Testament', pp. 225, 235, 241).

70. See Gérard Genette, *Paratexts: Thresholds of Interpretation* (trans. Jane E. Lewin; Cambridge: Cambridge University Press, 1997); Gérard Genette, 'Introduction to the Paratext', *New Literary History* 22 (1991), pp. 261-72; Gérard Genette, 'The Proustian Paratexte', *SubStance: A Review of Theory and Literary Criticism* 17 (1988), pp. 63-77; and Genette, *The Architext*, pp. 80-85. For critical interaction with Genette and/or his notion of paratext, see Maclean, 'Pretexts and Paratexts: The Art of the Peripheral', pp. 273-79; Georg Stanitzek, 'Texts and Paratexts in Media', *Critical Inquiry* 32 (2005), pp. 27-42; and Craig Dworkin, 'Textual Prostheses', *Comparative Literature* 57 (2005), pp. 1-24. For an application of paratextuality in a different intellectual sphere, see Susan Vanderborg, *Paratextual Communities: American Avant-Garde Poetry Since 1950* (Carbondale, IL: Southern Illinois University Press, 2002).

71. Allen, *Intertextuality*, p. 100; Genette, *Palimpsests*, pp. 1-3.

72. Genette, 'Proustian Paratexte', p. 63. Genette also states, 'By the word "paratext", I mean all of the marginal or supplementary data around the text. It comprises what one could call various thresholds: authorial and editorial (i.e. titles, insertions, dedications, epigraphs, prefaces and notes); media related (i.e. interviews with the author, official summaries) and private (i.e. correspondence, calculated or non-calculated disclosures), as well as those related to the material means of production and reception, such as groupings, segments, etc.' (p. 63). The paratext, in this sense, 'not only marks a zone of transition between text and non-text ("hors-texte"), but also a zone of transaction, a space that is essentially pragmatic and strategic' (p. 63).

73. Allen, *Intertextuality*, p. 101. Allen also notes that 'the paratext, for Genette, performs various functions which guide the text's readers and can be understood pragmat-

is that a 'text rarely appears in its naked state, without the reinforcement and accompaniment of a certain number of productions, themselves verbal or not'.[74] The realm of the paratext does not represent a 'limit or a sealed frontier' but rather a 'threshold' or a 'vestibule' which offers 'to anyone and everyone the possibility either of entering or of turning back'.[75] Observing that most texts go through some type of production process, Genette posits that 'one can probably suggest that there does not exist, and there never has existed, a text without paratext'.[76] What is more, these paratextual elements 'provide the text with a (variable) setting and sometimes a commentary, official or not, which even the purist among readers, those least inclined to external erudition, cannot always disregard as easily as they would like and as they claim to do'.[77]

In his theoretical framework for noting paratextual elements, Genette also addresses the inevitable questions swirling around the issue of intention. He makes a 'major distinction' in his analysis between 'authorial paratexts'

ically in terms of various simple questions, all concerned with the manner of the text's existence: when published? by whom? for what purpose? Such paratextual elements also help to establish the text's intentions: how it should be read, how it should not be read' (*Intertextuality*, p. 101). Genette develops these function questions in 'Introduction to the Paratext', pp. 263-65. He notes in this regard that 'these features essentially describe [the paratextual message's] spatial, temporal, substantial, pragmatic, and functional characteristics' (p. 263). In *Architext*, Genette discusses paratextuality in the context of a notion of 'textual transcendence', which he understands as 'everything that brings [the text] into relation (manifest or hidden) with other texts' (p. 81). He calls this 'textual transcendence' a form of transtextuality. Paratextuality, in this sense, is a subset of transtextuality. For Genette, paratextuality is 'transtextuality par excellence' (p. 82). He also includes in the notion of transtextuality 'that relationship of inclusion that links each text to the various types of discourse it belongs to' (p. 82). Regarding nomenclature, note Genette's reflective discussion of his development of these key terms in *Palimpsests*, pp. 1-7.

74. Genette, 'Introduction to the Paratext', p. 261. Among these 'accompaniments', Genette includes 'an author's name, a title, a preface, illustrations' (p. 261). Prior to his 'paratext' comments, Genette adumbrates his basic understanding of a text: 'The literary work consists, exhaustively or essentially, of a text, that is to say (a very minimal definition) in a more or less lengthy sequence of verbal utterances more or less containing meaning' (p. 261). Cf. Genette, *Palimpsests*, pp. 1-7.

75. Genette, 'Introduction to the Paratext', p. 261. Genette continues this image by stating that this threshold is like 'an "undecided zone" between the inside and the outside, itself without rigorous limits, either towards the interior (the text) or towards the exterior (the discourse of the world on the text), a border, or as Philippe Lejeune said, "the fringe of the printed text which, in reality, controls the whole reading"' (p. 261).

76. Genette, 'Introduction to the Paratext', p. 263. Genette also recognizes the obverse of his observation: 'Paradoxically, there do exist on the other hand, if only by accident, paratexts without text, since there exist, for example, disappeared or aborted works of which we only know the title' (p. 263).

77. Genette, *Palimpsests*, p. 3.

(generated by the original author) and 'allographic paratexts' (generated by someone other than the original author).[78] An authorial paratext might be the preface to a work by the author (i.e. 'the author's preface' or 'introduction'). An allographic paratext might be a critical introduction to a classic work by the editor of the book or the series in which the book is published.[79] The paratextual preface encourages the reader 'to read the text, and to instruct the reader how to read the text properly'.[80]

An example of the effect of paratextuality can be seen in the reception of a published work. The paratext, in Genette's understanding, is 'the means by which a text makes a book of itself and proposes itself as such to its readers, and more generally to the public'.[81] This paratextual feature of any published work has ramifications for its reception and perception. A self-published book is received much differently than a book in a modern scholarly series. Summarizing Genette's position at this point, Allen writes, 'we read such editions in a very different manner to the text's original readers and texts are radically transformed by the addition of these paratextual elements'.[82]

Though Genette works out his theoretical model of paratextuality within the field of literary studies, his basic categories can help nuance the way interpreters speak of the presence and nature of paratextual elements in the collection of biblical literature.[83] In the terms delineated above, the two main

78. See Allen, *Intertextuality*, p. 103. For the author-produced paratext, Genette uses both the term 'autographic' and 'authorial'. The term 'authorial' seems to articulate Genette's distinction here most pointedly.

79. On the notion of allographic paratexts, see Ursula Geitner, 'Allographie: Autorschaft und Paratext—im Fall der *Portugiesischen Briefe*', in *Paratexte in Literatur, Film, Fernsehen* (ed. Klaus Kreimeier and Georg Stanitzek; Berlin: Akademie Verlag, 2004), pp. 55-99. Cf. Stanitzek, 'Texts and Paratexts', pp. 41-42.

80. Allen, *Intertextuality*, p. 103. In 'Introduction to the Paratext', Genette explains, 'One does not always know if one should consider that [paratextual elements] belong to the text or not, but in any case they surround it and prolong it, precisely in order to *present* it, in the usual sense of this verb, but also in its strongest meaning: to *make it present*, to assure its presence in the world, its "reception" and its consumption, in the form, nowadays at least, of a book' (p. 261).

81. Genette, 'Introduction to the Paratext', p. 261. On this particular aspect of paratextuality, see Daisy Turrer, 'A Study on the Paratextual Space in Artists' Books', *Journal of Arts and Books* 29 (2011), pp. 27-31; and Jae Rossman, 'Reading Outside the Lines: Paratextual Analysis and Artists' Books', *Journal of Arts and Books* 23 (2008), pp. 30-41.

82. Allen, *Intertextuality*, p. 103.

83. Genette's discussion of the way paratextual elements form (e.g. the publication process) relates to the way the canon was formed, though there are important differences as well. For instance, there is a believing community involved in the composition, collection, and publication of the biblical literature. This emphasis on paratextuality also resonates with recent interest in the artifactual features of manuscripts and their

facets of studies in contextuality entail both the effect of simple literary juxtaposition ('mere contextuality') and also the effect of intentional paratextual elements (either authorial or allographic). Genette himself understands the paratextual elements to be closely tied to authorial intention. For Genette, a critical function of paratextuality is 'to ensure for the text a destiny consistent with the author's purpose'.[84] In this respect, 'the correctness of the authorial (and secondarily, of the publisher's) point of view is the implicit creed and spontaneous ideology of the paratext'.[85] The paratext

implications for historical reconstruction. In this sense, the artifactual features of a manuscript (e.g. dimensions, title, codex form, or handwriting) are paratextual elements that are rife with hermeneutical significance. Cf. the discussion of the 'Relevance of Manuscript Evidence' in Chapter 1. Though he does not use the 'paratextual' terminology, Barton comments on the hermeneutical effect of the 'typographical conventions' that are used in the modern publication of Bibles. He writes, 'The Bible in any of the forms it is encountered in the modern world gives out the strongest possible signals of unity, coherence, and closure. All the books have the same typography, the same style of translation, a consistent pagination, and a fixed order: features that arouse strong expectations that the contents will be a single "work"' (*Holy Writings, Sacred Text*, p. 151). These Bibles sell because their 'market' consists of a community that resonates with the commitments implied by these various paratextual elements. Barton also comments that in his perspective, 'one of the first and most obvious effects of historical criticism is that it disappoints all such expectations' (p. 151).

84. Genette, *Paratexts*, p. 407. See also Genette, 'Introduction to the Paratext', pp. 261-62: 'This fringe, in effect, always bearer of an authorial commentary either more or less legitimated by the author, constitutes, between the text and what lies outside of it, a zone not just of transition, but of *transaction*.' Drawing on speech act theory to articulate this aspect of the paratext, Maclean states that 'the paratext involves a series of first order illocutionary acts in which the author, the editor, or the prefacer are frequently using direct performatives. They are informing, persuading, advising, or indeed exhorting and commanding the reader' ('Pretexts and Paratexts', p. 274).

85. Genette, *Paratexts*, p. 408. For Genette, the 'more pertinent reading' is, naturally, the one more pertinent 'in the eyes of the author and his allies' ('Introduction to the Paratext', p. 262). He states more precisely that 'the definition of the paratext involves the necessity that someone should always be responsible for it, whether the author or one of his associates', though he does acknowledge that 'this necessity has various degrees' (p. 267). Allen notes also that this recognition of the importance of authorial intention puts Genette at odds with many sectors of both structuralist and poststructuralist 'theory and practice' (see *Intertextuality*, p. 104). For instance, see Stanitzek's pointed critique along these lines in 'Texts and Paratexts', pp. 34-40. Further, in their approaches to intertextuality, Julia Kristeva and Roland Barthes advocate an unlimited view of textuality that essentially precludes the role of the author (see the first part of Chapter 4). See also Hirsch's section on 'The Death of the Author' in the first chapter of *Validity*. On Genette's relation to his field, Marie-Rose Logan remarks that 'Genette has, like no other critic, managed to elaborate a reflection on critical discourse which incorporates a system, i.e. structuralism, without ever becoming entirely subservient to it' ('"Ut Figura Poiesis": The Work of Gérard Genette', in Gérard Genette, *Figures of Literary Discourse* [New York: Columbia University Press, 1982], p. vii).

is 'the place where the author displays intentions, where he or she speaks to the reader as sender to the receiver'.[86] These paratextual elements are 'hermeneutically privileged and powerful elements. They guide the reader's attention, influence how a text is read, and communicate such information as to give a texts its first contours, its manageable identity so to speak.'[87]

The notion of intention also highlights one of the differences between Sailhamer and Goswell's approaches to the study of contextuality. Goswell deliberately avoids any discussion of intentionality in his description of the paratextual feature of biblical ordering.[88] This allows him to examine the hermeneutical impact of the various biblical orders without having to account for whether or not this effect was intended by an author, editor, or community. Similarly, Sailhamer notes that a study of biblical contextuality does not necessarily address authorial intention. However, because of his compositional understanding of the canonization process, Sailhamer is also quick to discern an author's hand at work in the broader shaping of the

---

86. Maclean, 'Pretexts and Paratexts', p. 278. Maclean also clarifies that 'whether this message is successful or unsuccessful, honest or dishonest, does not affect the illocutionary status of the speech acts involved' (p. 278). Maclean touches on the prevailing question in literary studies as to whether or not an author can successful direct readers: 'The question is whether the author can successfully propose *the smaller, controlled strategies of the paratext as a model for the reading of the text as a whole* or only be "a caressing prefacer, stifling his reader, as a lover sometimes does a coy mistress, into silence"' (p. 278, emphasis added). For Maclean, then, 'the gap between intention and practice, between naming and performing, is also the sphere of the art of the peripheral' (p. 278).

87. Stanitzek, 'Texts and Paratexts', p. 32. Stanitzek notes that in this sense, paratexts function as 'indicators to be aimed for, as structures of literary expectations' (p. 32). Clarifying the import of Genette's point, Stanitzek says, 'When Genette describes paratexts as "accompanying productions" as opposed to the actual text, he does not mean that they are exceptional elements separate from the texts; to see them in such a role—often thought to be a typical poststructuralist interpretation—would be to misunderstand what Genette is saying' (p. 32).

88. This avoidance of the issue of intention is Koorevaar's primary contention with Goswell's approach: 'Goswell consciously excluded questions related to the history of the order of books in his article, and yet this matter is unavoidable' ('Torah Model', p. 64). Koorevar explains that 'if a particular order has a beautiful reading effect, but originated at a later date, then it is a later invention, after all. On the one hand, there has been a certain freedom in changing the existing order based on later insights and needs, but that does not change the fact that the earlier order was different, with a different effect on reading' (p. 64). These observations highlight for Koorevar the most pressing question, namely, whether or not 'there was ever such a thing as a first or original order, and if so, did this order have a clear reading objective or even a theological objective or did it not?' (p. 64). In the terms of the present study, these varying interpretive goals are not necessarily at odds. The major difference is that Koorevar focuses on *meant* contextuality and Goswell on *mere* contextuality.

biblical material.[89] As noted above, Genette also tends to connect paratextual elements to authorial intention. The diversity noted here notwithstanding, the basic insight that these scholars highlight about the meaningful effect that a broader literary context has on a particular individual writing is instructive. The categories that they articulate and develop also contribute to a nuanced understanding of the nature of biblical contextuality.

Meant Contextuality

On one hand, a study of contextuality that restricts itself to analyzing the effect that the broader context of the biblical collection has on an individual writing without recourse to intention (i.e. mere contextuality) has been solidly established by the scholars noted above and can bear hermeneutical fruit. On the other hand, the concept of canonical shaping, and canon-consciousness in particular, seems to allow for the possibility of an intended contextuality. This analysis moves from 'mere contextuality' to 'meant contextuality'. Indeed, the presence of a particular writing in a collected group of writings demonstrates that someone has *already* deemed the works to be connected in some way.[90] The presence of clear groupings (for which there

89. Chapman takes issue with this particular element of Sailhamer's understanding of the canon formation process (see 'Reclaiming Inspiration for the Bible', pp. 195-96). Chapman highlights the need to account for the 'canonical context' but denies that this context was generated by a particular author's intention. For instance, he writes that 'despite Sailhamer's strong effort to produce a "text-centered" Old Testament theology, he still maintains that the Pentateuch has one "composer" or "author"' and that 'a single individual was responsible for the final arrangement and organization of the Old Testament canon' (p. 195 n. 123). For the type of comment Chapman finds problematic, see Sailhamer, *Meaning of the Pentateuch*, pp. 50-52, 200-206. Despite this disagreement, Chapman still recognizes the value of Sailhamer's basic hermeneutical position ('No one in evangelical scholarship perceived as early or as perceptively as John Sailhamer how increased awareness of the biblical canon might helpfully reorient evangelical hermeneutics, especially in its thinking about history', p. 182).

90. Cf. Barton, *Holy Writings, Sacred Text*, p. 34: 'Collecting books together is potentially an interpretive process.' See also Chapter 2's discussion of intentional 'groupings'. In this regard, Jordan M. Scheetz speaks of 'the reality that certain texts have been intentionally placed together' (*The Concept of Canonical Intertextuality and the Book of Daniel* [Eugene, OR: Pickwick Publications, 2011], p. 32). In his study of canonical intertextuality and the book of Daniel, 'canonical' entails both 'a particular collection of literature' and also 'the fact that this literature has been *intentionally* placed together' (p. 33). Reflecting on this issue, Bockmuehl observes that 'the implied reader of the New Testament *as a whole* seems indeed to take the point of view that sees in the canonical side-by-side of authoritative but individualy disparate or even contradictory documents a purposeful montage or kaleidoscope of meaning. That is to say, the very fact of a biblical canon comes to represent an implicit invitation to an interpretive synthesis, to look for what is in common amid the all-too-evident tension and diversity—between the four Gospels, between James and Paul, between the New Testament and the Old, and so forth' (*Seeing the Word*, pp. 70-71).

is considerable historical evidence) indicates that during the composition and formation of the biblical corpora, specific associative moves were made whereby certain writings migrated toward one another.[91] As discussed (and argued for) in Chapters 1 and 2, there is plausible internal and external evidence that those making these associations were following the signposts and guidance of the biblical authors themselves (either directly in person or through their writings). In some cases, at least, the order of reading itself represents an interpretive move.[92] To give a standard example, the position of the Law and the Gospels at the beginning of the Old Testament/Hebrew Bible and New Testament, respectively, indicates their perceived foundational role.[93]

When engaging in a study of the contextuality present in the biblical canon, there is a 'canonical impulse' or a 'canonical pressure' put on the interpreter to begin thinking in terms of 'meant contextuality' rather than simply 'mere contextuality'. This interpretive tension can be seen in Bockmuehl's brief account of the New Testament's 'range of implied readings'.[94] After quickly surveying and describing a few elements of the shape of the New Testament, Bockmuehl acknowledges that 'taken by themselves, such observations are of course highly problematic and could easily incur the charge of anachronistic and almost superstitious biblicism'.[95] The reason for this caution is because 'the final shape of the canon was gradually consolidated over several centuries, and surface observations of this kind therefore necessarily part company with a "genetic" line of thought that would want to limit the meaning of texts to that which they had in their originally

91. Cf. Wall's comment regarding the formation of the Pauline corpus: 'At that moment when the canonizing, catholicizing community combined its two discrete Pauline corpora, ten-letter and three-letter, whatever the historical circumstance, it recognized that the Pauline witness was made complete at that moment and would no longer circulate among the congregations in any fraction of its earlier versions.' He also adds that 'the Pauline lists from an early period of Scripture's canonization would seem on balance to support this conclusion' ('Function of the Pastoral Letters', p. 36).

92. Cf. Goswell, 'Order of the Books of the New Testament', p. 235, who understands 'the character of paratext as (uninspired) commentary on the text'.

93. See the discussion below.

94. See the third chapter of *Seeing the Word*.

95. Bockmuehl, *Seeing the Word*, p. 111. Similarly, Barton argues that 'reading interpretive significance into the joins *between* the sections [in the New Testament] is thus particularly hazardous, as is the attempt to find a thematic unity in the whole Hebrew Bible or even the whole Christian Bible' (*Holy Writings, Sacred Text*, p. 150). Whereas Bockmuehl makes this caution, he nevertheless draws out the hermeneutical implications of the shape of the biblical material. For Barton, on the other hand, 'certainly it is wise to avoid asking about the "intentions" of the final redactors, and better to allow for a great deal of accident and chance in the process that gave us these collections' (*Holy Writings, Sacred Text*, p. 150).

disparate historical settings'.[96] Bockmuehl thus recognizes that many interpreters will eye holistic comments about the shape of the New Testament
with suspicion.

However, Bockmeuhl is quick to respond by arguing that 'the notion of
a canon is not just a contrived fourth-century clampdown by authoritarian
churchmen'.[97] Indeed, 'the issue of *unity* in the midst of complex diversity
is already strongly implicit in many of the individual documents in the New
Testament'.[98] 'What is more', Bockmuehl continues, 'in certain respects
the canon of the New Testament *itself* manifests a striking and by no means
incidental interrelation of form and content'.[99] He concludes his discussion
by noting strongly:

> Regardless of how *successful* one judges the collection of New Testament
> books to be in uniting around an identifiable common vision of truth, there
> is little question that both authors and framers of the canon *intended and
> expected* the individual texts and the collection to be understood in this fash-
> ion. The differences between the authors are indeed highly instructive for
> understanding both the historical origins and the present contours of Scrip-
> ture. But the fact is that New Testament interpretation can disregard the *inte-
> grating vision* in the texts only on the explicit assumption that the apostolic
> project has in fact failed.[100]

Further, if the notion of 'shape' is allowed to connect with meaning and
intention, one might speak of 'canonical intentionality', or the effect that
the shape of the overall collection is meant to evoke.[101] The concept of contextuality is 'an important component of a consideration of the semantics of
the shape of the Canon'.[102] The shape of the broader canonical collection is

96. Bockmeuhl, *Seeing the Word*, p. 111.

97. Bockmuehl, *Seeing the Word*, p. 111.

98. Bockmuehl, *Seeing the Word*, p. 111.

99. Bockmeuhl, *Seeing the Word*, p. 111. At this point, Bockmeuhl cites Trobisch's
work in *First Edition of the New Testament* and *Paul's Letter Collection*.

100. Bockmeuhl, *Seeing the Word*, p. 113.

101. Cf. Frei, *Eclipse of Biblical Narrative*, p. 11: 'Meaning and narrative shape bear
significantly on each other.' Sailhamer suggests that 'we must raise the question of the
specific shape of the OT Scriptures at the time of their formation as such and ask if that
shape reflects a consistent line of interpretation. Is there an "intelligent design" or purpose reflected in the final shape of the OT Scriptures as a whole? If so, what is the sense
of that design? Does the shape of the OT (Tanak) play into the shape and meaning of
the various parts of OT books such as the Pentateuch? Is there a meaningful design and
shape to the OT Scriptures?' (*Meaning of the Pentateuch*, p. 210).

102. Sailhamer, *Introduction*, p. 250. From a different angle, Robert W. Wall notes that
'while the interpreter should not place too much importance on the order of writings
within the New Testament, such a perspective does allow one to construct what Albert
Outler has called an overarching "canon-logic" that provides [an] added dimension of
meaning to the whole New Testament and to individual compositions within it. Stated

formed by the various groupings of the individual sections and also strategic texts that connect these corpora. Because there is viable historical evidence that the broad contours of these groupings was intended by those composing and gathering this material, there is (at least indirectly) evidence that the overall shape of the canonical context was intended (i.e. *meant* contextuality). This type of investigation seeks to discern and examine the intended paratextual features of the biblical collection.[103]

Regarding the identification of particular authors, it is possible that the ones responsible for shaping the biblical canon as a whole were also included in the group of traditionally recognized biblical writers. For example, it is possible that the Chronicler had a hand in shaping the Hebrew Bible and that the Apostle John played a similar role in the shaping of the New Testament canon.[104] Though identifying these authors (editors/redactors) is important, the value of noting the hermeneutical payoff of their compositional work is not diminished if they remain anonymous.[105]

The Shape of the Hebrew Bible. Concerning the Hebrew Bible, it is significant that the early church did not re-edit and dismantle the biblical

---

another way, the final shape of the New Testament reflects a "canonical grammar" that gives coherence to the New Testament message and purposes to aid the faith community in determining how it should use this biblical message to nurture its Christian worship and witness. The order of the different parts or units of the New Testament (Gospel, Acts, Pauline and non-Pauline Letters, Revelation) embeds a specific "grammar" that assigns a specific function to each successive unit of the whole New Testament. By following the implicit rules of this New Testament grammar, the interpreter is better able to make a meaning of a particular text or collection of texts that corresponds with the Bible's canonical role' ('The Apocalypse of the New Testament in Canonical Context', in *The New Testament as Canon: A Reader in Canonical Criticism* [ed. Robert W. Wall and Eugene E. Lemcio; Sheffield: Sheffield Academic Press, 1992], pp. 279-80).

103. On the study of intended paratextual elements, Koorevar reflects, 'it concerns text, actual text, that consists of words and belongs to a particular book, yet at the same time, this text was introduced for paratextual purposes: the formation of a block and sequential order... This relates to paratextual texts that have a double value. Because of them, the sequential order and subdivisions belong to the text of the canon itself and are of primary importance' ('Torah Model', p. 66).

104. Though these suggestions are perhaps tantalizing, they cannot be pursued within the scope of this study and are in some ways beside the point being made in this section on contextuality.

105. For instance, it might be interesting or fruitful to identify the individual who composed Deut. 34 as a conclusion to the Pentateuch. The chapter describes Moses' death (Deut. 34.5-12), so many have concluded that someone other than Moses recorded this particular portion of the text. Moses himself might have written it proleptically, Joshua might have written it to complete the 'Law' (suggested by *Baba Bathra* 14b-15a), or another prophet could have added this account on the basis of handed-down prophetic tradition. Important as this question is, it does not alter the function that Deut. 34 serves as a fitting conclusion to the narrative of Moses' life and the Pentateuch as a whole.

books.[106] Instead, they allowed the Old Testament to stand as a discrete witness. On a basic level, this preservation demonstrates that the early church recognized the importance of that Testament's overall shape. This observation seems to apply even with the variations present in the Septuagint (LXX). Though there is significant reordering, the shape of the corpora remain relatively stable. For instance, the Law is the same, and though they have been separated, the ordering within the Former and Latter Prophets is largely consistent.[107]

---

106. Cf. Sailhamer's observation that 'in due time, the early church produced its own NT rather than an "edited" version of the OT such as we find among the Dead Sea pesher scrolls. They left the OT intact as their "New Testament Scriptures", not changing anything. They simply added the NT to it as a continuation, not a replacement' (*Meaning of the Pentateuch*, p. 607). Chapman, 'The Canon Debate', p. 283, makes a similar point: 'Remarkably, however, neither faith tradition submitted Israel's ancient Scripture to a thoroughgoing revision but instead added new material, in different ways, onto the old.' For Chapman, this 'broad scale absence of revision again implies the recognition of some type of canonical authority, an authority reinforced rather than diminished by these patterns of canonical growth'. Childs, *Biblical Theology*, p. 75, also highlights the hermeneutical import of this historical reality: 'A most striking feature in the juxtaposition of the two testaments is actually the lack of Christian redactional activity on the Old Testament.' For Childs, this preservation suggests that 'the collection of Jewish scriptures was envisioned as closed and a new and different collection began which in time evolved into the New Testament'. Though the stability of the Old Testament collection among Christian communities is significant, not everyone agrees on the nature of this significance. In this regard, note the contrasting perspective of Aichele, *Control of Biblical Meaning*, pp. 30-35. Aichele argues that 'the relation between the two Christian canons is not a tranquil one. The "echoes" of scripture between the canons are not peaceful reverberations or natural metamorphoses of some prior intrinsic meaning. Instead they are monstrous distortions, skewed rewritings of the other text' (p. 34). For Aichele, this rewriting happens even if the shape of the Old Testament canon remains the same, as the 'whole' is assigned a new referent (i.e. Christ) that transmogrifies its meaning at a fundamental level.

107. Cf. J. Ross Wagner, 'The Septuagint and the "Search for the Christian Bible"', in *Scripture's Doctrine and Theology's Bible: How the New Testament Shapes Christian Dogmatics* (ed. Markus Bockmuehl and Alan J. Torrance; Grand Rapids, MI: Baker, 2008), pp. 17-28. Wagner argues that the LXX does not represent a rival entity to the Hebrew text. Rather, the various Greek translations exhibit a close relation to the Hebrew textual tradition (oftentimes the MT). Regarding the tension between the Hebrew Text and a putatively 'wider' LXX text, Wagner states that 'although the outer limits of the canon remain somewhat nebulous in the early Christian period, the New Testament authors appeal through their citations and retellings of the biblical narratives to a core set of Scriptures that includes a majority of the books of the present Hebrew canon' (pp. 22-23). See also the 'exkurs' by Thomas Hieke and Tobias Nicklas on what they label 'der sogenannte' Septuagint-canon in *'Die Worte der Prophetie dieses Buches' Offenbarung 22,6-21 als Schlussstein der Christlichen Bibel Alten und Neuen Testaments Gelesen* (Neukirchen–Vluyn, DE: Neukirchener, 2003), pp. 113-24. Cf. Seitz's discussion of

As the Hebrew Bible forms, the groupings of Law, Prophets, and Writings become an overarching framework by which to order the biblical material.[108] Undergirding this overall shape is a clear narrative impulse. The Law begins the narrative account of God's dealing with the world in general (Genesis 1–11) and Israel in particular (Genesis 12–50). Following the Pentateuch, the Prophets continue this narrative. The books of Joshua through Kings provide the prophetic narration and interpretation of the history of the nation of Israel.[109] This prophetic historiography becomes the lens through which subsequent biblical authors view the events of Israel's past and their relation to the future.[110]

The writings of the latter prophets of Isaiah, Jeremiah, Ezekiel, and the Twelve are situated within this prophetic history.[111] Many of the Writings,

the Hebrew and Greek canons in 'Canonical Approach and Theological Interpretation', pp. 90-96; and Lust, 'Septuagint and Canon', pp. 39-55. Lust concludes that 'there is no evidence of an Alexandrian Canon as opposed to a Palestinian Canon' and that 'the preserved data do not allow us to draw the conclusion that the Jewish communities in Egypt recognized a larger Canon than MT, comprising more biblical books in a different order' (p. 55). Cf. Brandt's comprehensive study of the diverse 'engestalten des Kanons' in Jewish and Christian historical communities in *Endgestalten des Kanons*, pp. 43-405.

108. See Stephen G. Dempster, 'Torah, Torah, Torah: The Emergence of the Tripartite Canon', in *Exploring the Origins of the Bible: Canon Formation in Historical, Literary, and Theological Perspective* (ed. Craig Evans and Emanuel Tov; Grand Rapids, MI: Baker, 2008), pp. 87-128. For a contrasting perspective, see Julio C.T. Barrera, 'Origins of a Tripartite Canon', in *The Canon Debate*, pp. 128-45.

109. Cf. Alexander, *Paradise to Promised Land*, p. 84: 'As they stand, the books of Genesis to Kings form a continuous narrative. This is apparent from both the overall picture provided and the way in which individual books are linked. Viewed as a whole, Genesis to Kings records selected events from the creation of the earth to the demise of the Davidic monarchy at the time of the Babylonian exile… Whatever the prior oral and/ or literary history of the individual books, it is obvious that they have been deliberately linked to form a continuous narrative.' Alexander also argues that 'by linking the books of Genesis to Kings, the final editor of this material produced an important metanarrative that provides a unique perspective on God's dealing with humanity. This ancient metanarrative not only recounts events that have taken place; it also significantly offers an authoritative explanation of them' (p. 110).

110. Cf. Shepherd, *Textual World*, pp. 5-14. For Shepherd, 'the constant reuse of a very familiar sequence of events to depict the past, present, and future is what makes the very fabric of biblical historiography and prophecy. The biblical authors depend upon their readers' knowledge of the narrative sequence from Genesis–Kings when they describe events in their own day or cast images of the future' (p. 5). To give one of Shepherd's many examples of this compositional technique, he observes that the creation narrative is used to describe Israel's past (Gen. 1–2), present (Gen. 8–9), and future (Isa. 65.17; 66.22).

111. For a thorough analysis of the way these interconnections actually work, see Stephen B. Chapman, *The Law and the Prophets: A Study in Old Testament Canon Formation* (Tübingen: Mohr Siebeck, 2000). Christopher R. Seitz does a similar study on the

then, provide reflection and commentary on significant events in the narrated history found in the Law and Prophets.[112] After this structural 'pause', the book of Chronicles picks up the narrative thread again and provides a panoramic recapitulation of the biblical narrative and draws out the implications of Israel's exile and return. Viewed as a unit, the Hebrew Bible 'encompasses the whole of its contents in a single narrative history that extends from creation to the return from exile'.[113] This macrostructural framework encourages readers to recognize that the Hebrew Bible represents a cohesive and interconnected history and interpretation of God's dealing with Israel.[114]

Within this overarching shape, the groups of writings that were initially conceived as a gathered corpus serve as a significant example of intended contextuality in the formation of the Hebrew Bible. As Sailhamer argues, 'the evident rationality behind the major divisions of the OT Canon, as well as that which lies behind the selection of books within each section, strongly suggests that the order of the books within the sections of the Canon is also intentional'. If this is the case, 'then some degree of montage or contextuality was at work in the process'.[115]

book of the Twelve in *The Goodly Fellowship of the Prophets: The Achievement of Association in Canon Formation* (Grand Rapids, MI: Baker, 2009).

112. Dempster, *Dominion and Dynasty*, sees this type of function for the Law, Prophets, and Writings in the overall shape of the Hebrew Bible. Cf. Karl Barth, *Church Dogmatics* (vol. I/2; London: Continuum, 2004), §19, p. 485: 'Among the older Protestant theologians there were some…who argued that when the prophets were added to the Law, which alone constituted Holy Scripture in the first instance, they did not make it more complete as such, i.e. as the Word of God, but as the expounding and confirming of the first witness by a second they made it clearer.' Luther, too, argues that the prophets 'based all their preaching of the important articles of the faith in Christ upon Moses' (Martin Luther, 'The Sermon the Risen Christ Preached to his Disciples', in *The Complete Sermons of Martin Luther* [vol. I/2; Grand Rapids, MI: Baker, 2000], p. 296). Making a similar connection, Luther argues that from the *proto-evangelium* in Gen. 3.15, 'an entire New Testament springs forth' (p. 297).

113. Cf. Sailhamer, *Introduction*, p. 250. Regarding the shape of Hebrew Bible, Koorevaar, 'The Torah Model', p. 79, suggests that an 'exile and return model' is a better structural fit than the 'Torah model'.

114. Stephen B. Chapman, 'What Are We Reading? Canonicity and the Old Testament', *Word & World* 29 (2009), pp. 334-47 (344), argues that 'the Old Testament, much more than has previously been appreciated, was produced as an internally cohesive and self-relating compositional unity'. Cf. Julius Steinberg, *Die Ketuvim: Ihr Aufbau und Ihre Botschaft* (Hamburg: Philo, 2006), p. 7: 'Die Makrostruktur des Hebräischen Bibelkanons ist hermeneutisch signifikant. Mit dem Ort eines jeden Buches im literarischen Gesamtgefüge weist sie diesem auch seinen Ort im theologischen Gesamtgefüge zu.'

115. Sailhamer, *Introduction*, p. 250. Sailhamer is quick, however, to include the reminder that 'con-textuality, like montage, is present with or without intentionality' (p. 250 n. 143).

For instance, among the Prophets, the book of the Twelve forms a coherent unit. Not only do these twelve prophetic books consistently appear together in the earliest manuscripts, internal analysis suggests that some of the books may have been composed and conceived with the others in view.[116] Further, within the Twelve, there is a presumed internal chronology that situates even the books that lack chronological indicators. For example, 'the fact that the book of Malachi is almost universally taken as the work of a postexilic prophet, when in fact there is no statement to that effect in the book itself, is strong evidence for the semantic effect of con-textuality'.[117]

Another possible example occurs within the Writings corpus. The book of Chronicles might have also been consciously written for the specific purpose of concluding the Hebrew Bible.[118] In this scenario, 'the dislocation of Chronicles at the end of the Hebrew canon may well be an intentional move in order to render an exilic perspective normative for the life of faith'.[119] If these case studies are legitimate, then at least some of the Old Testament authors wrote their texts with a specific purpose and canonical function in mind. These two examples are surveyed here to demonstrate the overall point. Other examples could also be pursued. For example, the individual Psalms in the book of Psalms have widely divergent dates of composition. However, at some point in Israel's history they were intentionally collected

116. See the discussion of the Minor Prophets as the book of the Twelve in Chapter 2. Cf. Mark E. Biddle, 'Obadiah-Jonah-Micah in Canonical Context: The Nature of Prophetic Literature and Hermeneutics', *Interpretation* 61 (2007), pp. 154-66.

117. Sailhamer, *Introduction*, p. 250.

118. Georg Steins suggests this role for the book of Chronicles in *Die Chronik als kanonisches Abschlussphänomen: Studien zur Entstehung and Theologie von 1/2 Chronik* (Beltz: Athenäum Verlag, 1995). Steins understands the book of Chronicles as a 'canonical closure phenomenon'. An important subsequent work on this subject is Hendrik J. Koorevaar, 'Die Chronik als intendierter Abschluß des alttestamentlichen Kanons', *Jahrbuch für Evangelikale Theologie* 11 (1997), pp. 42-76. Cf. Koorevaar, 'The Torah Model', p. 79: 'The book of Chronicles as a closure phenomenon at the end of the whole canon does show that the idea of a total functional canon must have been held by those involved in the finalisation.' Koorevar suggests that the author of the book of Chronicles was also the author of the Tanak as a whole. According to him, the primary purpose of the Chronicler in writing was 'eine Zusammenfassung und Bündelung der Botschaft des Alten Testamentes zu geben, um damit die Sammlung heiliger Schriften in einem Kanon abzuschließen und zu versiegeln' ('Chronik als intendierter Abschluß', p. 60). If this is the case, the final redactor of the shape of the Hebrew Bible would be one of its authors. Based largely on the minimal manuscript evidence (and heavily weighting LXX orderings), R.L. Harris argues against this closing function for the book of Chronicles in 'Chronicles and the Canon in New Testament Times', *JETS* 33 (1990), pp. 75-85.

119. Chapman, 'What Are We Reading', p. 344. Cf. John Sailhamer, *First and Second Chronicles* (Chicago: Moody Press, 1983), p. 9: 'The writer's purpose was not simply to retell these events but to explain and expound on their meaning in Israel's history... First and Second Chronicles may then be a commentary on the historical books.'

not only for the purpose of liturgical use but also for inclusion in the canon of Scriptures.[120]

The Shape of the New Testament. The New Testament also appears to bear marks of intelligent design. As the New Testament documents were written and collected, they quickly began circulating in groupings.[121] As these groupings form, they begin to be seen in light of each other.[122] The end result of this process is the shape of the New Testament. As will be discussed below, in this way, 'the shape of the New Testament itself [outlines] an implied interpretation of its own theology'.[123] This narrative framework generated by the shape of the New Testament's major corpora guide readers as they access its individual textual elements. As Bockmeuhl argues, 'Even the macrostructure of the New Testament canon can be seen to give important pointers to its implied meaning as a received whole.'[124] The corpora of

120. For a sampling of this type of reflection on the book of Psalms, see Gerald H. Wilson, 'Psalms and Psalter', in *Biblical Theology: Retrospect and Prospect* (ed. Scott J. Hafemann; Downers Grove, IL: IVP, 2002), pp. 100-10; Waltke, 'Canonical Process Approach to the Psalms', pp. 3-18; Childs, 'Reflections on the Modern Study of the Psalms', pp. 377-88; Erich Zenger, 'Der Psalter im Horizont von Tora und Prophetie. Kanonsgeschichtliche und kanonhermeneutische Perspecktiven', in *The Biblical Canons* (ed. J.M. Auwers and H.J. de Jonge (Leuven: Leuven University Press, 2003), pp. 111-34; and Susanne Gillmayr-Bucher, 'The Psalm Headings: A Canonical Reflecture of the Psalms', in *The Biblical Canons*, pp. 247-54. The book of Proverbs is an analogous example to the Psalter.

121. See the discussion of the formation of the New Testament in Chapter 2. Hill, *Who Chose the Gospels*, pp. 115-19, outlines the logistical steps taken in the gradual process of transferring biblical books (e.g. a Gospel) from scrolls to composite codices (e.g. the Gospels). Hill notes the implication involved in binding two separate books together in this form: 'You make a statement that, in *some* sense, these books belong together, and others don't belong' (p. 116). Cf. the similar judgment of Charles H. Scobie, 'A Canonical Approach to Interpreting Luke', in *Reading Luke: Interpretation, Reflection, Formation* (ed. Craig Bartholomew, *et al.*; Grand Rapids, MI: Zondervan, 2005), pp. 329-31.

122. Cf. the treatment of canonization in Chapter 2. For a brief overview of this process, see Bruce, *Canon of Scripture*, pp. 117-33. Kurt Aland and Barbara Aland, *The Text of the New Testament* (Grand Rapids, MI: Eerdmans, 1987), pp. 48-71, survey this same period with a focus on the transmission of the Greek manuscripts of the New Testament documents. Most scholars agree that the Gospel collection and the Pauline Epistles were the earliest corpora to be established.

123. Bockmuehl, *Seeing the Word*, p. 103. Bockmeuhl argues that 'there is in fact a strong case that the New Testament text itself begs to be read *systematically*, whether as a canonical whole or in its constituent parts' (p. 108). For him, the concern for a coherent unity within diversity is 'something to which the New Testament *itself* points as its implied reading' (p. 108). In addition to projecting a certain type of *reader*, 'the shape of its own text elicits at least the outline of a certain kind of *reading*' (p. 108).

124. Bockmeuhl, *Seeing the Word*, pp. 108-109.

Gospels, Acts/General Epistles, Paul's Letters, and Revelation can serve as the bedrock of the shape of this 'received whole'. Trobisch observes that 'many modern readers of the Bible have lost the feeling for the four literary units of the New Testament'.[125] Regaining a canon-conscious reading of the New Testament will take into account the effect that these literary units have on the reading process.

A benefit of using the literary corpora as a guide in discerning the New Testament's overall shape is the relative stability of these groupings. There is clearly some diversity in the manuscript traditions and in the later lists of the New Testament writings. There are alternate orders of both the major groupings and also the writings within these groupings. However, despite this real diversity, there remain discernible patterns in the way manuscripts were gathered, collected, and published.[126] The outline of the shape of the New Testament that follows is one possible way of describing the narrative that is generated by these writings. Alternative orderings would impact some elements of this overall picture. For instance, whether Acts is placed prior to the letters of Paul or prior to the General Epistles will affect the reading sequence.[127] Or whether the book of Hebrews is placed in the middle of the Pauline letters or at the end of the Pauline corpus will impact the way one encounters these writings within the collection.[128] Taking these variations into account does not mean, however, that an overarching framework

125. Trobisch, *Paul's Letter Collection*, p. 9.

126. To give an example, each of the four early Greek codex manuscripts begins with the four-fold Gospel corpus. Also, when Revelation is present, it comes at the end of the collection. Due to corruption, Vaticanus ends with Hebrews. Thus, it is theoretically possible it included Revelation toward the end at one point. In Sinaiticus, Alexandrinus, and Ephraemi Rescripti, Revelation appears at the end. In Sinaiticus, *Barnabas* and the *Shepherd* follow Revelation, and in Alexandrinus, Revelation is followed by *1–2 Clement*. On the nature of these types of patterns in the manuscript evidence, see the discussion in the 'Canon-Conscious Indications during Canonization' section in Chapter 2 and the manuscript lists in Appendix 1.

127. On the canonical function of Acts, see in particular Robert W. Wall, 'The Acts of the Apostles in Canonical Context', in *The New Testament as Canon: A Reader in Canonical Criticism* (ed. Robert W. Wall and E. Eugene Lemcio; Sheffield: Sheffield Academic Press, 1992), pp. 110-32. Wall argues that 'Acts is positioned between the Gospel and the Letter not only to link the two together in a "canonical conversation", but as a commentary on each' (p. 113). Cf. David E. Smith, *The Canonical Function of Acts: A Comparative Analysis* (Collegeville, MN: The Liturgical Press, 2002), pp. 14-34; and Childs, *New Testament as Canon*, pp. 234-40.

128. On the position of Hebrews in the manuscripts, see William H.P. Hatch, 'The Position of Hebrews in the Canon of the New Testament', *HTR* 29 (1936), pp. 133-51. For a recent treatment, see Childs, *Church's Guide for Reading Paul*, pp. 237-52. In this section, Childs also discusses the canonical location of the book of Acts and interacts with Wall's arguments (see n. 127, above).

cannot be discerned in the larger groupings. As will be discussed in the following outline, the broad framework provided by the major New Testament corpora is meaningful even in the light of minor variations in ordering. In sum, the reading that follows is one particular way of describing the structure and narrative shape of the New Testament based on patterns found in the early manuscript traditions.[129]

One historical observation that increases the probability that the shape of the New Testament canon is not a result of pure happenstance is that this type of literary collection was not necessarily an obvious development in the Christian community. Harnack in particular highlights this historical scenario and notes that a canon of New Testament documents was not the only option available at the time.[130] The shape of the New Testament, in other words, was not a foregone conclusion. There were other possibilities that could very well have materialized.

For instance, the church could have been content with the Old Testament Scriptures alone. They could also have reconfigured and enhanced the Old Testament canon with Christological additions and interpolations. Or they could simply have neglected the Old Testament and focused solely on the Gospels.[131] An additional option was a collection of the sayings of Jesus, or a type of concordance of prophesies that were fulfilled in New Testament times.[132] For Harnack, any of these possible options would have been understandable and even fitting. The one option that was, in Harnack's mind, most unlikely is what actually materialized, namely, a 'second authoritative collection'.[133] Consequently, a historian of the canon must ask how this col-

---

129. Further, a given interpreter/reader might still recognize the hermeneutical effect that a particular ordering or narrative shape has (mere contextuality) without necessarily ascribing intentionality to it (meant contextuality). Indeed, whether the origin of an ordering is arbitrary or the result of an intentional shaping, the hermeneutical effect on the reader is still a factor that is relevant to the interpretive task. Recognizing this distinction can also serve to provide common ground between proponents of divergent understandings of the history of the canon formation process. Additionally, a reader who is aware of the overall shape of the New Testament collection will be well equipped to account for the various orders on offer in the history of the canon.

130. See Harnack, *Origin of the New Testament*, pp. 1-41.

131. Ignatius expresses a form of this particular sentiment when he says, 'I believe nothing that I do not find in the Gospel' (Harnack's translation). See Ignatius, 'Epistle to the Philadelphians', in *ANF* 1.84. In the same letter, Ignatius also declares, 'I say that my archives are Jesus Christ, to disobey whom is manifest destruction. My authentic archives are His cross, and death, and resurrection, and the faith which bears on these things' (1.84).

132. Harnack notes that an authoritative collection of sayings very 'nearly happened' (*Origin of the New Testament*, p. 8 n. 3).

133. Harnack, *Origin of the New Testament*, p. 5: 'But we should have been absolutely unprepared for that which actually happened—a second authoritative collection.'

lection formed when the initial odds were not in its favor. That there were other viable options on offer forefronts the question of intention. Was the particular shape of the collection chosen (either directly or indirectly) as a better option than the alternatives? Further, the contemporary interpreter must grapple with the historical fact that the form and shape of the New Testament material has (in the past and present) an effect on its readers.

As the groupings come to be arranged, a distinct narrative thrust runs throughout the documents.[134] As is the case with the Old Testament, one might argue that the overarching shape of the New Testament canon generates a sufficient narrative framework in which to present its unified, coherent message.[135] Viewed as a whole, the narrative elements of the New Testament represent the continuation and complement of the narrative storyline

---

134. Cf. George E. Ladd's sketch of salvation history (*Heilsgeschichte*) in *A Theology of the New Testament* (Grand Rapids, MI: Eerdmans, 1993), p. 23: 'The Gospels record the works and words of Jesus; the Acts relates the establishment and extension of the movement set up by Jesus' ministry; the epistles explicate further the meaning of Jesus' redemptive mission; and the Revelation outlines the consummation of the redemptive work of Christ for the world and human history, which is made possible because of what he has done in history.' Ladd's point might be strengthened by noting more directly that this redemptive-historical narrative is generated by (or at least reflected in) the shape of the New Testament canon itself. In other words, readers only know that this is in fact the *heilsgeshichte* because of the narrative elements of the New Testament texts. As Ladd himself notes, 'God did not act in history in such a way that historical events were eloquent in and of themselves', but rather 'historical events are revelatory *only when they are accompanied by the revelatory word*' (p. 25). In much of the Bible, this 'revelatory word' takes the form of realistic narrative that supplies its overall shape.

135. Cf. Thomas R. Schreiner's 'defense of a thematic approach' to New Testament theology in *New Testament Theology: Magnifying God in Christ* (Grand Rapids, MI: Baker, 2008), pp. 9-13. Schreiner argues that a thematic approach is necessary in order to see an overarching organic unity in the New Testament. This is the case because 'none of the NT writings contains the whole of what is taught in the NT', each of them being 'accurate but partial and fragmentary witnesses' (p. 13). For Schreiner, 'a thematic approach to NT theology is invaluable because it attempts to capture the whole of what is taught by considering all twenty-seven books' (p. 13). Thus, Schreiner orders the themes of New Testament theology along the timeline of redemptive history. Seeking to proceed inductively so that his work might be 'anchored by the text' (p. 9), Schreiner wants to avoid 'deriving [his] outline or general train of thought from others' (p. 9). This intention is admirable, and the legion of parenthetical Scripture references attest to the fact that Schreiner has succeeded in weaving a good deal of textual real estate into the pages of his volume. However, it might be considered unfortunate that he did not tie his outline a little more closely to the structure of the New Testament itself. The present study seeks to demonstrate that the shape of the New Testament could provide at least a rudimentary 'redemptive-historical storyline' in which to fit the theology of the individual writings. Even these simple contextual observations might provide the type of cohesion that Schreiner finds lacking in a book-by-book approach. Cf. n. 134, above.

132 *A Canon-Conscious Reading of the Bible*

of the Hebrew Bible.[136] The chosen genre of the Gospel narratives also most closely aligns with these biblical historical narratives.[137]

The New Testament begins with the beginning of Jesus' ministry in the Gospels. This four-fold corpus contains four complementary perspectives on the life, ministry, death, and resurrection of Jesus.[138] This four-part story-line provides the 'identifying narrative' by which readers might understand the simple message, 'Jesus is risen'.[139] The first words of Matthew read,

---

136. Cf. Jenson, *Canon and Creed*, p. 23: 'The church read and reads the Old Testament in this way because the church's gospel is itself a narrative, even in its briefest statements, and because this gospel story identifies itself as the climax and content of a narrative told by the Old Testament.'

137. See the discussion of the genre of the Gospels (John in particular) in Andreas J. Köstenberger, *A Theology of John's Gospel and Letters* (Grand Rapids, MI: Zondervan, 2009), pp. 104-11. Köstenberger notes certain similarities between the Gospels and Greco-Roman biographies and other possible antecedents, but he ultimately concludes that 'it may be best to understand them as belonging to the genre of OT historical narrative' (p. 110). Cf. Loveday Alexander, 'What is a Gospel?', in *The Cambridge Companion to the Gospels* (ed. Stephen C. Barton; Cambridge: Cambridge University Press, 2006), pp. 13-33. Surprisingly, the option of 'biblical historical narrative' is not generally considered as a possible genre option for the Gospels (e.g., see its absence in Patzia's summary of this discussion in *Making of the New Testament*, pp. 87-88; and regarding Luke–Acts, see Darrell Bock's cursory dismissal of the category in *A Theology of Luke and Acts* [Grand Rapids, MI: Zondervan, 2012], pp. 43-48).

138. For a brief analysis of the way the four-fold Gospel collection functioned in the New Testament and in the early church, see Martin Hengel, 'The Four Gospels and the One Gospel of Jesus Christ', in *Earliest Gospels*, pp. 13-26 (this essay is a synopsis of his book *The Four Gospels and the One Gospel of Jesus Christ: An Investigation of the Collection and Origin of the Canonical Gospels* [trans. John Bowden; Harrisburg, PA: Trinity Press International, 2000]). Hengel says that 'it is part of the riddle of the New Testament that this *one* message of salvation has found written expression in *four* writings of a biographical kind, which often differ' (p. 13). See also Denis Farkasfalvy, 'The Apostolic Gospels in the Early Church: The Concept of Canon and the Formation of the Four-Gospel Canon', in *Canon and Biblical Interpretation*, pp. 111-22; Jack D. Kingsbury, 'The Gospel in Four Editions', *Interpretation* 33 (1979), pp. 363-75; and Goswell, 'The Order of the Books of the New Testament', pp. 227-32. Cf. J.K. Elliott, 'Manuscripts, the Codex and the Canon', *JSNT* 63 (1996), p. 107: 'Collecting the four chosen Gospels into one codex had the effect of according a special status to those four, but possibly more significant, helped to limit the number of Gospels to these four and no more.'

139. See Jenson, *Canon and Creed*, pp. 36-38. Jenson notes that 'whatever ancient literary genres may have shaped [Mark's] rhetorical moves and structures, and whatever sources may have provided his material, his Gospel as written is *logically* a single long proposition of the form "Jesus, the one who…and who…and who…is risen". Whatever Mark's immediate purpose in writing may have been, the text he produced served that purpose by expanding the proposition "Jesus is risen" for narrative identification of the subject and for dramatic insistence on the predicate.' In terms of this chapter, the canonical framework (of the four-fold Gospel corpus) supplies the shape and content of the 'identifying narrative' necessary to understand who Jesus is most fully.

'The book of the genealogies of Jesus Christ, Son of David, Son of Abraham' (Mt. 1.1). An individual that begins reading in Matthew is first introduced to the Gospel message as a 'book' (βίβλος).[140] The use of this term is one way that readers can understand the Gospel as a literary entity as well as an oral proclamation.[141] This understanding of the Gospel as a written entity stems from internal biblical evidence. There is also external historical evidence that suggests that 'the gospel' was understood in literary terms early in the life of the church.[142]

In terms of content, the Gospel of Matthew and the four-fold Gospel corpus represent a book of beginnings. Mark announces the 'beginning of the gospel of Jesus Christ' (Mk 1.1). Luke compiles his account of 'the things accomplished among us' by drawing on 'those who from the beginning were eyewitnesses and servants of the word' (Lk. 1.2). Reaching back to eternity past, John reveals what took place 'in the beginning' (Jn 1.1). As the Gospel writers present and interpret the new work of Jesus as the Messiah, they intentionally situate their accounts in line with the contours of the Old Testament. Childs notes the significance of this intertextual feature of the New Testament, arguing that 'the use of the Old Testament performs a major role in the canonical shaping of each of the Gospels and many of the New Testament letters as well'.[143] Indeed, 'without the Old Testament the

140. Hill, *Who Chose the Gospels*, p. 116, notes that after the mid-third century, 'over 2,000 handwritten codices survive which contain the four Gospels bound together in a single codex'. Cf. the linguistic discussion of the term βίβλος in Chapter 1.

141. Two early references to the 'Gospel' as a literary entity occur in Justin and Eusebius. Justin writes, 'For the apostles in the memoirs composed by them, which are called Gospels, thus handed down what was commanded them' (*1 Apol*. 66). Eusebius also mentions the 'books of the holy gospels' (*EH* III, 37.2). The *Didache* also exhorts Christians to pray 'just as the Lord commanded in his Gospel' (ὡς ἐκέλευσεν ὁ κύριος ἐν τῷ εὐαγγελίῳ αὐτοῦ, *Did* 8.2, *AF*, p. 355). Cf. G. Friedrich's comment on this transition in his entry on εὐαγγέλιον in *TDNT* (II, p. 735), 'Since the preaching bears witness to Christ and His words and acts, and since these constitute the essence of the Gospel, the writings which contain the life and words of Jesus come to be given the name "gospel".'

142. See, for instance, the numerous suggestions Hill makes to this effect in *Who Chose the Gospels*. After discussing Polycarp of Smyrna's use of 'gospel' alongside designators like 'law' and 'prophets', Hill notes that 'it is but a small and instinctive step to apply the apostolic preached gospel to the apostolic written Gospels' (p. 195). On the textualization of the gospel traditions, see the essays in Bockmuehl and Hagner (eds.), *The Written Gospel*.

143. Childs, *Biblical Theology*, p. 76. Similarly, von Campenhausen argues that 'in the Christian faith from the very first both elements, Jesus and the Scripture, were mutually and inseparably related' (*Formation of the Christian Bible*, p. 21). Cf. Vanhoozer, *Drama of Doctrine*, p. 222: 'Virtually all the New Testament writers expound on the significance of Jesus' person and work by forging links to the Old Testament.'

New Testament is simply a brute fact appearing as it were out of nowhere, a climax without a plot'.[144]

Even in the way they shape their narratives, the Gospel writers exhibit a 'canon-conscious' awareness of their location in the narrative world generated by the shape of Old Testament texts. In this sense, the Gospels are 'like theologies of the Hebrew Scriptures in story form'.[145] As Köstenberger contends, the Gospel writers 'demonstrably started out with a "canonical consciousness", that is, with a sense that they continued to write Scripture in continuity with antecedent Scripture. In keeping with this "canonical consciousness", the evangelists imitated and took their cue not only from the theology of the Hebrew Scriptures, but also from its underlying historiographic and linguistic conventions.'[146] To give one prominent example, the first sentence of the New Testament canon is inscrutable apart from the Pentateuch and the Former Prophets ('Son of David, Son of Abraham', Mt. 1.1). As a multifaceted and introductory narrative firmly grounded in a well-established textual plotline, the Gospels function as 'the subtext for all the writings that follow in the New Testament'.[147]

144. Dempster, 'Canon and Old Testament Interpretation', p. 160. Dempster also adds, 'Likewise, without the New Testament the Old Testament is a plot without a climax' (p. 160).

145. Shepherd, *Textual World of the Bible*, p. 83.

146. Köstenberger, *Theology of John's Gospel and Letters*, p. 108. The examples Köstenberger gives are Jn 1.1, Mk 1.1-3, and the Septuagintalisms in Lk. 1–2. On the way the Gospel narratives represent a continuation of Old Testament biblical narrative, see R.L. Brawley, 'Canonical Coherence in Reading Israel's Scriptures with a Sequel', in *The Biblical Canons*, pp. 627-34; and D. Moody Smith, 'When Did the Gospels Become Scripture?', *JBL* 119 (2000), pp. 3-20. Smith writes, 'The biblical narrative is the backbone of both Testaments. Although the narrative of the Tanak does not require the Gospel narrative of the NT as its completion, that narrative presupposes what has gone before. Moreover, the early Christian claim that the narrative and prophecies of old are fulfilled and continued in Jesus and the church prefigures, perhaps even demands, the production of more scripture, which will explain how this happened' (p. 12). He also notes that 'such scripture is required to explain this not first of all to outsiders but rather to Christians themselves. It becomes an essential part of their identity and self-understanding' (p. 12). Brawley argues that the New Testament 'bears the character of a sequel' because 'every book in the New Testament' presupposes the Old Testament characterization of God, presupposes the Old Testament narrative of God's relationship with Israel, and 'quotes and alludes to the Old Testament explicitly recognizing it at times as scripture' ('Canonical Coherence', pp. 629-30).

147. Robert W. Wall, 'The Significance of a Canonical Perspective of the Church's Scripture', in *The Canon Debate*, pp. 528-40 (536). On the function of the Gospel collection, Childs remarks, 'Naturally the juxtaposition of the four Gospels caused a strong effect on the reader because of the new and larger context created in spite of the lack of a single editorial intentionality' (*Biblical Theology*, p. 75). Childs also argues that 'the formation of a fourfold canonical corpus, at least by the middle of the second century,

On the heels of these gospel narratives, the book of Acts continues the story by charting the beginnings of the church at Pentecost and by following the two major movements of the Gospel to the Jews first and then to the Gentiles. The narrative structure of the book of Acts falls along these lines, as 'Acts 1–12 describes the growth and influence of the Jerusalem congregation under the leadership of Peter and the other authorities, whereas Acts 13–28 reports on the activities of Paul. The two parts are intertwined.'[148] Though Acts is typically associated with the Gospels (i.e. Luke–Acts), the manuscript evidence indicates that the book of Acts is more closely associated with the Epistles, and the General Epistles in particular.[149]

After the framework provided by Acts, the Pauline Corpus and the General Epistles represent the correspondence between the churches and their

---

confirmed and established the Church's confession that the reality of the one gospel found its authoritative form in a fourfold witness. The richness of the subject matter was such that it could not be reduced, flattened, or expanded with pious Gnostic speculations' ('One Gospel in Four Witnesses', p. 53). Cf. Schreiner's theological/devotional point: 'We have four Gospels because the depth and breadth of Jesus Christ could not be captured by a single one' (*New Testament Theology*, p. 12).

148. Trobisch, *First Edition of the New Testament*, pp. 81-82. For Trobisch, the 'narrative world' provided by Acts (including the portrayal of Luke as Paul's traveling companion) is historically suspect/unreliable. However, he recognizes that this narrative portrayal is an integral element of the text's final published form and thus part of the narrative's intended effect (at least by the publishers who produced it in the second century). For Trobisch, 'if the implied author and the implied literary setting are dismissed, the text will not function as it was designed to function when published' (Richard F. Ward and David Trobisch, *Bringing the Word to Life: Engaging the New Testament through Performing It* [Grand Rapids, MI: Eerdmans, 2013], pp. 59-60). Those who disagree with Trobisch's historical-critical conclusions can still benefit from his analysis of the canonical function of Acts within the New Testament and the logic of its own narrative structure. Cf. David Trobisch, 'The Book of Acts as a Narrative Commentary on the Letters of the New Testament: A Programmatic Essay', in *Rethinking the Unity and Reception of Luke and Acts* (ed. Andrew F. Gregory and C. Kavin Rowe; Columbia, SC: University of South Carolina Press, 2010), pp. 119-27; and Wall, 'Acts of the Apostles in Canonical Context', pp. 110-32.

149. Cf. Trobisch, *Paul's Letter Collection*, p. 10: 'With very rare exceptions no manuscripts exist that combine only the Gospels and Acts, or manuscripts of the general letters without Acts.' Consequently, 'Acts functions as the introduction to the general letters'. He also comments further that 'Whatever the reason might have been, it is clear from the older manuscript tradition that Acts and the general letters originally formed a unit.' On the function of the book of Acts in the New Testament and in the manuscript evidence, see the dialogue between Markus Bockmuehl, 'Why Not Let Acts Be Acts? In Conversation with C. Kavin Rowe', *JSNT* 28 (2005), pp. 163-66; and C. Kavin Rowe, 'History, Hermeneutics and the Unity of Luke–Acts', *JSNT* 28 (2005), pp. 131-57. Rowe continues this discussion in 'Literary Unity and Reception History: Reading Luke–Acts as Luke and Acts', *JSNT* 29 (2007), pp. 449-57.

apostolic leaders.[150] The epistle genre represents a significant portion of the New Testament canon and has an important effect on readers.[151] Structurally, the interconnections between the narratives and epistles of the New Testament are similar to the ones at work between the Former Prophets and the Latter Prophets in the Old Testament.[152] Though there are bits of historical accounts in the letters, the narrative flow of the New Testament is essentially put on hold. After a strong narrative beginning, there is a movement among the epistles into many directions with multiple apostles writing letters to a variety of churches in divergent geographic locations.[153] 1 Peter 1.1 ('Peter…to those who reside as aliens, scattered throughout Pontus, Galatia, Cappadocia, Asia, and Bithyna') and Jas 1.1 ('James…to the twelve tribes who are dispersed abroad') are two examples of this wide range of divergent locations and recipients. Galatians 1.1-2 ('Paul…and all the brethren who are with me, to the churches of Galatia') and Rev. 1.4 are also relevant in this regard ('John to the seven churches that are in Asia').

In light of the narrative framework previously established in the Gospels and Acts, readers can view the letters of the New Testament as dialogue between the figures introduced in the historical accounts of the earlier sections.[154] While the New Testament epistles function as a form of commentary on the Gospels or gospel message, the 'dialogue' metaphor high-

---

150. On the unity of the Pauline Corpus in the manuscripts, see 'The Letters of Paul' section in Chapter 2. Cf. Trobisch, *Paul's Letter Collection*, pp. 1-27. Trobisch suggests that Paul himself might have been the one to solidify a version of his own corpus of writings.

151. Cf. Stanley K. Stowers, *Letter Writing in Greco-Roman Antiquity* (Philadelphia, PA: Westminster Press, 1986), p. 15: 'Something about the nature of early Christianity made it a movement of letter writers.' This compositional impetus functioned within a robust literary cultural environment. As Patzia notes, 'Letter writing is one of Rome's most distinct legacies to the literature of the world' (*Making of the New Testament*, p. 43).

152. Cf. Sheppard, 'Canonization', p. 112: 'The potential of letting the theological views of a later period help define the meaning of earlier traditions is built similarly into the shape of the Hebrew Bible and the New Testament. In the former, the prophets whose books often predate the present Torah are, nonetheless, put after the Torah as though they are a commentary on it. So, in the New Testament, the letters of Paul which were written before are placed after the Gospels as theological commentary on the same subject.'

153. Cf. Childs, *Biblical Theology*, p. 295: 'The danger is acute of seeing the New Testament tradition emerging in a unilinear development when actually multiple directions can be discerned within the same period. Such a diversity hardly comes as a surprise when one considers the growth of early Christianity in the widely separated geographical areas of Egypt, Syria, Palestine, Asia Minor and the Aegean.'

154. See also the previous discussion regarding the nature of 'framing'. Trobisch notes in this regard that 'this combination makes good sense, for the main authors of the general letters—James, Peter and John—are the important leaders of the early church so vividly described in the first chapters of Acts' (*Paul's Letter Collection*, p. 10).

lights and accounts for the occasional and particular nature of most of the letters.[155] The notion of dialogue also alludes to the manner in which an author's writing in some ways mediates his presence. Paul, in particular, foregrounds this mediating quality of his written correspondence. For instance, in his second letter to the Corinthians, Paul writes, 'I do not want to appear to be frightening you with my letters. For they say, "His letters are weighty and strong, but his bodily presence is weak, and his speech of no account". Let such a person understand that what we say by letter when absent, we do when present' (ESV, 2 Cor. 10.9).[156] This type of notion was likewise common in the broader literary culture. In an ancient letter 'to my friend Isidorus in Philadelphia', for example, the sender writes, 'Upon reaching Antinoöpolis, I received your letter, through which I experienced the feeling of seeing you.'[157]

In this literary dialogue, the apostles essentially provide commentary on the gospel and reflect on how ordinary churches can live out that gospel in the midst of the vagaries of life.[158] Further, the nature of this dialogue

155. Further, the 'dialogue' metaphor better highlights the uniqueness of the epistolary genre and the effect it has among the New Testament literature. The epistles serve a similar but distinct purpose to that of the wisdom literature of the Old Testament (which can be understood to serve as a form of thoughtful reflection on Pentateuchal themes).

156. See also 2 Cor. 3.1-3; Gal. 6.11; and 2 Pet. 3.15-16. On this point, see Wall, 'Function of the Pastoral Letters', pp. 29-30. Wall notes that 'Paul himself offers support for the canonical perception that the New Testament collection of Pauline letters is an effective medium for continuing the true "spirit" of Paul's witness to God's gospel within the post-Pauline church' (p. 30). Wall argues further that 'even before the emergence of Pauline letter collections sometime early in the second century, there is the presumption— apparently proffered by the Apostle himself—of the immediate value of his writings to replace the irreplaceable Paul' (p. 30). See also 2 Jn 12 for an expression of the opposite sentiment.

157. The sender of this letter (whose name has been lost) continues by writing, 'I therefore urge you to keep writing continually, for in this way our friendship will be increased'. See Stowers, *Letter Writing*, pp. 62-63, for this translation (and an interpretation). Stowers argues that 'the idea that letters provide a surrogate for seeing or speaking with a friend is an important commonplace' (p. 62). In this connection, Stowers also cites a letter from the Roman stoic philosopher Seneca to Lucilus where Seneca writes, 'I never receive a letter from you without being in your company forthwith' (*Letter* 75.1). Cf. Peter Arzt-Grabner, '"I Was Intending To Visit You, But..." Clauses Explaining Delayed Visits and Their Importance in Papyrus Letters and in Paul', in *Jewish and Christian Scripture as Artifact and Canon* (ed. Craig A. Evans and H. Daniel Zacharias; London: T. & T. Clark, 2009), pp. 220-31.

158. The occasional nature of the epistolary literature of the New Testament has long been highlighted in New Testament studies, often understood as a 'hermeneutical problem'. See, e.g., Nils A. Dahl, 'The Particularity of the Pauline Epistles as a Problem in the Ancient Church', in *Neotestamentica et Patristica* (Leiden: Brill, 1962), pp. 261-71; and Robert W. Wall, 'The Problem of the Multiple Letter Canon of the New Testament',

is unified but by no means uniform. There is diversity in the way that Paul and the writers of the general epistles articulate their theological correspondence with the churches.[159] Because of the canonical framework, however, readers are encouraged to see this diversity as different notes in an ultimately coherent melody line rather than cacophonous disarray.[160] In other words, the shape of the (New Testament) canon allows diversity to function under the intended rubric of an overarching unity that is both theological and textual.[161]

in *The New Testament as Canon: A Reader in Canonical Criticism* (ed. Robert W. Wall and Eugene E. Lemcio; Sheffield: Sheffield Academic Press, 1992), pp. 161-83. Von Campenhausen notes that the Muratorian Fragment addresses this issue in particular: 'The author of the Muratorianum is here wrestling with a problem of which others too had been aware, and which was responsible, among other things, for the "catholicising" corrections to the Pauline epistles: namely that the particularity of the occasions which had given rise to the epistles seemed to be an obstacle to their universal relevance and their liturgical use' (*Formation of the Christian Bible*, p. 252). In many ways, Childs's final work on the Pauline Corpus is an attempt to answer the question, 'How could literature shaped by such contingent specificity serve as a religious norm for a wider Christian community?' (*Church's Guide for Reading Paul*, pp. 5-6).

159. The relationship between the way Paul and James speak of 'justification by faith' is perhaps the most pointed example. The differing tenor of Paul and Jude's discussion of eschatology is another clear example. Wall suggests further that 'Acts is reserved and positioned within the Second Testament as the context within which the canonical conversation between the Pauline and the non-Pauline collections is understood' ('Acts of the Apostles in Canonical Context', p. 120). In this regard, Wall argues that Acts, 'in accord with Gal. 2.1-10, retains the theological diversity found within the apostolic witnesses (see Acts 15.13-21)' (pp. 121-22). For Wall, the canonical function of Acts is to present this theological diversity 'as normative and necessary for the work of a God who calls both Jews and Gentiles to be the people of God' (p. 122). Wall expands on this theme in 'Problem of the Multiple Letter Canon', pp. 176-83.

160. Cf. Bockmuehl, *Seeing the Word*, pp. 107-108. The manuscript evidence bears out that the various epistolary literature was associated with one another. According to Trobisch's calculations, 34.79% of the Greek manuscripts of Paul's letters are grouped with the Acts/General Epistles (27.34% contain Paul's letters alone). He comments that 'in most cases the letters of Paul were bound together with Acts and the general letters' (*Paul's Letter Collection*, p. 10).

161. Cf. von Campenhausen's summary of a point Irenaeus makes in *Against Heresies*: 'The Gospels and Acts must therefore provide the fixed dogmatic framework within which his teachings—like the words of Jesus—find their "correct" setting, and can, as occasion arises, be elucidated and defined' (*Formation of the Christian Bible*, pp. 193-94). Von Campenhausen adds that for Irenaeus, 'the overall dogmatic interpretation of the new Scripture rests decisively on the opening exposition of the Gospels, and in particular of Acts' (p. 195). Further, 'With an easy mind [Irenaeus] juxtaposes the four different Gospels, places Acts next to both authentic and inauthentic Paulines, and explains that they all witness to the same Christ and to one and the same truth proclaimed by Christ' (p. 206). Examples like this from Irenaeus show that when the early church

After this widening effect of the two corpora of epistles, the book of Revelation picks up the narrative element that began with the Gospels and Acts. Because John's Apocalypse is technically an epistle as well, it is fitting that it occurs alongside the Pauline Corpus and the General Epistles.[162] This apocalyptic letter serves a crucial function in relation to the other letters found previously in the New Testament. In addition to being an epistle itself, the beginning of the book contains seven letters to seven churches, mirroring the middle section of the New Testament canon. One effect of these seven letters is that they structurally and thematically bind the book of Revelation to the rest of the New Testament documents. One element that strengthens the connection between the Revelation letters and the rest of the New Testament epistles is that each of the seven letters to the churches has a clear structure, highlighting that they are actual letters to actual churches. Each of the seven letters includes a greeting to the church leader, a description of Christ, words of either commendation or criticism, a warning, an exhortation, and a promise for those who persevere.[163]

Thus, after two major corpora of epistles, John's Apocalypse begins with a carefully crafted letter collection. Readers of the New Testament will be familiar with such a sequence of letters by an author to a number of churches. The Muratorian fragment makes the connection between the

leaders began to utilize the New Testament in their defense of Christianity against heretics and false teachers, they drew not only on individual texts (a common practice even among heretical teachers) but also on the shape of the New Testament (and Old Testament) as a holistic conceptual entity.

162. Goswell, 'Order of New Testament', p. 241, makes this connection and thus treats Revelation alongside the rest of the General Epistles. Recognizing that the 'letter form' has not 'materially influenced its content', Goswell maintains that 'its canonical positioning after *other* letters has the effect of making it another letter'. Robert W. Wall characterizes the book as 'an apocalyptic-prophetic epistle' (*Revelation* [Peabody, MA: Hendrickson, 1991], p. 39). Cf. also Wall's comment in 'Apocalypse of the New Testament in Canonical Context', p. 280: 'A consideration of the "special" relationship between the collection of New Testament letters and Revelation, itself a prophetic-apocalyptic letter, yields important clues for interpreting Revelation. While the letters and Revelation are discrete parts of the New Testament canon, their common literary form calls attention to their "special" relationship within the New Testament. Further, their common form suggests common intentions: the intention of every New Testament letter is to form the distinctive witness of a Christian people.'

163. Colin J. Hemer, *The Letters to the Seven Churches of Asia in Their Local Setting* (Sheffield: JSOT Press, 1986), p. 14, argues that the seven letters exhibit a 'highly formalized parallel structure' and appear 'quite distinct from the body of the Apocalypse, but prove on analysis to be intimately linked with it'. Cf. David E. Aune, 'The Form and Function of the Proclamations to the Seven Churches (Revelation 2–3)', *NTS* 36 (1990), pp. 182-204. See also the classic study done by William M. Ramsay, *The Letters to the Seven Churches of Asia and their Place in the Plan of the Apocalypse* (Peabody, MA: Hendrickson Publishers, 1994).

seven letters in Revelation 2–3 and the Pauline Corpus. In the middle of a discussion of Paul's epistles, the fragment reads, 'For John also in the Apocalypse, though he writes to seven churches, nevertheless speaks to all.'[164] What is more, John 'speaks to all' in one literary place, namely, his *book* of Revelation. One of the reasons these seven letters to the seven churches could be read by all is because they were 'all' in an embedded letter collection. This structural feature echoes and anticipates the shape of the New Testament collection.[165]

After the epistolary interlude of this letter section, John's vision then picks up the narrative thread again (Rev. 4.1), carrying it into the eschatological horizon of a new heavens and a new earth (Revelation 21–22). Accordingly, John's Apocalypse is the exclamation point of the biblical storyline, as redemptive history culminates in the vision he records in these final chapters of his book. The *Revelation* of Jesus Christ functions as a fitting canonical counterpart to the *Gospel* of Jesus Christ.[166] Thus, the overarching narrative framework of the New Testament provides the believing community with an exposition and interpretation of its origin (Gospels), expansion (Acts), and eschaton (Revelation).

Concluding Reflections

To sum up this section, both in the early pre-canonical groupings as well as in the shaping of its final form, the Christian canon as a whole hermeneutically informs the reading of the scriptural texts it contains. The church's guide for reading any given biblical book is the entire canonical context in which it is situated. In this way, readers are strongly encouraged to understand Christianity as 'a story that takes two Testaments to tell'.[167] A study of

164. For this translation, see Metzger, *Canon of the New Testament*, p. 307. Krister Stendahl, 'The Apocalypse of John and the Epistles of Paul in the Muratorian Fragment', in *Current Issues in New Testament Interpretation* (ed. William Klassen; New York: Harper & Brothers, 1962), pp. 239-45, draws out the significance of this connection.

165. Cf. Meade, 'Ancient Near Eastern Apocalypticism', pp. 318-19: 'That all seven "letters" are to be put in one "book" (βιβλίον) may give evidence of a growing consciousness that the particularity of individual messages are to be read within the context of a unified collection of an entire corpus.'

166. Cf. Bockmuehl, *Seeing the Word*, p. 111, who argues that in the final form of the New Testament canon, Mt. 1.1 and Rev. 22.18-21 form a 'suggestive canonical fastener around the New Testament as a whole'.

167. Seitz, *Prophecy and Hermeneutics*, p. 242. In this regard, von Campenhausen notes that 'from the beginning of the third century onwards no one anywhere knew of a different arrangement: the sacred Scripture of the orthodox Church consisted of an Old and a New Testament' (*Formation of the Christian Bible*, p. 269). Cf. Brevard S. Childs, 'The Nature of the Christian Bible: One Book, Two Testaments', in *The Rule of Faith* (ed. E. Radner and G. Sumner; Harrisburg, PA: Morehouse Publishers, 1998), pp. 115-25.

contextuality seeks to uncover and exposit this integrated textual feature of the biblical canon.

As developed in this chapter, there are two main levels in a study of the contextuality of the biblical collection, namely, *mere* contextuality and *meant* contextuality. Granting this distinction allows for a more carefully nuanced description of the effect that the canonical context has on readers. A study of mere contextuality seeks to describe the hermeneutical impact of reading an individual writing (the part) as a component of a broader collection (the whole). For instance, this type of analysis investigates the significance of the way the biblical books are ordered in various traditions and examines the meaningful associations/connections that are generated as a result of those arrangements. Further, this level of analysis does not address the issue of authorial intention but rather simply describes the effect of the biblical material in a particular form and in a particular order.

A study of meant contextuality complements a study of mere contextuality. The former investigates whether an author or editor of the biblical material has intended any of the features uncovered in the latter. Though these levels of investigation have different ultimate aims, their interpretive results can complement and inform the other. One way to begin an investigation of meant contextuality is by noting the shape of the biblical material within the broader canonical collection. The canonical context of the biblical writings has a particular shape and ordering. Uncovering the ordering principle or the canonical logic at work in the broader context encourages readers to ask whether this helpful and hermeneutically significant framework was the result of design rather than happenstance.

As argued in Chapter 2, there is internal and external historical evidence that the biblical authors and the believing community viewed certain writings in light of other writings. This associative process resulted in the formation of groupings within the biblical material. These groupings in turn were grouped within the larger context of the biblical canon. This movement toward mutual interdependence of the biblical literature represents plausible evidence for an active canon-consciousness at work among the biblical authors and the believing community during the composition and canonization of the canon formation process. Further, this reality lends legitimacy to the study of a canonical contextuality (both mere and meant). In Chapter 4, another line of evidence for discerning an intended contextual effect of the canonical context is examined, namely, the textual feature of biblical intertextuality. One way for a biblical author to influence the shape of the broader canonical context is through deliberately associating his work with other biblical literature through the use of intertextual references.

Chapter 4

INTERTEXTUALITY WITHIN THE CANONICAL CONTEXT

No man is an island, entire of itself; every man is a piece of the continent, a part of the main; if a clod be washed away by the sea, Europe is the less... any man's death diminishes me, because I am involved in mankind, and therefore never send to know for whom the bell tolls; it tolls for thee.[1]

No text is read independently of the reader's experience of other texts.[2]

No text is an island.[3]

The Study of Intertextuality

All authors have at their disposal a vast matrix of texts from which to draw on as they compose their works. In one sense, 'no text is an island', as every text is inherently informed by a complex nexus of precursor texts. In the current academic scene, the concept of intertextuality is in vogue.[4] Though biblical scholars have utilized elements of the discussion, contemporary dialogue about this textual phenomenon began in linguistic and purely literary disciplines.[5] Further, there is oftentimes a significant diversity in the

---

1. John Donne, 'Meditation XVII', in *The Works of John Donne* (ed. Henry Alford; London: John W. Parker, 1839), III, p. 575.

2. Umberto Eco, *The Role of the Reader: Explorations in the Semiotics of Texts* (Bloomington, IN: Indiana University Press, 1984), p. 21.

3. There is a place where someone has testified to this.

4. In this regard, Raymond Tallis laments, 'the contemporary obsession with "intertextuality"' (*Not Saussure: A Critique of Post-Saussurean Literary Theory* [London: MacMillan, 1995], p. 31).

5. For an overview of this vast field, see Thaïs E. Morgan, 'Is There an Intertext in this Text? Literary and Interdisciplinary Approaches to Intertextuality', *American Journal of Semiotics* 3 (1985), pp. 1-40; Susanne Friedman, 'Weavings: Intertextuality and the (Re)Birth of the Author', in *Influence and Intertextuality in Literary History* (ed. J. Clayton and E. Rothstein; Madison, WI: University of Wisconsin Press, 1991), pp. 146-80; and Susanne Gillmayr-Bucher, 'Intertextuality: Between Literary Theory and Text Analysis', in *The Intertextuality of the Epistles: Explorations of Theory and Practice* (ed. Thomas L. Brodie, Dennis R. MacDonald and Stanley E. Porter; Sheffield: Sheffield Academic Press, 2006), pp. 13-23.

way the notion of 'intertextuality' is employed and the way 'intertextual references' are identified and exposited.[6] Indeed, 'it is clear that intertextuality is no one thing and that the concept is in need of some clarification'.[7] Therefore, a working understanding of the origin and development of the term and concept is an important preliminary element of a discussion of biblical intertextuality.

Many literary critics and theorists understand the phenomenon of intertextuality in a broad and expansive fashion. For poststructuralist scholars such as Julia Kristeva (who coined the term) and Roland Barthes, intertextuality is a way of describing the nature of textuality in general.[8] In other

6. Cf. Richard Hays' introductory comments in a recent collection of essays: 'The difficulty, though, is that the term intertextuality is used in such diverse and imprecise ways that it becomes difficult to know what is meant by it and whether it points to anything like a method that can be applied reliably to the analysis of texts to facilitate coherent critical conversation' (*Reading the Bible Intertextually*, p. xi).Thomas L. Brodie, Dennis R. MacDonald, and Stanley E. Porter offer a similar assessment: 'The problem, however, is that the study of intertextuality, despite its potential, is quite underdeveloped. As a result, and in order to develop its potential as an interpretive tool, there is an acute need to clarify its scope, method and terminology' ('Introduction: Tracing the Development of the Epistles—The Potential and the Problem', in *The Intertextuality of the Epistle*, pp. 1-9 [1]).

7. Hays, *Reading the Bible Intertextually*, p. xii. Similarly, Allen observes that 'intertextuality is one of the most commonly used and misused terms in contemporary critical vocabulary' (*Intertextuality*, p. 2). He goes on to argue that 'intertextuality is and will remain a crucial element in the attempt to understand literature and culture in general' (p. 7).

8. Litwak, *Echoes of Scripture in Luke–Acts*, pp. 48-55, provides a helpful overview of the history of the contemporary discussion regarding intertextuality, beginning with the pioneering work of Kristeva and Barthes. After expositing the intertextual program of these figures, Litwak critiques their approach and offers reflection on how their emphasis on intertextuality can be reined in such that it can prove useful in the analysis of biblical texts. Alkier sketches an 'intellectual history' of the concept and its use in 'Intertextuality', pp. 3-11. Kristeva originally studied structuralism and post-structuralism as a student of Barthes in France. According to Allen, 'Kristeva's attempt to combine Saussurean and Bakhtinian theories of language and literature produced the first articulation of intertextual theory, in the late 1960s' (*Intertextuality*, p. 3). See also Gillmayr-Bucher, 'Intertextuality', pp. 13-16; and Kelly Oliver, *Reading Kristeva: Unraveling the Double-Bind* (Bloomington, IN: Indiana University Press, 1993), pp. 91-113. Oliver locates Kristeva's approach within her broader intellectual context (and particularly within twentieth century feminist thought). For a sampling of the tenor of post-structuralist accounts of language, textuality, and discourse, see the primary source essays in *Untying the Text: A Post-Structuralist Reader* (ed. Robert Young; Boston, MA: Routledge & Kegan Paul, 1981); Josué V. Harari (ed.), *Textual Strategies: Perspectives in Post-Structuralist Criticism* (Ithaca, NY: Cornell University Press, 1979); and Jonathan Culler, *On Deconstruction: Theory and Criticism after Structuralism* (Ithaca, NY: Cornell University Press, 2007).

words, all texts are composite creatures of all other texts, representing a kind of 'discursive space' where meaning is generated not necessarily in the act of writing but rather in the event of reading. This understanding of intertextuality is rooted in the field of semiotics. One of the central tenants of a semiotic approach to language is the *relationship* between the sign and the sign-system.[9] According to this postmodern discipline, 'the meaning of any text lies, not in the text as such, but rather in the intertextual operations of reading. Meaning is what readers produce using the semiotic machines at their disposal.'[10] In this approach, the phenomenon of intertextuality is 'not something that readers create, but it is something that creates readers'.[11] As Allen argues, 'this revolution in thought, which has been styled the "linguistic turn" in the human sciences, can be understood as one origin of the theory of intertextuality'.[12]

For Kristeva and proponents of her type of approach, 'intertextuality is about how readers weave together new texts from innumerable other texts and thus rewrite every text. In this perspective, everything is a text, not merely literary pieces. It is a key component of her perspective that intertextuality erases the boundaries between literary texts.'[13] Kristeva's concept of intertextuality is directed against the structuralist notion that a text is 'independent from its respective readings'.[14] For instance, in her discussion of 'the bounded text', Kristeva identifies *the text* as 'a permutation of texts, an intertextuality', which implies that 'in the space of a given text, several utterances, taken from other texts, intersect and neutralize one another'.[15] This way of looking at texts is 'characteristic of intertextuality'

---

9. Allen says that in semiotics, 'the relationship between sign and system is particularly important' (*Intertextuality*, p. 225). He also notes that 'Semiotics and semiology as developed in structuralism and poststructuralism can treat anything emanating from a signifying system as a text to be read' (p. 225). Chris Baldick, *The Concise Oxford Dictionary of Literary Terms* (Oxford: Oxford University Press, 1990), p. 201, defines semiotics as 'the systematic study of *signs*, or, more precisely, of the production of meanings from *sign-systems*, linguistic or non-linguistic'. Cf. Culler's discussion of 'Semiotics as a Theory of Reading' in *Pursuit of Signs*, pp. 51-87.

10. Aichele, *Control of Biblical Meaning*, p. 9. Allen observes that 'the term intertextuality was initially employed by poststructuralist theorists and critics in their attempt to disrupt notions of stable meaning and objective interpretation' (*Intertextuality*, p. 3).

11. Aichele, *Control of Biblical Meaning*, p. 19.

12. Allen, *Intertextuality*, p. 10.

13. Litwak, *Echoes of Scripture in Luke–Acts*, p. 49.

14. Alkier, 'Intertextuality', p. 4.

15. Julia Kristeva, *Desire in Language: A Semiotic Approach to Literature and Art* (New York: Columbia University Press, 1980), p. 36. Cf. Julia Kristeva, 'Word, Dialogue, and Novel', in *The Kristeva Reader* (ed. Toril Moi; New York: Columbia University Press, 1986), pp. 34-61.

and 'introduces a new way of reading which destroys the linearity of the text'.[16]

In this manner, Kristeva connects an inclusive understanding of textuality with the freeplay of a semiotic model of meaning and the vagaries of ideological analysis. For her, this conception of the 'text as ideologeme determines the very procedure of a semiotics that, by studying the text as intertextuality, considers it as such within (the text of) society and history'.[17] At key points, Kristeva demonstrates a strong affinity for the work of Mikhail Bakhtin.[18] In particular, she takes up his 'dialogic' understanding of texts, where 'any text is constructed as a mosaic of quotations; any text is the absorption and transformation of another'.[19] In Kristeva's perspective, 'Bakhtin was one of the first to replace the static hewing out of texts with a model where literary structure does not simply *exist* but is generated in relation to *another* structure.'[20]

---

16. Laurent Jenny, 'The Strategy of Forms', in *French Literary Theory Today: A Reader* (ed. T. Todorov; Cambridge: Cambridge University Press, 1982), pp. 34-63 (44). Cf. Harold Bloom's comment that 'a single text has only part of a meaning; it is itself a synecdoche for a larger whole including other texts. A text is a relational event, and not a substance to be analyzed' (*Kabbalah and Criticism* [New York: Seabury Press, 1975], p. 106).

17. Kristeva, *Desire in Language*, p. 37.

18. Kristeva cites and draws on Bakhtin directly in *Desire in Language*, pp. 64ff. Alkier, 'Intertextuality', pp. 4-5, also traces the movement 'from dialogicality to intertextuality' in Kristeva's thinking. Toril Moi (her translator and editor) observes that 'Kristeva was among the first to introduce Bakhtin's work to a Western audience' (*The Kristeva Reader*, p. 34).

19. Kristeva, *Desire in Language*, p. 66. She uses this language in other discussions of 'intertextuality' and adds that 'the notion of *intertextuality* replaces that of intersubjectivity, and poetic language is read as at least *double*' ('Word, Dialogue, and Novel', p. 37). In Bakhtin's terms, 'I give myself verbal shape from another's point of view, ultimately, from the point of view of the community to which I belong. A word is a bridge thrown between myself and another. If one end of the bridge depends on me, then the other depends upon my addressee. A word is territory shared by both addresser and addressee, by the speaker and his interlocuter' (Mikhail Bakhtin and Valentin N. Volosinov, *Marxism and the Philosophy of Language* [Cambridge, MA: Harvard University Press, 1986], p. 86). As Allen notes, 'it is this *addressivity* of the word and utterance, as Bakhtin will later term it, which must be the central focus of the study of language' (*Intertextuality*, p. 20).

20. Kristeva, 'Word, Dialogue, and Novel', pp. 35-36. Kristeva also contends that 'what allows a dynamic dimension to structuralism is [Bakhtin's] conception of the "literary word" as an *intersection of textual surfaces* rather than a *point* (a fixed meaning), as a dialogue among several writings: that of the writer, the addressee (or the character), and the contemporary or earlier cultural context' (p. 36). In Kristeva's approach, then, 'Intertextuality thus becomes less a name for a work's relation to prior texts than a designation of its participation in the discursive space of a culture' (Culler, *Pursuit of*

Roland Barthes memorably articulates this poststructuralist view of textuality, asserting (before the development of the term 'intertextuality' by Kristeva) that 'we know now that a text is not a line of words releasing a single "theological" meaning (the "message" of the Author-God) but a multi-dimensional space in which a variety of writings, none of them original, blend and clash'.[21] For Barthes, 'the text is a tissue of quotations drawn from the innumerable centres of culture'.[22] This destabilized understanding of authorial intention and textuality is a hallmark of the way the notion of intertextuality was originally developed and employed.

An important figure for those pursuing a chastened form of intertextual analysis in contradistinction to the climate of postmodern semiotic studies

Signs, p. 114). Cf. Hays, *Echoes of Scripture*, p. 15: 'All discourse, in this view, is necessarily intertextual in the sense that its conditions of intelligibility are given by and in relation to a previously given body of discourse.'

21. Roland Barthes, 'The Death of the Author', in *Image–Music–Text* (trans. Stephen Heath; London: Fontana, 1977), p. 146. On the relationship between Kristeva and Barthes in the development of the concept of 'intertextuality', see Mary Orr, *Intertextuality: Debates and Contexts* (Cambridge: Polity Press, 2003), pp. 20-36. Orr addresses at length the question, 'Why has Kristeva's version of intertextuality been sidelined, even actively discredited, whereas Barthes's among others has not? Is such discrediting of Kristeva as coiner and theorist of intertextuality deliberate, or justifiable?' (p. 21). Cf. Judith Still and Michael Worton's introduction to Kristeva's oeuvre and its connection to Barthes in *Intertextuality: Theories and Practices* (ed. Michael Worton and Judith Still; Manchester: Manchester University Press, 1990), pp. 1-44.

22. Barthes, 'Death of the Author', p. 146. In another context, Barthes similarly argues that 'the plural of the Text' depends 'not on the ambiguity of its content but on what might be called the *stereographic plurality* of its weave of signifiers (etymologically, the text is a tissue, a woven fabric). The reader of the Text may be compared to someone at a loose end' ('From Work to Text', in *Image–Music–Text*, p. 159). Cf. Allen, *Intertextuality*, p. 13: 'Informed by Saussurean linguistics and its theoretical legacy, Barthes announces the death of the Author on the basis of a recognition of the relational nature of the world.' Barthes' 'death sentence' has been engaged in the scholarly court of appeals from both literary and theological lines of inquiry. In *Validity in Interpretation*, Hirsch attempts to refute Barthes' argument against authorial intention as a determinative factor in discerning textual meaning. In *Meaning in this Text*, Vanhoozer seeks to deal directly with the 'theological' claim implicit in Barthes' literary argument about textuality. Throughout his career, Barthes maintained an interest in biblical interpretation (e.g. see *Structural Analysis and Biblical Exegesis: Interpretational Essays* [ed. Roland Barthes *et al.*; Pittsburgh, PA: Pickwick Press, 1974]). For a sampling of the continued interaction with Barthes, see James Michels, 'Roland Barthes: Against Language', *ETC: A Review of General Semantics* 52 (1995), pp. 155-73; and Elena Oxman, 'Sensing the Image: Roland Barthes and the Affect of the Visual', *Substance: A Review of Theory & Literary Criticism* 39 (2010), pp. 71-90. Cf. Annette Lavers, *Roland Barthes: Structuralism and After* (London: Meuthen, 1982); Jonathan Culler, *Barthes: A Very Short Introduction* (Oxford: Oxford University Press, 2002); and Graham Allen, *Roland Barthes* (London: Routledge, 2003).

is literary theorist Jonathan Culler.[23] Culler critiques Kristeva's expansive notion of intertextuality, incisively noting that a *purely* intertextual understanding of textuality is not sustainable *on its own terms*. He observes that 'the attempt to demonstrate the importance of intertextuality leads one to focus on the other discourses identifiable in and behind a discourse and to try to specify them'.[24] From an analysis of Kristeva's own work, Culler concludes that intertextuality must inevitably be circumscribed, but more narrowly focusing the parameters of investigation undermines the 'general concept of intertextuality in whose name we are working'.[25]

For Culler, 'Kristeva's procedure is instructive because it illustrates the way in which the concept of intertextuality leads the critic who wishes to work with it to concentrate on cases that put in question the general theory.'[26] Further, 'to restrict the concept of intertextuality for practical reasons—to mark out a manageable area of investigation—is not an innocent strategy. It poses questions about the claims made for the larger concept.'[27] Summarizing Culler's main points, Litwak observes, 'Kristeva's program fails from

---

23. See Jonathan Culler, *The Pursuit of Signs: Semiotics, Literature, Deconstruction* (London: Routledge, 2001). In Chapter 5 of this volume ('Presupposition and Intertextuality', pp. 110-31), Culler deals directly with Kristeva and the poststructuralist account of intertextuality. Thiselton introduces Culler's approach by lamenting, 'It is a source of regret that many of those biblical specialists who have drawn *intertextuality* as a model for biblical research seem to owe more to Barthesian perspectives than to the careful and precise sub-categorizations and sympathetic but perceptive warnings put forward on this subject by Jonathan Culler' (*New Horizons in Hermeneutics* [Grand Rapids, MI: Zondervan, 1992], p. 504). See also Culler's methodological interaction with Umberto Eco in *Interpretation and Overinterpretation* (ed. Stefan Collini; Cambridge: Cambridge University Press, 1992). In this dialogue, Culler defends a form of readerly 'overinterpretation' that emphasizes the manifold reading contexts that are possible in textual engagement.

24. Culler, *Pursuit of Signs*, p. 122. Culler is responding directly to Kristeva's statement that 'the poetic signified refers to (relates to) other discursive signifieds, so that in a poetic utterance can be read numerous other discourses' (p. 116). Culler comments that 'anyone thinking that the point of intertextuality is to take us beyond the study of identifiable sources is brought up short' by examples of Kristeva's own textual analysis (p. 117). The point, Culler reflects, is not 'that such questions are uninteresting or insignificant but only that a situation in which one can track down sources with such precision cannot serve as the paradigm for a description of intertextuality, if intertextuality is the general discursive space that makes a text intelligible' (pp. 117-18).

25. Culler, *Pursuit of Signs*, p. 122. In a similar vein, Genette observes that any notion of intertextuality must be inevitably narrowed in some measure because to engage in actual textual analysis is to examine 'semantic-semiotic microstructures, observed at the level of the sentence, a fragment, or a short, generally poetic, text' (*Palimpsests*, p. 2).

26. Culler, *Pursuit of Signs*, p. 118.

27. Culler, *Pursuit of Signs*, p. 116.

its self-definition. She cannot explicate intertextuality as she understands it without using the very type of pretext comparisons to which Kristeva claims intertextuality is opposed'.[28]

The Study of Biblical Intertextuality

Though there are possible pitfalls in using such an approach without methodological reflection, the concept of intertextuality can prove beneficial if it is carefully defined and consistently employed.[29] After all, the object of biblical interpretation is a text, and this text is made up of multiple texts that often reference each other. Further, these texts have authors who have intended to communicate meaning to their readers. One way these authors communicate is through references to other texts. Indeed, it is difficult to read any part of the canon without hearing 'rumbles of intertextuality'.[30] As Thiselton observes, 'In the biblical traditions inter-textuality in its broad sense is simply a fact of life.'[31] A study of biblical intertextuality also seeks

28. Litwak, *Echoes of Scripture in Luke–Acts*, p. 51. Cf. also Allen's survey of critiques of Kristeva's central assertions from within the field of poststructuralist semiotics, particularly her adoption and development of Bakhtin's ideas (*Intertextuality*, pp. 55-58).

29. Cf. Hays, *Reading the Bible Intertextually*, pp. xiii-xiv: 'Theological interpretation has much to gain, therefore, from greater attention to the theoretical complexities of intertextuality and to the revisionary transformations that take place when a skillful writer (Luke, for example) employs intertextual strategies of narration.' Note also the caution of Allen, *Intertextuality*, p. 56, who notes that 'intertextuality, as a concept, has a history of different articulations which reflect the distinct historical situations out of which it has emerged' and that 'any application of it now will itself be an intertextual or transpositional event'.

30. The phrase 'rumbles of intertextuality' comes from Umberto Eco, 'Intertextual Irony and Levels of Reading', in *Umberto Eco on Literature* (Orlando: Harcourt, 2004), pp. 212-35 (235).

31. Thiselton, *New Horizons*, p. 42. Thiselton critically interacts with various approaches to intertextuality (e.g. the post-structuralist account) and weighs their merits for biblical interpretation (e.g. pp. 499-507). By 'broad sense', Thiselton means that at a minimum, it is well established (among scholars and biblical readers) that biblical writers frequently draw on other biblical texts. He writes, 'It is also possible to work with simpler models of intertextuality as a starting-point' that notes 'simply examples of texts which become framed or re-contextualitzed in different ways within different biblical texts' (p. 39). Similarly, Hays states that 'the phenomenon of intertextuality— the imbedding of fragments of an earlier text within a later one—has always played a major role in the cultural traditions that are heir to Israel's Scriptures: the voice of Scripture, regarded as authoritative in one way or another, continues to speak in and through later texts that both depend on and transform the earlier' (*Echoes of Scripture*, p. 14). Cf. Peter Phillips, 'Biblical Studies and Intertextuality: Should the Work of Genette and Eco Broaden our Horizons?', in *The Intertextuality of the Epistles*, pp. 35-45.

to draw out the sometimes neglected insight that the biblical *authors* were also biblical *readers*.

Consequently, literary categories are helpful, and perhaps necessary, in dealing with this literary phenomenon. Some interpreters that are uncomfortable using the concept of intertextuality because of its connection to literary studies do not recognize that the notions of 'quotation' and 'allusion' are literary concepts themselves. Any hermeneutical approach that has a *text* as its object of interpretation will need to utilize tools that are suited to textual analysis.[32] The study of inter*text*uality is well suited to this type of textual task.[33]

32. Cf. Stephen D. Moore, 'A Modest Manifesto for New Testament Literary Criticism: How to Interface with a Literary Studies Field that is Post-Literary, Post-Theoretical, and Post-Methodological', *Biblical Interpretation* 15 (2007), pp. 1-25; and Stanley E. Porter, 'Literary Approaches to the New Testament: From Formalism to Deconstruction and Back', in *Approaches to New Testament Study* (ed. Stanley E. Porter and David Tombs; Sheffield: Sheffield Academic Press, 1995), pp. 77-128. Porter reflects on both the benefits and limitations of integrating elements of literary criticism into biblical studies. He comments initially that 'despite the fact that literary-critical exegesis of the New Testament is of only fairly recent provenance, the New Testament itself suggests that literary sensitivity has been necessary from the start' (p. 77). Similarly, Brodie, MacDonald, and Porter note that 'access to the text is through the words that the text consists of. Until there is some clarity about the literary nature of the text—the nature of the words, their origin and context, and the literary environment in which they find themselves—it is not possible to have a clear understanding of the text' ('Introduction', p 3). One of Sternberg's central arguments in *Poetics of Biblical Narrative* is that the 'literary' nature of biblical narrative is inescapable. Therefore, a 'poetics' of biblical narrative (a study of how narratives work) is not only justifiable but also *necessary* (for a development of these points see *Poetics of Biblical Narrative*, pp. 1-57). For a brief reflection on the vagaries of defining the contours of 'literature' and 'literary analysis' even from within the discipline, see Jonathan Culler, *Literary Theory* (New York: Sterling, 2009), especially pp. 23-54; and Peter Widdowson, *Literature* (London: Routledge, 1999), pp. 1-25. Gérard Genette interacts with this methodological issue at length (highlighting its aesthetic dimension) in *Fiction and Diction* (trans. Catherine Porter; Ithaca, NY: Cornell University Press, 1993), esp. the lead essay, 'Fiction and Diction' (pp. 1-29).

33. Though the originators of the concept of 'intertextuality' eschew the 'source-hunting' of traditional biblical studies, the term actually lends itself to the type of appropriation biblical scholars have made use of (inter**text**uality). In fact, this textual focus of many proponents of 'intertextual studies' led Kristeva herself to employ a modified nomenclature. In *Revolution in Poetic Language* (New York: Columbia University Press, 1985), Kristeva writes, 'The term *inter-textuality* denotes this transposition of one (or several) sign-system(s) into another; but since the term has often been understood in the banal sense of 'study of sources', we prefer the term *transposition* because it specifies that the passage from one signifying system to another demands a new articulation of the thetic—of enunciative and denotative positionality' (pp. 59-60). She confirms her movement away from the stability of textual meaning by noting that

A Production-Oriented Approach to Intertextuality
Recognizing the wide and unwieldy spectrum of approaches flying under
the banner of intertextuality, biblical scholars often make use of the concept
in order to help explain the way one biblical writer draws upon the text of
another. A minimal definition of intertextuality along these lines is the study
of the relationship between two or more literary texts. More specifically,
intertextuality is the study of the 'presence of one text within another'.[34]
From this definition, there are two major streams of intertextual analysis:
reception-oriented approaches and production-oriented approaches.[35] A

'transposition' (what she means when she speaks of intertextuality) 'implies the aban-
donment of a former sign system, the passage to a second via an instinctual interme-
diary common to the two systems, and the articulation of the new system with its new
respresentability' (p. 60).

    34. Genette, *Palimpsests*, pp. 1-2. Genette writes, 'For my part I define [intertex-
tuality], no doubt in a more restrictive sense, as a relationship of copresence between
two texts or among several texts: that is to say, eidetically and typically as the actual
presence of one text within another' (pp. 1-2). Genette includes the technical categories of quotation, plagiarism, and allusion under the heading of intertextuality.
Attempting to account for the variegated nature of intertextual influence, Allan H.
Pasco delineates 'three kinds of intertextualities: of imitation, opposition, and allusion' (*Allusion: A Literary Graft* [Toronto: University of Toronto Press, 2002], p. 3).
Pasco also characterizes allusions as 'literary grafts'. Culler 'introduces a modest
intertextuality' that relates 'sentences of a text to another set of sentences which they
presuppose' (*Pursuit of Signs*, p. 124). Culler, in particular, stresses the relationship
between the notions of intertextuality and presupposition. He examines three types
of presuppositions and the way they invoke intertextual connections (logical, rhetorical, and pragmatic). Analyzing the role of these various presuppositions in discourse
is part of Culler's suggestions for a 'limited approach' to intertextuality.

    35. For a summary of these categories, see the helpful discussion of Stefan Alkier,
'Intertextuality and the Semiotics of Biblical Texts', in *Reading the Bible Intertextually* (ed. Richard B. Hays, Stefan Alkier, and Leroy A. Huizenga; Waco, TX: Baylor
University Press, 2009), pp. 7-11. Drawing on the resources of 'categorical semiotics',
Alkier favors an unlimited conception of intertextuality based upon an inclusive model
of textuality. For those in the field of literary theory, a 'production-oriented' or circumscribed use of intertextuality is often negatively characterized as a misguided structuralist use of intertextuality versus the typical liberating poststructural use of the concept
(cf. Allen, *Intertextuality*, pp. 92-94). Allen notes that 'Structuralists retain a belief in
criticism's ability to locate, describe and thus stabilize a text's significance, even if that
significance concerns an intertextul relation between a text and other texts' (p. 94). Cf.
also the categories developed by Annette Merz in 'The Fictitious Self-Exposition of
Paul: How Might Intertextual Theory Suggest a Reformulation of the Hermeneutics of
Pseudepigraphy?', in *The Intertextuality of the Epistles*, pp. 113-32. Merz discusses
non-intended intertextuality that is 'introduced to a text by its recipient in a manner
not envisaged by the author' (p. 119), *intended intertextuality* which is 'the term given
to references to earlier texts which the (real and implied) author consciously intends
the reader to perceive' (p. 120), and *veiled intertextuality*, which is 'a specific instance

reception-oriented approach is oriented toward the reading experience and focuses on the types of intertextual connections that a reader might make between two or more texts.[36] The poststructuralist accounts of intertextuality surveyed above are examples of a thoroughgoing reception-oriented perspective.

Conversely, a production-oriented approach to intertextuality investigates the intertextual connections that are 'produced' and intended by the author of a text. In line with this perspective, the intertextual references that the interpreter seeks are the ones embedded in the text by the author. These connections are somehow marked in the text and are part of the 'intertextual potential' of the original composition. The production-oriented perspective relies on a narrow/limited conception of intertextuality. In this model, texts contain intentional or circumstantial 'markings' that serve as pointers to intertextual references. This understanding of intertextuality also functions within a closed model of textuality. Here intertextuality is understood not only as a feature of a *reader's* response, but also as a compositional strategy of an *author*.[37] Thus, a production-oriented approach to intertextual analysis adopts a textual-canonical starting point rather than a historical-critical one.[38] Depending on which starting point an interpreter chooses, the pursuit of an author's intended meaning will look quite different (i.e. a primarily *textual* task versus a primarily *historical* task).

This view of authorial intention associates verbal meaning with the embodied intention of an author in a text (i.e. an author's 'textual intent').

of intended intertextuality, where the (real) author is fully conscious of the references made to earlier texts, but more or less deliberately conceals these from the reader' (p. 120).

36. For an example of a reader-oriented intertextual approach, see Michael Riffaterre, 'Compulsory Reader Response: The Intertextual Drive', in *Intertextuality: Theories and Practices* (ed. Michael Worton and Judith Still; Manchester: Manchester University Press, 1990), pp. 56-78. Genette contrasts his own approach with Riffaterre's, noting that for Riffaterre, 'An intertext…is the perception, by the reader, of the relationship between a work and others that have either preceded or followed it' (*Palimpsests*, p. 2).

37. Contra Barthes, 'Death of the Author', p. 148: 'A text's unity lies not in its origin but in its destination.' He explains this idea by arguing that 'a text is made of multiple writings, drawn from many cultures and entering into mutual relations of dialogue, parody, contestation, but there is one place where this multiplicity is focused, and that place is the reader, not, as was hitherto said, the author. The reader is the space on which all the quotations that make up a writing are inscribed without any of them being lost' (p. 148). In Barthes' well-cited formulation, the 'birth of the reader' comes at 'the cost of the death of the Author' (p. 148). Barthes understands intertextuality as a phenomenon that almost directly contrasts the 'production-oriented' view.

38. Cf. Childs, *Church's Guide for Reading Paul*, pp. 10-17, who compares and contrasts 'historical criticism' and the 'canonical context' as possible starting points in the pursuit of the meaning of biblical texts.

The goal is not to discover an author's mental state at the time of writing, but rather what an author has actually done in the communicative act of composing a text. Understanding and articulating 'authorial intention' in this manner mitigates the charge of the 'intentional fallacy'. In 1946, William K. Wimsatt and Monroe Beardsley heavily critiqued the use of an author's intentions as a criterion for interpretation and a determiner of meaning.[39] They deny the 'claim of the author's "intention" upon the critic's judgment' and argue that 'the design or intention of the author is neither available nor desirable as a standard for judging the success of a work of literary art'.[40] For them, an 'intention' is the 'design or plan in the author's mind' and has 'obvious affinities for the author's attitude toward his work, the way he felt, what made him write'.[41] Defining the scope of intention in

39. See William K. Wimsatt and Monroe Beardsley, 'The Intentional Fallacy', *Sewanee Review* 54 (1946), pp. 468-88. This often-quoted article was reprinted in *On Literary Intention: Critical Essays Selected and Introduced* (ed. David Newton-de-Molina; Edinburgh: Edinburgh University Press, 1976), pp. 1-13. See also William K. Wimsatt, 'Genesis: A Fallacy Revisited', in *The Disciplines of Criticism: Essays in Literary Theory, Interpretation, and History* (ed. Peter Demetz, Thomas Greene and Lowry Nelson; New Haven, CT: Yale University Press, 1968), pp. 193-225; Monroe C. Beardsley, 'Textual Meaning and Authorial Meaning', *Genre* 1 (1968), pp. 169-81; and Monroe C. Beardsley, 'Intentions and Interpretations: A Fallacy Revived', in *The Aesthetic Point of View: Selected Essays* (ed. Michael J. Wreen and Donald M. Callen; Ithaca, NY: Cornell University Press, 1982), pp. 188-207. For a recent defense of Wimsatt and Beardsley's position, see George Dickie and W. Kent Wilson, 'The Intentional Fallacy: Defending Beardsley', *The Journal of Aesthetics and Art Criticism* 53 (1995), pp. 233-50; and B. Rosebury, 'Irrecoverable Intentions and Literary Interpretation', *British Journal of Aesthetics* 37 (1997), pp. 15-30. Cf. John Maynard, *Literary Intention, Literary Interpretation, and Readers* (Ontario: Broadview Press, 2009); and Rachael Fernflores, 'Beyond the Intentional Fallacy', *Literature and Aesthetics* 20 (2010), pp. 56-73.

40. Wimsatt and Beardsley, 'Intentional Fallacy', p. 1. The argument of their essay relates specifically to poetic texts, though their paradigmatic statement of the problem of authorial intention has been applied by subsequent scholars to most other types of literature.

41. Wimsatt and Beardsley, 'Intentional Fallacy', p. 1. According to Wimsatt and Beardsley, the pursuit of this type of authorial intention was a hallmark of the Romantic period ('it is not so much a historical statement as a definition to say that the intentional fallacy is a romantic one', p. 3). They also argue that a poem is 'detached from the author at birth and goes about the world beyond his power to intend about it or control it' (p. 3). C.S. Lewis characterizes the intentional fallacy as the 'personal heresy'. See his dialogue (c. 1930s) on this issue with Milton scholar Eustace M.W. Tillyard in *The Personal Heresy: A Controversy* (ed. Joel D. Heck; Austin, TX: Concordia University Press, 2008). Concerned about the rising prominence of 'biography in our literary studies', Lewis seeks to push back on the 'proposition that all poetry is *about* the poet's state of mind' and that poetry 'must be the expression of [the poet's] personality' (p. 4). The poet/author's mental makeup 'is precisely what does not count' in

this manner, they reject the notion that a reader has access to the whims, desires, and mental state at the time of writing. These specific arguments are generally persuasive due in large measure to the vague parameters of this aspect of an individual writer's psychology.[42] However, granting the inability of readers and later interpreters to access the 'mental state/mind of the author', one can still speak of a circumscribed notion of an author's communicative intention.

This precise level of investigation asks, 'What has the author communicated in his or her text?' Further, 'what an author has intended' is understood in light of 'what an author has actually done' in/with a text compositionally. Thus, an interpreter/reader can focus on an author's *textual intention* while fully recognizing that an author's *psychological intention* is beyond access. That an author's psychological intention is inexplicable does not necessarily mean that his or her textual intention cannot be discerned or explained.[43]

interpreting his or her work (p. 19). 'The value of a poem consisting in what it does to the readers', Lewis concludes, 'all questions about the poet's attitude to his utterance are irrelevant' (p. 98).

42. Wimsatt and Beardsley observe that 'there is a gross body of life, of sensory and mental experience, which lies behind and in some sense causes every poem, but can never be and need not be known in the verbal and hence intellectual composition which is the poem' ('Intentional Fallacy', p. 8). Cf. Stefan Collini's characterization of the intentional fallacy: 'The supposed mistake of believing that evidence about the author's pretextual intentions might be relevant to establishing the "meaning" of the "verbal icon" (to use Wimsatt's phrase) that was the work of literature' ('Introduction: Interpretation Terminable and Interminable', in *Interpretation and Overinterpretation*, p. 6). Cf. Kevin J. Vanhoozer, 'Intention/Intentional Fallacy', in *DTIB*, pp. 327-30. Vanhoozer summarizes the perceived 'fallacy' of intentionalism: 'to mistake a *historical* inquiry about authors for a properly *interpretive* study of texts' (p. 237). Acknowledging the recent framing of the debate, Vanhoozer notes that 'the notion of authorial intention crops up throughout the history of biblical interpretation and has bearing on a number of crucial hermeneutical issues, including the nature of the text, the meaning of meaning, and the aims and norms of reading' (p. 327). Accordingly, Vanhoozer highlights the implications of authorial intention for theological and biblical studies.

43. As Vanhoozer notes, 'It is only fallacious to appeal to intention when the appeal is to some mental, pre-textual event, rather than to the intention embodied in the text' (*Meaning in this Text*, p. 253). In the 'Preface to the Anniversary Edition' of *Meaning in this Text*, Vanhoozer reiterates that 'a text is thus a means and medium of authorial action' and that 'meaning is an affair not of "planning" but "performing"' (*Meaning in this Text*, p. 5). For Vanhoozer, 'a text is a set of verbal signs intended by an author to bring about understanding in a reader' ('Intention/Intentional Fallacy', p. 329). Consequently, 'Intention pertains to what authors are doing *in tending* to their words. To interpret is to describe what an author is doing in a particular sentence or passage by paying attention both to its formal features (e.g. the words, the structure) and to its broader context, to the text as a whole (e.g. the literary genre)' (p. 329). Similarly, Brown sets the task of interpretation in the context of a communication model and

This focus on the *textual intention* of an author allows an interpreter to keep the process of interpretation in the realm of text and also maintains the role of the author as a central contributor/producer of verbal meaning.[44]

Intertextual Quotations. Proponents of a modest understanding of intertextuality generally recognize two broad types of intertextual references, namely, quotations and allusions. First, an author may employ a direct citation or quotation of another text (e.g. a New Testament author utilizing a passage from the Old Testament). This type of reference may include an introductory formula and sometimes an identification of the source. In either case, the author explicitly alerts the reader that he is utilizing a different text.[45] The biblical writer might cite the author, the book, or simply

defines meaning as 'the complex pattern of what an author intends to communicate with his or her audience for the purposes of engagement, which is inscribed in the text' (*Scripture as Communication*, p. 48). Both Vanhoozer and Brown draw on and modify the notion of verbal meaning developed by Hirsch in *Validity in Interpretation*.

44. Hirsch in particular has championed the relevance of an author's intention for the determination of verbal meaning. Thus, Hirsch is a central dialogue partner in many of the intentionalist/anti-intentionalist debates. See Hirsch, *Validity in Interpretation*; E.D. Hirsch, 'Objective Interpretation', *PMLA* 75 (1960), pp. 463-79; and E.D. Hirsch, 'Current Issues in Theory of Interpretation', *Journal of Religion* 55 (1975), pp. 298-312. Dickie and Wilson summarize this theoretical divide in 'Defending Beardsley', p. 235: 'The dispute between Beardsley [anti-intentionalist] and Hirsch [intentionalist] can be stated quite sharply. Beardsley claims that combinations of words can have a specific meaning independently of anyone's intention. Hirsch claims that combinations of words cannot have a specific meaning unless that meaning is intended by its author and further that an author's intention *determines* the meaning his combinations of words have.' In their article, Dickie and Wilson summarize the position of anti-intentionalism (primarily Wimsatt and Beardsley) and then seek to refute various arguments for intentionalism (e.g. those espoused by Hirsch and Paul Grice), including the notion of 'hypothetical intentionalism' developed by William Tolhurst. In subsequent works, Hirsch somewhat softens his strict distinction between 'meaning' and 'significance' (attempting to take into account the shifting contexts of future readers), though he maintains the relevance of the author's intention in the determining of meaning. In this regard, see E.D. Hirsch, *The Aims of Interpretation* (Chicago: The University of Chicago Press, 1976); E.D. Hirsch, 'Meaning and Significance Reinterpreted', *Critical Inquiry* 11 (1984), pp. 202-25; and E.D. Hirsch, 'Transhistorical Intentions and the Persistence of Allegory', *New Literary History* 25 (1994), pp. 549-67. Cf. Evan Watkins, 'Criticism and Method: Hirsch, Frye, Barthes', *Soundings* 58 (1975), pp. 257-80; Dale Leschert, 'A Change of Meaning, Not a Change of Mind: The Clarification of a Suspected Defection in the Hermeneutical Theory of E.D. Hirsch, Jr', *JETS* 35 (1992), pp. 183-87; Kate McLoughlin and Carl Gardner, 'When Is Authorial Intention Not Authorial Intention?', *European Journal of English Studies* 11 (2007), pp. 93-105; and Linda O'Neil, 'Hermeneutic Haunting: E.D. Hirsch, Jr and the Ghost of Interpretive Validity', *Educational Studies* 47 (2011), pp. 451-68.

45. Steve Moyise defines an 'explicit quotation' as an instance where 'an author

note that he is quoting 'Scripture'. The task of the interpreter is then to identify the source of the quotation or citation on the basis of parallels in wording with the original text. Most of the time, identifying quotations is a relatively straightforward process. The verbal elements of a quotation frequently either match the source text verbatim or resemble it closely enough to remove uncertainty regarding the connection.[46]

For instance, in John's passion narrative in John 19, the intertextual uses of Psalm 22, Psalm 34, and Zech. 12.10 can be classified as explicit quotations or direct citations, as each is prefaced with an introductory formula that identifies the quoted text as 'Scripture'.[47] Further, each can be identified on the basis of significant verbal parallels.[48] By quoting these passages, John asserts in a striking fashion that specific details of Jesus' crucifixion scene correspond to the scene of suffering depicted in Psalm 22. That other specific details of the Psalm correspond to John's account further highlights John's interest in showing a connection between the two texts. Jesus' thirst (19.28/Ps. 22.15), his pierced hands and feet (19.23/Ps. 22.16), and his preserved bones (19.33/Ps. 22.17) all resonate with the psalmist's depiction. Through these intertexts, John allows the quoted context of Psalm 22 to resonate in his own narrative composition.

The pattern of Matthew's fulfillment formulae in the first two chapters of his Gospel also serves as a clear example of intertextual quotation.[49]

---

clearly indicates that the words that follow are not his or her own but are taken from another source' ('Quotations', in *As it is Written: Studying Paul's Use of Scripture* [ed. Stanley E. Porter and Christopher D. Stanley; Atlanta, GA: SBL, 2008], p. 15). He also notes that 'if the text is particularly well known, it is possible to introduce it without any marker at all' (p. 15). Daly-Denton also notes that the 'narrative setting' of a quotation sometimes 'functions *in lieu* of such a formula', especially when 'its textual fidelity to its source is beyond question' (*David in the Fourth Gospel: The Johannine Reception of the Psalms* [Leiden: Brill, 2000], p. 10).

46. When the quotation differs from any known source text, the author could either have altered the phraseology for stylistic or theological reasons, or utilized a source no longer extant. Cf. Moyise's statements in relation to Paul in 'Quotations', p. 17.

47. The exact texts are 19.24 (Ps. 22.18); 19.36 (Exod. 12.46/Num. 9.12 and Ps. 34.20); and 19.37 (Zech. 12.10).

48. To give one example, the Greek text of Ps. 22.18 (LXX 21.19) reads διεμερίσαντο τὰ ἱμάτιά μου ἑαυτοῖς καὶ ἐπὶ τὸν ἱματισμόν μου ἔβαλον κλῆρον, and the NA^{27} text of Jn 19.24 reads ἵνα ἡ γραφὴ πληρωθῇ [ἡ λέγουσα]· διεμερίσαντο τὰ ἱμάτιά μου ἑαυτοῖς καὶ ἐπὶ τὸν ἱματισμόν μου ἔβαλον κλῆρον ('they divided my outer garments among them, and for my clothing they cast lots'). These texts are verbatim over an extended linguistic sequence, thus providing evidence of an intertextual quotation. Though some cases are not as clear as Jn 19.24, this text illustrates the solid evidence that verbal parallels provide.

49. The specific connections are Mt. 1.22-23/Isa. 7.14; Mt. 2.5-6/Mic. 5.2; Mt. 2.15/Hos. 11.1; Mt. 2.17-18/Jer. 31.15; Mt. 2.23/Isa. 11.1; and Mt. 4.14-15/Isa. 9.1-2. For a survey of these 'formula-quotations', see R.T. France, *The Gospel of Matthew*

Further, because of their initial and final locations in the four-fold Gospel corpus, these sections of Matthew and John, respectively, provide book-ends to one of the overarching themes of the gospel proclamation, namely, that Jesus represents the fulfillment of Scripture. An attentive reader of the four-fold Gospel is thus encouraged to view the four Gospels in light of key Old Testament quotations.[50] This pattern of intertextual activity is also an example of the way the compositional strategies of the biblical authors help solidify the canonical context in the mind of the reader (contextuality).[51]

Intertextual Allusions. Another type of intertextual connection is an allusion. In this case, an author simply alludes to another biblical text without noting the source or even indicating that s/he is utilizing another text. A literary allusion is a textual reference designed to bring something to the mind of a reader without mentioning it directly.[52] Though indirect, the allusive reference has a purpose and is part of the author's intended meaning.[53] The allusive connection is 'an enunciation whose full meaning

(NICNT; Grand Rapids, MI: Eerdmans, 2007), pp. 10-14. France notes that this quotation pattern is 'a distinctive feature of this gospel' (p. 11). Cf. also Michael P. Knowles, 'Scripture, History, Messiah: Scriptural Fulfillment and the Fullness of Time in Matthew's Gospel', in *Hearing the Old Testament in the New Testament* (ed. Stanley E. Porter; Grand Rapids, MI: Eerdmans, 2006), pp. 59-82.

50. Cf. Phillips, 'Biblical Studies and Intertextuality', pp. 39-40. Commenting on the reference to Isaiah in Mk 1.1, Phillips reflects on the wide-ranging effect of the quoted text: 'The intertextual role of this beginning is clear—the text is to be interpreted within the light of the Hebrew Scriptures and in particular the prophecy of Second Isaiah. However, there is more intertextuality here than the direct reference to Isaiah. The beginning of the Gospel refers explicitly to Isaiah, but implicitly, through the compound quotation, it refers also to Exodus, Malachi and to the general pattern of the salvation history of Israel by introducing themes of Exodus, Exile and Return. Since the intertextual function of the beginning is to set the milieu within which the text must be interpreted, Mark's Gospel has to be interpreted within the light of Isaiah and the Hebrew Bible specifically, if not the whole of Jewish salvation history in general.'

51. See the theoretical discussion of 'Contextuality' in Chapter 3.

52. Cf. Stanley Porter's definition in 'Allusions and Echoes', in *As it is Written: Studying Paul's Use of Scripture* (ed. Stanley E. Porter and Christopher D. Stanley; Atlanta, GA: SBL, 2008), p. 30: 'The term *allusion* is used for a figure of speech that makes indirect extratextual references.' See also Porter's discussion in 'Further Comments on the Use of the Old Testament in the New Testament', in *The Intertextuality of the Epistles*, pp. 98-110.

53. Porter, summarizing a variety of definitions, notes that 'allusion is a figure used by the author to reference specific types of material for a functional purpose' ('Allusions and Echoes', p. 31). Cf. Daly-Denton's point that 'allusions, although more fragmentary and periphrastic, must still be recognizable if they are to perform their function' (*David in the Fourth Gospel*, p. 9).

presupposes the perception of a relationship between it and another text, to which it necessarily refers by some inflections that would otherwise remain unintelligible'.[54] Some allusions are readily discernable due to the prominence of the text they refer to or the clear verbal parallels between the two texts. Other allusions make more opaque reference to sometimes fragmentary sources.[55]

As mentioned above, John's passion narrative makes use of a series of intertextual quotations. These quotations have a deliberate citation formula to highlight directly the connection between the texts cited. In Matthew's passion narrative, he makes use of a series of intertexts. However, Matthew primarily alludes rather than quotes in the construction of his narrative of Jesus' crucifixion. Though he does not employ quotation, Matthew nevertheless weaves textual allusions to Psalm 22 throughout his narrative in Mt. 27.33-54. There are four main points of contact with Psalm 22 in Matthew's text. Matthew mentions the actual crucifixion almost in passing ('And when they had crucified him…') and moves quickly to the details that give meaning to this historical event. In his description of the soldiers dividing up 'his garments among themselves by casting lots' (Mt. 27.35), Matthew alludes to Ps. 22.18.[56]

In his description of the insults Jesus receives on the cross in Mt. 27.39-44, Matthew alludes to the words of the enemies of the Lord in Ps. 22.7-8. Those 'hurling abuse' at Jesus were 'wagging their heads' as they taunted him.[57] The words of Ps. 22.8 are in the mouths of the Jewish leaders mocking Jesus, saying, 'he trusts in God; Let God rescue him now, if he delights in him' (Mt. 22.43).[58] Jesus' dialogue in this scene too is a clear allusion

54. Genette, *Palimpsests*, p. 2.

55. Cf. Thiselton, *New Horizons*, p. 40: 'It is notoriously difficult to distinguish between resonances and shared uses of familiar imagery or language and conscious quotation.' In order to engage in the way allusions actually function in a text, they can be broadly categorized in terms of verbal and thematic allusions. A verbal allusion can refer to individual/specific words or themes, and a thematic allusion can also refer to words or themes more expansively. For an outline of these broad classifications, see Ian Paul, 'The Use of the Old Testament in Revelation 12', in *The Old Testament in the New Testament: Essays in Honour of J.L. North* (ed. Steve Moyise; Sheffield: Sheffield Academic Press, 2000), pp. 257-63. The clarification of authorial intention above seeks to address Paul's critique of Jon Paulien regarding this issue (see discussion below). If the author's communicative meaning is seen as embodied in the text, then the 'intention of the author' and the 'coherence of the text' will be closely aligned.

56. Ps. 22.18: 'They divide my garments among them, And for my clothing they cast lots'.

57. Ps. 22.7-8: 'All who see me sneer at me; They separate with the lip, they wag the head, saying, Commit yourself to the Lord; let him deliver him; Let him rescue him, because he delights in him'.

58. In this section (Mt. 27.38-44), Matthew twice notes that Jesus was surrounded

to the opening words of Ps. 22.1: 'My God, my God, why have you forsaken me?' (Mt. 27.46). After Jesus yields up his spirit and the veil of the temple is torn, Matthew 'flashes forward' to give a glimpse of the resurrection (Mt. 27.52-54).[59] This glimpse of the near future resonates with the climax of Psalm 22, where the Psalmist recounts that the Lord 'has not despised nor abhorred the affliction of the afflicted; Nor has he hidden his face from him' (Ps 22.24). Rather, 'when he cried to him for help, he heard' (Ps. 22.24). With the context of Psalm 22 in view, Matthew's flash forward is a confirmation to the readers that the Lord did in fact hear the prayers of his anointed one when he cried out intertextually informed words of despair (Mt. 27.46).

Through this sequence of intertextual allusions, Matthew 'fills out' the scene of Psalm 22. Each of the allusions noted above require exegetical analysis and interpretive verification.[60] However, a study of the technical details of Matthew's use of the Old Testament need not distract interpreters from his larger compositional purposes. Opting to employ the more subtle method of allusion allows Matthew to build a powerfully evocative narrative tapestry. The effect of this intertextual narration is cumulative. Readers familiar with Psalm 22 will catch the full force of Matthew's intertextual activity. Through his connections to the Psalmist's text, Matthew juxtaposes the scenes and generates a field of textual connections. In Psalm 22, the enemies of the Lord are the ones sneering, mocking, and wagging their heads at the afflicted David. In a startling reversal, in Matthew 27, the leaders of

---

by 'two robbers', even specifying, 'one on the right and one on the left' (27.38) and that 'the robbers who had been crucified with him were also insulting him with the same words' (27.44). This detail could also allude to the scene of Psalm 22, where the enemies of God engulf the afflicted one: 'Many bulls have surrounded me; Strong bulls of Bashan have encircled me... For dogs have surrounded me; a band of evildoers has encompassed me' (22.12, 16).

59. A close reading of the deictic elements of the narrative of 27.52-54 seems to indicate swift shifts in the temporal sequence. After Jesus yields up his spirit (27.50), the veil is torn, the earth shakes and the rocks are split (27.51), and the tombs were opened and many saints were raised (27.52). Then, Matthew notes that they came out of their tombs '*after* his resurrection' and entered Jerusalem and appeared to many (27.53). Immediately following this note, Matthew flashes back to the narrative present of the crucifixion scene: '*Now* the centurion, and those who were with him keeping guard over Jesus, *when* they saw the earthquake and the things that were happening...' (27.54). The narrated temporal sequence then proceeds as normal (27.57: 'When it was evening, there came a rich man from Arimathea...').

60. New Testament scholars typically recognize most of the specific allusions noted above. E.g., see the entries for Psalm 22 in UBS[4]'s 'index of allusions and verbal parallels' (UBS[4], p. 895). Cf. Craig L. Blomberg's survey in 'Matthew', in *Commentary on the New Testament Use of the Old Testament* (ed. G.K. Beale and D.A. Carson; Grand Rapids, MI: Baker, 2007), pp. 97-100.

Israel are the ones wagging their head and hurling the insults of the enemies of God at the crucified Christ. In this sense, Matthew's account of
Jesus' cry from the cross functions as an indictment on the leaders of Israel
for provoking those words by crucifying him and for playing the part of the
villains of that very scene from the Psalter. The art of allusion allows Matthew to harness not only the power of the literary genre of narrative but also
to enhance that narrative with a strategic scene from Israel's textual past.
Thus, along with quotations, intertextual allusions are important and often
utilized elements in the authorial arsenal of the biblical writers.

Intertextual Echoes. A subcategory of allusion is the concept of an intertextual echo.[61] The 'echo' is a particular form (a subtype) of an intertextual
allusion. In Hays' terms, 'an allusive echo functions to suggest to the reader
that text B should be understood in light of a broad interplay with text A,
encompassing aspects of A beyond those explicitly echoed'.[62] Having both
categories active and available enables a reader to appreciate subtle literary elements otherwise unrecoverable (or at least difficult to describe). In
the scheme outlined here, quotations, allusions, and echoes are on a spectrum of authorial purpose and use, moving from direct, to indirect, to subtle,
respectively.[63]

61. The study of intertextual echoes has received increased attention since the publication of Richard B. Hays' *Echoes of Scripture in the Letters of Paul* (New Haven, CT:
Yale University Press, 1989). See also Richard B. Hays, *The Conversion of the Imagi-
nation: Paul as Interpreter of Israel's Scripture* (Grand Rapids, MI: Eerdmans, 2005).
In this work, Hays responds to critics of his earlier work (pp. 163-89). In this regard,
note also Richard B. Hays, 'On the Rebound: A Response to Critiques of *Echoes of
Scripture in the Letters of Paul*', in *Paul and the Scriptures of Israel* (ed. Craig A.
Evans and James A. Sanders; Sheffield: Sheffield Academic Press, 1993), pp. 70-96.
Porter provides a number of methdological cautions and critiques of Hays' approach
in 'Further Comments on the Use of the Old Testament', pp. 99-106; and Stanley
E. Porter, 'The Use of the Old Testament in the New Testament: A Brief Comment
on Method and Terminology', in *Early Christian Interpretation of the Scriptures of
Israel: Investigations and Proposals* (ed. Craig A. Evans and James A. Sanders; Sheffield: Sheffield Academic Press, 1997), pp. 79-96.
62. Hays, *Echoes of Scripture*, p. 20. He also says that 'when a literary echo links
the text in which it occurs to an earlier text, the figurative effect of the echo can lie
in the unstated or suppressed (transumed) points of resonance between the two texts'
(p. 20).
63. Daly-Denton calls this continuum a '"sliding scale" of diminishing intentionality
on the part of the author and decreasing visibility on the surface of the text, requiring a
correspondingly increasing competence on the part of the reader' (*David in the Fourth
Gospel*, p. 9). Hays comments, 'Quotation, allusion, and echo may be seen as points
along a spectrum of intertextual reference, moving from the explicit to the subliminal.
As we move farther away from overt citation, the source recedes into the discursive distance, the intertextual relations become less determinate, and the demand placed on the

For some, the category of 'echo' is a way to avoid any discussion of authorial intention. John Hollander and Richard Hays characterize an echo as 'a metaphor of, and for, alluding, and does not depend on conscious intention'.[64] In their formulation, a literary echo is an unintended indirect reference to a text.[65] Clearly, discerning this type of intertextual reference is difficult and can sometimes rely based solely on a reader's response to a text. However, this category can be helpful if the distinction between echo and allusion remains loosely intact.[66]

Moreover, recognizing the multifaceted manner in which authors utilize texts in their own compositional work, one might distinguish various authorial purposes in the 'echoing' of scriptural texts, themes, and literary patterns/shapes. Though there are certainly unintended echoes that a given reader might hear, there could also be 'echo effects' embedded in a text with the design of evoking a certain set of associations or reactions. These instances of intertextual echoes are intended by the author but for a different purpose than an intertextual allusion. An author can both allude to and echo a text according to the design of his/her compositional strategy. When connecting the 'echo effect' of a text to an author's compositional strategy, there is a similarity between the notions of a 'strong echo' and a 'subtle allusion'. The 'echo' terminology is valuable to interpreters because it provides a nuanced category to describe the artful textual elements of a literary composition. The effects that intertextuality generates in the writing and reading

reader's listening powers grows greater' (*Echoes of Scripture*, p. 23). Paulien notes that 'the assessment of an ancient author's intention with regard to allusions will always be an exercise in probability. There will always be an element of art in the process as well as science' ('Elusive Allusions in the Apocalypse', p. 63). Cf. the helpful table depicting the 'sliding scale of allusion probability' drawn up by Köstenberger and Patterson in *Invitation to Hermeneutics*, p. 543. Arguing for heightened methodological rigor in the analysis of intertextual connections, Porter too emphasizes the value of recognizing the 'variety of ways in which a text might be cited' and arranging these 'along a cline or continuum of possible uses' ('Further Comments on the Use of the Old Testament', p. 106). For Porter, the five main categories on this continuum are formulaic quotation, direct quotation, paraphrase, allusion, and echo (see pp. 107-110).

64. John Hollander, *The Figure of Echo: A Model of Allusion in Milton and After* (Berkeley, CA: University of California Press, 1981); Hays, *Echoes of Scripture*, p. 29.

65. In order to sidestep the issue of authorial intention and audience reception, Hays opts to 'make no systematic distinction between the terms'. In his work, '*allusion* is used of obvious intertextual references, *echo* of subtler ones' (*Echoes of Scripture*, p. 29).

66. This methodological step here and in the following paragraph represents a departure from Hays' less strict distinction between the nature of an 'echo' and an 'allusion'. Cf. the work of Jon Paulien (see n. 67, below), who argues for a strict distinction between an allusion and an echo (with authorial intention being connected to the former and not the latter).

of biblical texts is no less *intended* because it is *understated*. Even when the rumbles of intertextuality are heard only as whispers of other texts, they nevertheless render their effect in meaningful ways.

Discerning Intertextual Connections

When engaging or appropriating this type of intertextual analysis, the pressing need is criteria by which intertextual references are to be discerned. Intertextual allusions in particular are oftentimes notoriously difficult to discern and thus represent a challenge to any interpreter. A reflective set of methodological 'controls' for discerning allusive references can go a long way toward making these allusions a little less elusive.[67] In line with a production-oriented concept of intertextuality, the allusions that the interpreter seeks to discern are the ones placed/embedded in the text by the author.[68]

Because a production-oriented perspective investigates the intertextual connections that are 'produced' by an author, these connections are somehow marked in the text and are part of the intertextual potential of the original composition. In this model, texts contain intentional or circumstantial 'markings' that serve as pointers to intertextual references.[69] Accordingly,

67. For a helpful introduction to the 'elusive' task of identifying the embarrassment of Old Testament allusions in the New Testament (Revelation in particular), see Jon Paulien, 'Elusive Allusions: The Problematic Use of the Old Testament in Revelation', *Biblical Research* 22 (1988), pp. 37-53; and Jon Paulien, 'Criteria and Assessment of Allusions to the Old Testament in the Book of Revelation', in *Studies in the Book of Revelation* (ed. Steve Moyise; Edinburgh: T. & T. Clark, 2001), pp. 113-29. Paulien reflects on the state of the scholarly discussion on this issue in 'Elusive Allusions in the Apocalypse: Two Decades of Research into John's Use of the Old Testament', in *The Intertextuality of the Epistles*, pp. 61-68.

68. This perspective relies on a narrow/limited (i.e. 'modest') conception of intertextuality and also functions within a closed model of textuality. On these categories, see Alkier, 'Intertextuality', pp. 7-11.

69. On the notion of a text 'marking out' an intertextual reference, see Ziva Ben-Porat, 'The Poetics of Literary Allusion', *PTL: A Journal for Descriptive Poetics and Theory of Literature* 1 (1978), pp. 105-28 (108). Ben-Porat argues that a literary allusion embeds a 'built-in directional signal' (i.e. a 'marker') that is 'identifiable as an element or pattern belonging to another independent text'. Robert H. Suh, 'The Use of Ezekiel 37 in Ephesians 2', *JETS* 50 (2007), pp. 715-33 (718), observes that the 'shared vocabulary' of two literary compositions can be 'used in ways that function as distinctive markers that call to mind the source text'. Riffaterre speaks of the 'intertextual trace' in 'La Trace de l'intertexte', *La Pensée* 215 (1980), pp. 4-18. Cf. Gillmayr-Bucher, 'Intertextuality', pp. 18-19: 'Every understanding of a relation between texts starts essentially with the recognition of the relation. There has to be some kind of intertextual marker to guide the process of reading to an intertextual reading and understanding. It first needs a sign that is recognized as a marker in order to attract the readers' attention and make them aware of another text. In this process, every sign in a text can trigger an intertextual relation.'

the relevant allusive connections are the ones that plausibly fit into the compositional strategy of the author.[70] This way of viewing the nature of intertextual allusions assumes that the allusion was produced by the author, that it would be historically possible for the author to allude to a particular text, and that the allusion serves an actual function in the author's text.[71]

---

70. For Hays, 'to limit our interpretation of Paul's scriptural echoes to what he intended by them is to impose a severe and arbitrary hermeneutical restriction' (*Echoes of Scripture*, p. 33). However, seeking to take into account the context of interpretive communities, Hays makes an important methodological decision (and one that separates him from proponents of an unlimited reception-oriented approach to intertextuality): 'Claims about intertextual meaning effects are strongest where it can credibly be demonstrated that they occur within the literary structure of the text and that they can plausibly be ascribed to the intention of the author and the competence of the original readers' (p. 28). Accordingly, Hays examines 'the phenomenon of intertextuality in Paul's letters in a more limited sense, focusing on his actual citations of and allusions to specific texts' (p. 15). Daly-Denton notes that to avoid succumbing to parallelomania, 'the echoed text must be reasonably distinctive' (*David in the Fourth Gospel*, p. 11). She states further that 'the claim that the author is echoing Scripture in a particular passage must be in line with what we know of the conventions for Scripture interpretation during the NT period' and 'must also cohere with the author's general line of argument' (p. 11).

71. Hays outlines several criteria for determining the presence of an 'echo' in *Echoes of Scripture*, pp. 25-33 (a section entitled, 'Hermeneutical Reflections and Constraints'). His seven tests for 'hearing echoes' in a text include:

1. *Availability:* 'Was the proposed source of the echo available to the author and/ or original readers?'
2. *Volume:* 'The volume of an echo is determined primarily by the degree of explicit repetition of words or syntactical patterns, but other factors may also be relevant.'
3. *Recurrence:* 'How often does Paul elsewhere cite or allude to the same scriptural passage?'
4. *Thematic Coherence:* 'How well does the alleged echo fit into the line of argument that Paul is developing? Is its meaning effect consonant with other quotations in the same letter or elsewhere in the Pauline corpus?'
5. *Historical Plausibility:* 'Could Paul have intended the alleged meaning effect? Could his readers have understood it?'
6. *History of Interpretation:* 'Have other readers, both critical and pre-critical, heard the same echoes? The readings of our predecessors can both check and stimulate our perception of scriptural echoes in Paul.'
7. *Satisfaction:* 'With or without clear confirmation from the other criteria listed here, does the proposed reading make sense? Does it illuminate the surrounding discourse? Does it produce for the reader a satisfying account of the effect of the intertextual relation?'

Hays acknowledges that 'there are always only shades of certainty when these criteria are applied to particular texts' but also that 'the more of them that fall clearly into place, the more confident we can be in rendering an interpretation of the echo effect in

Consequently, one of the most important elements in discerning an allusion is the author's textual intent.[72] If an author's meaning can be discerned by examining their text, then the presence of verbal, thematic, and structural parallels can function as a set of criteria for determining whether or not an author actually has a precursor text in view.[73] These parallels can often adequately indicate the meaning of the author.

a given passage' (p. 32). See also Suh, 'Use of Ezekiel 37 in Ephesians 2', pp. 715-33. Suh argues that Ezekiel's account of the valley of dry bones that come to life parallels Paul's account of a salvation that involves the bringing to life of those who were once 'dead in their transgressions'. He establishes 'points of contact' between these two texts by 'seeking out verbal, structural, and conceptual/thematic parallels' (p. 717). Suh concludes that 'whatever Paul's intention, he used Ezekiel 37 as a framework for building his own argument in Ephesians 2' (p. 733). Köstenberger and Patterson employ a set of five criteria for discerning a literary allusion (*Invitation to Biblical Interpretation*, pp. 544-47): (1) linguistic parallels; (2) theological significance; (3) contextual consistency; (4) transitivity ('transitivity denotes the ability of the audience to grasp and comprehend the allusion and its source text', p. 545); and (5) availability. Jeffery M. Leonard engages the task of discerning the nature of allusions at length in 'Identifying Inner-Biblical Allusions: Psalm 78 as a Test Case', *JBL* 127 (2008), pp. 241-65. Leonard asks specifically, 'If a link between texts can be established, what evidence is needed to ascertain the direction of the textual or traditional influence?' (p. 242). For him, 'to be valid [an intertextual allusion] must rest on genuine textual connection whose direction of dependence can actually be established' (p. 243). Stressing the importance of verbal links, Leonard posits 'shared language' as the 'single most important factor in establishing a textual connection' (p. 246). Cf. also Daly-Denton's methodological discussion in *David in the Fourth Gospel*, pp. 9-12. Though these various sets of criteria cannot be rigidly applied to every instance of intertextual connection, they provide an important attempt at articulating what a limited/modest approach to intertextuality might look like in the context of biblical studies.

72. Note also, in this regard, Eco's caution: 'When a text unleashes the mechanism of intertextual irony, it has to expect that it will not produce just the allusions intended by the author, since the possibility of having a double reading depends on the breadth of the reader's own textual encyclopedia, and this encyclopedia varies from reader to reader' ('Intertextual Irony', pp. 228-29). In a similar vein, it is also helpful to remember that 'allusion is a natural and expected feature of literature, and is not always a specific attempt by the author to refer explicitly to a second specific text. Texts, as part of the Intertext, habitually exhibit intertextuality' (Phillips, 'Biblical Studies and Intertextuality', p. 44). Cf. the discussion in Chapter 5 of the terms 'encyclopedia' and 'universe of discourse' in relation to an author's textual intention.

73. These three types of parallels are developed by Paulien in 'Elusive Allusions', pp. 41-44. Paulien categorizes intertextual references into four main groups: citations, quotations, allusions, and echoes. He argues that 'with citations and quotations, we are certain that an author had a specific previous text in mind. With allusion, we are reasonably certain of the same. With an echo, we are reasonably certain that there is no intention on the part of the author to refer the reader to a particular pretext' ('Elusive Allusions in the Apocalypse', p. 67). He also cautions, 'Results will be compromised if an author's intention to allude to the Old Testament is ignored or if intention

Intertextuality within the Canonical Context
Interpreters working from a modest approach to intertextuality can greatly benefit from a canon-conscious understanding of the interpretive task. The concept of canon can serve a crucial function in the intertextual conversation. Though accepting canonical limits does exclude many intertextual connections (e.g. Conan the Barbarian or *Gone with the Wind*), this limitation can actually be a benefit in the interpretive task rather than a burden.[74] The concept of canon can provide a helpful way to limit the scope of examined discourse while avoiding completely arbitrary or *ad hoc* strictures. This restriction can be understood as a 'voluntary' and intentional restraint on the part of both biblical writers and biblical interpreters. In this sense, interpreters accept the 'plane' or conditions set by the author of the text being read.[75] In this way, the concept of 'canon' facilitates and governs the process of forming controls for the limitless possibilities of meaning.

The reality of intertextuality is an organic feature of the wide-ranging canonical collection.[76] As developed above, the task of identifying intertex-

is seen where it was not intended' (p. 67). See also Paul's reflection on and critique of Paulien's categories in 'Use of the Old Testament in Revelation 12', pp. 257-63. He argues that an 'evaluation of allusions' needs two dimensions: 'an axis of confidence (the reader's perpective); and an axis of significance (the author's/text's perspective)' (p. 261).

74. Adopting an unlimited view of textuality and intertextuality, George Aichele investigates the intertextual connections between the Gospel passion narratives and the Conan the Barbarian storylines ('Canon as Intertext: Restraint or Liberation?', in *Reading the Bible Intertextually*, pp. 148-55), and Tina Pippin brings into dialogue diverse characterizations of the infamous figure of Jezebel from (inter alia) 2 Kings 9, Revelation 2, and the novel *Gone with the Wind* ('Jezebel Re-Vamped', in *A Feminist Companion to Samuel and Kings* [ed. Athalya Brenner; Sheffield: Sheffield Academic Press, 1994], pp. 196-206). Pippin asks rhetorically in her conclusion, 'What have we done with the story of Jezebel? Is her story continually recolonized, reopened, the brief scenes of her life re-enacted and reinscribed?' (p. 206). Cf. George W.E. Nickelsburg, 'Tobit, Genesis, and the Odyssey: A Complex Web of Intertextuality', in *Mimesis and Intertextuality in Antiquity and Christianity* (ed. Dennis R. MacDonald; Harrisburg, PA: Trinity Press International, 2001), pp. 41-55; and the wide range of essays in *Those Outside: Noncanonical Readings of the Canonical Gospels* (ed. George Aichele and Richard Walsh; New York: T. & T. Clark, 2005). Further, in a recent commentary, Aichele brings Jude and 2 Peter into intertextual dialogue with the 1956 science fiction film, *Invasion of the Body Snatchers*. See George Aichele, *The Letters of Jude and Second Peter: Paranoia and the Slaves of Christ* (Sheffield: Sheffield Phoenix Press, 2002). Aichele comments, '*Invasion of the Body Snatchers* and the letter of Jude illuminate one another, even as they cast intertextual light on "paranoid despotic regimes"' (p. 39).

75. Cf. Chapter 5's discussion of what is involved in becoming the ideal reader of the biblical text.

76. Scheetz speaks of the 'complex issues one faces with the biblical text, which is

tual connections is crucial because they are woven into the fabric of most of the biblical material within that collection.[77] One of the benefits of viewing references to the Old Testament in terms of intertextuality involves the context of these referenced texts. A hallmark of intertextual studies is the focus on the broader 'universe of discourse' generated by the text used by an author. By making reference to another text, an author unavoidably invokes the larger context of that original text.[78] The abovementioned difficulty of identifying the texts referenced by the biblical authors is mollified by the fact that they 'repeatedly situate' their discourse 'within the symbolic field created by a single great textual precursor: Israel's Scripture'.[79] The largest

at the same time a singular text and yet many texts' (*Concept of Canonical Intertextuality*, p. vii). He also notes that within a canonical context, intertextuality 'speaks of the dialogue inherent in the canonical text because of the canon and canonical process. There are points of dialogue between the context that gave rise to a particular text, the text that was consequently written, the greater literary context(s) in which the text has been gathered, and the reuse of text(s) in another context' (p. 33). Seeking to combine the insights of both 'Kristevan influenced intertextuality' and 'canon criticism', Scheetz's 'goal is an attempt to understand the actual composition of the text of scripture that is at the same time a text and many texts' (p. 32).

77. Cf. Hugh Holman, *A Handbook to Literature* (Indianapolis, IN: Bobbs-Merrill, 1980), p. 127: 'Discovering the meaning and value of the allusions is frequently essential to understanding [a] work.'

78. Of course, this assertion is strongly contested by some. For a snapshot of the debate on this issue between C.H. Dodd and Albert Sundberg, see I. Howard Marshall, 'An Assessment of Recent Developments', in *It is Written: Scripture Citing Scripture* (ed. D.A. Carson and H.G.M. Williamson; Cambridge: Cambridge University Press, 1988), pp. 1-21. For Dodd, strategic 'fields' of Old Testament texts form the 'substructure' of the New Testament's theological message. See C.H. Dodd, *According to the Scriptures: The Substructure of New Testament Theology* (London: James Nisbet, 1952). For a recent defense of the position that the New Testament authors did *not* recognize and respect the context of the OT passages they quoted, see Martin Pickup, 'New Testament Interpretation of the Old Testament: The Theological Rationale of Midrashic Exegesis', *JETS* 51 (2008), pp. 253-82. See also the spectrum presented by Walter Kaiser, Darrel Bock, and Peter Enns in *Three Views on the New Testament Use of the Old Testament* (ed. Kenneth Berding and Jonathan Lunde; Grand Rapids, MI: Zondervan, 2009). The discussion below engages the biblical writers' multifaceted use of textual contexts. Cf. Daly-Denton, *David in the Fourth Gospel*, p. 1: 'The literary theory of intertextuality acknowledges that texts do not exist in isolation. When a quotation from an earlier work is introduced into a later work, it brings in its train manifold resonances of other texts already associated with it.'

79. Hays, *Echoes of Scripture*, p. 15. Hays makes this statement specifically in relation to Paul, but it holds true for the rest of the New Testament writers as well. Hays believes that this feature of Paul's letters is something he imitates from the Old Testament material itself. In this sense, Paul 'allows Scripture to echo into the text of his letters in such a way that the echoes suggest patterns of meaning wider than his own overt interpretive claims. Paul's own discourse recapitulates the allusive complexity of his great subtext' (p. 155).

and most extensive entry in the biblical authors' conceptual library of possible intertextual connections is labeled, 'The Hebrew Bible'. Because the
biblical authors consistently draw upon the narrative world generated by
other biblical texts, the developing canon is a prevailing textual context for
the writing and reading of the Scriptures.[80] In other words, the canon both
guides and governs a biblical interpreter's detection and interpretation of
intertextual references and their fertile potential for rich biblical meaning.

While there are a variety of possible sources that inform the writings of
the biblical authors that should be taken into account, other biblical writings
remain the most prominent.[81] For example, both the prophets and poets of
Israel take their bearings from the theological themes and narrative world of
the Pentateuch. Subsequent biblical writers and leaders of Israel meditate on
the Law of Moses day and night, and this practice is reflected in their writings (cf. Josh. 1.7-8; Ps. 1.2; Mal. 4.4, etc.).[82] In the New Testament literature,
this phenomenon is similarly pronounced. The Gospels frame their narrative

---

80. In interacting with Barr's contention (in *Holy Scripture*) that the 'cross-
referencing' within the Old Testament is insignificant, Provan highlights this intertextual feature, noting that 'it is not a trivial or marginal matter, this reality of
cross-referencing. It is, rather, a central matter' ('Canons to the Left of Him', p. 8).
Provan argues further that it is 'an intrinsic feature of the nature of our OT narrative
texts that they have come into their present form in relationship with each other and
with Torah and prophetic texts, the very form in which they are written inviting reference time and time again to these other scriptural texts' (p. 8). He illustrates this principle by observing that in the book of Kings 'the whole way in which the story is told is
designed to get readers thinking about the broader context of the story in Torah, especially in Deuteronomy; to cause them to reflect on the way in which earlier events and
characters in the story of Joshua-Samuel illuminate the events and characters of Kings;
and to bring to mind also prophetic perspectives on the story' (pp. 8-9). For his development of these exegetical observations, see Ian W. Provan, *1 and 2 Kings* (Peabody,
MA: Hendrickson, 1995).

81. For a survey of extra-biblical documents that were significant to varying degrees
during the formation of the canon, see John H. Charlesworth, 'Writings Ostensibly
Outside the Canon', in *Exploring the Origins of the Bible* (ed. Craig Evans and Emanuel Tov; Grand Rapids, MI: Baker, 2008), pp. 57-86. Charlesworth argues for a late
date for the closing of both the Old Testament and the New Testament (if they ever
closed at all) and views extrabiblical literature as formative for the biblical writings.
For a contrasting perspective, see the discussion in Chapters 1-2.

82. Cf. Dempster, 'Canon and Old Testament Interpretation', p. 169: 'When prophets began to record their words to preserve them as evidence of their truthfulness,
many of their condemnations are comprehensible only with the assumption of a body
of earlier, authoritative texts—the Torah—and many of their promises are clothed with
the language of previous descriptions of pivotal events in Israel's early history.' To
illustrate, Dempster points to Hosea's use of the 'ten words' (Hos. 4.1-3), the covenant
(Hos. 1.9), and the exodus image (Hos. 1.10-11) from the Pentateuch in his prophetic
discourse.

about Jesus in the grammar and syntax of the Hebrew Scriptures.[83] Jesus argues that his story was anticipated in the Old Testament and that Moses and the Prophets built a path that directly led to him (cf. Jn 5.46). Moreover, the New Testament writers enlist a large cast of supporting characters from Old Testament narratives in portraying their messianic protagonist. In sum, the overwhelming majority of verifiable quotations, allusions, and echoes made by biblical writers are drawn from other locations in the canon. This interconnected feature of the canonical context is hermeneutically significant.[84]

The task of the interpreter is then to recognize the meaningful *effect* that the referenced text has on an author's work. When an element of one textual context is woven into a new textual context, there is a meaning-full effect on the reading of both texts.[85] The new textual context invariably transforms and is transformed by the quoted material.[86] Noting this hermeneutical effect is what makes the use of the notion of intertextuality more than simply a popularized form or trendy way of speaking of historical-critical 'source-hunting'.[87] 'To identify allusions', as Hays notes, 'is only the begin-

---

83. Sailhamer makes this point about the narratives of Genesis 1–3. He writes, 'the world depicted in the biblical narratives is crucial for the identity of the Christian Gospel... Notions as pervasive as "God" and "the world" are derived in the NT and in our own day from the narratives of the OT' (*Introduction to Old Testament Theology*, p. 217). In other words, 'these narratives are, in fact, the very "grammar" and "lexicon" by which we learn the meaning of the Gospel and in which the Gospel makes sense and can be shown to be unique' (p. 217).

84. Cf. the development of the general examples mentioned in this paragraph in Chapter 3's discussion of contextuality.

85. In one sense, a subsequent writer does not change the source text in the least by utilizing it in his own work. However, readers of the new text will be influenced by the author's use of that source text in a fresh composition. Readers of the canon will likely be readers of both texts. This reading situation is hermeneutically significant.

86. Moyise consistently makes this methodological point in his writings on the New Testament's use of the Old Testament. E.g., see Steve Moyise, 'Intertextuality and the Study of the Old Testament in the New Testament', in *The Old Testament in the New Testament* (ed. Steve Moyise; London: T. & T. Clark, 2000), pp. 14-41; Steve Moyise, 'Intertextuality and Biblical Studies: A Review', *Verbum et Ecclesia* 23 (2002), pp. 418-31; Steve Moyise, 'Intertextuality and Historical Approaches to the Use of Scripture in the New Testament', in *Reading the Bible Intertextually*, pp. 23-32; Steve Moyise, *The Old Testament in the New* (London: T. & T. Clark, 2004); and Steve Moyise, *Evoking Scripture: Seeing the Old Testament in the New* (London: T. & T. Clark, 2008).

87. Harold Bloom characterizes the type of analysis used in a limited approach to intertextuality as a 'wearisome industry of source-hunting, of allusion-counting, an industry that will soon touch apocalypse anyway when it passes from scholars to computers' (*Anxiety of Influence* [New York: Oxford University Press, 1973], p. 31). As noted above, Kristeva similarly castigates the 'banal sense of "study of sources"' (*Revolution in Poetic Language*, p. 59).

ning of the interpretive process'.[88] In fact, one of the reasons the academic discussion of intertextuality is helpful/relevant to biblical studies is because these categories can equip interpreters to articulate both the various ways that biblical authors draw on other texts (quotations/allusions/echoes) and also the manifold and meaning-full effects that these interwoven intertexts evoke.[89] This feature of intertextuality also recovers the important role of the reader who perceives or misperceives these connections and feels their meaning-full effect (let the reader understand!) while still maintaining a strategic place for the author's textual intention.[90]

---

88. Hays, *Echoes of Scripture*, p. 17. For Hays, 'the critical task, then, would be to see what poetic effects and larger meanings are produced by the poet's device of echoing predecessors' (p. 18).

89. Hays colorfully comments on the 'spontaneous power of particular intertextual conjunctions' by noting that 'despite all the careful hedges that we plant around texts, meaning has a way of leaping over, like sparks. Texts are not inert; they burn and throw fragments of flame on their rising heat. Often we succeed in containing the energy, but sometimes the sparks escape and kindle new blazes, reprises of the original fire' (*Echoes of Scripture*, pp. 32-33). See also Hays' development of the notion of 'intertextual narration' in 'The Liberation of Israel in Luke–Acts: Intertextual Narration as Countercultural Practice', in *Reading the Bible Intertextually*, pp. 101-17. Many of Hays' metaphors/images (echo, fire, narration) are designed to highlight and illuminate the complex hermeneutical effects that intertextual connections produce. This type of inquiry involves asking, 'What poetic linkages of sound or imagery make this sort of imaginative leap possible, what effects are produced in the argument by it, and what sort of response does it invite from the sympathetic reader's imagination?' (*Echoes of Scripture*, p. 14).

90. In his writings on the subject, Georg Steins connects the role of the reader to the study of intertextuality within a canonical context (*Kanonisch-Intertextuelle Lektüre*). See Georg Steins, *Die Bindung Isaaks im Kanon, Grundlagen und Programm einer Kanonisch-Intertextuellen Lektüre* (Frieburg: Herder, 1999); Georg Steins, 'Kanonisch-Intertextuelle Bibellektüre—My Way', in *Intertextualität: Perspektiven auf ein interdisziplinäres Arbeitsfeld* (ed. Karin Herrmann and Sandra Hübenthal; Aachen: Shaker, 2007), pp. 55-68; Georg Steins, 'Der Bibelkanon als Denkmal und Text: Zu einigen methodologischen Aspekten kanonischer Schriftauslegung', in *The Biblical Canons* (ed. J.M. Auwers and H.J. de Jonge; Leuven: Leuven University Press, 2003), pp. 177-98; and Steins, 'Kanon und Anamnese', pp. 110-29. For Steins, 'Der Bibelkanon als Gestalt gewordener Dialog erfordert die Mitarbeit der Rezipienten; ihre Lektüre ist zu beschreiben als ein fortwährende intertextualisierung im priviligierten Raum des Kanons' (*Die Bindung Isaaks im Kanon (Gen 22)*, p. 84). 'Die Kanon und das intertextuelle Lesen' are not secondary considerations, but rather 'wirken von Anfang an bei der Sinnkonstitution mit' (p. 89). In sum, 'Im Horizont des Bibelkanons und der von ihm vorstrukturierten Intertextualität stellt sich die Lektüre als 'interplay' von Text und Leser in einem Prozeß permanenter Neukontextualisierung dar' (p. 97). Steins critically interacts directly with Childs's canonical approach (pp. 9-44), stressing the need to supplement it with a fuller accounting of the role of the *kanonische leser*. See also Childs's response to Steins in 'Critique of Recent

Moreover, an important (though sometimes neglected) aspect of this discussion is the likelihood that biblical authors use the context of an intertext for a variety of purposes.[91] Some authors may use the intertext's context for a contrast (e.g. irony, as a foil) and others use it for similarity (e.g. as an illustration or a piece of their argument). Further, an individual author might use an intertextual quotation or allusion for a variety of purposes in a single text or passage.[92] Recognizing this multifaceted use of context can help nuance the way interpreters might describe one biblical author's use of another's text.[93]

Intertextual Canonical Interpretation', *ZAW* 115 (2003), pp. 173-84. Though Childs critiques Steins for shifting focus to the reader, Scheetz points out that Steins does in fact 'speak explicitly of the canon as the place of privileged intertextuality' (*Concept of Canonical Intertextuality*, p. 31). Cf. the critical interaction with Steins in Brandt, *Endgestalten des Kanons*, pp. 36-42; and Driver, *Brevard Childs*, pp. 137-59 (comparing and contrasting Childs and Steins' understanding of canonical intertextuality).

91. On the diverse ways an author might use an intertextual connection, see Manfred Pfister, 'Konzepte der Intertextualität', in *Intertextualität: Formen, Funktionen, Anglistische Fallstudien* (ed. Ulrich Broich and Manfred Pfister; Tübingen: Niemeyer, 1985), pp. 1-30. Gillmayr-Bucher, 'Intertextuality', pp. 21-23, summarizes Pfister's categories. Of particular note, in this regard, is the notion of *Dialogizität* (dialogism), which 'considers the intention of references to another text' (p. 22). A given intertext might accord 'with its original meaning; it may support the new text; or the new text can turn against the text it refers to, ridicule it, and aim at a totally different or contrasting meaning' (p. 22). Cf. Scheetz, *Concept of Canonical Intertextuality*, p. 33: The intertextual dialogue 'reflects points of continuity, where there are similar terms, phrases, and values, and points of discontinuity where these terms, phrases, and values have shifted in meaning. What may be of secondary importance in another context, and a term or phrase in one context is used in a different way in another context, all of which reflects not static textual units but a dialogue between smaller texts and a larger context.'

92. See Marshall's summary of the diverse ways that New Testament writers draw on Old Testament texts ('Assessment of Recent Developments', pp. 204-205). For Marshall, 'if anything is clear, it is that a variety of types of use must be recognised' (p. 204). One of the burdens of Hays' work in *Echoes of Scripture* is to point out the varied 'strategies of intertextual echo' that Paul employs (e.g. pp. 173-78). Hays also draws on the 'analytic framework' of Thomas M. Greene in *The Light in Troy: Imitation and Discovery in Renaissance Poetry* (New Haven, CT: Yale University Press, 1982), pp. 16-19, 37-53. The categories Greene develops for understanding an author's imitation of a precursor text are sacramental, eclectic, heuristic, and dialectic imitation. In relation to these categories, Hays posits that Paul's intertextual practices 'characteristically require the reader to engage in serious sustained deliberation about the relation between Scripture's *mundus significans* and the new situation that Paul is addressing' (*Echoes of Scripture*, p. 175).

93. One way authors make use of written works is by utilizing them as source material for sections of their composition. There is a distinction between an author's use of a written entity as a source and an author's use of another text as an intertextual

For example, in Exodus 34, the Lord declares to Moses that 'the Lord, the Lord God' is 'compassionate and gracious, slow to anger, and abounding in loving kindness and truth' (Exod. 34.6). The Lord 'keeps loving kindness for thousands', 'forgives iniquity, transgression and sin', but also 'will by no means leave the guilty unpunished' (Exod. 34.7). Subsequent biblical authors draw on this important statement of God's character in a variety of ways. In Jon. 4.2, Jonah alludes to these words after Ninevah repents and is spared from the Lord's judgment.[94] In Nah. 4.2, the prophetic word alludes to these same words in order to pronounce judgment on Ninevah for failing to respond in repentance (Nah. 1.1-3).[95] Thus, the same intertextual allusion to a discursive statement from the Pentateuchal narrative of Exodus 34 ('The Lord is slow to anger...') can function as a *reminder* of God's promise of mercy and also a *warning* of his certain judgment.[96]

reference. The task of an author writing a historical narrative is to make sense of the historical data that he is using (e.g. literary documents, oral testimony, memory) and to order and present it as a coherent whole. Biblical books such as the Pentateuch, Kings, Chronicles, and the Gospels seem to be written in this way. There are many explicit references throughout the canon to other literary entities that have been used as sources by a biblical author (e.g. Gen. 5.1, Exod. 24.3-7, Exod. 31.18, Num. 21.14, 21.17-18, 21.27, Josh. 10.13, 1–2 Kings as source material for 1–2 Chronicles, etc.). The possible uses of traditional material in Paul's letters and the complexities of the Synoptic problem are relevant in this regard as well. Whereas source criticism or form criticism might try to isolate these sources in the text and then reconstruct or analyze them independently, a compositional approach asks how the author has made use of those sources in his text. This approach does not focus on the parts per se, but rather (once the parts are discerned using textual tools) the focus is on how those parts contribute to the meaning of the whole. In the categories of the present chapter, intertextuality and the use of literary entities as source material are both compositional strategies that an author has at his disposal when composing a text. Though both of these practices are clear examples of an author drawing on another text, it can be helpful to distinguish between the former and the latter (the present study focuses on the former).

94. Displeased and angry, Jonah prays, 'Please Lord, was not this what I said while I was still in my own country? Therefore in order to forestall this I fled to Tarshish, for I knew that you are a gracious and compassionate God, slow to anger and abundant in lovingkindness, and one who relents concerning calamity' (Jon. 4.1-2).

95. The book of Nahum begins, 'The oracle of Ninevah' (1.1). This reference to the 'great city' connects the prophetic books of Nahum and Jonah within the literary context of the book of the Twelve. The judgment of Ninevah in Nahum is emphasized in its closing words: 'There is no relief for your breakdown, your wound is incurable' (Nah. 3.19).

96. Thiselton argues that 'it may sometimes be worth while to observe a distinction between image, picture, or representational or propositional content and function or illocutionary force' (*New Horizons*, pp. 40-41). Statements in the biblical text (e.g. Nah. 1.3) can 'be *used* in various ways or operate with different *force* in different speech-acts: the words could be spoken as a *warning*, as an act of *comfort*, or to lend support to a *promise*' (p. 41). Accordingly, 'when we speak of "re-using" or

As an 'intertextual collection of Scriptures', the biblical canon showcases the relationships that are present between biblical passages, sections, and books.[97] By highlighting the organic relationships that exist within a diverse set of texts, the canonical context provides a space where intertextual connections are realized.[98] There is here an important connection between studies of intertextuality and contextuality because oftentimes the shaping of a collection of writings is actualized and solidified by means of intertextual connections. In this model, intertextual connections function within the atmosphere provided by the canon and do not need to journey into the outer space of extratextuality in order to generate fruitful meaning. Readers who hold to a production-oriented view of intertextuality and are interested in the communicative intention of the author as evidenced in a text will see the canon as a constructive place for the generation of meaning. Further, when both the text and the precursor text are present in the same collection, the intertextual relationship becomes less tenuous. In this sense, an intertextually informed concept of canon enables and encourages Scripture to interpret Scripture.

If the above considerations are taken into account, then the interpretive task takes on a limited and manageable scope. In this setting, the task of the alert reader is to discern which texts inform a given work under investigation. The interpreter looks first to other canonical texts in order to discern an author's intended textual connection. Recognizing that canonical authors draw upon other canonical texts (an observation gained by study of the biblical texts themselves), then the interpretive task involves discerning and reflecting on these connections with the context of the canon in view. By executing this task, interpreters make the scope of their conceptual context match the expectation of the biblical authors themselves. In this scenario, the reader develops a canon-consciousness that corresponds to the canon-consciousness of the biblical writers. By allowing the full context of the canon to influence and direct the interpretive task, the interpreter situates him/herself within the horizon of the implied reader of Scripture.[99]

"re-applying" textual meaning', interpreters should ask questions like, 'are we speaking of transforming a propositional content, of re-directing an illocutionary force, or some change of meaning such as an innovative extension of a metaphor?' (p. 41).

97. The helpful phrase 'intertextual collection of Scriptures' is drawn from Chapman, *The Law and the Prophets*, pp. 109, 285. See also Chapman's discussion in 'The Canon Debate', pp. 291-92, where he argues that any definition of canon should take into account 'the literary interrelatedenss found among the various writings contained within the biblical corpus'. Chapman urges interpreters to reckon with 'the intertextual nuance of canon' (p. 292).

98. Cf. Fiddes, 'Canon as Space and Place', p. 128: 'The area within the canonical boundaries can in fact appear to the interpreter to be limitless, as an endlessly open field within which to wander.'

99. Cf. Chapter 5's development of the 'ideal reader' of the Christian canon. See

The Contextual and Intertextual Function of The
Book of Revelation within the Canonical Context

One way to illustrate the value of the study of biblical contextuality and biblical intertextuality is by exploring the hermeneutical significance that the book of Revelation has in its current position as the final book of the Christian Bible. Located at the end of the canon, the book as a whole functions as the last word of God's written revelation and serves as a fitting conclusion to both the Old Testament and the New Testament. The important role that John's Apocalypse plays in the canonical context of the Bible is a feature of biblical contextuality.

Further, the intertextual allusions found in the final chapters of Revelation 21–22 are particularly relevant for the way the book of Revelation functions as a conclusion. Contextually and intertextually, this final section of the book effectively seals the message of Scripture and conceptually closes the canon. The profoundly intertextual nature of this book illustrates the pressing need for careful reflection on the way intertextual connections are made and how they function in the microstructures and macrostructures of an individual composition. This type of intertextual study also highlights the relevance of an author's compositional strategy to the interpretation of their work. A further aim is to suggest the relevance of this internal textual analysis to a historical investigation of the canon formation process.

The Book of Revelation Fittingly Concludes the New Testament Canon

Viewing the interpretive task as the pursuit of an author's textual intention, an examination of the book of Revelation seeks to discern John's compositional strategy. Accordingly, though there are a multitude of vexing hermeneutical issues involved in the interpretation of this book, the elements highlighted in the following investigation seek to forefront the features of John's compositional strategy that contribute to its overall effect in the context of the New Testament canon. As a carefully structured composition, the book concludes the New Testament as a whole.[100] In this regard, there are

also Fiddes, 'Canon as Space and Place', p. 136, who notes that 'with regard to the Christian community, as long as we count ourselves part of it we have a demand laid upon us to read, interpret and wrestle with its canon in a manner that no other texts ask from us'.

100. The book of Revelation appears at the end of most of the major manuscript traditions from the fourth century onward (see Appendix 1). On Revelation as a conclusion to the New Testament, see (inter alia) Wall, 'Apocalypse of the New Testament in Canonical Context', pp. 274-98; Clarke, 'Canonical Criticism', pp. 204-20; Goswell, 'Order of New Testament', pp. 239-41; and Tobias Nicklas, 'The Apocalypse in the Framework of the Canon', in *Revelation and the Politics of Apocalyptic Interpretation* (ed. Richard B. Hays and Stefan Alkier; Waco, TX: Baylor University Press, 2012), pp. 143-53.

structural, verbal, and thematic connections between the shape of the book of Revelation and the shape of the rest of the New Testament.

Structural Connections. As noted and developed in Chapter 3, there is a distinct narrative thrust that runs throughout the writings of the New Testament.[101] The overarching shape of the New Testament canon generates a sufficient narrative framework in which to present its unified, coherent message. In this overall shape, the Gospels present the beginning and end of Jesus' life and ministry; the book of Acts presents the beginning and expansion of the life of the church by means of the ministry of apostles; and the Pauline Corpus and the General Epistles represent dialogue between the churches and the apostles. After the widening effect of the two corpora of epistles, the book of Revelation picks up the narrative element that began with the Gospels and Acts. After the epistolary interlude of the New Testament letters, John's vision then picks up the narrative thread again (Rev. 4.1), carrying it into the eschatological horizon.[102] Thus, the overarching narrative framework of the New Testament provides the church with an exposition and interpretation of its origin (Gospels), expansion (Acts), and eschaton (Revelation).

The book of Revelation presents itself as the final word of the central figure in this New Testament storyline, namely, the risen Christ. The narrative assumes that the readers know and are familiar with Jesus and also John

101. This paragraph represents a distilled version of the 'Shape of the New Testament' section of Chapter 3.

102. Though there is much debate regarding the exact chronological sequence of the events described in the book, John gives a definite shape to the narrative as a whole that helps readers access its message. The narrative begins on earth with John located on the island of Patmos. Though the bulk of the book involves the recounting of an eschatological narrative, a straightforward historical narrative frames the book. After greeting his readers (1.4-7), John begins telling a story in first person. This narrative is crucial for understanding the book of Revelation as a whole. The apocalyptic events and visions that occur throughout the bulk of the book are set within this narrative framework. John provides the setting for his narrative by recounting that he was on the 'island called Patmos' because of the 'word of God and the testimony of Jesus' (1.9). More specifically, John was 'in the Spirit on the Lord's day' (1.10) when he hears behind him the voice that he soon realizes comes from the risen Christ (1.12-16). Jesus then commands him to write letters to seven churches (Rev. 2–3) and then one of his messengers shows John a vision about what will 'soon take place' (Rev. 4–22). The narrative ends after the vision concludes and John falls at the feet of the 'angel who showed [him] these things' (22.8-9). After a closing sequence of dialogue, John ends the book with a characteristic epistolary greeting ('The grace of the lord Jesus be with all. Amen', 22.21). Though these narrative sections obviously require much exegetical effort and analysis, the point here is that they are clearly narratives and are presented in an overarching narrative framework provided by Rev. 1 and Rev. 22.

as his trustworthy bondservant.[103] Readers of the New Testament will naturally connect this book to the Gospel narratives about Jesus and the writings of the apostle John.[104] Only assumed knowledge of other portions of the New Testament canon can fully account for the opening words of this apocalyptic book: 'The Revelation of Jesus Christ, which God gave him... and he sent and communicated it by his angel to his bond-servant John, who testified...to all that he saw' (1.1-2).

Verbal and Thematic Connections. In addition to this significant narrative element, there are also a number of notable verbal and thematic connections that reach across the New Testament canon. Just as there are interesting links between the beginning and the end of the book of Revelation itself, there are also important connections between the first and last book of the New Testament.

Jesus' Book. As noted above, the command to 'write' is significant in Revelation along with the concept of a 'book'. The content of Revelation is characterized as the 'words of the prophecy of this book' (τοὺς λόγους τῆς

---

103. The prologue of Rev. 1.1-3 alerts readers to the character of the witnesses that testify in 'this book'. The book's subject matter is the 'revelation of Jesus Christ' ('Ἀποκάλυψις Ἰησοῦ Χριστοῦ). This revelation has its ultimate source in God ('which God gave him'), and its purpose is 'to show to his bond-servants the things which must soon take place' (1.1). Further, the revelatory vision of the future is mediated through God's angel who communicates the message to God's bond-servant. John in turn testifies (ὃς ἐμαρτύρησεν) to the word of God (τὸν λόγον τοῦ θεοῦ) and to the testimony of Jesus Christ (τὴν μαρτυρίαν Ἰησοῦ Χριστοῦ). John himself is identified here as a faithful and comprehensive witness who testifies to all that he sees (ὅσα εἶδεν). In 22.6, the angelic messenger reiterates, 'these words are faithful and true' (cf. John and Jesus' self-testimony in 22.8 and 22.16 respectively). The message of the book is thus vouchsafed by the trustworthiness of the apostle, the angel, Jesus Christ, and ultimately God himself. Close readers of the New Testament who encounter this characterization of John as a trustworthy eyewitness will likely hear echoes of the similar statements about John's character in John's Gospel (e.g. Jn 19.35; 21.24; 1 Jn 1.1-4).

104. Cf. Smith, 'When Did the Gospels Become Scripture?', p. 15: 'Strikingly, the initial NT book is a Gospel that begins with a royal, Davidic genealogy and the final one is an apocalypse that characterizes itself as prophecy (1.3; 22.18). Of course, although Revelation has no explicit scriptural citation, it is replete with scriptural, especially prophetic, language. Whether or not some individual planned the NT that way (Trobisch), the meaning and significance are clear enough. Revelation implies the continuation and culmination of the biblical story.' Regarding the two-testament canonical context, Brawley reflects, 'The Christian canon of two Testament means also that each Testament has its own coherence even as each is composed of plural voices—the coherence of a theocentric story before Jesus and its sequel after Jesus' ('Canonical Coherence', p. 634). The book of Revelation similarly assumes a 'canonical coherence' with other parts of the New Testament (e.g. the gospel message developed in the Gospel corpus).

προφητείας τοῦ βιβλίου τούτου). Forms of the word βιβλίον occur elsewhere in the New Testament, but perhaps its most prominent position occurs in Mt. 1.1. Because this verse begins the first book of the four-fold Gospel corpus, βίβλος is the first word of the New Testament. Mt. 1.1 reads, βίβλος γενέσεως Ἰησοῦ Χριστοῦ υἱοῦ Δαυὶδ υἱοῦ Ἀβραάμ (ESV, 'The book of the geneaology of Jesus Christ, the son of David, the son of Abraham'). In addition to encapsulating the textual and theological themes of Matthew's narrative and connecting it to a range of Old Testament contexts, this densely packed sentence also generates readerly expectations regarding the textual nature of the ensuing Gospel. An individual that begins reading Matthew is first introduced to the Gospel message as a 'book'.[105] This is one way that the Gospel can be understood as a literary entity as well as an oral proclamation.

The Gospel of Matthew and the four-fold Gospel corpus recounts the Ἀρχὴ τοῦ εὐαγγελίου Ἰησοῦ Χριστοῦ (Mk 1.1, 'The beginning of the gospel of Jesus Christ') and the book of Revelation recounts the Ἀποκάλυψις Ἰησοῦ Χριστοῦ (Rev. 1.1, 'The revelation of Jesus Christ'). In particular, John reveals what took place in the beginning (Jn 1.1) and what will transpire in the end (Revelation 21–22). The New Testament thus sheds light on all of temporal history; a history focused on Jesus, the Christ. Matthew's book begins and John's book ends the overarching narrative of the New Testament.[106] They are the first and last chapters of a multifaceted βίβλος.

Jesus' Lineage. Another important verbal link that spans the New Testament is the assertion that Jesus hails from the lineage of David. In Revelation 22, there is a mention of Jesus being the descendent of David. In both the Old Testament and the New Testament, Davidic imagery is fraught with messianic significance. Thus, a mention of David is frequently strategic and rarely inconsequential. Just before the final sequence of the book of Revelation, Jesus makes a statement about his identity, saying 'I am the root and the descendant of David, the bright morning star' (22.16, ἐγὼ εἰμι ἡ ῥίζα καὶ τὸ γένος Δαυίδ, ὁ ἀστὴρ ὁ λαμπὸς πρωϊνός).[107] Here Jesus empha-

---

105. Cf. BDAG, s.v. 'βίβλος'. See also the discussion of βίβλος in Chapter 1.

106. Cf. Thomas Hieke's discussion of Matthew's use of βίβλος in 'Biblos Geneseos— Mt 1,1 vom Buch Genesis her gelesen', in *The Biblical Canons*, pp. 635-50.

107. In this passage, there is also an important intertextual allusion to the messianic promises of the Pentateuch. In Rev. 22.16, Jesus identifies himself as the bright morning star (ὁ ἀστὴρ ὁ λαμπρὸς ὁ πρωῖνός). In Num. 24.17, Balaam says that 'A star shall come forth from Jacob (LXX: ἀνατελεῖ ἄστρον ἐξ Ἰακὼβ) / A scepter shall rise from Israel / And shall crush through the forehead of Moab / and tear down all the sons of Sheth.' In the latter part of the book of Revelation (e.g. Rev. 19–20), the Davidic messiah is seen conquering the enemies of God, thus fulfilling the picture hinted at in the Numbers passage. Cf. 2 Pet. 1.19 and the discussion of the Davidic Messiah in Appendix 3.

sizes in two ways his Davidic lineage. He is 'the root' (ἡ ῥίζα) and also 'the descendent' (τὸ γένος) of David.[108] This characterization parallels the description one of the elders gives of Jesus in Rev. 5.5. Urging John to 'Stop weeping', he says, 'Behold, the lion that is from the tribe of Judah (ὁ λέων ὁ ἐκ τῆ φυλῆς Ἰούδα), the root of David (ἡ ῥίζα Δαυίδ), has overcome so as to open the book and its seven seals' (5.5).[109] The Jesus spoken of throughout John's Apocalypse is here identified as the Davidic 'anointed one' of messianic prophecy.

Jesus is spoken of in Davidic terms elsewhere in the New Testament, but a particularly strategic usage again occurs in the first sentence of the first book. Mt. 1.1 begins with a reference to Jesus as 'the Son of David, the Son of Abraham': υἱοῦ Δαυὶδ υἱοῦ Ἀβραάμ.[110] In the rest of his Gospel, Matthew records the title of 'Son of David' in strategic places in his narrative.[111]

108. A ῥίζα is simply 'the underground part of a plant' or 'that which grows from a root' (BDAG, s.v. 'ῥίζα'). Here the term is being used figuratively in terms of 'descendent'. The word γένος is 'expressive of relationship of various degrees and kinds', and here clearly indicates 'ancestral stock' (BDAG, s.v. 'γένος'). The combination of these similar terms drawn from Old Testament imagery highlights Jesus' Davidic/Messianic heritage. Louw-Nida observe that 'here ῥίζα and γένος are very similar in meaning, and it is often best to coalesce the two terms into a single expression, for example, "I am a descendant of David" or "I belong to the lineage of David"'. The combination of these two terms emphasizes the beginning (the roots) and continuance (descent) of Jesus' Davidic/Messianic heritage. From beginning to end, Jesus lives the life of the Messiah that the life of David anticipated and prefigured.

109. This verse also has an interesting analogous connection that is hermeneutically suggestive: Jesus is the key to unlocking the structural mystery of the Apocalypse. As noted above, the 'series of sevens' is a clear structural device in the mysterious vision section of the book (the most extensive as well). Here, John records that Jesus is the one who is able to 'unseal' or 'unlock' the content of this mysterious book of visions. This is another way that John's structural framework centers on the person of the risen Lord Jesus. In this sense, his 'book' of Revelation is what contains and is able to explicate the book of mysterious revelations (5.5, ἀνοῖξαι τὸ βιβλίον καὶ τὰς ἑπτὰ Σφραγῖ δας αὐτοῦ).

110. By reversing the chronological order of these two historical figures, Matthew puts David in the emphatic position. If the reason for this reversal is the prominence of the promise of the Davidic covenant (e.g. 2 Sam. 7; 1 Chron. 17) in the Old Testament and in Matthew's compositional strategy (which is capable of demonstration), then Matthew has provided a canon-conscious reading of Israel's history in these few words. The rest of Matthew's first chapter confirms this reading (for instance, the nature of Matthew's genealogy and its structural/thematic focus on David and the exile can be read as a structural allusion/echo of the first nine chapters of the book of Chronicles). Cf. the connections Koorevar draws between Chronicles and Matthew in 'Chronik als intendierter Abschluß', pp. 75-76.

111. See Mt. 1.20; 9.27; 12.23; 15.22; 20.30-31; 21.9; and 21.5. Many of these uses are connected to Jesus' ministry of healing. Cf. Jack Kingsbury, 'The Title "Son of David" in Matthew's Gospel', *JBL* 95 (1976), pp. 591-602.

In both Matthew 1 and Revelation 22, the reference is specifically to the 'descendent' of David. What Matthew recounts is the book of the 'genealogies' (γενέσεως) of Jesus.[112] There is enough overlap in the semantic domain of these words to include them in the connections between these two areas of the New Testament canon.[113] Rev. 22.16 alludes to Jesus being a descendent (γένος) of David, and Mt. 1.1 provides the details of that line of succession (γενέσεως).

Though Matthew is the writer who makes the most intentional use of the 'Son of David' title in particular, Mark, Luke, and John also make significant use of Davidic imagery.[114] Underlying all of these references is the clear and repeated reference to Jesus as the 'Christ' (Ἰησοῦ Χριστοῦ). That Jesus is the Christ of Davidic lineage is perhaps the most basic unifying element in all of the New Testament.[115] In this regard, Jn 20.31 serves as a sum-

112. The word γένεσις here most likely involves 'an account of someone's life' in terms of their background or history. In Greek literature, the term also entails the notion of 'ancestry as point of origin'. See BDAG, s.v. 'γένεσις'. The phrase βίβλος γενέσεως is usually translated as either 'the book of genealogy' (ESV, NKJV), or 'the record of the genealogy' (NASB). The phraseology is drawn from the LXX translation of Gen. 2.4; 5.1 (αὕτη ἡ βίβλος γενέσεως ἀνθρώπων). In fact, the English title of Genesis comes from this usage. See the extensive discussion of this connection in Hieke, 'Biblos Geneseos', pp. 638-44. Hieke analyzes the way the phrase βίβλος γενέσεως functions in the books of Genesis and Matthew and also how Matthew's Greek text relates to the LXX and the MT text forms.

113. The terms γενέσεως and γένος are related in that they both deal with the origins of an individual (i.e. where someone came from). The former highlights the beginnings and the latter highlights that there is a connection. See the closely related entries 1339 and 1351 in Louw-Nida.

114. In Luke, Gabriel tells Mary that the Lord God will give Jesus 'the throne of his father David; and he will reign over the house of Jacob forever, and his kingdom will have no end' (Lk. 1.33). Zacharias also blesses the 'Lord God of Israel' for raising up 'a horn of salvation for us in the house of David his servant…to show mercy toward our fathers, and to remember his holy covenant' (1.67-72). John also recounts the musings of the people about Jesus. They were saying, 'This is the Christ' (Jn 7.41). Others said, 'Has not the Scripture said that the Christ comes from the descendants of David, and from Bethlehem, the village where David was?' (7.42). This heated discussion of the identity of the Messaiah affected people's perception of Jesus: 'So a division occurred in the crowd because of him' (7.43). Cf. Mk 2.25-26; 10.46-48; 11.9-10; 12.34-37. For a survey and exposition of this Davidic imagery, see D.R. Bauer, 'Son of David', in *Dictionary of Jesus and the Gospels* (ed. Joel B. Green and Scott McKnight; Downers Grove, IL: IVP, 1992), pp. 766-69.

115. See also the 'Renewed Promise' section of Appendix 3. As noted above, Davidic imagery is rife in the Gospels. Jesus' identity as the Davidic Messiah is also an integral feature of Paul's understanding of the nature of the gospel. Paul characterizes the 'gospel of God' as a message that was 'promised beforehand through his prophets in the holy Scriptures, concerning his Son, who was born of a descendant of David according to the flesh…' (Rom. 1.1-3). He also exhorts Timothy to 'remember Jesus

mary purpose statement for both the Gospels and the New Testament as a whole: 'These have been written so that you may believe that Jesus is the Christ' (ταῦτα δὲ γέγραπται ἵνα πιστεύσητε ὅτι Ἰησοῦς ἐστιν ὁ χριστός).

In sum, an examination of the beginning and the ending of the New Testament canon yields a cluster of verbal, structural, and thematic intertextual links and connections. The *Revelation* of Jesus Christ functions as a fitting canonical counterpart to the *Gospel* of Jesus Christ. John's Apocalypse, then, aptly completes the New Testament canon. Carefully observing the intertextual connections present within these texts enhances a reader's ability to make sense of the New Testament as a whole. Taking these types of textual features into account enables readers of the New Testament canon to develop a canon-conscious mindset and to conceive of (i.e. keep 'in mind') a discernable and tangibly shaped New Testament canonical context when reading individual books and passages.

The Book of Revelation Fittingly Concludes the Christian Canon
One of the ways that the New Testament as a whole connects to the Old Testament is through a deluge of intertextual references. This use of the Old Testament by New Testament authors is perhaps the most compelling evidence of an organic connection between the two Testaments.[116] As noted above, the writers of the New Testament expect and demand their readers to know and be familiar with a panorama of Old Testament texts.[117] In fact,

---

Christ, risen from the dead, descendant of David, according to my gospel...' (2 Tim. 2.8). These paradigmatic statements at the beginning and end of the Pauline corpus inform Paul's consistent characterization of Jesus as 'Jesus Christ' and 'Christ Jesus' in his apostolic correspondence. Cf. Sailhamer, *Meaning of the Pentateuch*, p. 461, who states that the identification of Jesus as the Davidic anointed one of messianic prophecy might be 'the canonical integrating element within the whole of the OT and the NT'.

116. The use of the Old Testament in the New Testament is one of the most important elements of biblical theology. For an introduction to the textual, hermeneutical, and theological issues involved in this type of study, see G.K. Beale (ed.), *The Right Doctrine from the Wrong Texts? Essays on the Use of the Old Testament in the New* (Grand Rapids, MI: Baker Books, 1994); Steve Moyise (ed.), *The Old Testament in the New Testament: Essays in Honour of J.L. North* (Sheffield: Sheffield Academic Press, 2000); Stanley E. Porter (ed.), *Hearing the Old Testament in the New Testament* (Grand Rapids, MI: Eerdmans, 2006); and G.K. Beale, *Handbook on the New Testament Use of the Old Testament: Exegesis and Interpretation* (Grand Rapids, MI: Baker, 2012). For a survey of the actual textual connections, see D.A. Carson and G.K. Beale (eds.), *Commentary on the New Testament Use of the Old Testament* (Grand Rapids, MI: Baker, 2007). These works represent a small sampling of the substantial body of secondary literature devoted to this field. Cf. also Seitz's methodological cautions and proposals throughout *Character of Christian Scripture*.

117. The fact that New Testament writers expected their readers to know their

they 'repeatedly situate' their discourse 'within the symbolic field created by a single great textual precursor: Israel's Scripture'.[118]

In this setting, the book of Revelation functions as a fitting and intertextually connected conclusion to the Christian canon as a whole. Here, the Christian canon is understood as the Bible consisting of the Old and New Testaments.[119] In examining the position of Revelation in that canon, a relevant question is the shape of the Old Testament. For the purpose of this investigation, it is not necessary to choose between the ordering of the Hebrew Bible and the Greek Septuagint translation.[120] Though there are significant differences in the arrangement of these two versions, the shape of the various corpora remain relatively stable. The New Testament that ends with the book of Revelation concludes the Old Testament that begins with the book of Genesis.[121] John's Apocalypse is thus the second bookend of the Christian Bible.

The pervasive use of the Old Testament in the book of Revelation is in line with the hermeneutical methodology of the rest of the New Testament authors.[122] In fact, the entire book brims with Old Testament allusion and

references can be seen in how they oftentimes omit an exposition or an introduction to key Old Testament texts and figures. They simply utilize these canonical figures in their writings. A memorable example of this technique is Mark's comment after the 'abomination of desolation' is mentioned by Jesus: 'Let the reader understand!' (Mk 13.14).

118. Hays, *Echoes of Scripture*, p. 15.

119. As mentioned in Chapters 1–2, the four major Greek manuscript traditions of the fourth century (Codex Sinaiticus; Codex Vaticanus; Codex Alexandrinus; Codex Ephraemi Rescriptus) include a version of the Hebrew Bible along with the New Testament. These editions indicate the presence of a previously accepted body of literature. See Trobisch, *First Edition of the New Testament*, pp. 24-25. Also observe that in different communities, consolidation takes slightly different forms. This accounts for the various orders and inclusion of individual books that occur in some communities but not in others.

120. See Seitz's discussion of the Hebrew and Greek canons in 'Canonical Approach and Theological Interpretation', in *Canon and Biblical Interpretation*, pp. 90-96. Cf. also the 'exkurs' by Thomas Hieke and Tobias Nicklas on what they label 'der sogenannte' Septuagint-canon in *Die Worte der Prophetie dieses Buches*, pp. 113-24.

121. Cf. Hieke, 'Biblische Texte als Texte der Bibel Auslegen', p. 333: 'The knowledge here obtained through a canonical reading fits almost all Christian canon-forms: Rev. 22.6-21 is the capstone (*schlusstein*) of every Christian Bible that begins with Genesis and ends with the book of Revelation of John—and at the minimum contains the texts (and their contexts) which Rev. 22.6-21 necessarily presupposes for its understanding' (my translation).

122. John's pervasive yet subtle use of the Old Testament has been studied at length from a number of perspectives. For a representative overview of this issue, see G.K. Beale, *John's Use of the Old Testament in Revelation* (Sheffield: Sheffield Academic Press, 1998); Steve Moyise, *The Old Testament in the Book of Revelation* (Sheffield:

echo from beginning to end, making it a sort of climax of the New Testament's reliance on the Old Testament for its imagery, modes of thought, and theology.[123] Specifically, John's use of Old Testament imagery in Revelation 21–22 is one of the key features of the book as a conclusion of the Christian canon. As Matthewson asserts, 'nearly every verse' in these chapters 'provides a point of departure for probing the author's use of the Old Testament in this text, making it a suitable basis for further inquiry'.[124]

Important themes mentioned here originate and are developed throughout the Old and New Testaments.[125] Genesis begins with the creation of the heavens and the earth (Gen. 1.1), and Revelation ends with the creation of a *new* heavens and a *new* earth. In the final chapters of his book, John develops the way the work of God in the risen Christ brings about the renewal of all creation, the restoration of God's original purpose for humanity, and the enduring promise of a coming redeemer. Each of these themes is supported by verbal, thematic, or structural links to significant texts from the Hebrew Bible.[126] In particular, through a network of intertextual allusions to the Pentateuchal narratives of Genesis 1–3, John creates a macrostructural inclusio for the biblical canon and storyline.

In sum, the moment recounted by John in the vision of Revelation 21–22 fulfills God's purpose of creation and represents the goal of biblical

Sheffield Academic Press, 1995); and Steve Moyise, 'Models for Intertextual Interpretation of Revelation', in *Revelation and the Politics of Apocalyptic Interpretation*, pp. 31-45.

123. Moyise argues that 'John's method is not to quote Scripture formally but to weave its "words, images, phrases and patterns" into his own composition' (*Old Testament in the Book of Revelation*, p. 145). On this point, cross-reference also the relevant methodological reflection by Paulien, 'Elusive Allusions', pp. 37-53; and Mathewson, 'Assessing Old Testament Allusions in the Book of Revelation', pp. 311-25.

124. David Mathewson, *A New Heaven and a New Earth: The Meaning and Function of the Old Testament in Revelation 21.1–22.5* (London: Sheffield Academic Press, 2003), p. 3. He also argues that 'John's visionary denouement must be read in constant intertextual relationship with the Old Testament, not just to isolate and validate allusions, but to explore the semantic correspondences and interpretive significance of allusions and echoes' (pp. 23-24).

125. See William J. Dumbrell, *The End of the Beginning: Revelation 21–22 and the Old Testament* (New South Wales: Lancer, 1985). Dumbrell identifies five major themes/allusions that occur in Rev. 21–22, namely, the New Jerusalem, the New Temple, the New Covenant, the New Israel, and the New Creation. Dumbrell notes that these chapters are 'such an appropriate way not only to finish the Book of Revelation but to conclude the story of the entire Bible' and also investigates how these themes 'changed or developed down through the Bible's story' (p. i). Cf. Paul Sevier Minear, *Christians and the New Creation: Genesis Motifs in the New Testament* (Louisville, KY: Westminster/John Knox Press, 1994).

126. For a development of these themes and their intertextual connection to the texts of the Hebrew Bible (Gen. 1–3 in particular), see Appendix 3.

revelation and the hope of the church, namely, that 'they will see his face, and his name will be on their foreheads' (22.4).[127] The scene is one depicting a redeemed people beholding their God and bearing the name that defines them. The 'Lord God' (κύριος ὁ θεὸς) is their light, and they will with him 'reign forever and ever' (22.5). This glimpse of what it will be like at the beginning of the end of days concludes the vision John receives on the island of Patmos. Accordingly, John's Apocalypse is the exclamation point of the biblical storyline, as redemptive history culminates in the vision he records in these final chapters of his book. Moreover, the earth-shaking implications of this apocalyptic message are made possible by its rumbles of intertextuality.

Summary
The goal of this illustrative investigation has been to suggest that the book of Revelation is best interpreted in light of its compositional shape, as an integral part of the New Testament canon, and as an integral part of the Christian canon as a whole. Seen on this canonical horizon, the function of the book as a conclusion of God's written revelation can be fully appreciated. Biblical readers would be impoverished without the book of Revelation, and readers of John's Apocalypse would likewise be impoverished without the rest of the canon. In other words, the church's surest guide for reading the book of Revelation is the entire canonical context in which it is situated.

A Brief Historical Postscript
In addition to highlighting these hermeneutical implications, this investigation also suggests the relevance of these textual observations to the historical process of canon formation. By means of the internal features surveyed above, it is possible that the book of Revelation amplified the concept of closure that the early church then utilized in subsequent discussions regarding the extent and content of the biblical writings. The concept of a closed canon that was present among leaders in the early church could very well be in part a result of the effect that the book of Revelation had on its readers.[128]

---

127. Mathewson, *A New Heaven and A New Earth*, p. 206, traces the connection between this phrase and the theme of God's glory being made manifest to the entire world. Cf. Schreiner, *New Testament Theology*, p. 37, who argues that 'the capstone of all biblical theology is summed up in the words "they will see his face"' (Rev. 22.4).

128. In the early church, the 'integrity formula' of Rev. 22.18-19 (cf. Deut. 4.2; Prov. 30.5-6) is echoed in patristic literature (e.g. *Didache* 4.13 and *Barnabas* 19.11). Papias (*EH* 3.39.15), Dionysius of Corinth (*EH* 4.23.12), and Irenaeus (*Against Heresies* 5.13.1) also allude to this mindset using these words. Jewish writers such as Josephus (*Apion* 1.42), *1 Enoch* (104.9-10), *1 Macc.* (8.30), and the *Letter of Aristeas* (310-11) pick up on the same language (likely from Deut. 4.2). Cf. Michael J. Kruger,

Conversely, von Campenhausen states strongly that 'in the earliest stages of forming the new canon the apocalypses played no important part, and attracted hardly any attention'.[129] One basis for von Campenhausen's contrary assertion is that he recognizes 'the process began with the Gospels and Paul' and that 'interest in the original teaching and tradition was its most prominent feature'.[130] Though von Campenhausen's point is well taken, it may be that the Apocalypse played a more prominent role in the thinking of the early church at the *end* of the canonization process rather than at the *beginning*. The early extant manuscript evidence (e.g. among the Oxyrhynchus papyri) indicates that the book of Revelation was as widely used and circulated as other important New Testament writings.[131] Thus, it is historically possible that the circulation of this book influenced the discussion regarding the collection in which it would eventually reside and function as a conclusion.

Concluding Reflections

This chapter seeks to relate the concept of canon to the study of biblical intertextuality. The formation of a literary collection generates textual connections (contextuality), and also helps limit the vast array of texts that hypothetically could inform any given biblical writing (intertextuality). A circumscribed understanding of the literary study of intertextuality can help describe what the biblical authors are doing as they utilize other biblical texts. These intertextual references to other texts found within the

'Early Christian Attitudes Toward the Reproduction of Texts', in *The Early Text of the New Testament* (ed. Charles E. Hill and Michael J. Kruger; Oxford: Oxford University Press, 2012), pp. 63-80.

129. Von Campenhausen, *Formation of the Christian Bible*, p. 218. He is arguing in particular against views such as H. Windisch, 'Der Apokalyptiker Johannes als Begründer des neutestamentlichen Kanons', *ZNW* 10 (1909), pp. 148-74. Windisch contends that it was John who first 'gave the impulse to the formation of the Canon... first of all by the fact that he wrote and published the first new canonical book, and secondly, because his book both in form and content legitimated the canonisation of other writings' (translation in *Formation*, p. 218 n. 48).

130. Von Campenhausen, *Formation of the Christian Bible*, pp. 218-19.

131. Two important early manuscripts of Revelation include P.IFAO 2.31 and P.Oxy. 1079. Both are opisthographs and date from the second and third centuries. See Hurtado, *Earliest Christian Artifacts*, pp. 31-32. Hurtado notes that there are 'at least four early copies of Revelation, which puts it in a three-way tie with Romans and Hebrews as the fifth-most-attested New Testament writing (behind John, Matthew, Luke, and Acts)'. Thus, 'in spite of the lengthy time that it took for Revelation to be accepted as part of the emerging New Testament canon, particularly in the East, it appears to have enjoyed a reasonable popularity, at least among Christian circles reflected in the earliest extant papyri' (p. 32).

boundaries of the canon help bind together the associations described in a study of contextuality. In other words, the shape of the biblical material (contextuality) is often generated by the way a biblical author uses and relates his writing to other biblical material (intertextuality).

In order to illustrate the nature and value of a study of biblical contextuality and biblical intertextuality, the function of the book of Revelation in the Christian canon proves a useful example. In terms of mere contextuality, the reader notices that the book of Revelation serves as a fitting conclusion both to the New Testament and the Christian canon as a whole. A reader also notices that there seem to be intentional intertextual allusions throughout the book of Revelation to passages from the Old Testament, especially the prophecies of Isaiah and the creation narratives of Genesis 1–3. These intertextual connections provide evidence of the possibility that the function of Revelation is the result of meant contextuality and not only mere contextuality. This examination also illustrates the types of analysis that are possible when the concept of canon is active in the mind of the interpreter. A canon-conscious textual orientation helps a reader discern the rich textual features in the biblical literature and the various textual strategies employed by the biblical authors.

Chapter 5

IDENTIFYING AND BECOMING THE IDEAL
READER OF THE BIBLICAL CANON

Μακάριος ὁ ἀναγινώσκων ('Blessed is he who reads', Rev. 1.3).

A further implication of allowing the concept of canon to function as a control on the interpretive task involves the identification of the intended audience of the Bible as a whole. The question of 'original' or intended audience is a perennial issue in the interpretation of any ancient text. In biblical studies, the historical-critical pursuit of the original audience of a biblical writing is standard fare. One alternative to this historical-critical task is to attempt a description of the intended audience that is implied by the text itself. This type of investigation asks whether the author envisions only a certain group of readers (an 'original audience') or also a certain type of reader (an 'implied audience'). Determining the original audience of a text is primarily a historical task, whereas identifying the implied audience of a text is primarily a literary task. A literary approach is not necessarily incompatible with a historical approach; however, the aims and resources used to attain the objective are different.

In the following analysis, I explore the insights of literary and semiotic studies into the role of the reader and also ask whether the fruit of these studies can yield any insight into interpreting the texts in the biblical canon. Further, I examine whether these insights can function alongside a communication model of meaning and a production-oriented understanding of the 'implied reader'. Dialoguing with the fields of literary and semiotic studies in this area is helpful because the questions and issues these scholars raise and engage regarding language, texts, and the act of reading are central to the task of textual interpretation in general and biblical interpretation in particular. The notion of 'implied reader' invokes a series of hermeneutically significant questions: What is it? Who produces it? How can it be identified? These questions naturally lead to a further query: What is the relationship between this *implied* reader of a text and an *actual* reader of a text? After interacting with these important literary issues, the following section pursues the implications these observations can have for readers of the canonical collection. In this section, I seek to demonstrate that strategic biblical texts envision an 'ideal reader', namely, an actual reader who seeks to identify *with* the implied reader.

Identifying the Implied Reader of a Literary Text

There are a number of ways to express the notion of an intended reader-ship of a particular text. In his study of the function of the novel genre form, Wolfgang Iser utilizes the category of the 'implied reader'.[1] Iser is concerned with the 'literary effects and responses' that attend to the reading of novels. Iser observes that the novel is a unique genre 'in which reader involvement coincides with meaning production'.[2] Because novels subtly critique social and historical norms by projecting narrative worlds that require conceptual interaction, 'readers of the novel, are then forced to take an active part in the composition of the novel's meaning'.[3] For Iser, 'this active participation is fundamental to the novel'.[4]

1. See Wolfgang Iser, *The Implied Reader: Patterns of Communication in Prose Fiction from Bunyan to Beckett* (Baltimore, MD: The Johns Hopkins University Press, 1974). Iser works out a theoretical framework for the notion of 'implied reader' in *The Act of Reading: A Theory of Aesthetic Response* (Baltimore, MD: The Johns Hopkins University Press, 1980); Wolfgang Iser, *Prospecting: From Reader Response to Literary Anthropology* (Baltimore, MD: The Johns Hopkins University Press, 1989); and Wolfgang Iser, 'The Reading Process: A Phenomenological Approach', in *Reader-Response Criticism: From Formalism to Post-Structuralism* (ed. Jane P. Tompkins; Baltimore, MD: The Johns Hopkins University Press, 1980), pp. 50-69. Cf. Wolfgang Iser, *The Range of Interpretation* (New York: Columbia University Press, 2000). For a recent critical interaction with Iser, see Zoltán Schwáb, 'Mind the Gap: The Impact of Wolfgang Iser's Reader-Response Criticism on Biblical Studies—A Critical Assessment', *Literature and Theology* 17 (2003), pp. 170-81. Umberto Eco interacts with Iser's notion of the 'implied reader' in *The Limits of Interpretation* (Bloomington, IN: Indiana University Press, 1994), pp. 46-48; and *Six Walks in the Fictional Woods* (Cambridge, MA: Harvard University Press, 1994), pp. 15-16.
2. Iser, *Implied Reader*, p. xi.
3. Iser, *Implied Reader*, p. xii. Cf. Boris Uspensky's description of the 'narrative world' of a novel in *Poetics of Composition* (Berkeley, CA: University of California Press, 1973), p. 137: 'In a work of art, there is presented to us a special world, with its own space and time, its own ideological system, and its own standards of behavior. In relation to that world, we assume (at least in our first perceptions of it) the position of an alien spectator, which is necessarily external. Gradually, we enter into it, become more familiar with its standards, accustoming ourselves to it, until we begin to perceive that world as if from within.'
4. Iser, *Implied Reader*, p. xii. Cf. Wolfgang Iser, 'Indeterminacy and the Reader's Response in Prose Fiction', in *Aspects of Narrative: Selected Papers from the English Institute* (ed. J. Hillis Miller; New York: Columbia University Press, 1971), pp. 1-45; and Iser, *Prospecting*, pp. 31-41.

Iser uses the term 'implied reader' to describe the nature of this active participation. He understands the term to incorporate 'both the prestructuring of the potential meaning by the text' and also 'the reader's actualization of this potential through the reading process'.[5] Texts do not overtly expound on every detail of every object presented in a story or a discourse. There are gaps in every verbal presentation that are 'filled in' by the reader.[6] The implied reader goes through a process of meaningful discovery that is guided but not overtly dictated by the author. 'In order for this complex process to be put into operation', Iser contends, the author uses 'a variety of cunning stratagems to nudge the reader unknowingly into making the "right" discoveries'.[7] For Iser, then, the category of 'implied reader' is a helpful window into 'the fascinating process of reading and reacting'.[8]

Literary theorist Umberto Eco has examined this important role of the reader and has sought to develop the concept within a semiotic framework.[9]

---

5. Iser, *Implied Reader*, p. xii. Iser also immediately qualifies his definition by stating that the term 'refers to the active nature of this process—which will vary historically from one age to another—and not to a typology of possible readers' (p. xii). Reflecting on Iser's distinction here, Daniel W. Wilson, 'Readers in Texts', *PMLA* 96 (1981), pp. 848-63 (850), observes that 'Iser believes that the implied reader consists of both an objectively determinable structure in the text (*Textstruktur*) and the varying subjective actualizations of the structure by real readers (*Aktstruktur*).' Wilson also points out that Iser has a phenomenological (though perhaps inconsistent) understanding of authorial intention (contra Hirsch's approach in *Validity*). Cf. Iser, 'Reading Process: A Phenomenological Approach', pp. 50-69.

6. See Iser, *Act of Reading*, pp. 20-52, 107-34. Iser contends that 'effects and responses are properties neither of the text nor of the reader; the text represents a potential effect that is realized in the reading process' (p. ix). Thiselton observes that 'the text often does not specify whether an object has certain properties (for example whether a table is wooden or plastic, or has three or four legs) but we regularly "fill in" what we *presuppose* and *construe*. The notion of the reader's activity in "filling in blanks" in the text becomes a central theme in Iser's theory' (*New Horizons*, p. 517). In Iser's terms, a gap or a 'blank' is a 'vacancy in the overall system of the text, the filling of which brings about an interaction of textual patterns' (*Act of Reading*, p. 231). Cf. Eco, *Six Walks*, p. 3: 'Any narrative fiction is necessarily and fatally swift because, in building a world that comprises myriad events and characters, it cannot say everything about this world. It hints at it and then asks the reader to fill in a whole series of gaps.' From an independent theoretical basis, Sternberg understands 'the literary work as a system of gaps' and discusses 'gaps, ambiguity, and the reading process' in *Poetics of Biblical Narrative*, pp. 186-229.

7. Iser, *Implied Reader*, p. xiv. Cf. Iser, *Act of Reading*, p. 33: 'The intended reader, then, marks certain positions and attitudes in the text, but these are not yet identical to the reader's role, for many of these positions are conceived ironically...so that the reader is not expected to accept the attitude offered him, but rather to react to it.'

8. Iser, *Implied Reader*, p. xiv.

9. See especially Eco, *Role of the Reader*; Umberto Eco, *Semiotics and the Philosophy of Language* (Bloomington, IN: Indiana University Press, 1984); and Eco, *Limits*

Drawing on a semiotic understanding of texts, Eco asserts that readers are active participants in the production of meaning, and in fact, are a constitutive element in the meaning-making process.[10] Eco characterizes the notion of the implied reader as the 'model reader'. For Eco, all authors have at least a minimal mental construct of the type of individual that they envision reading or encountering their work.[11] In order to communicate, an author has 'to assume that the ensemble of codes he relies upon is the same as that shared by his possible reader'.[12]

These shareable 'codes' could be complex signifying elements, or they could simply be the particular language being used to construct the text.[13]

---

of Interpretation, pp. 1-63. Germane also is the dialogue on display in *Interpretation and Overinterpretation*. Eco here interacts with Richard Rorty, Jonathan Culler, and Christine Brooke-Rose. Cf. the critical interaction with Eco's thought in *Umberto Eco and the Open Text: Semiotics, Fiction, Popular Culture* (ed. Peter Bondanella; Cambridge: Cambridge University Press, 2005); and *New Essays on Umberto Eco* (ed. Peter Bondanella; Cambridge: Cambridge University Press, 2009). On the relationship between Eco's model reader and Iser's implied reader, see Eco, *Six Walks*, pp. 15-16. Eco notes, 'My Model Reader is, for instance, very similar to the Implied Reader of Wolfgang Iser' (p. 15). He also notes key differences in their concepts in relation to how much meaning-making power is given to the reader (pp. 15-16). Eco's focus in the model reader construct is 'that "fictitious reader" portrayed in the text, assuming that the main business of interpretation is to figure out the nature of this reader, in spite of its ghostly existence' (p. 16). Though Eco is clearly interested in the pervasive 'role of the reader', he is also convinced that the 'model reader' is wrapped up in the 'sinews' of the text and its 'genetic imprinting' (p. 16).

10. For instance, Eco begins his study on the role of the reader with the heading, 'How to Produce Texts by Reading Them' (*Role*, p. 3). Though Eco stresses the role of the reader in this fashion, he nevertheless argues that the text itself constrains the free construction of meaning in the reading process (see the discussion of his notion of *intentio operis* below). Iser, too, allows for a 'narrowing down' of meaning-full possibilities available to the reader (e.g. *Act of Reading*, pp. 183-85). By contrast, see Stanley Fish, *Is There a Text in This Class? The Authority of Interpretive Communities* (Cambridge, MA: Harvard University Press, 1980), p. 3: 'The reader's response is not *to* the meaning: it *is* the meaning.' For radical reader-response critics like Fish, 'Interpretation is the source of texts, facts, authors, and intention' (p. 17).

11. Cf. Eco, *Interpretation and Overinterpretation*, p. 64: 'A text is a device conceived in order to produce its model reader.'

12. Eco, *Role*, p. 7. Thiselton summarizes Eco, stating that 'every text envisages, or "selects" by its nature, a "model reader". This is the construct-reader who shares the ensemble of codes presupposed by the author' (*New Horizons*, p. 526). Cf. Eco, *Six Walks*, p. 10: 'One must therefore observe the rules of the game, and the model reader is someone eager to play such a game.' Accordingly, the 'model author' is the 'voice' that is manifested as a 'narrative strategy', that is, 'as a set of instructions which is given to us step by step and which we have to follow when we decide to act as the model reader' (p. 15).

13. Eco, *Role*, p. 7, explains that 'to organize a text, its author has to rely upon a series of codes that assign given contents to the expressions he uses'.

In order to communicate, the author must 'foresee a model of the possible reader...supposedly able to deal interpretatively with the expressions in the same way as the author deals generatively with them'.[14] Through these basic choices, authors generate at least an implicit 'model reader'.[15] By reading the text and noting the nature of its network of expectations, a reader can discern the minimal makeup of the model reader of that text. If an author uses technical jargon without explanation or makes literary allusions to certain texts, then one can assume that the author's model reader is one that understands or at least knows how to process that information.[16] In other words, the model reader is the type of reader the author has in mind.

Further, the model reader is generated or created by the producer of a text. The cues that the reader picks up on are constructed by the author (or text). In Eco's terms, at the same time the text *expects* certain things from a reader, it also '*creates* the competence of its Model Reader'.[17] The way to know the makeup of the model reader is to read the text and note the

---

14. Eco, *Role*, p. 7. Culler characterizes the 'literary work' as a 'linguistic event which projects a fictional world that includes speaker, actors, events, and an implied audience (an audience that takes shape through the work's decisions about what must be explained and what the audience is presumed to know)' (*Literary Theory*, p. 40). For Culler, the role of the reader is an 'important fact' that must be engaged. Literary critics must not obscure the fact 'that a text is addressed to and thus posits a reader, and that the elucidation of this role (what is this reader supposed to know or accept?) is crucial to the understanding of the operations of the text' (*Pursuit of Signs*, p. xxi).

15. Cf. Eco, *Role*, p. 7: 'At the minimal level, every type of text explicitly selects a very general model of possible reader through the choice (i) of a specific linguistic code, (ii) of a certain literary style, and (iii) of specific specialization indices.'

16. Cf. Eco, *Six Walks*, p. 6: 'A story may be more or less quick—that is to say, more or less elliptic—but how elliptic it may be is determined by the sort of reader it is addressed to... In a narrative text, the reader is forced to make choices all the time.' Though Eco focuses on narrative texts, he also notes that every type of text projects an intended readership. 'In other words', Eco avers, 'there is a model reader not only for *Finnegans Wake* but also for a railway timetable, and the texts expect a different kind of cooperation from each of them. Obviously, we are more excited by Joyce's instructions for "an ideal reader affected by an ideal insomnia", but we should also pay attention to the set of reading instructions provided by the timetable' (p. 17). Further, after noting that 'the model author and the model reader are entities that become clear to each other only in the process of reading, so that each one creates the other', Eco reflects, 'I think this is true not only for narrative texts but for any sort of text' (p. 24).

17. Eco, *Role*, p. 7. After quoting a passage from a novel called *Waverley* that uses key names to allude to other similar stories/traditions, Eco notes that 'after having read this passage, whoever approaches *Waverley* (even one century later and even—if the book has been translated into another language—from the point of view of a different intertextual competence) is asked to *assume* that certain epithets are meaning « chivalry » and that there is a whole tradition of chivalric romances displaying certain deprecatory stylistic and narrative properties'.

expectations of the author (or text). In this sense, 'a well-organized text on the one hand presupposes a model of competence coming, so to speak, from outside the text, but on the other hand works to build up, by merely textual means, such a competence'.[18] There is thus an interconnection and overlap between the textual and readerly spheres at play in the reading event. For Eco, empirical authors and readers are not the immediate concern. When he speaks of 'authors' and 'readers' he refers to the 'textual strategies' of implied author and implied reader.[19] In this sense, Eco is interested in a *text*'s intention rather than an author's *textual* intention.[20]

18. Eco, *Role*, p. 8. In *Six Walks*, Eco describes the model reader as 'a sort of ideal type whom the text not only foresees as a collaborator but also tries to create. If a text begins with "Once upon a time", it sends out a signal that immediately enables it to select its own model reader, who must be a child, or at least somebody willing to accept something that goes beyond the commonsensical and reasonable' (p. 9).

19. Eco writes, 'In the following paragraphs I shall renounce the use of the term / author/ if not as a mere metaphor for « textual strategy »... In other words, the Model Reader is a textually established set of felicity conditions to be met in order to have a macro-speech act (such as a text is) fully actualized' (*Role*, p. 11).

20. Cf. the discussion of authorial intention in Chapter 4. As previously discussed, there is a debate between finding the locus of meaning either in the author's intention or in the reader's response. Eco seeks to offer a third possibility: 'Between the intention of the author (very difficult to find out and frequently irrelevant for the interpretation of a text) and the intention of the interpreter who (to quote Richard Rorty) simply "beats the text into a shape which will serve for his purpose", there is a third possibility. There is an *intention of the text*' (*Interpretation and Overinterpretation*, p. 25). In this way, Eco generates a spectrum of an author's intention (*intentio auctoris*), a text's intention (*intentio operis*), and a reader's intention/response (*intentio lectoris*). Because 'it is possible to speak of the text's intention only as the result of a conjecture on the part of the reader', Eco attempts to maintain 'a dialectic link' between the *intentio operis* and the *intentio lectoris*. In contrast to genuine reader-response criticism, Eco argues that the 'text as a coherent whole' controls and directs the *intentio operis*. 'In this sense', Eco concludes, 'the internal textual coherence controls the otherwise uncontrollable drives of the reader' (p. 65). In sum, 'to recognize the *intentio operis* is to recognize a semiotic strategy' (p. 64). See Eco's development of this approach in '*Intentio Lectoris*: The State of the Art', in *The Limits of Interpretation*, pp. 44-63. In light of the development of the notion of an author's *textual intention* in Chapter 4, one might say that by speaking of the 'text's intention' in terms of a semiotic *strategy* seems to reap the benefits of an author's compositional strategy but then in turn attributes that meaning to the text as a semiotic object. The author, in Eco's model, works behind the scenes as a phantom-like ghostwriter, producing an effect but never quite making it into the credits. However, Eco's acknowledgement of the constraining force of the 'text' distances him from Fish's movement beyond these categories. Fish recounts his journey: 'Whereas I had once agreed with my predecessors on the need to control interpretation lest it overwhelm and obscure texts, facts, authors, and intentions, I now believe that interpretation is the source of texts, facts, authors, and intentions. Or to put it another way, the entities that were once seen as

An important concept related to the model reader is the notion of a 'universe of discourse'. This phrase denotes the shared contextual world in the mind of the author and reader. In other words, 'the universe of discourse is what an utterer and interpreter must share so that communication can result'.[21] For an author to give his work communicative force, he must utilize a specific web of signifying elements.[22] This intended matrix of potentially meaningful elements is the universe of discourse within which the words and concepts of a given work function. The model reader uses intratextual analysis and works within the text's universe of discourse.[23] The universe of discourse is similar to the presuppositional pool that the author expects the reader to share.[24] As Alkier articulates, 'The universe of dis-

competing for the right to constrain interpretation (text, reader, author) are now all seen to be the *products* of interpretation' (*Text in this Classroom*, pp. 16-17). For Fish, the attempt to formulate 'controls' on interpretation is a misadventure. Rather than spending a 'great deal of time in a search for the ways to limit and constrain interpretation' (p. 321), interpreters (like Hirsch or Eco) should simply embrace the relativism inherent in the task. Fish's 'message to them is finally not challenging, but consoling—not to worry' (p. 321). Vanhoozer's *Is There Meaning in this Text?* is a book-length response to Fish's *Is There A Text in this Class?*

21. James Jakob Liszka, *A General Introduction to the Semiotics of Charles Sanders Peirce* (Bloomington, IN: Indiana University Press, 1996), p. 92. Alkier draws on both Liszka and Peirce for his understanding of the field of semiotics. He quotes Peirce's argument that 'a given sign can consequently only function as a sign if it is ordered to a world—to a universe of discourse of the sign connection—inside of whose conditions it can generate meanings'. Alkier notes also that speaking of communicative intent moves the discussion from semiotic grammar to semiotic rhetoric (see Alkier, 'Categorical Semiotics', p. 231).

22. Alkier notes that the possible 'sign connections' relevant to a given work 'constitute an entire given culture, which is therefore to be understood not as monadic and monological but rather as relational and dialogical. Cultures are based on the communally conventionalized, created, and often contradictory use of signs.' For Alkier, cultures themselves 'are connections of signs' ('Categorical Semiotics', p. 230).

23. Alkier, 'Categorical Semiotics', p. 240.

24. Cf. Alkier, 'Categorical Semiotics', p. 231, who calls the universe of discourse the 'concretely perceptible sign connection'. Cynthia Westfall notes that 'participants and entities that the author believes can be inferred from a discourse item already introduced or from shared information is an *inferable*' (*A Discourse Analysis of the Letter to the Hebrews: The Relationship Between Form and Meaning* [London: T. & T. Clark, 2005], p. 86). For an interaction with the notion of 'presuppositional pool', see Peter Cotterell and Max Turner, *Linguistics and Biblical Interpretation* (Downers Grove, IL: IVP, 1989), pp. 90-97, 257-59. The presuppositional pool 'contains information constituted from the situative context…as well as the new information from the completed part of the discourse itself' (p. 90). This conceptual area informs one's 'perception of the significance of an utterance' (p. 91). They also reckon with the 'presuppositions held by the hearer that he does not share with the speaker' (p. 94). In sum, 'the presupposition pool we engage as we listen to any particular discourse has immediate

course of a given sign connection, for example, of a text, is then the world that this text establishes and assumes so that what is told by or claimed by the text can plausibly function.'[25] In this regard, the model reader of semiotic studies serves the same function as the implied reader of literary studies. An author of a text assumes and projects a reader who has a certain universe of discourse. This shared context allows for (and is necessary for) the production and/or relaying of meaning.[26]

When considering the projected expectations of the reader, it is helpful to distinguish between the reader's 'universe of discourse' and the reader's cultural 'encyclopedia'.[27] Whereas the universe of discourse is generated by the author and the text ('sign system') the author employs, the reader's encyclopedia is the open-ended contextual information made up of a person's knowledge, perception, and experience of their surrounding culture. The former can be circumscribed by finite boundaries, while the latter can never be controlled or even fully grasped by any one individual or any one articulation of the mass of variegated signifying elements. In contrast to the universe of discourse which is always tied to a given communicative sign, the encyclopedia 'encompasses the conventionalized knowledge of a given society and thus breaches the boundaries of individual sign relations by virtue of the concept of the universe of discourse'.[28] The encyclopedia

consequences for our perception of that discourse' (p. 94). Cotterell and Turner give Peter's use of Deut. 21.22-23 in Acts 5.30 as an example of the way an author/speaker draws on the shared presuppositions of their audience. Brown and Yule note that 'each participant in a discourse has a presupposition pool and his pool is added to as the discourse proceeds. Each participant also behaves as if there exists only one presupposition pool shared by all participants in the discourse' (*Discourse Analysis* [Cambridge: Cambridge University Press, 1983], p. 80; see also pp. 79-83). Cf. Joel B. Green, 'Discourse Analysis and New Testament Interpretation', in *Hearing the New Testament* (ed. Joel B. Green; Grand Rapids, MI: Eerdmans, 1995), pp. 183-86.

25. Alkier, 'Categorical Semiotics', p. 231. He also notes that 'the theory of the universe of discourse limits the validity of statements to a clearly defined realm; it designates the scope of statements' (p. 232). As an example, Alkier notes that Matthew's narrative context and the Pauline corpus might be perceived as a text's 'universe of discourse'. In this sense, 'the proper scope of a universe of discourse can be judged in different ways' (p. 232).

26. Culler notes in this regard that 'in the act of writing or speaking', an author or speaker 'inevitably postulates an intersubjective body of knowledge' (*Pursuit of Signs*, p. 112).

27. See Alkier's comparison and contrast of these two elements in 'Intertextuality', pp. 8, 35-37; and Alkier, 'Categorical Semiotics', pp. 230-37. Cf. Eco's interaction with this textual feature in a range of fictional works (e.g. Alexandre Dumas' *The Three Musketeers*) in *Six Walks*, pp. 97-116; and 'Intertextual Irony and Levels of Reading', pp. 212-35.

28. Alkier, 'Categorical Semiotics', p. 233. Eco speaks of a reader's 'competence in language as a social treasury' (*Interpretation and Overinterpretation*, p. 67). He

is 'the cultural framework in which the text is situated and from which the gaps of the text are filled'.[29] This feature of a reader's encyclopedia makes it 'necessarily virtual and impossible to grasp fully due to its complexity'.[30]

Distinguishing between the two concepts of a universe of discourse and a reader's encyclopedia can help nuance the way interpreters speak of the requisite knowledge/background information required for the proper interpretation of a text.[31] An understanding of a particular text's universe of discourse is gleaned from a study of the text itself. It includes *elements* of the projected reader's encyclopedia, but it also *directs* the reader to assign meaningful significance to certain elements of that vast array to actualize in the understanding of the given communicative act.[32] To interpret any text, at least a minimal skeleton of the author and reader's cultural encyclopedia must be accessed.[33] For example, at the least, idiomatic expressions,

continues, 'I mean by social treasury not only a given language as a set of grammatical rules, but also the whole encyclopedia that the performances of that language have implemented, namely, the cultural conventions that the language has produced and the very history of the previous interpretations of many texts, comprehending the text that the reader is in the course of reading' (pp. 67-68).

29. Alkier, 'Intertextuality', p. 8. Summarizing Eco and János Petöfi, Alkier explains that 'the conventionalized encyclopedia is a regulative hypothesis that is supposed to explain what we do when we use signs' ('Categorical Semiotics', p. 235). Cf. Eco, *Role*, pp. 17-23.

30. Alkier, 'Categorical Semiotics', p. 233.

31. Eco makes a distinction between an open-ended cultural encyclopedia and the universe of discourse that is necessary to understand a given textual meaning: 'Every act of reading is a difficult transaction between the competence of the reader (the reader's world knowledge) and the kind of competence that a given text postulates in order to be read in an economic way' (*Interpretation and Overinterpretation*, p. 68).

32. Brown and Yule observe that 'those aspects of the context which are directly reflected in the text, and which need to be called upon to interpret the text, we shall refer to as *activated features of context* and suggest that they constitute the contextual framework within which the topic is constituted, that is, *the topic framework*' (*Discourse Analysis*, p. 75). In these terms, the author's textual intention helps guide readers to recognize which features of the cultural encyclopedia need to be accessed and 'activated' in order to understand adequately the meaning of a text. Cf. Green, 'Context', p. 131: 'Textual meaning cannot simply be identified with or reduced to the historical situation of [its origin] since, from this perspective, cultural products such as texts have the capacity to speak to and also beyond the situations within which they were formed.'

33. Cf. Alkier, 'Categorical Semiotics', p. 233: 'No one communicates only in texts; no text functions without a connection to other sign systems.' Part of the importance of a cultural encyclopedia is that it 'consists not only of linguistic knowledge but also of the knowledge of forms of address, norms of behavior, technical and practical knowledge, and so forth'. Cf. Robert Wuthnow, *Communities of Discourse: Ideology and Social Structure in Reformation, the Enlightenment, and European Socialism* (Cambridge, MA: Harvard University Press, 1989), p. 3, who notes that authors 'draw

cultural conventions, and linguistic developments will need to be taken into account. Any time readers encounter a text, they must process elements of their cultural encyclopedia in order to achieve understanding.[34] Beyond the minimal framework, though, the universe of discourse is more helpful in relating the vast amount of background information to the interpretation of a particular communicative speech act inscribed in a text. When reading or interpreting a text, both concepts are at least implicitly active.[35]

Though there are concerning issues with Iser's understanding of the 'implied reader' and Eco's articulation and development of the notion of the 'model reader' and its related concepts, the basic insight that texts project certain readerly expectations is instructive. This valuable observation can be maintained and utilized even in light of the methodological diversity of the literary theorists who have developed and employed the concept.[36] Many of the serious concerns relate to finding the locus of meaning

resources, insights, and inspiration from the environment: they reflect it, speak to it, and make themselves relevant to it. And yet they also remain autonomous enough from their social environment to acquire a broader even universal and timeless appeal'.

34. Alkier argues that 'reading a text or listening to a conversation partner is not a passive process of pure reception but rather an interactive process that requires the creative cooperation of the reader or hearer'. Drawing on Eco again, Alkier notes that 'the work of reading (or hearing, for that matter) demands…the activation or anesthetizing of cultural encyclopedic knowledge, which permits that which is deciphered or heard to become a meaningful whole' ('Categorical Semiotics', p. 235). See also Eco, *Role*, pp. 13-37.

35. Alkier, 'Categorical Semiotics', p. 236, argues that the universe of discourse and the encyclopedia 'stand in a hermeneutically reciprocal relationship'. He explains, 'only on the basis of the research of individual universes of discourse can reasonable entries be made into a virtual encyclopedia, but only through recourse to a postulated encyclopedia are manifested expressions actualized as content' (p. 236).

36. Briggs offers a similar assessment: 'I suggest that Iser, Chatman, Booth, and Eco are describing aspects of a model for understanding reading in a way that allows us to draw on the basic idea of a reader appropriate to a text without us being drawn into the finer points of the differences between their respective approaches' (*Virtuous Reader*, pp. 37-38). Briggs' own stripped down definition of an implied reader as a 'reader appropriate to a text' is helpful. For Green, Iser and Eco represent 'more moderate forms of reception theory' ('Context', p. 132). That Iser is 'more moderate' in his proposals, for instance, is confirmed by the critique he receives from more radical reader-response critics. E.g., see Stanley Fish, 'Why No One's Afraid of Wolfgang Iser', in *Doing What Comes Naturally: Change, Rhetoric, and the Practice of Theory in Literary and Legal Studies* (Oxford: Clarendon Press, 1989), pp. 68-86; and Wolfgang Iser, 'Talk Like Whales: A Reply to Stanly Fish', *Diacritics* 11 (1981), pp. 82-87. As Thiselton notes, Iser (contra Fish) does not 'question the "givenness" of stable constraints in textual meaning, but underlines their potential and indeterminate status independent of actualization by the reading process' (*New Horizons*, p. 517). For a less sympathetic treatment of Iser along with a pointed critique of Fish, see Stanley E.

in a reader's response rather than an author's textual intention, a firm commitment to a thoroughgoing semiotic understanding of language, and the related commitment to an unlimited view of textuality. Despite these clarifying methodological concerns, a circumscribed notion of these concepts can maintain the insights from this area of literary study. The notion of an implied or model reader can prove especially helpful in understanding certain genres of literature (e.g. narrative). Further, a carefully defined use of the terms 'universe of discourse' and 'encyclopedia' can complement a limited view of intertextuality and textuality.[37] In these ways, the concept of implied reader can put 'in a moral and theological form some of the valid insights of reader-response theory'.[38]

In biblical studies, the notion of an implied reader has been used to elucidate the function of narrative texts and the way they organically invite readerly participation. Jeannine Brown defines the implied reader as 'the textually constructed reader presupposed by the narrative text'.[39] She explains that the implied reader 'reflects the intended response the author envisions for the text'.[40] In this way, the implied reader 'functions as the embodiment of the right response at every turn to the author's communicative intention'.[41] This reader

Porter, 'Why Hasn't Reader-Response Criticism Caught On in New Testament Studies?', *Literature and Theology* 4 (1990), pp. 278-92. Porter also responds directly to Thiselton's interaction in Stanley E. Porter, 'Reader-Response Criticism and New Testament Study: A Response to A.C. Thiselton's *New Horizons in Hermeneutics*', *Literature and Theology* 8 (1994), pp. 94-102. Cf. also Porter, 'Literary Approaches to the New Testament', pp. 83-93, 106-110.

37. Alkier, 'Categorical Semiotics', p. 230, admits the possibility of this usage. He argues that 'the proper scope of a universe of discourse can be judged in different ways' and that 'the universe of discourse can be narrowly or widely set' (p. 232). See also the relevant discussions of Chapter 4.

38. R.W.L. Moberly as cited by Briggs, *Virtuous Reader*, p. 38. Moberly refers here to the work of Stephen Fowl and L. Gregory Jones.

39. Brown, *Scripture as Communication*, p. 40. Cf. Wilson's definition of the implied reader in 'Readers in Texts', p. 848: 'The behavior, attitudes, and background—presupposed or defined, usually indirectly, in the text itself—necessary for a proper understanding of the text. This idealized reader may be consciously or unconsciously conceived by the author, but he or she exists in every work, since almost every "message" presupposes a certain kind of recipient and implicitly defines him or her to some extent.' For R. Alan Culpepper, *Anatomy of the Fourth Gospel: A Study in Literary Design* (Philadelphia, PA: Fortress Press, 1983), the implied reader 'embodies all those predispositions necessary for a literary work to exercise its effect' (p. 209).

40. Brown, *Scripture as Communication*, p. 40. She also adds that 'while actual readers may respond in all sorts of ways to a text, the implied reader responds only as the author intends'. Cf. Briggs' definition: 'The implied reader is a literary-critical category relating to the notion of how a text "expects" to be read' (*Virtuous Reader*, p. 36).

41. Brown, *Scripture as Communication*, p. 40. For Brown, the concept of implied

'does exactly what the author wants the reader to do' and is thus 'an approximation of the fulfillment of the author's perlocutionary intention'.[42] One of the reasons Brown's articulation of this literary phenomenon is instructive is because it is set within a communication model of meaning. This understanding is a production-oriented compositional understanding of this literary feature. The implied reader and the projected universe of discourse are features of the author's textual intent and compositional strategy.[43]

Brown's study of the disciples in the Gospel of Matthew employs narrative criticism with a focus on the function of the implied reader. The first task for Brown is to trace Matthew's narrative portrayal of the disciples in his Gospel.[44] She concludes that in Matthew, 'the disciples are consistently portrayed as misunderstanding Jesus' mission and message, as exhibiting inadequate faith, and as falling short of the significant role intended for them as Jesus' disciples'.[45] The portrait shows the disciples sometimes showing positive signs of belief but also mixed with a consistent pattern of 'little faith'. This characterization of the disciples continues throughout the narrative, as the disciples are 'consistently portrayed as prone to misunderstand and as wavering in their faith'.[46]

reader 'can help us flesh out what active reception of a text is meant to look like'. Cf. her definition in *The Disciples In Narrative Perspective: The Portrayal and Function of the Matthean Disciples* (Atlanta, GA: SBL, 2002), p. 123: 'The implied reader will be defined as the persona constructed from the narrative text that responds appropriately to the text's rhetorical devices and thus fulfills the goals of the text.' In light of relevant research in literary criticism, Brown 'affirms there is a textually-derived implied reader who responds appropriately to the text's goals and this implied reader is a valid aim of narrative criticism' (p. 125). After a definitional discussion, Brown provides her fully nuanced understanding of 'implied reader' (p. 128).

42. Brown, *Scripture as Communication*, p. 129. Brown notes also that Wayne Booth uses the complementary phrase 'postulated reader' in *The Rhetoric of Fiction* (Chicago: University of Chicago Press, 1983), p. 177. Cf. Eco, *Role*, p. 10: 'It will be only the text itself—such as it is made—that tells us which kind of reader it postulates.'

43. This understanding is a contrast to Eco's view of the locus of textual meaning. Eco locates meaning in a 'text's intention' (*intentio operis*) and understands 'author' and 'reader' to be textual strategies (*ad hoc* or heuristic constructs) versus actual meaning-making entities. See also the discussion of authorial intention in Chapter 4.

44. See Brown, *Disciples*, pp. 39-58. Brown uses Mt. 16.21–20.28 as a paradigm for how Matthew portrays the disciples in the Gospel as a whole.

45. Brown, *Disciples*, p. 119. Brown notes also that this conclusion about the function of the disciples in Matthew contrasts with the typical results of redaction and historical-critical approaches.

46. Brown, *Disciples*, p. 120. Brown comments that 'the disciples do not progress [in] their understanding (or move toward greater faith) as the narrative comes to a conclusion' (pp. 119-20).

Brown then asks about the effect that this narrative presentation of the disciples has on the implied readers of the Gospel. One of her primary points is that 'the way Matthew's implied author characterizes the disciples directly impacts the creation of a reader who fulfills the goals of the text'. In other words, 'understanding the impact of the disciples upon the implied reader is one step toward illuminating the goals of the implied author'.[47] Initially, for readers of Matthew's Gospel, 'the disciples' positive response to Jesus engenders identification because the reader has been predisposed by the preceding narrative to respond positively to Jesus'.[48] At points in the narrative when the disciples are portrayed positively, the reader is encouraged to identify with them.[49] However, Matthew's presentation also invokes a contrasting response. As Brown notes, 'the reader is soon confronted with a number of negative characterizations of the disciples (e.g. their "little faith")'.[50] In this sense, 'the disciples' negative portrayal works as a foil in the narrative, challenging the reader to follow Jesus more faithfully than the disciples do'.[51]

Ultimately, Brown utilizes the concept of the implied reader to describe the effect of Matthew's narrative (in this case the narrative portrayal of the disciples) on potential readers. The way that Matthew has compositionally shaped his narrative has a meaningful effect on the way its readers understand his message regarding the nature and content of discipleship.[52] In

47. Brown, *Disciples*, p. 128.

48. Brown, *Disciples*, p. 129.

49. Cf. Ronald Thiemann's comments on this textual feature in 'Radiance and Obscurity in Biblical Narrative', in *Scriptural Authority and Narrative Interpretation* (ed. Garrett Green; Philadelphia, PA: Fortress Press, 1987), pp. 21-41. Thiemann reflects on the way Matthew's narrative elements 'summon the reader to enter the world of the text' (pp. 35-36). In this way, Matthew generates 'narrative space for his readers within the Gospel story' (p. 37).

50. Brown, *Disciples*, p. 129.

51. Brown, *Disciples*, p. 130. Brown continues by arguing that 'one way to conceive of the disciples' function at the discourse level, then, is as *an incentive to the implied reader toward ideal discipleship*. Ideal discipleship might be defined as the Matthean ideal for discipleship envisioned in Jesus' teaching and exemplified by various characters in Matthew's gospel who in some way fulfill that vision' (p. 130).

52. Brown summarizes the effect of the narrative portrayal of the disciples by stating that 'the implied reader will both identify with the more positive aspects of the disciples' portrayal and distance himself from their negative characterization. Both positive and negative aspects of the disciples' portrayal, therefore, function as an incentive for the implied reader toward the Matthean ideal of discipleship. In addition, the implied reader derives hope and encouragement from Jesus' gracious treatment of the disciples in spite of their failures and faults' (*Disciples*, p. 133). See also Jeannine K. Brown, 'Direct Engagement of the Reader in Matthew's Discourses: Rhetorical Techniques and Scholarly Consensus', *NTS* 51 (2005), pp. 19-35. In this article, Brown traces the

some scenarios in the narrative, readers are endeared to the disciples, and in others they are repelled. This cycle of identification with and distancing from the disciples is part of the effect of Matthew's narrative. Brown's work highlights the exegetical payoff of taking the literary category of 'implied reader' into account when attempting to read a narrative closely and carefully with an eye toward the textual intention of the author.[53]

The notion of an implied reader can also help connect the literary and theological horizons of biblical texts in particular. In a programmatic work, Markus Bockmuehl takes up the notion of the implied reader in order to 'derive from this a range of criteria for appropriate spiritual and theological engagement with the text'.[54] Bockmuehl first notes that the 'troubled fortunes of New Testament scholarship' have been exacerbated by (inter alia) a lack of agreement on basic procedures and presuppositions. In light of this methodological quagmire, Bockmuehl argues that closer attention to the effective history of texts (*Wirkungsgeschichte*) and the readings those texts *imply* can help move the discipline further in a responsible and congenial

way 'Matthew's five great discourses move from addressing the story's audience to direct engagement with the reader' (p. 19).

53. Cf. Richard Bauckham, 'John for Readers of Mark', in *The Gospels for All Christians: Rethinking the Gospel Audiences* (ed. Richard Bauckham; Grand Rapids, MI: Eerdmans, 1998), pp. 147-71. Bauckham uses the notion of 'implied reader' to help explain John's compositional strategy and entertains the possibility that John writes his Gospel with readers of Mark in view. In this sense, the implied reader of the Gospel of John is a reader of the Gospels (Mark in particular). Bauckham demonstrates that at least the parenthetical editorial comments in Jn 3.24 (about John the Baptist) and Jn 11.2 (about Mary) presuppose knowledge of narrative events and characters found only in Mark's Gospel. For Bauckham, this expectation of the implied reader 'belongs to the deliberate design of the Fourth Gospel' (p. 159). In this sense, the Gospel of John 'presupposes that many of its reader/hearers will know Mark and will expect to be able to relate John's narrative to Mark's' (p. 159). Bauckham summarizes his analysis by reflecting, 'It seems unlikely that such a result is accidental, and the value of the two parenthetical explanations we have studied (3.24; 11.2) is that they are points where the text of the Gospel virtually requires to be understood as inviting readers/hearers who also know Mark to relate the two Gospel narratives in a complementary way' (p. 170). See also, in this vein, Francis J. Moloney, 'Who is "The Reader" In/Of The Fourth Gospel?', *Australian Biblical Review* 40 (1992), pp. 20-33; Jeff Staley, *The Print's First Kiss: A Rhetorical Investigation of the Implied Reader in the Fourth Gospel* (Atlanta, GA: Scholars Press, 1988); and Culpepper, *Anatomy of the Fourth Gospel*, pp. 203-27.

54. Bockmuehl, *Seeing the Word*, p. 68. Aside from the fact that Bockmuehl self-consciously critiques the discipline and offers a line of sight for a way forward (see his similitude involving a modern-day C.H. Dodd), his book is also the lead volume in Baker's Studies in Theological Interpretation series, edited by Craig G. Bartholomew, Joel B. Green, and Christopher R. Seitz.

way.[55] His understanding of the implied reader draws initially on literary studies (e.g. Iser and Eco), but he moves quickly to the theological and historical implications that this type of hermeneutical construct can have for an interpreter of the New Testament.

His sketch of the implied reader thus highlights five basic theological commitments that the New Testament authors seem to expect of their readers. These convictions form a composite core theological profile of the projected reader of biblical texts. First, the implied reader of the New Testament 'has a personal stake in the truth reference of what it asserts'.[56] This reader understands the New Testament documents as a witness to the revelation and saving work of God in Christ.[57] Second, the implied reader has 'undergone a religious, moral, and intellectual *conversion* to the gospel of which the documents speak'.[58] The New Testament authors 'assume that the readers share a stance of Christian faith, that they look to the Christian gospel as both formative and normative in their lives'.[59]

Third, the implied reader also views the New Testament documents as authoritative. On this point, Bockmuehl argues that 'the stance of the texts themselves already presupposes a kind of canonical momentum'.[60] Because the implied reader comes to the texts as part of a canonical whole, they see unity in the diversity and hold them to be authoritative in (perhaps in spite of) that interrelationship.[61] Fourth, the implied readers are 'ecclesially situ-

---

55. The effective history (*Wirkungsgeschichte*) of a text is also known as 'reception history' (*Rezeptionsgeschichte*). For recent developments in this field, see *The Oxford Handbook of The Reception History of the Bible* (ed. Michael Lieb, Emma Mason, and Jonathan Roberts; Oxford: Oxford University Press, 2011); and James G. Crossley, *Reading the New Testament: Contemporary Approaches* (London: Routledge, 2010), pp. 115-49 (Crossley surveys Bockmuehl's approach, pp. 171-73). In his recent commentary on 1 and 2 Thessalonians in the Blackwell Bible Commentaries series, Thiselton interacts with the history of interpretation under the rubric of reception history. See Anthony C. Thiselton, *1 & 2 Thessalonians Through the Centuries* (Malden, MA: Wiley-Blackwell, 2010).

56. Bockmuehl, *Seeing the Word*, p. 69. Cf. also p. 232.

57. Bockmeuhl cites Lk. 1.4 and 1 Pet. 1.8 to illustrate the concern for believing 'the certainty of the things' about Jesus even though these readers are those who 'have not seen him'. He writes, 'it matters that these things are true—and at least to that (admittedly limited) extent it matters that they are true to history' (*Seeing the Word*, p. 69).

58. Bockmuehl, *Seeing the Word*, p. 70.

59. Bockmuehl, *Seeing the Word*, p. 70.

60. Bockmuehl, *Seeing the Word*, p. 70. For this concept of 'canonical momentum', Bockmuehl draws on Thomas Söding, 'Inmitten der Theologie des Neuen Testaments: Zu den Voraussetzungen Und Zielen Neutestamentlicher Exegese', *NTS* 42 (1996), pp. 161-84, esp. p. 165. He mentions the concept of canonical momentum again in a later section, also with reference to Söding (see p. 112).

61. Bockmuehl, *Seeing the Word*, pp. 70-71.

ated'. Rather than isolated individuals, the implied readers are 'assumed to be related to the (or a) body of Christian believers, either as full members or at least as sympathizers and hangers-on'.[62] Finally, the implied reader is 'evidently assumed to be "inspired", in the sense of Spirit filled'.[63] For Bockmuehl, 'the documents appear to take for granted that their envisaged reader will in the act of reading be empowered to receive the saving divine reality of which the text speaks'.[64] The 'present-tense perspective of the texts themselves' confirms this important trait expected of the reader.[65]

Identifying with *the Implied Readers of the Biblical Text*

After discussing the notion of an 'implied reader' and also sketching a few examples of the expectations that biblical authors have for their pro-jected readers, the issue of the relationship between the implied reader and the actual (or 'real') reader comes to the forefront.[66] As Briggs memorably states, 'No blood flows in the veins of implied readers.'[67] By its nature, the 'implied reader' of a text is a compositional construct and remains distinct

---

62. Bockmuehl, *Seeing the Word*, p. 71. He adds that 'the chronological priority of the church over the New Testament has in effect surrounded the text with a cloud of presupposed ecclesial witnesses' (p. 71). Bockmuehl's qualifier ('chronological') is important, as he is not asserting an *ontological* priority of the church over the New Testament.

63. Bockmuehl, *Seeing the Word*, p. 72.

64. Bockmuehl, *Seeing the Word*, p. 72.

65. Bockmuehl, *Seeing the Word*, p. 72. To illustrate this concept, Bockmuehl cites Rev. 2.7, 1 Thess. 2.13, and Mt. 28.20. He argues that 'in these three cases and many others, the implied reader is drawn into an act of reading that involves an active part on stage rather than the discreet view from the upper balcony' (p. 72).

66. In studies of the implied readers, the individuals who tangibly access the work are variously called 'actual' readers, 'real' readers, or 'empirical' readers. In *Role*, Eco prefers to contrast the model reader with the empirical reader (e.g. pp. 4, 8, 11). In *Six Walks*, he writes, 'the model reader of a story is not the empirical reader. The empirical reader is you, me, anyone, when we read a text. Empirical readers can read in many ways, and there is no law that tells them how to read.' For a brief delineation of these terms from the perspective of narrative criticism, see Mark A. Powell, *What is Narrative Criticism?* (Minneapolis, MN: Fortress Press, 1990), pp. 27-31. Cf. William Nelles, 'Historical and Implied Authors and Readers', *Comparative Literature* 45 (1993), pp. 22-46 (esp. his interaction with Wayne Booth's notion of 'implied author', pp. 33-35); and Walter J. Slatoff, *With Respect to Readers: Dimensions of Literary Response* (Ithaca, NY: Cornell University Press, 1970). In 'Readers in Texts', pp. 848-63, Wilson seeks to bridge the gap between English and German literary scholarship on this critical issue.

67. Briggs, *Virtuous Reader*, p. 206. He continues by explaining that the implied readers are 'literary-critical constructs, ideal (no pun intended) for getting at the kinds of interpretive judgments required of any reader of a given text'.

from the individual actually reading that text. However, there is an inevitable and mutually informing interconnection between the horizon of the implied reader and that of the real reader. To understand a work that has an embedded readerly expectation, the individual reading that work must necessarily perceive at least elements of the hermeneutical profile expected of him or her. When a reader perceives the expectations generated by the reading of a text, that reader has a significant decision to make: to be or not to be the implied reader. While reading a text, 'the real reader needs to judge the desirability of occupying the space of the implied reader'.[68] In this manner, readers might 'aspire to imitate the implied reader, but the two categories remain distinct'.[69]

If readers are reading seeking understanding, they will be invariably confronted with the implied reader. For biblical texts, recognizing the character and content of the implied reader is not a neutral experience. Because of the communicative nature of the biblical text as a medium of encounter, the real reader is forced to either accept or reject the intended perlocutionary effect of transformation.[70] In order for a real reader to become the implied reader

---

68. Briggs, *Virtuous Reader*, p. 206. Briggs notes that the real reader might wish to say 'in practice, "I am not like Moses", or "The construct is too male", or "Too many problematic passages undermine my ability to trust the ones that seem to offer more life-giving possibilities"' (pp. 206-207). In this sense, real readers 'can say that while they understand the "offer" of the text (assuming that some exercise of interpretive empathy has allowed them to see it for what it is), they are not themselves interested in aspiring to be the kind of person such an implied reader models' (pp. 207-208). Cf. Moloney, 'Who is the Reader', p. 21: 'The implied reader is part of the spatial gaps and temporal flow of the narrative itself. However, the Christian tradition of reading the Bible, and the community of readers through the ages which produced the Bible, presupposes that a relationship is established between the implied reader *in* the text and the real reader *of* the text. The relationship may sometimes be uncomfortable. The text may produce pleasure, pain, ambiguity and even hostility, but some form of relationship between an implied reader in the text and a real reader of the text must exist.'

69. Briggs, *Virtuous Reader*, p. 207.

70. Gerhard Maier describes the Bible as a 'medium of encounter' in *Biblical Hermeneutics* (trans. Robert W. Yarbrough; Wheaton, IL: Crossway, 1994), p. 25. For Maier, this revelatory and theological feature of the Bible is a central motivation and justification for a 'special hermeneutic' (a *hermeneutica sacra*). Similarly, Brown encourages 'a more interpersonal model of reading and interpreting, one that lives up to the implicitly relational idea of the biblical text as communication—and therefore one that does justice to the dialogical nature of interpretation and contextualization' (*Scripture as Communication*, p. 15). Vanhoozer characterizes the 'macrogenre of Scripture' as 'divine address' (*Drama of Doctrine*, p. 224). John Webster, *Word and Church* (Edinburgh: T. & T. Clark, 2001), p. 77, also highlights the way God speaks through canonical texts: 'The reader is an actor within a larger web of events and activities, supreme among which is God's act in which God speaks God's Word through the text of the Bible to the people of God... As a participant in this historical process, the reader is *spoken to* in the text.'

(and the texts overwhelmingly encourage a reader to do so), then he or she must submit to the restraints of the implied reader.[71] As Bockmuehl articulates, 'There may well be a sense in which one cannot long pursue the question of how the text's implied reader relates to its truth before one stumbles over the more delicate issue of how the modern interpreter for his or her part relates to it.'[72] He continues by noting that the act of 'braketing this issue temporarily may well be an illuminating exercise', but that 'sidestepping it over the long term requires increasingly taxing and implausible amounts of fancy footwork'.[73] In the terms developed above, the ideal reader of the biblical writings is an actual reader who seeks to identify *with* the implied reader generated by the biblical writings.

By way of summary, the primary characteristics of the implied reader of the Christian canon can be grouped under two main headings, one theological and the other hermeneutical. In Matthew's Gospel, there is an interplay between blocks of discourse and blocks of narrative. At the end of one of these discourse sections, Jesus asks his disciples, 'Have you understood all these things?' (Mt. 13.51). In the preceding chapters, Matthew recounts Jesus' teaching on the kingdom (often in parables) and on the nature of discipleship. After the disciples answer in the affirmative to Jesus' query, Jesus makes an important comment. He says, 'Therefore, every scribe who has become a disciple of the kingdom of heaven is like a head of a household, who brings out of his treasure things new and old' (Mt. 13.52). Jesus' words here are a good representation of two of the expectations that the biblical authors have for their readers. First, the implied reader of the Christian canon is a believing disciple, a 'disciple of the kingdom'. As Bockmuehl argues, 'Both Testaments of Scripture clearly presuppose such an interpreter. The implied interpreter of the Christian Scripture is a *disciple*, just as that disciple's implied reading of the text is its witness to Christ.'[74]

---

71. Bockmuehl, *Seeing the Word*, p. 73: 'In other words, the texts appear to envisage a reader who freely explores certain lines of interpretation while avoiding others.' Cf. Vanhoozer, *Drama of Doctrine*, pp. 18-21. For Vanhoozer, this tension between the implied reader and the actual reader is part of the 'drama of biblical interpretation'. He writes, 'The drama of reading Scripture ultimately involves the fate of text and reader alike: Will the text succeed in establishing its worldview? Will the reader be decisively shaped through the process? There is potential for dramatic conflict not merely within the story but in the very process of reading in which the reader struggles, sometimes spiritually, with the text' (p. 19).

72. Bockmuehl, *Seeing the Word*, p. 74.

73. Bockmuehl, *Seeing the Word*, p. 74. In a discussion of 'new historicism', Bockmuehl also asserts that 'in dealing with the New Testament's inalienably theological subject matter there can be no objective history—and certainly no neutral historian' (p. 45).

74. Bockmuehl, *Seeing the Word*, p. 92. Cf. the title of his essay, 'Reason, Wisdom

In addition to this theological characteristic, there is also a complementary hermeneutical one. The implied reader of the biblical text is one whose eye has been trained to recognize the contours of those very texts. Jesus tells his followers that a *scribe* (one trained in the interpretation of texts) who has become a disciple (one trained to know God) can produce great things for the kingdom of heaven. At this place in Matthew's narrative, the issue of interpretation is prominent. In fact, the immediately preceding section of discourse focuses on the presentation and right interpretation of Jesus' words (e.g. his sayings and parables).[75] Accordingly, Jesus' query to his disciples encompasses the broader discourse context and is loaded with hermeneutical freight: 'Have you *understood* all these things?' (Mt. 13.51, Συνήκατε ταῦτα πάντα).[76] Further, Jesus now highlights the importance of the personal involvement of his followers in the 'kingdom of heaven', a concept that he has been filling with meaning.[77] Jesus here envisions a cer-

---

and the Implied Disciple of Scripture', in *Reading Texts, Seeking Wisdom: Scripture and Theology* (ed. D.F. Ford and G.N. Stanton; London: SCM Press, 2003), pp. 53-68.

75. Matthew's narrative in Matthew 13 is full of Jesus' words/teaching in the form of parabolic discourse. Matthew recounts that Jesus 'spoke many things to them in parables' (13.2). The disciples ask Jesus, 'Why do you speak to them in parables?' (13.10). Jesus connects his use of parables when speaking to the people to the prophecy of Isaiah (13.14-15/Isa. 6.9-10; 13.34-35/Ps. 78.2) and tells his disciples, 'To you it has been granted to know the mysteries of the kingdom of heaven, but to them it has not been granted' (13.11). Jesus prefaces his own interpretation by exhorting them, 'Hear then the parable of the sower' (13.18). Jesus then presents a sequence of parables about what the kingdom of heaven 'is like' (13.24, 31, 44-47). In the middle of this discourse section, Matthew recounts, 'All these things Jesus spoke to the crowds in parables, and he did not speak to them without a parable' (13.34). To conclude this particular section of discourse, Matthew summarizes, 'When Jesus had finished these parables, he departed from there' (13.53). The presentation and interpretation of the parabolic words of Jesus, then, serve as the thematic content and structural markers of the discourse recounted in Matthew 13.

76. The verb συνίημι conveys the sense of having 'an intelligent grasp of something that challenges one's thinking or practice' (BDAG, s.v. 'συνίημι'). In the immediate context of Matthew 13, the issue of 'understanding' or 'comprehending' what Jesus is saying is paramount. The reason Jesus gives for speaking in parables is to actualize ('fulfill') the prophecy of Isaiah: 'because while seeing they do not see, and while hearing they do not hear, nor do they understand' (Mt. 13.13, οὐδὲ συνίουσιν). By contrast, he tells the disciples, 'But blessed are your eyes, because they see; and your ears, because they hear' (13.16). The implied reader of this text identifies with Jesus' portrayal of his true disciples. Through Matthew's compositional work, he has enabled subsequent generations to see, hear, and understand the words of Jesus. This textual feature enables a careful and sympathetic reader of Matthew's Gospel to answer Jesus' query, 'Yes, I do understand these things.'

77. The string of parables that precedes Jesus' comment about the 'scribe who has become a disciple' emphasizes the identity of the kingdom of heaven (i.e. 'the kingdom

tain type of 'scribe' (πᾶς γραμματεὺς), in other words, a certain type of reader/interpreter.[78] The scribal figure that Jesus envisions ('implies') is one who has been 'discipled in the ways of the kingdom' (μαθητευθεὶς τῇ βασιλείᾳ) through grappling with Jesus' own words and the Hebrew Scriptures that are so often invoked by those words.

Jesus likens ('is like', ὅστις ἐστιν) this individual to a 'head of a household' who 'brings out of his treasure things new and old' (13.52, ὅστις ἐκβάλλει ἐκ τοῦ θησουροῦ αὐτου καινὰ καὶ μαλαιά). The word picture that Jesus paints here suggests that the task of 'brining out' things from the treasure or storehouse is not a simplistic one but rather involves a strategic selection. As a complex entity, the content of the 'treasure' must be gathered and stored together in some sort of structure. The head of the household then brings out of that storehouse what is needed at the appropriate or 'fitting' time. There is also an implicit hermeneutical task involved in the process. The presentation of goods involves selecting elements from a diverse store. Both new and old things must be ordered and presented. What is more, they are presented in a dialectic, mutually defining relationship.[79] In striking fashion, Jesus' words resonate with the burning issue of the relationship of the authority of the Scriptures (the Law and the Prophets) and the authority of Jesus himself (the Lord and the apostles). This is both a theological and a literary question, as the authority of both the old covenant and the new covenant is quickly bound up with sacred texts that share that authority. By stressing the new and the old, Jesus simultaneously affirms both the unity/interrelatedness and the diversity/distinctiveness of the two elements involved (i.e. the man 'brings out' both new *and* old).

In this regard, Jesus' description of the scribe who has become a disciple can serve as an analogy to readers seeking to read individual parts of Scripture in light of the whole canonical context.[80] Just as Jesus exhorts his orig-

---

of heaven is like…'). In this verse there is a shift to the identity of a citizen of that kingdom (i.e. 'every scribe…is like'). In light of the repeated refrains of the preceding parables, this shift makes Jesus' point about this scribal kingdom activity emphatic.

78. The word translated 'scribe' (γραμματεύς) generally refers to someone 'who has special functions in connection with documents' (see BDAG, s.v. 'γραμματεύς'). The typical sense of γραμματεύς in the New Testament relates to an individual who had expertise 'in matters relating to divine revelation', and more specifically to 'experts' or 'scholars versed in the law'. Scribes are often mentioned in association with the Jewish leaders (e.g. Mt. 2.4; 16.21; 20.18; 21.15; and 27.41). The usage in Mt. 13.52 is likely an extension of this sense, applied to the interpretation of the words of Jesus.

79. In other words, the elements are defined in relationship to one another (καινὰ καὶ μαλαιά). The oldness of the 'old' (μαλαιά) is perceived because of the presence of the new, and the newness of the 'new' (καινὰ) is seen in relation to the old.

80. The notion of scribe implies the literary realm and so the image of the householder bringing out new and old things from his treasure already bears an analogous connection to textual activity.

inal followers to view his own words in light of the Scriptures, Matthew's
readers are likewise encouraged to view the import of this pericope (i.e. the
part) within the broader context of the surrounding discourse, the book of
Matthew, the Gospel-corpus, the New Testament, and the Two-Testament
Christian canon (i.e. the whole). Part of Matthew's compositional strategy
is to present a carefully crafted selection of those dominical words so that
readers (both ancient and contemporary) can access them and thus follow
Jesus' hermeneutical guidance.[81] Moreover, the canonical context (OT and
NT) within which readers encounter Matthew's narrative includes the texts
that are most germane to the interpretation of Jesus' words.

As discussed and developed in Chapter 2 (on canon-consciousness),
Chapter 3 (on canonical contextuality), and Chapter 4 (on canonical intertextuality), the canonical context has a number of hermeneutically significant features. Each of these areas describe the natural hermeneutical effects
that a collection of writings has on readers ('mere') and also the elements of
these features that have been intentionally produced by the authors and editors of the biblical material itself ('meant').[82] The implied reader of the biblical collection skillfully takes note of this multifaceted matrix of canonical
features. In other words, the implied reader of the Christian Scriptures is
one that has a robust canon-consciousness. Accordingly, the implied reader
affirms the *authority* of the canonical documents (Canon 1) and also accepts
the *guidance* of the canonical framework (Canon 2). The *believing* community is also to be a *reading* community. In this sense, the implied audience is
the community that notes, 'this is the framework provided by the canonical
collection, and we know that its testimony is true'.

One way to move toward being transformed into the implied reader projected by the biblical authors is to move toward a canon-conscious reading
of Scripture. In this sense, the ideal reader is a Christian, but more specifically one reading particular Christian *texts* in a particular way. These
texts have a shape that has contributed to the formation of that reader's
understanding of what it means to be the ideal reader of those texts. Thus,
the notion of the ideal reader can form a crucial part of the foundation of
a confessional view of the doctrine of Scripture, and it can also function
as an integrated element of one's hermeneutical approach to reading those

---

81. In this sense, as author of a Gospel narrative, Mathew himself represents a
scribe who has become a disciple. Cf. Ezra's characterization as a 'scribe skilled in the
law of Moses, which the Lord God of Israel had given' (Ezra 7.6) and as one who 'had
set his heart to study the law of the Lord and to practice it, and to teach his statutes and
ordinances' (7.10). This strategic training and devotion in turn allowed Ezra to lead the
people in reading, understanding, and responding to the 'book of the Law of Moses'.
See Neh. 8.1-12.

82. Broadly, the distinction between 'mere' and 'meant' can be likened to the distinction between 'reception-oriented' and 'production-oriented' textual features.

authoritative texts. The ideal reader of the Christian canon is a disciple (one who follows Jesus) who is also a scribe (one who skillfully reads texts). The ones who can pick up these texts and follow the author's intention are the same ones who have picked up their cross and followed Jesus.

Identifying and Becoming the Ideal Readers of the Biblical Canon

Taking the shape of the biblical material into account allows biblical readers to identify and voluntarily associate with the expectations generated by a closed authoritative canon. As noted above, the canon as a whole guides its readers through the biblical material by limiting and generating meaning. In turn, the ideal reader of the canon is one who accepts this guidance.[83] This type of real reader, in effect, '[exemplifies] the wisdom of the implied exegete'.[84]

---

83. By analogy, the 'ideal reader' is similar to what Wayne Booth calls the 'credulous listener' (i.e. the narrative audience in a work of fiction). The credulous listener 'believes that it all really happened as reported by the teller' and 'accepts all its norms as permanent, unqualified by "aesthetic distance" or by any sense of a possible return to a realer life: this *is* real life' and 'who takes all narrators at their word'. See Nelles, 'Historical and Implied Authors and Readers', p. 34. A historical example of a reading of the Testaments that follows the guidance of the canonical shaping is the use of the 'rule of faith' in the Patristic period. In relation to a two-testament Bible, this rule of faith also provides confirmation that those in the early church (e.g. Irenaeus and Tertullian) thought in terms of the broader collection and broader context of Scripture. The rule of faith assures that the relationship between the Testaments, however it is construed, will remain intact. The rule of faith asserts that the 'God of Abraham, Isaac, and Jacob' (Exod. 3.6) is 'the God and father of our Lord Jesus Christ' (Eph. 1.3). The God of the Old Testament is not at odds with the God of the New Testament. The rule is often recognized as a summary of the scriptural storyline. By deliberately binding the overall message of both Testaments, the rule of faith functions as a canon-conscious summary of the storyline of Scripture in the early church's discipleship and defense against heresy. Though there is an important historical development that takes place as the New Testament forms, the relationship between the canon and the rule of faith should not be understood as adversarial. The rule concisely points to the character of the two-testament canon of the churches. Driver notes in this regard that 'it is altogether unlikely that the church's two testament canon should have no relation whatsoever to its *canon et regula fidei* in the period before questions of the New Testament's scope were settled' (*Brevard Childs*, p. 27). Cf. Kathryn Green-McCreight, 'Rule of Faith', in *DTIB*, pp. 703-704; Paul M. Blowers, 'The *Regula Fidei* and the Narrative Character of Early Christian Faith', *Pro Ecclesia* 6 (1997), pp. 199-228; Seitz, *Character of Christian Scripture*, pp. 191-203; and Vanhoozer, *Drama of Doctrine*, pp. 203-10. For Vanhoozer, 'Reading according to the Rule of Faith means, concretely, reading the Old Testament in relation to the New (e.g. christocentrically, eschatologically) and holding together God the Creator with God the Father of Jesus Christ' (p. 204).

84. Bockmeuhl, *Seeing the Word*, p. 99, makes this comment with reference to an artistic portrayal of Thomas Aquinas in the role of scriptural interpreter.

As noted in Chapters 3 and 4, the function of the book of Revelation in the Christian canon is a feature of its contextual culmination of the New Testament narrative and its intertextual use of creation imagery drawn from the narratives of Genesis 1–3.[85] By means of its content and position in relation to the rest of the biblical corpora (as adumbrated above), the book of Revelation generates an implicit expectation that no new written revelation is necessary 'until he comes' (cf. Rev. 22.18-19). Thus, the fruit of John's compositional activity is a sealed Apocalypse, a sealed New Testament, and a sealed Christian canon. As a result of this closing function, the Bible as a whole is now ostensively sealed from further addition, subtraction, or modification.

One might point out that any talk of the book of Revelation sealing the canon contradicts a clear statement to the contrary in Rev. 22.10, where the angel clearly tells John, 'Do not seal up the words of this prophecy.' However, the function of the book of Revelation as a conclusion to the canon actually complements the directive here. At the end of the book of Daniel, the prophet is commanded to seal up the prophecy because the time of fulfillment had not yet come (Dan. 12.4, 9). By drawing on this Daniel text, the angel in Rev. 22.10 demonstrates that the revelation given to John pictures the fulfillment of the prophecies described in the book of Daniel.[86] In Christ himself, the end of days has dawned. Consequently, the message of the gospel and the message of the book of Revelation are to be proclaimed without hesitation. Rather than contradicting this mandate, by composing his book, John carries it out.[87]

This phenomenon is another way Revelation helps provide a concept of closure that can be found within the boundaries of the biblical canon. By closing the canon and committing the divine revelation to writing, the message of that text is now widely available to readers (22.6-9). Thomas Hieke draws out the significance of the 'words of the prophecy' being written down (*schriftlich*) in a 'book' that is widely available to anyone who

---

85. See the final section of Chapter 4.

86. See G.K. Beale and Sean M. McDonough, 'Revelation', in *Commentary on the New Testament Use of the Old Testament* (ed. G.K. Beale and D.A. Carson; Grand Rapids, MI: Baker, 2007), p. 1156. They note that this allusion to Daniel 'expresses awareness that Daniel's prophecy is commencing fulfillment in John's own time and that genuine believers should discern this revelation and respond positively'.

87. Cf. Michael Fishbane, *Biblical Interpretation in Ancient Israel* (Oxford: Oxford University Press, 1985), p. 445, who argues that 'the essential hermeneutical role of oracular exegesis is twofold: to reopen or prolong confidence in an oracle's content; and, more importantly, to establish its *closure*, i.e. to show how the oracle has been, or will soon be, actualized'. By extensively drawing on Daniel's prophecy, this dual hermeneutical function is at work in the book of Revelation (especially in 22.6-21).

might take it and read. The medium of a book makes it possible for the written form (*schrift-form*) to exceed the 'space-time limitation' of speech and proclamation.[88] This type of effect applies not only to John's Apocalypse but also to the rest of written revelation.[89] In other words, by sealing the canon, its message is unsealed.[90] There is thus a dialectical relationship at work here. Both the gracious invitation to read and the stern prohibition against changing the contents of this 'book' in any way (22.18-19) exist alongside one another.

In addition to this canonical function, the book of Revelation as a whole also helps identify the ideal reader of the biblical canon. A central element of John's compositional strategy is to focus deliberately on the activity of reading and writing, to encourage his readers to view his work as a 'book', and to exhort them to become certain types of readers. The overall framework of the book of Revelation contains textual clues that help guide readers in their understanding of its literary meaning, its theological message, and its expectation for those reading this 'book'.[91]

88. This understanding of the function of written texts contrasts the poststructuralist critique of the traditional understanding of the nature of writing. As Barthes articulates it, 'The classical sign is a sealed unit, whose closure arrests meaning, prevents it from trembling or becoming double, or wandering. The same goes for the classical text: it closes the work, chains it to its letter, rivets it to its signified' ('Theory of the Text', in *Untying the Text: A Post-Structuralist Reader* [ed. Robert Young; London: Routledge, 1981], pp. 31-37 [33]).

89. See Thomas Hieke, 'Biblische Texte als Texte der Bibel Auslegen—Dargestellt am Beispiel von Offb 22,6-21 und Anderen Kanonrelevanten Texten', in *Der Bibel-kanon in der Bibelauslegung* (ed. Egbert Ballhorn and Georg Steins; Stuttgart: W. Kohlhammer Verlag, 2007), pp. 333-34.

90. Vanhoozer articulates this idea when he notes that 'without its normative specification in the canon, the gospel could neither be proclaimed nor taught' (*Drama of Doctrine*, p. 229).

91. One of the best ways of discerning the shape of the book is through a close reading of its beginning and ending. The prologue and epilogue of a literary work often provide readers with important clues for understanding the content that lies between. Trobisch notes in this regard that 'the editorial intention very often is expressed clearly at the beginning or at the end of a text. These passages are very apt to contain editorial changes' (*Paul's Letter Collection*, p. 88). Childs also comments that 'the purpose of the author is often most clearly stated in the prescript or in the conclusion' (*New Testament as Canon*, p. 49). Regarding the overall shape of Revelation, Childs maintains that the most helpful approach is 'to take the final form of the present book seriously and seek to determine how the complex structure functions within the book as a whole' (p. 510). The prologue and epilogue of Revelation are crucial elements of this final form. Accordingly, there are many innertextual verbal connections between Revelation 1 and Revelation 22 that serve as clear bookends for the work and help bind the various narrative threads together. Chapter

An important theme present throughout John's Apocalypse is the compositional emphasis on *writing* a *book*. At the beginning of John's vision, he hears behind him 'a loud voice like the sound of a trumpet' (1.10). From the context, the voice belongs to the risen Christ, the living one who was dead but is 'alive forevermore' (1.18). His first words to his bondservant John come in the form of a compositional mandate. Jesus commands John 'to write in a book what he sees' (ὃ βλέπεις γράψον εἰς βιβλίον) and to send it to the seven churches (1.11). After describing the appearance of Jesus, John recounts that he 'fell at his feet like a dead man' (1.17). After Jesus tells him not to be afraid and comforts him with the truth that he is the 'first and the last' and has dominion even over death and Hades (1.18), Jesus gives a further command to write. He tells John, 'Write the things which you have seen, and the things which are, and the things which will take place after these things' (1.19).[92] The imperative γράψον comes from the general verb γράφω, which conveys the process of expressing thoughts in writing, and in this context, the recounting of 'pronouncements and solemn proceedings'.[93] These commands to write affirm the literary context of the book as a whole and provide a framework for the narrative and discourse that follows. The next two chapters echo these verses, as Jesus tells John to compose individual letters for each of the seven churches.[94]

1 contains a prologue (1.1-3), an epistolary introduction (1.4-6), and the beginning of the book's narrative sequence (1.9). The final chapter completes the narrative begun in the first chapter (22.1-5), contains an epistolary conclusion by John, and provides a sequence of closing editorial comments (22.10-20), followed by a benediction (22.21). These similarities provide a reader with an initial sense of cohesion for the complex content of the rest of the book.

92. Jesus' words here perhaps indicate a rough outline of the book's contents. For a detailed analysis of 'the disputed significance of Rev. 1.19 as an interpretive key to the book', see G.K. Beale, *The Book of Revelation: A Commentary on the Greek Text* (Grand Rapids, MI: Eerdmans, 1999), pp. 152-70. Beale surveys a number of interpretive options and concludes that the phrase 'what will happen after these things' is 'an allusion to Daniel 2 with an "already-and-not-yet" sense' and affirms that 'each of the three object clauses in v. 19 refers equally to the entire book' (p. 168). However one understands these specific elements, there is at least a form of structural sequence in Jesus' statement. For the point being made here, the past, present, and future temporal elements are an indication of the narrative framework that situates the visions of Rev. 4.1–22.5. Cf. the wording of Rev. 1.8.

93. See BDAG, s.v. 'γράφω'. Forms of γράφω occur frequently throughout the New Testament, but the imperative is found almost exclusively in Revelation.

94. E.g., to the first church, Jesus commands, Τῷ ἀγγέλῳ τῆς ἐν Ἐφέσῳ ἐκκλησίας γράψον. The same phrasing is used in Jesus' comments to the church in Ephesus (2.1), Smyrna (2.8), Pergamum (2.12), Thyatira (2.18), Sardis (3.1), Philadelphia (3.7), and Laodicea (2.14).

Thus, the compositional command 'to write' is a consistent refrain in the first few chapters of the book.[95] What John sees, he is to write down.[96]

More specifically, John is to write these things down *in a book* (εἰς βιβλίον). The word βιβλίον here has the sense of a complex, intentional composition.[97] Thus, the command from Jesus is not a generic directive. John is to behold divinely inspired visions and recount them in a specific book that he is carefully to compose. He is tasked with the active role of author as well as the relatively passive role of viewer. Here the fact that the general verb 'to write' is connected to the concept of a written composition is significant. The prophecy that will be handed down consists of 'the things which are written' (1.3, τὰ ἐν αὐτῇ γεγραμμένα). Those who read 'The Apocalypse of John' are encountering the fruit of his obedience to this command to write what he sees in a book.[98] After occurring once in the first chapter, the word βιβλίον does not occur again in the same sense until the final chapters.[99] After the books and the 'Lamb's book of life' (τῷ βιβλίῳ τῆς ζωῆς τοῦ ἀρνίου) are mentioned as part of the eschatological vision (20.11-15), there is a significant concentration of occurrences in 22.6-21. In this section, βιβλίον occurs seven times. Four of these uses occur in the important phrase, 'the words of the prophecy of this book'

95. Of the twelve instances of the imperative γράψον in the book, nine of them occur in chaps. 1–3. See 1.11, 19; 2.1, 8, 12, 18; 3.1, 7, and 14. The other instances are in 14.13; 19.9; and 21.5. This imperative is only found elsewhere in the New Testament in Lk. 16.6-7, where it is used in a legal context.

96. The compositional mandate itself is an echo of a well-established pattern in the prophetic literature of the Old Testament. See, e.g., Isa. 30.8: 'Now go, write it on a tablet before them and inscribe it on a scroll, that it may serve in the time to come as a witness forever'; and Hab. 2.2: 'Then the Lord answered me and said, "Record the vision and inscribe it on tablets, that the one who reads it may run"'. Cf. Deut. 27.8 ('You shall write on the stones all the words of this law very distinctly'), and Isa. 8.1 ('Then the Lord said to me, "Take for yourself a large tablet and write on it in ordinary letters…"').

97. See BDAG, s.v. 'βιβλίον'. As mentioned in Chapter 1, the word can mean either a 'brief written message' in general (e.g. a certificate of divorce in Mt. 19.7) or a 'long written composition'. Etymologically, the word derives from βύβλος, the word for Egyptian papyrus. The bark of this papyrus was used in the production of writing materials. Cf. Ronald L. Trail, *An Exegetical Summary of Revelation 1–11* (Dallas, TX: SIL International, 2003), pp. 33-34.

98. Drawn from the words of Rev. 1.1, 'The Apocalypse of John' is the title this book bears in most of the Greek manuscripts. See Trobisch, *First Edition of the New Testament*, pp. 40-41.

99. The word βιβλίον is used nine times to signify a 'scroll' that can be 'opened' and 'rolled up' (5.1, 2, 3, 4, 5, 8, 9; 6.14; and 10.8). In the latter parts of John's vision, βιβλίον is used to indicate the Lamb's 'book of life' that records the names of God's people (13.8; 17.8; 20.12; 21.27).

(τοὺς λόγους τῆς προφητείας τοῦ βιβλίου τούτου).[100] From beginning to end, then, John's Apocalypse presents itself as a specific type of communicative entity, a 'book'.

Parallel to these commands regarding the *writing* of this book, there are also complementary guidelines given regarding the *reading* of this book. In the introduction, before the epistolary greeting, a blessing is pronounced for those who read and hear these words: 'Blessed is he who reads and those who hear the words of the prophecy, and heed the things which are written in it' (Rev. 1.3, Μακάριος ὁ ἀναγινώσκων καὶ οἱ ἀκούοντες τοὺς λόγους τῆς προφητείας). This striking statement ends the prologue and builds a high expectation for the content that follows. This strong comment is matched by an almost verbatim expression at the end of the book. In 22.7, the words of Jesus appear for the first time since the end of chap. 3, the end of the last letter to the churches. Jesus urgently and emphatically states, 'Behold, I am coming quickly.'[101] He then pronounces a blessing that echoes the introduction: 'Blessed is he who heeds the words of the prophecy of this book' (Rev. 22.7, μακάριος ὁ τηρῶν τοὺς λόγους τῆς προφητείας τοῦ βιβλίου τούτου). In this form, the recipient of the blessing is specified as one who 'heeds' (τηρῶν) the words of the prophecy of this book.[102]

These two statements are important in demonstrating the compositional shape of the book of Revelation. In 22.7, the reader discovers that the strong word of commendation to the readers of this book ultimately derives from the risen Christ himself. The introductory statement expands on Jesus' concluding words by emphasizing the three actions of reading, hearing, and heeding. Jesus himself is the one who blesses the reading and heeding of the revelation that centers on him.[103]

After this promise of *blessing* to the reader, there follows in Rev. 22.18-19 a promise of *curses* to any individual who alters the words of this book.[104]

100. This phrase occurs in 22.7, 10; 22.18, 19. The other three uses refer to things written in 'this book' (22.9, 18, 19).
101. All three elements of this statement (Ἰδοὺ ἔρχομαι ταχύ) heighten the immediacy of Jesus' assertion.
102. For a discussion of what is involved in this 'heeding', see fn 114 below.
103. Cf. Rev. 22.14: 'Blessed are those who wash their robes, so that they may have the right to the tree of life, and may enter by the gates into the city.' The focus on blessing in relation to the reading of this book in 22.7 may be the framework for understanding the blessing of 22.14.
104. Hieke, 'Biblische Texte als Texte der Bibel Auslegen', p. 332, calls the pronouncement in Rev. 22.18-19 a 'text assurance formula' (*textsicherungsformel*) that ensures the extent and continued existence of the revealed text. He observes that such a statement 'draws attention to *what* exactly is now to be protected' (my translation). Cf. Tobias Nicklas, '"The Words of the Prophecy of this Book": Playing with Scriptural Authority in the Book of Revelation', in *Authoritative Scriptures in Ancient Judaism* (ed. M. Popović; Leiden: Brill, 2010), pp. 309-26.

5. *Identifying and Becoming the Ideal Reader of the Biblical Canon* 211

Jesus again issues a stern warning to 'everyone who hears the words of the prophecy of this book' (22.18a, παντὶ τῷ ἀκούοντι τοὺς λόγους τῆς προφητείας τοῦ βιβλίου τούτου). For the one who adds to these words, 'God will add to him the plagues which are written in this book' (22.18b). Conversely, for the one who takes away words from this book, 'God will take away his part from the tree of life and from the holy city, which are written in this book' (22.19).[105]

One who adds or takes away from these words is in essence doing the exact opposite of heeding and guarding them. Accordingly, the exact opposite recompense is the result. These strong words allude to the 'canonical formula' of Old Testament prophetic literature that goes all the way back to the Pentateuch.[106] Toward the beginning and end of the book of Deuteronomy, Moses gives a warning concerning the people's reception of the Law of the Lord. He commands the people to 'listen to the statues and the judgments' which the Lord had given to him in order to teach the people (Deut. 4.1). He states, 'You shall not add to the word which I am commanding you, nor take away from it, that you may keep the commandments of the Lord your God which I command you' (Deut. 4.2).[107]

Toward the end of Deuteronomy, Moses gives a similar set of warnings. God will make prosper those who obey the Lord and 'keep his commandments and his statutes which are written in this book of the law' (30.10). However, those who do not keep the commands and heed the words of the Lord will be punished 'according to all the curses of the covenant which are written in this book of the law' (29.21). Thus, in Deuteronomy, there is a close connection between 'adding' and 'taking away' from the words of the book of covenant and failing to heed and obey those words. In Rev.

---

105. In this short passage, there is an emphasis by verbal repetition of the things that are 'written in this book' (γεγραμμένας ἐν τῷ βιβλίῳ τούτῳ).

106. On the 'canonical formula' in Deut. 4.2 (and extrabiblical parallels), see Gerhard von Rad, *Deuteronomy* (Philadelphia, PA: Westminster/John Knox Press, 1966), pp. 48-49; and Peter C. Craigie, *The Book of Deuteronomy* (Grand Rapids, MI: Eerdmans, 1976), pp. 129-30. Bruce K. Waltke, *The Book of Proverbs: Chapters 15-31* (Grand Rapids, MI: Eerdmans, 2005), pp. 476-77, relates this phraseology to Agur's similar words in Prov. 30.6. Johannes Taschner argues that the 'canonical formula' (*die kanonformel*) of Deut. 4.2 is the 'hermeneutical key' (*hermeneutischer Schlüssel*) of the Pentateuch in '"Fügt nichts zu dem hinzu, was ich euch gebiete, und streicht nichts heraus!" Die Kanonformel in Deuteronomium 4,2 als hermeneutischer Schlüssel der Tora', in *Kanonisierung—die Hebräische Bibel im Werden* (ed. Georg Steins and Johannes Tascher; Göttingen: Neukirchener Theologie, 2010), pp. 46-63. Cf. Johannes Taschner, 'Das Deuteronomium als Abschluss der Tora', in *Kanonisierung*, pp. 64-92.

107. The notion of keeping the commandments of the Lord in Deut. 4.2 verbally parallels the notion of keeping/guarding the things written in Rev. 1.3.

22.18-19, a similar relationship is envisioned between the people of God and the 'book' that claims to convey his word to them.[108]

This passage puts an authoritative stamp on the content of Revelation and effectively seals the book and the message it contains from further addition or subtraction. The closing formula also emphasizes the divine authority and origin of the book.[109] The 'words of the prophecy of this book' of Revelation are to be treated with as much respect and submission as was attributed to the Law. By his use of intertextual allusions to the book of Deuteronomy, John makes the bold claim that the authority of the book of Revelation parallels that of the Torah. For the Jewish people, there is no higher claim.[110] Because it contains the 'revelation of Jesus Christ', the book should be guarded as a treasured word from the highest authority.

Along with the blessing to the reader in 22.7, the warning of 22.18-19 functions as a fitting conclusion to the book and helps solidify its overall structure. Rather than a disordered array of divergent symbols, images, and fragmentary pericopes, the abovementioned features suggest that the book of Revelation is a carefully constructed composition that generates a complex but coherent narrative and interpretation of the end of days.[111] Moreover, through the way he composes his text, John encourages readers to take note of the book's structural framework and to read and locate it within a broader canonical horizon. In other words, the 'implied reader' of the book of Revelation is an intended feature of John's compositional strategy. The 'ideal reader' of the book, in turn, is the reader who takes note of these readerly expectations and seeks to embody them (i.e. he or she not only *reads*, but also *heeds*).

The final narrative sequence of the book in Rev. 22.8-9 is significant in this regard. John confesses that he is the one 'who heard and saw these things' and then he describes what his reaction to this staggering vision

108. Cf. Beale and McDonough, 'Revelation', pp. 1157-58.

109. Cf. von Campenhausen, *Formation of the Christian Bible*, p. 216: 'A claim such as belongs to every inspired text by its very nature is here given conscious, conceptually precise formulation.' Regarding the blessing to the reader in Rev. 1.3, von Campenhausen comments, 'His revelations are backed by the highest authority known to Christianity, and the apocalyptist explicitly transfers to his own book the sacred validity of that authority' (p. 216).

110. For a survey of the way the Torah functioned as both a supreme authority and as the foundational element of the Hebrew Bible and thus the Christian canon as a whole, see Stephen G. Dempster, 'Torah, Torah, Torah', pp. 87-128. Cf. this discussion in Chapter 2.

111. Cf. David L. Barr, 'The Apocalypse as a Symbolic Transformation of the World: A Literary Analysis', *Interpretation* 38 (1984), pp. 39-50 (43): 'Whereas our concern is to divide the book, John's concern was to bind it together'. For a survey of the 'macrostructural' considerations involved in determining the shape of the book, see Bauckham's essay in *Climax of Prophecy*, pp. 1-37.

entailed. He recounts, 'When I heard and saw, I fell down to worship at the feet of the angel who showed me these things' (22.8).[112] The angel acts quickly and decisively to rectify this inappropriate action, commanding John, 'Do not do that.' The angel then provides the reason why John's act of deference was inappropriate, saying, 'I am a fellow servant of yours and of your brethren the prophets and of those who heed the words of this book' (22.9). By identifying with John, the angel makes clear that he does not share divine status. As the readers know, the angel is only the messenger of this vision (cf. Rev. 1.1-3) and is not worthy of John's worship.

In his statement to John, the angel makes a series of associations. First, the angel associates himself with John. He then associates both of them with the prophets ('your brethren the prophets', τῶν ἀδελφῶν σου τῶν προφητῶν). These associations come as no surprise to those familiar with the biblical storyline. The prophets and apostles are grouped together and serve a function similar to the angels, who are God's messengers. The phrase 'prophets and apostles' is also sometimes used in relation to God's revelation through Scripture. For instance, in 2 Pet. 3.2, Peter tells his readers that they 'should remember the words spoken beforehand by the holy prophets and the commandment of the Lord and Savior spoken by your apostles'. Similarly, Paul describes believers as part of a household that has been 'built on the foundation of the apostles and prophets, Christ Jesus himself being the corner stone' (Eph. 2.20). In Heb. 1.14, the angels are described as 'ministering spirits, sent out to render service for the sake of those who will inherit salvation'. These descriptions complement the associations made in Rev. 22.9. These figures are fellow bondservants who serve a common Lord, Christ himself.

What is stunning about the angel's words is who comes next in this list, namely, *biblical readers*. The angel asserts that 'those who heed the words of this book' are 'fellow servants' (σύνδουλος) along with angels, prophets, and apostles. The noun σύνδουλος identifies 'one who, along with others, is in a relationship of total obedience to one master'.[113] None of the types of individuals in this list deserve this type of service and worship. Only one merits that honor, as the angel commands with his next words, 'Worship God' (22.9, τῷ θεῷ προσκύνησον).

---

112. Compare with Rev. 19.10, where an analogous exchange between John and the angel occurs. Cf. also the similar scenes in Acts involving Peter (Acts 10.25-26) and Paul (Acts 14.14-15).

113. See BDAG, s.v. 'σύνδουλος'. The editors of BDAG comment regarding the use of σύνδουλος in relation to God that 'since it is a truism that one can be a slave to only one master, such self-identification, far from being a declaration of mean servility, served notice that ultimate allegiance was owed to God or Christ alone'. In Col. 4.7, Paul's use of σύνδουλος parallels the associations the angel makes in Rev. 22.9: 'As to all my affairs, Tychicus, our beloved brother and faithful servant and fellow bondservant in the Lord, will bring you information.'

The implied corollary of this sequence is that one of the ways an individual might worship God is by heeding these words. In Rev. 1.3, there is a similar blessing promised for the one who 'heeds' or 'keeps' what is written in this book.[114] This task involves preserving the text but also treasuring and submitting to its contents. The book of Revelation presents the culmination of the biblical metanarrative. The blessing is for one who accepts and preserves the book that generates that comprehensive worldview. *Following Jesus now also means reading his book and heeding its message.* Seen within the context of the Christian canon, Revelation 22 serves an exceedingly fitting role in providing closure to the biblical storyline and the canon in which that story is told. In this sense, the hermeneutically loaded exhortation to the reader of the book of Revelation in Rev. 22.18-19 can serve both a local and a global function.

Hieke and Nicklas discuss the way this passage functions locally in relation to the book of Revelation, but also globally as a comment relating to the Christian canon as a whole. They point out the importance of the two images of the tree of life and the Holy City as symbols that represent the entirety of the biblical material. For them, the 'textsicherungsformel' of Rev. 22.19 frames a 'textkorpus' that extends from the tree of life to the Holy City (i.e. Genesis to Revelation). For a biblical reader, this passage applies immediately to the book but also to the 'great textual context' (*textzusammenhang*) of both Testaments in tandem.[115]

The emphasis on the reading of this book parallels the sentiment at work in strategic texts of the Old Testament. Along with other places, in Joshua 1, Psalm 1, and Malachi 4, readers are overtly encouraged to meditate day and night on the 'Law of the Lord'.[116] These texts function as 'macrocompositional seams' and connect 'the quest for wisdom and understanding to an individual daily reading and meditation on Scripture'.[117] These texts are 'strategic' because they appear at the major divisions of the Hebrew Bible.

---

114. The verb τηρέω (translated, 'to keep') is associated with the action of 'watching over' and preserving the state of something, or 'to cause a state, condition, or activity to continue'. In Revelation 1, the word likely means also 'to persist in obedience' with regard to what is written. See BDAG, s.v. 'τηρέω'. Cf. Trail, *Exegetical Summary of Revelation 1–11*, p. 16.

115. See Hieke and Nicklas, *Worte der Prophetie dieses Buches*, pp. 61-83.

116. The specific references are Josh. 1.7-8, Ps. 1.1-3, and Mal. 4.4. Cf. Shepherd, *Textual World of the Bible*, p. 90: 'At every major juncture in the composition of the Hebrew Bible (Moses-Prophets, Prophets-Pss, Dan-Chr) the message is the same: read Scripture to find revelation of the future work of God in Christ.'

117. Sailhamer, *Meaning of the Pentateuch*, p. 574. Chapman, 'What Are We Reading', p. 343, calls them 'editorial framing notices'. See also Blenkinsopp, *Prophecy and Canon*, pp. 120-23. Cf. Koorevaar's critique of the 'Torah Model' generated by these connections in 'The Torah Model', pp. 68-70.

An implication of the claim made in Revelation is that this book of Moses should now be read within the context of the entire Christian canon. In Psalm 1, the 'blessed' man is the one whose 'delight is in the law of the Lord', on which he 'meditates day and night' (1.2). Just as those who meditate on the first book of the Bible (the Law) are blessed, so too are the readers of the last book of the Bible (Μακάριος ὁ ἀναγινώσκων, 'Blessed is the one who reads'). The ideal reader of the Christian canon is one who devotes himself to diligent reading and re-reading of these biblical 'books'. In this sense, the ideal reader of the canon is one who consistently engages its contents.[118]

The ending of the historical phase of the composition of biblical writings does not mean that God no longer speaks or that the Spirit was 'chased into a book'.[119] Rather, the biblical writings imply that he now speaks in *just this book*, in *just these words*.[120] The book of Revelation is an example of the way God 'continues to confront the church through the pages of Scripture'.[121] The conclusion of the canon points its readers forward and demands of them a posture of anticipation. John's Apocalypse assumes that God's written revelation is completed and sufficient, *until he comes* (Rev. 22.20). As the last book of the Christian canon, the book of Revelation contains the last words of the risen Lord to the churches.[122] Jesus himself is the one who testifies to these things, and he says, 'Yes, I am coming quickly' (22.20). The ideal reader of the book of Revelation and thus the entire Christian canon is identified as the one who replies to these words, 'Amen. Come, Lord Jesus' (22.20, Ἀμήν, ἔρχου κύριε Ἰησοῦ).[123]

---

118. Cf. Fiddes, 'Canon as Space and Place', p. 136, who argues that a canonical boundary demands interaction. He writes, 'A community which holds its identity through a certain body of material has an obligation to engage with it. It cannot ignore it. The boundary marks out an area, sets up a space, in which exploration is required.'

119. Harnack argues that the closing of the New Testament meant that the 'era of enthusiasm' was over and that the Spirit was 'chased into a book!' (*Origin of the New Testament*, p. 36). For Harnack, 'the narcotic of Scriptural authority paralysed the intellect in its restless search for truth' (p. 152). The distinct effect of a normative set of documents led Harnack to describe 'men's minds' of the post-apostolic period as 'ever haunted by the spectre of the Canon' (p. 152).

120. Cf. David Yeago, 'The Bible', in *Knowing the Triune God* (ed. James J. Buckley and David Yeago; Grand Rapids, MI: Eerdmans, 2001), pp. 49-94 (66): 'It is *this* discourse, what is said in *these* writings, textually fixed in just *this* fashion, which the church knows as the "divine discourse" of the Holy Spirit.'

121. Childs, *Biblical Theology in Crisis*, p. 100.

122. In this regard, note how many times Jesus employs the phrase, 'I am' (ἐγώ εἰμι) in Revelation 22.

123. Cf. Bauckham, *Climax of Prophecy*, p. 168: 'The prayer for the *parousia* is at the heart of Christian living according to the Apocalypse.'

CONCLUSION

Embracing a Canon-Conscious Reading of Scripture

This book seeks to answer two broad and basic questions. First, 'How did the biblical canon come to be?' Second, 'What effect does that canon have on its readers?' The former is a historical question; the latter is a hermeneutical question. The former relates to the formation of the biblical canon; the latter relates to the function of the biblical canon. Though these questions have often been pursued in virtual isolation from one another, there are considerable gains from noting the inherent interconnections between the two lines of inquiry. The common element that binds them together is their shared object of study, namely, the collection of texts known as the Christian canon.

The above analysis has further aimed at providing a sketch of the theoretical and hermeneutical considerations that might support a canonical approach to the interpretive task. The first part considers the historical and theological questions that surround the formation of the canon (Chapters 1-2), and the second part considers the hermeneutical issues that surround the function of the canon in the reading community (Chapters 3-5). This theoretical basis can aid biblical readers in their own pursuit of a thoroughgoing canon-consciousness in a contemporary setting.[1] In other words, questions of 'canon' should be on the minds of historians and theologians, but also biblical interpreters.

In tracing out the formation of the biblical canon, the historian is inextricably faced with the question of definition: What is *a* canon? What is the

---

1. Developing this type of mindset will be especially important as contemporary communication paradigms continue to shift away from the book form. Many have noted the connection between the open-ended nature of theories of textuality and intertextuality of postmodernity and the proliferation of internet technology. For instance, Marcel O'Gorman observes that 'somewhere in the early 1990s, the major tenets of deconstruction (death of the Author, intertextuality, etc.) were displaced into technology, that is hypertext...philosophy was transformed, liquidated even, into the materiality of new media' (*Digital Media, Critical Theory, and the Humanities* [Toronto: University of Toronto, 2005], p. xv). For a provisional reflection on the role the concept of canon might play in the world of new media, see Spellman, 'Canon After Google', pp. 39-42.

biblical canon? In Chapter 1, I seek to bring clarity to this definitional issue. Anyone examining the actual etymology and usage of the term 'canon' in the early church will quickly note that simplistic definitions will not suffice. The usage of this term includes historical, theological, and hermeneutical connotations. The 'canon' entails both the idea of authority and normativity (Canon 1, 'canon as rule') as well as the tangible notion of boundaries and shaping (Canon 2, 'canon as list'). Because of this multiplex function of the term and concept, the 'narrow view' of the meaning of 'canon' is not the most appropriate understanding.

One of the reasons to adopt a broader view of the notion of canon is because it is more appropriate to the historical usage and also because it can then describe and account for the 'canon-consciousness' that is at work in the composition and canonization phase of the formation of the biblical canon prior to final consolidation in various communities. In Chapter 2, I outline the type of evidence that demonstrates the presence of a form of canon-consciousness at work among both the biblical authors who were writing the texts of Scripture and also the believing community that was copying, preserving, and treasuring those texts as they passed them on to later generations.

A hoped-for byproduct of this investigation (its intended perlocutionary effect!) is to provide theoretically viable means by which an interpreter can justify taking the concept of canon into account when interpreting a given section of scriptural writing. The argument as a whole seeks to connect some of the most important fields that address the canon question. After establishing the importance of canon-consciousness in the historical process of canon formation, the notion can also have significance for the interpretive task. Indeed, if the internal biblical evidence implies a canon-consciousness among the biblical authors, and the external historical evidence suggests the presence of a compatible mentality among the believing community, *then the concept of canon can legitimately function as a control on the interpretive task.* If this trajectory reflects reality, then the appeal to canon (in all its multifaceted connotations) is not arbitrary but rather acknowledges the 'inner logic of Scripture's textual authority'.[2] In this way, a robust canon-consciousness is not a notion foreign to biblical texts but a feature that lays 'deep within the formation of the literature'.[3] The hermeneutical payoff of this governing function is that the canon helps guide contemporary readers through the biblical material by limiting and generating textual connections, and also helps identify the intended audience of the Christian Bible as a whole.

---

2. This helpful phrase comes from Brevard S. Childs, 'Retrospective Reading of the Old Testament Prophets', *ZAW* 108 (1996), pp. 362-77 (376).

3. Childs, *Biblical Theology*, p. 70.

Consequently, in Chapters 3-5, I seek to provide a theoretical framework for how the concept of canon functions for the canon-conscious interpreter. In Chapter 3, I describe the guiding function of the canonical collection in terms of *mere* and *meant* contextuality. Noting the *mere* contextuality at work in a literary collection involves describing the effect that the ordering, arrangement, and overall shape of the biblical material has on readers. This analysis notes these effects without regard to the question of intention. *Meant* contextuality, then, asks whether an author or an editor intended any of these effects. If the biblical authors and those who were collecting the biblical writings were aware of a larger body of literature, then it is plausible that they could have strategically composed and arranged certain writings in particular ways in order to create a particular intended effect. With these two categories in place, one can readily describe the shape that is generated by the groupings found within the canonical boundaries (i.e. Law, Prophets, Writings, Gospels, Acts, Epistles, Revelation). These groupings generate an overarching narrative within which the individual scriptural writings serve a function.

After noting this shape that is generated by the broad canonical context, in Chapter 4 I investigate how the concept of canon informs the study of biblical intertextuality. The formation of a literary collection generates textual connections (contextuality), and also helps limit the vast array of texts that hypothetically could inform any given biblical writing (intertextuality). A circumscribed understanding of the literary study of intertextuality can help describe what the biblical authors are doing as they utilize other biblical texts. These intertextual references to other texts found within the boundaries of the canon help bind together the associations described in a study of contextuality. In fact, the shape of the biblical material (contextuality) is often generated by the way a biblical author uses and relates his writing to other biblical material (intertextuality).

As an intertextual collection of Scriptures, the biblical canon showcases the relationships that are present between biblical passages, sections, and books. By highlighting the organic relationships that exist within a diverse set of texts, the canonical context provides a space where intertextual connections are realized. There is here an important connection between intertextual and contextual studies because oftentimes the shaping of a collection of writings is actualized and solidified by means of intertextual connections. Readers who hold to a production-oriented view of intertextuality and are interested in the communicative intention of the author as evidenced in a text will see the canon as a constructive place for the generation of meaning. Further, when both the text and the precursor text are present in the same collection, the intertextual relationship becomes less tenuous. In this sense, an intertextually informed concept of canon enables and encourages Scripture to interpret Scripture.

Investigating the contextual and intertextual function of the book of Revelation within the canonical context illustrates the nature and value of these two types of investigation. In terms of mere contextuality, the reader notices that the book of Revelation serves as a fitting thematic and structural conclusion both to the New Testament and the Christian canon as a whole. A reader also notices that there seem to be intentional intertextual allusions throughout the book of Revelation to passages from the Old Testament, especially the prophecies of Isaiah and the creation narratives of Genesis 1–3. These intertextual connections provide evidence of the possibility that the canonical function of Revelation is the result of meant contextuality in addition to mere contextuality. This line of inquiry also illustrates the types of investigation that are possible when the concept of canon is active in the mind of the interpreter. Maintaining a textual orientation and allowing the concept of canon to inform the interpretive task enables a reader to discern more fully the various compositional strategies employed by the biblical authors.

A further implication of allowing the concept of canon to function as a control on the interpretive task involves the identification of the intended audience of the Bible as a whole. In Chapter 5, I note that the biblical authors envision a certain type of reader and a certain type of response that their writings will produce. This 'implied reader' is accessed by reading the text and noting the expectations that the biblical author anticipates. In order for a real reader to become the implied reader (and the texts overwhelmingly encourage a reader to do so), then he or she must submit to the restraints required of the implied reader.

As discussed and developed in Chapter 2 (on canon-consciousness), Chapter 3 (on canonical contextuality), and Chapter 4 (on canonical intertextuality), the canonical context bears a number of hermeneutically significant features. Each of these areas describe the natural hermeneutical effects that a collection of writings has on readers ('mere') and also the elements of these features that have been intentionally produced by the authors and editors of the biblical material itself ('meant'). The implied reader of the biblical collection skillfully takes note of this multifaceted matrix of canonical features. In other words, the implied reader of the Christian Scriptures is one that possesses a robust canon-consciousness. What is more, the profile of this implied reader of the biblical canon is a cumulative feature of the biblical authors' compositional strategies. Accordingly, strategic biblical texts envision an 'ideal reader', namely, an actual reader who seeks to identify *with* this implied reader. The book of Revelation again highlights the way the canonical context serves as a hermeneutical guide. The ideal reader of the book of Revelation (and the Bible as a whole) is one who keeps and treasures it as a 'revelation' from the risen Lord.

In sum, the concept of canon effectively guides biblical readers as they investigate the context of a biblical writing (*contextuality*), certain elements of the compositional strategy of its author (*intertextuality*), and the proper response demanded by that author's textually mediated message (*ideal reader*). The above investigations of the theological, historical, and hermeneutical facets of the Christian canon have sought to demonstrate that interpreters of the Bible have legitimate grounds for utilizing the concept of canon as a control on the interpretive task. Further, this type of move toward a canon-conscious reading of the Bible would perhaps be a move toward reading the Bible as it was designed to be read.

Let the reader understand!

Appendix 1

ORDERING OF THE GREEK UNCIAL CODEX MANUSCRIPTS OF THE FOURTH AND FIFTH CENTURY

Old Testament

Sinaiticus (א 01)	Alexandrinus (A 02)	Vaticanus (B 03)	Ephraemi Rescriptus (C 04)
Gen.	Gen.	Gen.	
—	Exod.	Exod.	
—	Lev.	Lev.	
Num.	Num.	Num.	
—	Deut.	Deut.	
—	Josh.	Josh.	
—	Judg.	Judg.	
—	Ruth	Ruth	
—	1–4 Kgs	1–4 Kgs.	
1 Chron.	1–2 Chron.	1–2 Chron.	
[2 Chron.]		1–2 Esd.	(…)
[1 Esd.]	Hos.		
2 Esd.	Amos	Pss.	Job
Esther	Mic.	Prov.	Prov.
Tob.	Joel	Eccl.	Eccl.
Jdt	Obad.	Song	Song
1 Macc.	Jon.	Job	*Wis.*
4 Macc.	Nah.	*Wis.*	*Ecclesiasticus*
	Hab.	*Sir.*	
Isa.	Zeph.	Esther	(…)
Jer.	Hag.	*Jdt*	
Lam.	Zech.	*Tob.*	
Joel	Mal.		
Obad.	Isa.	Hos.	
Jon.	Jer.	Amos	
Nah.	*Bar.*	Mic.	
Hab.	Lam.	Joel	
Zeph.	*Ep. Jer.*	Obad.	
		Jon.	
		Nah.	
		Hab.	
		Zeph.	

Hag.	Ezek.	Hag.	
Zech.	Dan.	Zech.	
Mal.		Mal.	
	Esther	Isa.	
Pss.	*Tob.*	Jer.	
Prov.	*Jdt*	*Bar.*	
Eccl.	1–2 Esd.	Lam.	
Song	*1–4 Macc.*	*Ep. Jer.*	
Wis.	Pss.	Ezek.	
Sir.	*Ps. 151*	Dan.	
Job	Job		
	Prov.		
	Eccl.		
	Song		
	Wis.		
	Sir. – Ps. Sol.		

New Testament

Sinaiticus (ℵ01)	Alexandrinus (A 02)	Vaticanus (B 03)	Ephraemi Rescriptus (C 04)
Mt.	Mt.	Mt.	Mt.
Mk	Mk	Mk	Mk
Lk.	Lk.	Lk.	Lk.
Jn	Jn	Jn	Jn
Rom.	Acts	Acts	Acts
1 Cor.	Jas.	Jas.	
2 Cor.	1 Pet.	1 Pet.	Rom.
Gal.	2 Pet.	2 Pet.	1 Cor.
Eph.	1 Jn	1 Jn	2 Cor.
Phil.	2 Jn	2 Jn	Gal.
Col.	3 Jn	3 Jn	Eph.
1 Thess.	Jude	Jude	Phil.
2 Thess.			Col.
Heb.	Rom.	Rom.	1 Thess.
1 Tim.	1 Cor.	1 Cor.	[2 Thess.]
2 Tim.	2 Cor.	2 Cor.	1 Tim.
Tit.	Gal.	Gal.	2 Tim.
Phlm.	Eph.	Eph.	Tit.
	Phil.	Phil.	Phlm.
Acts	Col.	Col.	Heb.
Jas	1 Thess.	1 Thess.	
1 Pet.	2 Thess.	2 Thess.	Jas.
2 Pet.	Heb.	Heb.	1 Pet.
1 Jn	1 Tim.		2 Pet.
2 Jn	2 Tim.	(…)	1 Jn

3 Jn	Tit.		[2 Jn]
Jude	Phlm.		3 Jn
			Jude
Rev.	Rev.		
Barn.	*1 Clem.*		Rev.
Herm.	*2 Clem.*		

Notes: (…) indicates where the manuscript breaks off; double hyphens – represent lacunae most likely due to corruption of the manuscript; brackets [ ] represent an omission; *italics* represent apocryphal (non-canonical) literature.

Sources: Metzger, 'Appendix II: Variations in the Sequence of the Books of the New Testament', in *Canon*, pp. 295-300; McDonald, 'Appendix B: Lists and Catalogues of Old Testament Collections' and 'Appendix C: Lists and Catalogues of New Testament Collections', in *Biblical Canon*, pp. 439-51; Henry B. Swete, *An Introduction to the Old Testament in Greek* (Cambridge: Cambridge University Press, 1902), pp. 122-31, 201-202; Costantin von Tischendorf, *Codex Ephraemi Syri Rescriptus sive Fragmenta Novi Testamenti*. Leipzig, 1843.

Appendix 2

ORDERING OF THE HEBREW BIBLE IN THE TALMUDIC AND MASORETIC TRADITIONS

Baba Bathra 14b (Talmud)	Josephus	Jerome	Leningrad Codex
Gen.	Gen.	Gen.	Gen.
Exod.	Exod.	Exod.	Exod.
Lev.	Lev.	Lev.	Lev.
Num.	Num.	Num.	Num.
Deut.	Deut.	Deut.	Deut.
Josh.	Job	Josh.	Josh.
Judg.	Josh.	Judg.–Ruth	Judg.
Sam.	Judg.	1–2 Kgs	Sam.
Kgs	Ruth	3–4 Kgs	Kgs
Jer.	Sam.	Isa.	Isa.
Ezek.	Kgs	Jer.	Jer.
Isa.	Isa.	Ezek.	Ezek.
The Twelve	Jer.–Lam.	The Twelve	The Twelve
	Ezek.		
Ruth	The Twelve	Job	Chron.
Pss.		Pss.	Pss.
Job		Prov.	Job
Prov.	Pss.	Eccl.	Prov.
Eccl.	Prov.	Song	Ruth
Song	Eccl.	Dan.	Song
Lam.	Song	1–2 Chron.	Eccl.
Dan.		1–2 Esd.	Lam.
Est.		Est.	Est.
Ezra (Neh.)			Dan.
Chron.			Ezra–Neh.

Sources: *The Talmud of Babylonia: An American Translation, Volume 22A: Tractate Baba Batra Chapters 1-2* (trans. Jacob Neusner; Atlanta, GA: Scholars Press, 1992), pp. 68-72 (14b-15a); Jerome, *Preface to the Books of Samuel and Kings*, in *NPNF*, 2.6.489-91; *Biblia Hebraica Stuttgartensia* (ed. K. Ellinger and W. Rudolph; Stuttgart: Deutsche Bibelstiftung, 1977); and McDonald, 'Appendix B: Lists and Catalogues of Old Testament Collections' in *Biblical Canon*, pp. 439-44.

Appendix 3

SURVEY OF INTERTEXTUAL CONNECTIONS BETWEEN
GENESIS 1–3 AND REVELATION 21–22

As mentioned in Chapter 4, the creation narratives of Genesis 1–3 are of
critical importance for a study of biblical intertextuality. Important themes
mentioned here originate and are developed throughout the Old and New
Testaments.[1] Genesis begins with the creation of the heavens and the earth
(Gen. 1.1), and Revelation ends with the creation of a *new* heavens and a
new earth. In the final chapters of his book, John develops the way the work
of God in the risen Christ brings about the renewal of all creation, the restoration of God's original purpose for humanity, and the enduring promise of
a coming redeemer. Each of these themes is supported by verbal, thematic,
or structural links to significant texts from the Hebrew Bible. In particular,
through a network of intertextual allusions to the Pentateuchal narratives of
Genesis 1–3, John creates in Revelation 21–22 a macrostructural inclusio
for the biblical canon and storyline.

Renewed Creation
After the judgment at the great white throne (20.11-15), John recounts, 'Then
I saw a new heaven and a new earth' (21.1, Καὶ εἶδον οὐρανὸν καινὸν καὶ
γῆν καινήν).[2] Next, John sees 'the holy city, new Jerusalem coming down

---

1. See William J. Dumbrell, *The End of the Beginning: Revelation 21-22 and
the Old Testament* (New South Wales: Lancer, 1985). Dumbrell identifies five major
themes/allusions that occur in Revelation 21–22, namely, the New Jerusalem, the New
Temple, the New Covenant, the New Israel, and the New Creation. Dumbrell notes that
these chapters are 'such an appropriate way not only to finish the Book of Revelation
but to conclude the story of the entire Bible' and also investigates how these themes
'changed or developed down through the Bible's story' (p. i). Cf. Paul Sevier Minear,
Christians and the New Creation: Genesis Motifs in the New Testament (Louisville,
KY: Westminster/John Knox Press, 1994).
2. The newness of this new creation is indicated by the fact that 'the first heaven
and the first earth passed away', and as a result 'there is no longer any sea'. Pilchan
Lee, *The New Jerusalem in the Book of Revelation: A Study of Revelation 21–22 in the
Light of its Background in Jewish Tradition* (Tübingen: Mohr Siebeck, 2001), p. 268,
notes that the use of the word καινὸν here indicates 'the creation of a universe which,

out of heaven from God, made ready as a bride adorned for her husband' (21.2). After this creative event, 'a loud voice from the throne' provides an interpretation of what John has just seen which emphasizes the incredible effect the divine presence has on the worship of God's people (21.3-4).

In the following paragraph, 'He who sits on the throne' makes a summary pronouncement over this new creation: 'Behold, I am making all things new' (21.5).[3] John is then again commanded, 'Write, for these words are faithful and true' (21.5). God then tells John with a note of finality, 'It is done. I am the Alpha and the Omega, the beginning and the end' (γέγοναν. ἐγώ εἰμι τὸ ἄλφα καὶ τὸ ὦ, ἡ ἀρχὴ καὶ τὸ τέλος). Thus ends the sequence of creative actions in these last chapters of Revelation. The remainder of Rev. 21.6–22.5 contains description and explanation of the new creation that takes place in 21.1-5. After proclaiming the end of the new creation, God essentially offers blessings for those who believe and overcome and curses for those who are cowardly and do not believe (21.7).[4] After beholding God fashion a new creation, John then gets a guided tour of the new Jerusalem (21.10-27), the river of the water of life (22.1), and the tree of life (22.2). The pastoral imagery and heavenly vision of Rev. 21.1–22.5 is set within the framework of God's creative activity.

This theme of creation is foundational for much of the biblical and prophetic understanding of the world. God as creator of the heavens and the earth is one of the most important characterizations of Israel's God. The theme is prominent in the Law, Prophets, Writings, and the rest of the New Testament.[5] Accordingly, the idea of *new* creation is just as important and builds on the theology of God as creator. Indeed, the concept of new

though it has been gloriously and radically renewed in quality or nature, stands in continuity with the present one'. Similarly, Wall, *Revelation*, p. 247, calls καινὸν an 'eschatological catchword' that conveys the consummation and renewal of the 'old order'.

3.   The statement 'I am making all things new' (21.5) might be the most hermeneutically significant element of this section of the book of Revelation.

4.   In the description of this scene, there is an interesting parallel between the two kinds of water presented. Those whose names are in the book of life are invited to drink from the 'water of life', but those who reject Christ are banished to the 'lake of fire'.

5.   Cf., e.g., Pss. 8; 19; 104; Jon. 1. For a more extensive survey of similar texts, see Richard Bauckham, *God Crucified: Monotheism and Christology in the New Testament* (Grand Rapids, MI; Eerdmans, 1999). Bauckham highlights this characterization of God as sovereign creator in the Old Testament and in the literature of second temple Judaism. He then uses this observation to argue for the presence of an 'early high Christology' throughout the New Testament. For Bauckham, when New Testament authors speak of Jesus as creator, they are asserting that he partakes in the divine identity of Yahweh himself.

creation is one of the driving forces behind the progress of God's revelation.[6] This foundational theme is heavily utilized in Isaiah and Ezekiel, but it is important to note in particular that the bedrock of creation imagery in the Christian Bible is the creation account found in the first chapters of the Pentateuch.[7] The words that begin the Hebrew Bible also begin the characterization of God as creator of the universe and are stunning in scope: 'In the beginning God created the heavens and the earth.'[8] The phrase 'the heavens and the earth' here is a figure of speech that has all of creation in view.[9] Thus, Gen. 1.1 asserts in striking fashion that God is not only the creator of Israel, but of the entire world. Because he is creator, all things under heaven and earth fall under his sovereignty.[10]

---

6. Dumbrell, *End of the Beginning*, states that new creation 'is the goal to which the Book of Revelation and the Bible itself has moved' (p. ii) and is 'the axis around which all biblical theology turns' (p. 196).

7. Texts and images from Isaiah 65–66 and Ezekiel 40–48 are prominent in Revelation 21. Regarding new creation, Isa. 65.17 is particularly important: 'For behold, I create new heavens and a new earth; And the former things will not be remembered or come to mind.' One of the most substantive recent studies on the role of Isaiah in Revelation is Jan Fekkes, *Isaiah and Prophetic Traditions in the Book of Revelation: Visionary Antecedents and Their Development* (Sheffield: Sheffield Academic Press, 1994). Fekkes is methodologically keen on the allusive nature of John's use of the Old Testament. For a similar analysis of the use of Ezekiel in Revelation, see J.P. Ruiz, *Ezekiel in the Apocalypse: The Transformation of Prophetic Language in Revelation 16:17–19:10* (Frankfurt am Main: Peter Lang, 1989); and Beate Kowalski, *Die Rezeption des Propheten Ezechiel in der Ofeenbarung des Johannes* (Stuttgart: Kotholische Bibelwerk, 2004). Paulien characterizes Kowalksi's volume as 'the state of the art on assessment of allusions in biblical studies' ('Elusive Allusions in the Apocalypse', p. 63).

8. In the LXX translation of this verse, there are verbal links to Rev. 21.1-5. The text in Gen. 1.1 reads, ἐν ἀρχῇ ἐποίησεν ὁ θεὸς τὸν οὐρανὸν καὶ τὴν γῆν. Rev. 21.1 reads, Καὶ εἶδον οὐρανὸν καινὸν καὶ γῆν καινήν.

9. The phrase is most likely a merism, which is a 'literary device that uses an abbreviated list to suggest the whole' and often 'cites the poles of a list to suggest everything in between'. In this sense, the device is a form of synecdoche. See Tremper Longman, 'Merism', in *Dictionary of the Old Testament: Wisdom, Poetry, and Writings* (ed. Tremper Longman and Peter Enns; Downers Grove, IL: IVP, 2008), pp. 464-66. John H. Sailhamer, *The Pentateuch as Narrative: A Biblical-Theological Commentary* (Grand Rapids, MI: Zondervan, 1992), p. 84, notes that the phrase is 'a figure of speech for the expression of totality'.

10. Cf. Rendtorff, *Canonical Hebrew Bible*, p. 90: 'Whatever kinds of questions and doubts and claims to the contrary may emerge in the course of the history of Israel, the fact that God is *one* and that besides him there are no other gods and that this one created the whole world and humanity, is pronounced incontrovertibly in the first sentence of the Hebrew Bible as the basis and precondition of everything that will follow: "In the beginning God created the heavens and the earth". For God there is no beginning, and besides God there is no creator.'

Another key element of the creation account is the manner in which the sequence of creation progresses in Gen 1.3-31. God calls forth the world with the power of his words. God *speaks* and light begins to emanate (1.3), expanses move into place (1.6), dry land materializes (1.9), vegetation begins to grow (1.11), the sun and the moon are given purpose (1.14), the waters begin to teem with sea creatures, birds begin to soar above the earth (1.20), land animals begin to populate the fields (1.24), and a special creature is made in God's own image and given dominion over all of these things (1.26-30). God then gives his commentary on this litany of creative speech acts. He surveys 'all that he had made' and makes a comprehensive pronouncement: 'it was very good' (1.31).[11] The creation account that begins the book of Genesis is the foundation of the biblical portrait of God's character and purpose. The God of Israel is creator of the heavens and the earth, and he is good. These traits are what identify the God of Israel among the false gods of the nations throughout biblical history.[12] Just as in the Genesis account, 'he who sits on the throne' in Rev. 21.5 speaks, and *all things* are made new: 'Behold, I am making all things new' (ἰδοὺ καινὰ ποιῶ πάντα).[13]

Renewed Worship
Continuing the parallel with the creation narratives, the scene pictured in Rev. 21.6–22.5 displays a scene that essentially 'fills out' the original purpose of creation. Before the fall into sin that is recounted in Genesis 3, a snapshot of the purpose of mankind on the earth is provided in Genesis 2. Adam and Eve are placed in the garden in order to serve God and enjoy his presence. They were brought into being in order to worship and obey their creator. The scene in Genesis 2 indicates their created purpose. The verbs in Gen. 2.15 translated as 'work' and 'keep' are elsewhere used to describe the worship of Israel, specifically the priestly 'service' and 'guarding' of

---

11. The author notes that only here did God say that what he saw was 'very' good (וְהִנֵּה־טוֹב מְאֹד), for the purpose of creation was to make mankind a place to dwell and worship God. The creation of mankind is the pinnacle of his creative purpose and ends the sequence of creative acts in Genesis 1. Cf. the LXX of Gen. 1.31: καὶ ἰδοὺ καλὰ λίαν.

12. For instance, in Isaiah 44, the Lord mocks the idols made by the hands of men. These wooden idols cannot speak the future or claim any sovereignty, because they themselves are created things. In contrast, the Lord, 'the King of Israel', declares, 'I, the Lord, am the maker of all things' (Isa. 44.24). This foundational characteristic trumps all other claims to deity and brooks no rivals.

13. Cf. Wall, 'Apocalypse in Canonical Context', p. 280: 'Read as the Bible's *inclusio*, Revelation gives theological coherence to the Christian Scriptures: everything from Genesis to Revelation should be interpreted by a "canon-logic" which asserts that a faithful Creator God has kept the promise to restore all things for the Lord and for good.'

the tabernacle.[14] By using these terms, the author shows that one of mankind's created purposes is 'to worship and obey' the Lord, by keeping his commands and guarding the covenant relationship he has entered into with them. This idea is confirmed in the following verse where Adam is given a commandment from God that he is to obey (Gen. 2.16).[15] They were to be God's people, and the Lord was to be their God.

This purpose is the foundational element of the various covenant relationships that occur in subsequent biblical narratives. The Garden of Eden was intended to be the place where God met with his people. The later Old Testament institutions of the tabernacle and the temple serve a similar worship-oriented function. The garden, the tabernacle, and the temple are all means by which God is able to be present among his people. A series of intertextual references and allusions are present between the biblical narratives recounting the creation of the garden (Genesis 1–2), the construction of the tabernacle (Exodus 35–40), and the construction of the temple (2 Chron. 3–5). Thus, there are textual reasons to associate these three places.[16]

In his account of the eschatological recreation in Revelation 21–22, John makes use of all three of these locations. After beholding the new heaven and new earth (Rev. 21.1), John sees 'the holy city, new Jerusalem, coming down out of heaven from God' (21.2). The covenantal overtones are indicated by the use of marriage imagery. The holy city has been 'made ready as a bride adorned for her husband' (21.2).[17] This city represents God's divine presence. The description of the New Jerusalem in Rev. 21.10-21 draws on prophetic descriptions of the future temple.[18] The details of this description

14. E.g. Num. 3.7-8; 8.25-26; 18.5-6; 1 Chron. 23.32; and Ezek. 44.14.

15. For an exposition and defense of this interpretation, see Sailhamer, *Pentateuch as Narrative*, pp. 100-102. Cf. the compatible analysis of Gordon J. Wenham, *Genesis 1–15* (Nashville, TN: Thomas Nelson Publishers, 1987), pp. 66-67.

16. See Gordon J. Wenham, 'Sanctuary Symbolism in the Garden of Eden Story', in *I Studied Inscriptions from Before the Flood: Ancient Near Eastern, Literary and Linguistic Approaches to Genesis 1–11* (ed. Richard S. Hess and David T. Tsumura; Winona Lake, IN: Eisenbrauns, 1994), pp. 399-404; and T. Desmond Alexander, *From Eden to the New Jerusalem: An Introduction to Biblical Theology* (Grand Rapids, MI: Kregel, 2008), pp. 13-73. Cf. Sailhamer, *Pentateuch as Narrative*, p. 298; and Beale, *The Book of the Revelation*, pp. 1110-12.

17. Note the connection between a marriage at the beginning of the Bible (Genesis 2) and a marriage at the end of the Bible (Revelation 19, 21). Isa. 61.10 and 62.5 pick up the marriage imagery as well. Fekkes, *Isaiah*, p. 247, argues that 'nuptial imagery is at the heart of John's evocation of the New Jerusalem'. Cf. Jan Fekkes, '"His Bride Has Prepared Herself" Revelation 19–21 and Isaian Nuptial Imagery', *JBL* 109 (1990), pp. 269-87.

18. The details John records regarding the holy city are imbued with imagery from Ezekiel 40–48. For a survey of the intertextual allusions, see Beale and McDonough, 'Revelation', pp. 1151-56. Lee, *New Jerusalem in the Book of Revelation*, p. 229, notes

demonstrate that the city itself has been constructed with the most precious of materials. Everything in the city demonstrates its exceeding value and worth. However, the rarity and worth of the city is ultimately derived from the one who dwells there: God himself. The brilliance of the city is only seen rightly in relation to its most profound characteristic; namely, it has 'the glory of God' (21.11, τὴν δόξαν τοῦ θεοῦ).[19]

That the portrayal and purpose of the holy city points to God's divine presence with his people is confirmed by references to the tabernacle before and the temple after the description of the New Jerusalem's specifications. In Rev. 21.3, John hears a voice say, 'Behold, the tabernacle of God is among men' (ἰδοὺ ἡ σκηνὴ τοῦ θεοῦ μετὰ τῶν ἀνθρώπων). The voice then provides another expression of covenantal relationship by saying that 'they shall be his people, and God himself will be among them' (21.3).[20] After the description of the city (21.10-21), John notes the absence of a temple in its midst: 'I saw no temple in it' (21.2, Καὶ ναὸν οὐκ εἶδον ἐν αὐτῇ). John then explains that the divine presence removes the need for a temple. He reasons, 'for the Lord God the Almighty and the Lamb are its temple' (21.22).

The city also no longer needs the light of the sun or the moon, 'for the glory of God has illumined it, and its lamp is the Lamb' (21.23). This detail regarding the obsolete function of the sun and the moon is one of the indications that the new creation far surpasses the old creation. Whereas before, the sun and moon lit up the world of humanity, the Lamb who was slain for them now performs that function. This is a profound fulfillment of what John says in the prologue of his Gospel: 'There was the true light which coming into the world, enlightens every man' (Jn 1.6). This light illumines not only Israel, but also the nations 'who will walk by its light' and the kings of the earth who will 'bring their glory into it' (21.24). The illumination

---

also that 'Ezekiel 40–48 and Isaiah 40–66 are the most important texts for describing the New/Heavenly Temple/Jerusalem in the early Jewish literature.' Lee concludes that these 'Jewish writers seem to treat OT prophecies quite freely, not very literalistically, varying the details in all sorts of ways'.

19. Bauckham, *Climax of Prophecy*, pp. 4-6, notes the parallel between the section in 17.1–19.10, which describes the fall of Babylon, and 21.9–22.9, which pictures the establishment of the New Jerusalem. These sections represent 'the climax towards which the whole book has aimed: the destruction of Babylon and her replacement by the New Jerusalem. The intimate connexion between the two parallel sections is further indicated by the announcement of the Lamb's marriage to his bride at the end of the rejoicing over the fall of Babylon.' Lee, *New Jerusalem in the Book of Revelation*, pp. 264-66, surveys the details of these 'antithetical parallels'.

20. Cf. the wording of Jn 1.14: 'And the word became flesh, and dwelt among us, and we saw his glory, glory as of the only begotten from the father, full of grace and truth.'

resulting from the divine presence recounted here reorders the way the universe works.[21]

Renewed Eden

One of the most striking elements of this new creation is the removal of sin and the reversal of the curse.[22] John is shown a 'river of the water of life, clear as crystal coming from the throne of God and of the Lamb in the middle of its street' (22.1-2). Alongside this crystal clear river is 'the tree of life' (ξύλον ζωῆς) that bears twelve kinds of fruit and which yields its fruit every month.[23] This idyllic scene strongly echoes the Garden of Eden narratives in Genesis 2. However, this garden is altogether different, for here there is no serpent lurking in the shadows.[24] The leaves of this tree are no longer a reminder of transgression but are 'for the healing of the nations' (22.2). Though Genesis 3 recounts the consequences of disobedience among the trees in the garden, on this day 'there will no longer be any curse' (καὶ πᾶν κατάθεμα οὐκ ἔσται ἔτι).[25] The eschatological garden will be the throne

---

21. For instance, 'In the daytime (for there will be no night there) its gates will never be closed' (Rev. 21.25). The details given here parallel the scene in Isa. 60.19-22. Lee, *New Jerusalem in the Book of Revelation*, p. 293, notes that these passages 'emphasize the brightness of the New Jerusalem illuminated by the glory of God' and not necessarily the 'redundancy of the sun and the moon'.

22. The description of the new creation paradise in 22.1-5 concludes the major section of 21.1–22.5. Matthewson, *A New Heaven and a New Earth*, p. 215, observes that 'structurally, the inclusion of paradise motifs establishes clear links with 21.1-5a, where the new creation exhibits paradise-like features, thus forming a sort of inclusion with that section'. In this sense, 22.3-5 serves as the 'climax to John's vision'.

23. Though Ezekiel mentions 'many trees' in his vision (Ezek. 47.7), the 'tree of life' in Rev. 22.2 ultimately originates in the Genesis creation narrative (Gen. 2.9). For further argumentation along these lines, see Mathewson, *A New Heaven and a New Earth*, pp. 189-90.

24. In Rev. 12.9, John identifies 'the great dragon' who was thrown down out of heaven as 'the serpent of old who is called the devil and Satan, who deceives the whole world'. This same 'serpent of old' is bound for a thousand years in 20.2 and then in 20.10 is thrown into the lake of fire to be 'tormented day and night forever and ever'. Thus, readers of Revelation will know at this point in the book why there is no serpent found in this eschatological garden.

25. The concept of 'curse' (κατάθεμα) here relates to the 'ban of destruction' that the Lord directed Israel to put on the enemies of Israel and the enemies of God (e.g. Zech. 14.11). The scene in Revelation 22 is significant because the nations are worshiping the Lord along with Israel, and there is no curse on them because they are no longer his enemies. Barbara Friberg, Timothy Friberg and Neva F. Miller, *Analytical Lexicon of the Greek New Testament* (Victoria, BC: Trafford Publishing, 2005), pp. 217-18, understand κατάθεμα to refer to 'something that has been delivered over to divine wrath'. Cf. Bauckham, *Climax of Prophecy*, pp. 316-17; and BDAG, s.v. 'κατάθεμα'. Because of the Edenic setting of 22.1-5, the curse concept should also be ultimately

room of God and the lamb, and 'his bond-servants will serve him' (22.3, οἱ δοῦλοι αὐτοῦ λατρεύσουσιν αὐτῷ).[26] This reversal of the effects of the curse is anticipated in 21.4-5.[27] In a recognition of the pain and suffering that has taken place between the Garden of Eden and the New Jerusalem, the voice tells John that God 'will wipe away every tear from their eyes' and 'there will no longer be any death; there will no longer be any mourning, or crying or pain' (21.4). This scene provides a picture of the fulfillment of the new covenant. Sins have been forgiven, pain is no more, and the curse has been reversed. In short, paradise has been restored.

Renewed Promise
A final connection between Revelation 21–22 and Genesis 1–3 involves the identification of the one who accomplishes this redemption. Biblical writers make clear that the work of the lamb is the sole reason God's people are able to experience his presence in this new creation. In Revelation, the lamb is the one who has 'released us from our sins by his blood' (Rev. 1.5). As mentioned above, John's vision also reveals that this *lamb* of God is also the *lion* of Judah. John recounts in Rev. 5.5 that Jesus is 'the lion that is from the tribe of Judah, the root of David'. These references to 'the lion of Judah' (ὁ λέων ὁ ἐκ τῆς φυλῆς Ἰούδα) and 'the root of David' (ἡ ῥίζα Δαυίδ) are clear thematic allusions to messianic texts of the Old Testament.[28] Then, in Rev. 22.16, Jesus himself declares, 'I am the root and the descendent of David, the bright morning star.'[29] The characterization John notes in these places strongly resonates with the expectation found in the Hebrew Bible

related to the curse that resulted from Adam's disobedience in the garden. A comparison and contrast of the scenes in Genesis 2–3 and Rev. 22.1-5 yields a number of fruitful intertextual connections. See Wall, *Revelation,* pp. 256-57; and Clarke, 'Canonical Criticism', p. 210.

26. This service is the consummation of God's created purpose for humanity (see previous discussion regarding the command and expectation for humanity to worship and obey their creator).

27. These details of the reversal of the curse strongly resonate with Isa. 65.19-25. Revelation 21–22 thus represents a profound fulfillment of these prophetic promises.

28. The 'lion of Judah' phrase is drawn from Gen. 49.9, and the 'root of David' comes from Isa. 11.1, 10 (cf. Paul's use of this text in Rom. 15.12). These images are further utilized in Jer. 11.10; 23.5; 33.15; and Zech. 3.8.

29. On the lexical significance of the images of 'root' and 'descendent', see the discussion in the last section of Chapter 4. Rev. 22.16, in particular, makes an important intertextual reference to one of these Messianic passages. Jesus identifies himself as the bright morning star (ὁ ἀστὴρ ὁ λαμπρὸς ὁ πρωϊνός). In Num. 24.17, Balaam says that 'A star shall come forth from Jacob / A scepter shall rise from Israel / And shall crush through the forehead of Moab / and tear down all the sons of Sheth.' In the latter part of the book of Revelation, the Davidic messiah is seen conquering the enemies of God, thus fulfilling the picture hinted at in the Numbers passage. Cf. 2 Pet. 1.19.

concerning the coming Davidic king. The expectation of a coming king from the tribe of Judah, who will crush God's enemies, rule in power, and receive the obedience of the people stems from promises of the Pentateuch (e.g. Gen. 49.8-10; Num. 24.7-9).[30]

This kingly promise is later joined with God's covenant promise to David in 2 Samuel 7. The coming king of the Pentateuch will be a son of David. In the Old Testament, the eschatological king of Israel comes from David's seed. John's mention of Jesus as the Davidic king is therefore highly significant. Subsequent biblical writers who often cast hope for the future in terms of a Davidic kingdom pick up on this composite image. For instance, the Chronicler reiterates the promise to David made in 2 Samuel 7 in his narrative that focuses messianic expectation on a coming son of David. Though all of Judah's subsequent kings fail to fulfill this promise, the Chronicler holds out hope that one is coming who will. In the Psalter too, one of the main figures is the anointed king of Psalm 2. In the rest of the book of Psalms, David represents the ideal king who prefigures the coming Messiah.[31] Accordingly, in the Hebrew Bible, when the coming king is mentioned, the eschatological son of David is usually in view or at least lurking nearby.[32] By strategically highlighting Jesus as the son of David, John makes use of an important biblical image.[33] Just as the focus on Jesus as the Christ ties the book of Revelation to the rest of the New Testament, so too does

30. The promise of a redeemer begins even as the curse is being pronounced in Gen. 3.15. The future oriented perspective of the kingly blessing in Genesis 49 is drawn from the 'end of days' perspective of Jacob's blessing (Gen. 49.1).

31. Demonstrating that the book of Psalms and the book of Chronicles are messianic documents lies beyond the scope of this study. For one example of this interpretation, see Stephen G. Dempster, *Dominion and Dynasty: A Theology of the Hebrew Bible* (Downers Grove, IL: IVP, 2003). Regarding the Psalter, Dempster's heading reads 'The Psalms: David, David and David'. Regarding the book of Chronicles, cross-reference the comment of John Sailhamer, *First and Second Chronicles* (Chicago: Moody Press, 1983), p. 11: 'The message of Chronicles is "messianic"; that is, it looks forward to the coming King who will rule over God's people forever. In the historical books, the Psalms, and the prophets, the term *Messiah* stands for the Davidic King. The centrality of the Davidic King in the narrative therefore makes this story "messianic". It is the messiah, the Christ, the Son of David, who will bring peace to His own people and blessings to all men. In the New Testament we learn that this King's name is Jesus.'

32. So, e.g., the king of the prophecy in Zechariah 9–14 is most likely Davidic. That the expected king and shepherd of these passages are related to David is confirmed by the mentions of David's house in the surrounding context: 12.7, 8, 10, 12; 13.1. For a sampling of similar expectation in the prophets focused on a 'coming David', see e.g. Isa. 9.7; Jer. 23.5; Hos. 3.5; Amos 9.11.

33. Cf. the Davidic scene in Rev. 11.15 where voices in heaven proclaim that 'the kingdom of the world has become the kingdom of our Lord and of his Christ'. In a marked manner, this scene fills out (i.e. fulfills) the enthronement setting of Psalm 2.

this emphasis bind it to the Old Testament. Indeed, that Jesus is the Davidic anointed one of messianic prophecy might be 'the canonical integrating element within the whole of the OT and the NT'.[34] Only in this coming king is hope of new creation and new life made a reality.

34. See Sailhamer, *Meaning of the Pentateuch*, p. 461. Sailhamer notes that the biblical portrait of Jesus is 'the Jesus we know from reading the OT and the NT as a single book. It is the Jesus we know from reading all the biblical texts, and since evangelicals hold these text to be the Word of God, it is this Jesus whom they stand behind as the one and only historical Jesus'. Von Campenhausen argues in this regard that 'the Christian Bible—and this is the first and absolutely unshakeable fact that we know about it—comes into existence from the start as the *book of Christ*. The "scriptures of the Lord" testify to the Lord—the Old Testament prophetically, the New Testament historically. Christ speaks in both Testaments and is their true content. This alone is what makes the Bible the Christian Bible, the book of the Christian Church' (*Formation of the Christian Bible*, pp. 327-28).

BIBLIOGRAPHY

Books and Monographs

Aichele, George, *The Control of Biblical Meaning: Canon as Semiotic Mechanism* (Harrisburg, PA: Trinity Press International, 2001).

—*The Letters of Jude and Second Peter: Paranoia and the Slaves of Christ* (Phoenix Guides to the New Testament, 19; Sheffield: Sheffield Phoenix Press, 2012).

Aichele, George, and Richard Walsh (eds.), *Those Outside: Noncanonical Readings of Canonical Gospels* (New York: T. & T. Clark, 2005).

Ackroyd, Peter R., *Continuity: A Contribution to the Study of the Old Testament Religious Tradition* (Oxford: Blackwell, 1962).

Aland, Kurt, and Barbara Aland, *The Text of the New Testament: An Introduction to the Critical Editions and to the Theory and Practice of Modern Textual Criticism* (trans. Erroll F. Rhodes; Grand Rapids, MI: Eerdmans, 1987).

Alexander, T. Desmond, *From Eden to the New Jerusalem: An Introduction to Biblical Theology* (Grand Rapids, MI: Kregel, 2008).

—*From Paradise to the Promised Land: An Introduction to the Pentateuch* (Grand Rapids, MI: Baker, 3rd edn, 2012).

Allen, Graham, *Roland Barthes* (London and New York: Routledge, 2003).

—*Intertextuality* (The New Critical Idiom Series; London and New York: Routledge, 2nd edn, 2011).

Allert, Craig D., *Revelation, Truth, Canon and Interpretation: Studies in Justin Martyr's Dialogue with Tryhpo* (Supplements to Vigiliae Christiane; Leiden: Brill, 2002).

—*A High View of Scripture? The Authority of the Bible and the Formation of the New Testament Canon* (Evangelical Ressourcement Series; Grand Rapids, MI: Baker, 2007).

Auwer, J.M., and H.J. de Jonge (eds.), *The Biblical Canons* (BETL, CLXIII; Leuven: Leuven University Press, 2003).

Bakhtin, Mikhail, and Valentin N. Volosinov, *Marxism and the Philosophy of Language* (Cambridge, MA: Harvard University Press, 1986).

Baldick, Chris, *The Concise Oxford Dictionary of Literary Terms* (Oxford: Oxford University Press, 1990).

Balla, Peter, *Challenges to New Testament Theology: An Attempt to Justify the Enterprise* (Tübingen: Mohr Siebeck, 1997).

Barr, James, *Holy Scripture: Canon, Authority, Criticism* (Philadelphia, PA: Westminster Press, 1983).

—*The Concept of Biblical Theology: An Old Testament Perspective* (London: SCM Press, 1999).

Barth, Karl, *Church Dogmatics* (vol. I/ii; London: Continuum, 2004).

Barthes, Roland, Francois Bovon, F.J. Leenhardt, R. Martin-Achard and J. Starobinski (eds.), *Structural Analysis and Biblical Exegesis: Interpretational Essays* (trans. Alfred M. Johnson, Jr; Pittsburgh, PA: Pickwick Press, 1974).

Barton, John, *Holy Writings, Sacred Text: The Canon in Early Christianity* (Louisville, KY: Westminster/John Knox Press, 1997).
—*How the Bible Came to Be* (Louisville, KY: Westminster/John Knox Press, 1997).
—*The Spirit and the Letter: Studies in the Biblical Canon* (London: SPCK, 1997).
—*The Old Testament: Canon, Literature and Theology: Collected Essays of John Barton* (Society for Old Testament Studies Series; Burlington, VT: Ashgate Publishing Company, 2007).
Bauckham, Richard, *The Climax of Prophecy: Studies on the Book of Revelation* (Edinburgh: T. & T. Clark, 1993).
—*God Crucified: Monotheism and Christology in the New Testament* (Grand Rapids, MI: Eerdmans, 1999).
—*Jesus and the Eyewitnesses: The Gospels as Eyewitness Testimony* (Grand Rapids, MI: Eerdmans, 2007).
Bayard, Pierre, *How to Talk about Books You Haven't Read* (London: Granta Books, 2007).
Beale, G.K., *John's Use of the Old Testament in Revelation* (Sheffield: Sheffield Academic Press, 1998).
—*The Book of Revelation: A Commentary on the Greek Text* (The New International Greek Testament Commentary; Grand Rapids, MI: Eerdmans, 1999).
—*Handbook on the New Testament Use of the Old Testament: Exegesis and Interpretation* (Grand Rapids, MI: Baker, 2012).
Beale, G.K. (ed.), *The Right Doctrine from the Wrong Texts? Essays on the Use of the Old Testament in the New* (Grand Rapids, MI: Baker Books, 1994).
Beckwith, Roger T., *The Old Testament Canon of the New Testament Church and Its Background in Early Judaism* (Grand Rapids, MI: Eerdmans, 1985).
Berding, Kenneth, and Jonathan Lunde (eds.), *Three Views on the New Testament Use of the Old Testament* (Zondervan Counterpoints Series; Grand Rapids, MI: Zondervan, 2009).
Blenkinsopp, Joseph, *Prophecy and Canon: A Contribution to the Study of Jewish Origins* (University of Notre Dame Center For The Study of Judaism and Christianity in Antiquity, 3; Notre Dame, IN: Notre Dame University Press, 1977).
Bloom, Harold, *The Anxiety of Influence* (New York: Oxford University Press, 1973).
—*Kabbalah and Criticism* (New York: Seabury Press, 1975).
—*Maps of Misreading* (New York: Oxford University Press, 1975).
Bock, Darrell L., *A Theology of Luke and Acts: God's Promised Program, Realized for All Nations* (Biblical Theology of the New Testament Series; Grand Rapids, MI: Zondervan, 2012).
Bockmuehl, Markus, *Seeing the Word: Refocusing New Testament Study* (Studies in Theological Interpretation Series; Grand Rapids, MI: Baker, 2006).
Bondanella, Peter, *Umberto Eco and the Open Text: Semiotics, Fiction, Popular Culture* (Cambridge: Cambridge University Press, 2005).
Bondanella, Peter (ed.), *New Essays on Umberto Eco* (Cambridge: Cambridge University Press, 2009).
Booth, Wayne C., *The Rhetoric of Fiction* (Chicago: University of Chicago Press, 2nd edn, 1983).
Briggs, Richard S., *The Virtuous Reader: Old Testament Narrative and Interpretive Virtue* (Studies in Theological Interpretation Series; Grand Rapids, MI: Baker, 2010).

Brandt, Peter, *Endgestalten des Kanons. Das Arrangement der Schriften Israels in der Judischen und Christlichen Bibel* (Berlin: Philo, 2001).
Brodie, Thomas L., Dennis R. MacDonald and Stanley E. Porter (eds.), *The Intertextuality of the Epistles: Explorations of Theory and Practice* (New Testament Monographs, 16; Sheffield: Sheffield Academic Press, 2006).
Brown, Gillian, and George Yule, *Discourse Analysis* (Cambridge: Cambridge University Press, 1983).
Brown, Jeannine K., *The Disciples In Narrative Perspective: The Portrayal and Function of the Matthean Disciples* (Atlanta, GA: Society of Biblical Literature, 2002).
—*Scripture as Communication: Introducing Biblical Hermeneutics* (Grand Rapids, MI: Baker, 2007).
Bruce, F.F., *The Canon of Scripture* (Downers Grove, IL: InterVarsity Press, 1988).
—*The Books and the Parchments: Some Chapters on the Transmission of the Bible* (London: Marshall Pickering, rev. edn, 1991).
Campenhausen, Hans von, *The Formation of the Christian Bible* (Philadelphia, PA: Fortress Press, 1971).
Carson, D.A., and Douglas J. Moo, *An Introduction to the New Testament* (Grand Rapids, MI: Zondervan, 2005).
Carson, D.A., and G.K. Beale (eds.), *Commentary on the New Testament Use of the Old Testament* (Grand Rapids, MI: Baker, 2007).
Chapman, Stephen B., *The Law and the Prophets: A Study in Old Testament Canon Formation* (Forschungen zum Alten Testament, 27; Tübingen: Mohr Siebeck, 2000).
Charles, Robert Henry, *A Critical and Exegetical Commentary on the Revelation of St. John* (The International Critical Commentary Series; 2 vol.; Edinburgh: T. & T. Clark, 1920).
Childs, Brevard S., *Biblical Theology in Crisis* (Philadelphia, PA: Westminster Press, 1970).
—*Introduction to the Old Testament as Scripture* (Philadelphia, PA: Fortress Press, 1979).
—*The New Testament as Canon: An Introduction* (Philadelphia, PA: Fortress Press, 1984).
—*Biblical Theology of the Old and New Testaments: Theological Reflection on the Christian Bible* (Minneapolis, MN: Fortress Press, 1992).
—'Retrospective Reading of the Old Testament Prophets', *ZAW* 108 (1996), pp. 362-77.
—*The Church's Guide for Reading Paul: The Canonical Shaping of the Pauline Corpus* (Grand Rapids, MI: Eerdmans, 2008).
Comfort, Phillip W., and David P. Barrett (eds.), *The Text of the Earliest New Testament Greek Manuscripts: New and Complete Transcriptions with Photographs* (Wheaton, IL: Tyndale House, 2001).
Comfort, Phillip W., *Encountering the Manuscripts: An Introduction to New Testament Paleography and Textual Criticism* (Nashville, TN: B & H, 2005).
Cotterell, Peter, and Max Turner, *Linguistics and Biblical Interpretation* (Downers Grove, IL: InterVarsity Press, 1989).
Craigie, Peter C., *The Book of Deuteronomy* (The New International Commentary on the Old Testament; Grand Rapids, MI: Eerdmans, 1976).
Crossley, James G., *Reading the New Testament: Contemporary Approaches* (London and New York: Routledge, 2010).
Culler, Jonathan, *The Pursuit of Signs: Semiotics, Literature, Deconstruction* (London and New York: Routledge, 2001).
—*Barthes: A Very Short Introduction* (Oxford: Oxford University Press, 2002).

238 *A Canon-Conscious Reading of the Bible*

—*Structuralist Poetics: Structuralism, Linguistics and the Study of Literature* (London and New York: Routledge, 2002).

—*On Deconstruction: Theory and Criticism after Structuralism* (Ithaca, NY: Cornell University Press, 2007).

—*The Literary in Theory* (Culture Memory in the Present Series; Stanford, CA: Stanford University Press, 2007).

—*Literary Theory* (New York: Sterling, 2009).

Culpepper, R. Alan, *Anatomy of the Fourth Gospel: A Study in Literary Design* (Philadelphia, PA: Fortress Press, 1983).

Daly-Denton, Margaret, *David in the Fourth Gospel: The Johannine Reception of the Psalms* (Arbeiten zur Geschichte des Antiken Judentums und des Urchristentums, 47; Leiden: Brill, 2000).

Dell, Katharine, and Will Kynes (eds.), *Reading Job Intertextually* (London: T. & T. Clark, 2012).

Dempster, Stephen G., *Dominion and Dynasty: A Theology of the Hebrew Bible* (Downers Grove, IL: InterVarsity Press, 2003).

Dickens, Charles, *Hard Times: For These Times* (London: Penguin Books, 2003).

Dodd, Charles H., *According to the Scriptures: The Sub-Structure of New Testament Theology* (London: Nisbet, 1952).

Dohmen, Christoph, *Die Bibel und ihre Auslegung* (Munich: C.H. Beck, 2006).

Dohmen, Christoph, and Manfred Oeming, *Biblischer Kanon: Warum und Wozu? Eine Kanontheologie* (Freiburg: Herder, 1992).

Draisma, Spike, *Intertextuality in Biblical Writings. Essays in Honour of Bas van Iersel* (Kampen: Kok, 1989).

Driver, Daniel R., *Brevard Childs, Biblical Theologian: For the Church's One Bible* (Forschungen zum Alten Testament 2 Reihe, 46; Tübingen: Mohr Siebeck, 2010).

Dumbrell, William J., *The End of the Beginning: Revelation 21–22 and the Old Testament* (New South Wales: Lancer, 1985).

Dungan, David L., *Constantine's Bible: Politics and the Making of the New Testament* (Minneapolis, MN: Fortress Press, 2007).

Eco, Umberto, *Semiotics and the Philosophy of Language* (Bloomington, IN: Indiana University Press, 1984).

—*The Role of the Reader: Explorations in the Semiotics of Texts* (Bloomington, IN: Indiana University Press, 1984).

—*Six Walks in the Fictional Woods* (Cambridge, MA: Harvard University Press, 1994).

—*The Limits of Interpretation* (Bloomington, MA: Indiana University Press, 1994).

—*The Name of the Rose* (trans. William Weaver; San Diego, CA: Harcourt, 1994).

Eisenstein, Elizabeth L., *The Printing Press as an Agent of Change* (Cambridge: Cambridge University Press, 1980).

Eisenstein, Sergei, *The Film Sense* (trans. Jay Leyda; New York: Harcourt Brace, 1942).

Ellis, E. Earle, *Paul's Use of the Old Testament* (Wissenschaftliche Untersuchungen zum Neuen Testament, 18; Grand Rapids, MI: Eerdmans, 1957).

—*The Old Testament in Early Christianity: Canon and Interpretation in the Light of Modern Research* (Wissenschaftliche Untersuchungen zum Zeuen Neuen Testament, 54; Grand Rapids, MI: Baker, 1992).

Fekkes, Jan, *Isaiah and Prophetic Traditions in the Book of Revelation: Visionary Antecedents and Their Development* (Journal for the Study of the New Testament Supplement Series, 93; Sheffield: Sheffield Academic Press, 1994).

Fish, Stanley, *Is There a Text in This Class? The Authority of Interpretive Communities* (Cambridge, MA: Harvard University Press, 1980).

Fishbane, Michael, *Biblical Interpretation in Ancient Israel* (Oxford: Oxford University Press, 1985).

Fitzmyer, Joseph A., *The Gospel According to Luke (X-XXIV): Introduction, Translation, and Notes* (The Anchor Bible Commentary Series; Garden City, NY: Doubleday, 1985).

Fowl, Stephen E., and L. Gregory Jones, *Reading in Communion: Scripture and Ethics in Christian Life* (Biblical Foundations in Theology Series; London: SPCK, 1991).

France, R.T., *The Gospel of Matthew* (New International Commentary on the New Testament; Grand Rapids, MI: Eerdmans, 2007).

Frank, Isidor, *Der Sinn der Kanonbildung: Eine historisch-theologische Untersuchung der Zeit vom 1. Clemensbrief bis Irenäus von Lyon* (Freiburg: Herder, 1971).

Freedman, David Noel, *The Unity of the Hebrew Bible* (The Distinguished Senior Faculty Series; Ann Arbor, MI: University of Michigan Press, 1993).

Frei, Hans W., *The Eclipse of Biblical Narrative: A Study in Eighteenth and Nineteenth Century Hermeneutics* (New Haven, CT: Yale University Press, 1974).

Friberg, Barbara, Timothy Friberg and Neva F. Miller, *Analytical Lexicon of the Greek New Testament* (Victoria, BC: Trafford Publishing, 2005).

Gamble, Harry Y., *The New Testament Canon: Its Making and Meaning* (Philadelphia, PA: Fortress Press, 1985).

—*Books and Readers in the Early Church: A History of Early Christian Texts* (New Haven, CT: Yale University Press, 1995).

—*The Architext: An Introduction* (trans. Jane E. Lewin; Berkeley, CA: University of California Press, 1992).

Genette, Gérard, *Fiction and Diction* (trans. Catherine Porter; Ithaca, NY: Cornell University Press, 1993).

—*Palimpsests: Literature in the Second Degree* (trans. Channa Newman and Claude Doubinsky; Lincoln, NE: University of Nebraska Press, 1997).

—*Paratexts: Thresholds of Interpretation* (trans. Jane E. Lewin; Cambridge, MA: Cambridge University Press, 1997).

Gillespie, David C., *Early Soviet Cinema: Innovation, Ideology and Propaganda* (London: Wallflower Press, 2000).

Greene, Thomas M., *The Light in Troy: Imitation and Discovery in Renaissance Poetry* (New Haven, CT: Yale University Press, 1982).

Grice, Paul, *Studies in the Way of Words* (Cambridge, MA: Harvard University Press, 1989).

Hahneman, Geoffrey Mark, *The Muratorian Fragment and the Development of the Canon* (Oxford: Clarendon Press, 1992).

Harari, Josué V. (ed.), *Textual Strategies: Perspectives in Post-Structuralist Criticism* (Ithaca, NY: Cornell University Press, 1979).

Harnack, Adolf von, *What is Christianity? Lectures Delivered in the University of Berlin during the Winter-Term, 1899–1900* (London: Williams & Norgate, 1901).

—*Marcion: Das Evangelium vom fremden Gott* (Leipzig: Hinrichs, 2nd edn, 1924).

—*The Origin of the New Testament and the Most Important Consequences of the New Creation* (trans. J.R. Wilkinson; London: Williams & Norgate, 1925).

Hays, Richard B., *Echoes of Scripture in the Letters of Paul* (New Haven, CT: Yale University Press, 1989).

—*The Conversion of the Imagination: Paul as Interpreter of Israel's Scripture* (Grand Rapids, MI: Eerdmans, 2005).

Hemer, Colin J., *The Letters to the Seven Churches of Asia in Their Local Setting* (Journal for the Study of the New Testament Supplement Series, 11; Sheffield: Journal for the Study of the New Testament Press, 1986).

Hengel, Martin, *The Four Gospels and the One Gospel of Jesus Christ: An Investigation of the Collection and Origin of the Canonical Gospels* (trans. John Bowden; Harrisburg, PA: Trinity Press International, 2000).

Heskett, Randall, and Brian Irwin (eds.), *The Bible as Human Witness: Hearing the Word of God Through Historically Dissimilar Traditions* (Library of Biblical Studies; London: T. & T. Clark, 2010).

Hibbard, J. Todd, *Intertextuality in Isaiah 24–27* (Forschungen zum Alten Testament 2. Reihe, 16; Tübingen: Mohr Siebeck, 2006).

Hieke, Thomas, and Tobias Nicklas, *'Die Worte der Prophetie dieses Buches' Offenbarung 22,6-21 als Schlussstein der Christlichen Bibel Alten und Neuen Testaments Gelesen* (Neukirchen–Vluyn, DE: Neukirchener Verlag, 2003).

Hill, Charles E., *The Johannine Corpus in the Early Church* (Oxford: Oxford University Press, 2004).

—*Who Chose the Gospels? Probing the Great Gospel Conspiracy* (Oxford: Oxford University Press, 2010).

Hill, Charles E., and Michael J. Kruger (eds.), *The Early Text of the New Testament* (Oxford: Oxford University Press, 2012).

Hirsch, E.D., Jr, *Validity in Interpretation* (New Haven, CT: Yale University Press, 1967).

—*The Aims of Interpretation* (Chicago: University of Chicago Press, 1976).

Holman, C. Hugh, *A Handbook to Literature* (Indianapolis, IN: Bobbs-Merrill, 1980).

Horton, Charles (ed.), *The Earliest Gospels: The Origins and Transmission of the Earliest Christian Gospels—The Contribution of the Chester Beatty Gospel Codex P45* (Journal for the Study of the New Testament Supplement Series, 258; London: T. & T. Clark, 2004).

House, Paul, *The Unity of the Twelve* (Sheffield: Almond Press, 1990).

Hurtado, Larry W., *The Earliest Christian Artifacts: Manuscripts and Christian Origins* (Grand Rapids, MI: Eerdmans, 2006).

Iser, Wolfgang, *The Implied Reader: Patterns of Communication in Prose Fiction from Bunyan to Beckett* (Baltimore, MD: The Johns Hopkins University Press, 1974).

—*The Act of Reading: A Theory of Aesthetic Response* (Baltimore, MD: The Johns Hopkins University Press, 1980).

—*Prospecting: From Reader Response to Literary Anthropology* (Baltimore, MD: The Johns Hopkins University Press, 1989).

—*The Range of Interpretation* (New York: Columbia University Press, 2000).

Jensen, Peter, *The Revelation of God* (Contours of Christian Theology; Downers Grove, IL: InterVarsity Press, 2002).

Jenson, Robert W., *Canon and Creed* (Interpretation: Resources for the Use of Scripture in the Church; Louisville, KY: Westminster/John Knox Press, 2010).

Jones, Barry Alan, *The Formation of the Book of the Twelve: A Study in Text and Canon* (Atlanta, GA: Scholars Press, 1995).

Käsemann, Ernst (ed.), *Das Neue Testament als Kanon* (Göttingen: Vandenhoeck & Ruprecht, 1970).

Klink, Edward W., III, and Darian R. Lockett, *Understanding Biblical Theology: A Comparison of Theory and Practice* (Grand Rapids, MI: Zondervan, 2012).

Knight, Arthur, *The Liveliest Art: A Panoramic History of the Movies* (London: Macmillan, 1957).

Köstenberger, Andreas J., *A Theology of John's Gospel and Letters* (Biblical Theology of the New Testament; Grand Rapids, MI: Zondervan, 2009).

Köstenberger, Andreas J., and Richard D. Patterson, *Invitation to Biblical Interpretation: Exploring the Hermeneutical Triad of History, Literature, and Theology* (Grand Rapids, MI: Kregel, 2011).

Kowalski, Beate, *Die Rezeption des Propheten Ezechiel in der Ofeenbarung des Johannes* (Stuttgarter biblische Beiträge, 52; Stuttgart: Kotholische Bibelwerk, 2004).

Kristeva, Julia, *Desire in Language: A Semiotic Approach to Literature and Art* (ed. Leon S. Roudiez; trans. Thomas Gora, Alice Jardine, and Leon S. Roudiez; New York: Columbia University Press, 1980).

—*Revolution in Poetic Language* (New York: Columbia University Press, 1985).

Kruger, Michael J., *Canon Revisited: Establishing the Origins and Authority of the New Testament Books* (Wheaton, IL: Crossway, 2012).

Ladd, George E., *A Theology of the New Testament* (Grand Rapids, MI: Eerdmans, 1993).

Lavers, Annette, *Roland Barthes: Structuralism and After* (London: Meuthen, 1982).

Lee, Pilchan, *The New Jerusalem in the Book of Revelation: A Study of Revelation 21–22 in the Light of its Background in Jewish Tradition* (Wissenschaftliche Untersuchungen zum Neuen Testament 2. Reihe, 129; Tübingen: Mohr Siebeck, 2001).

Lewis, C.S., and Eustace M.W. Tillyard, *The Personal Heresy: A Controversy* (ed. Joel D. Heck; Austin, TX: Concordia University Press, 2008).

Lieb, Michael, Emma Mason and Jonathan Roberts (eds.), *The Oxford Handbook of The Reception History of the Bible* (Oxford: Oxford University Press, 2011).

Liszka, James Jakob, *A General Introduction to the Semiotics of Charles Sanders Peirce* (Bloomington, IN: Indiana University Press, 1996).

Litwak, Kenneth Duncan, *Echoes of Scripture in Luke–Acts: Telling the History of God's People Intertextually* (London: T. & T. Clark, 2005).

Louw, J.P., and E.A. Nida, *Greek-English Lexicon of the New Testament: Based on Semantic Domains* (New York: United Bible Society, 1989).

Lyotard, Jean-Francois, *The Postmodern Condition: A Report on Knowledge* (Minneapolis, MN: University of Minnesota Press, 1984).

MacLachlan, Gale L., and Ian Reid, *Framing and Interpretation* (Carlton: Melborne University Press, 1994).

Maier, Gerhard, *Biblical Hermeneutics* (trans. Robert W. Yarbrough; Wheaton, IL: Crossway, 1994).

Marshall, I. Howard, *The Gospel of Luke: A Commentary on the Greek Text* (The New International Greek Testament Commentary; Grand Rapids, MI: Eerdmans, 1978).

—*A Critical and Exegetical Commentary on the Pastoral Epistles* (International Critical Commentary; Edinburgh: T. & T. Clark, 1999).

Marti, D. Karl, *Das Dodekapropheton* (Kurzer Hand-Commentar zum Alten Testament, 13; Tübigen: Mohr Siebeck, 1904).

Mathewson, David, *A New Heaven and a New Earth: The Meaning and Function of the Old Testament in Revelation 21.1–22.5* (Sheffield: Sheffield Academic Press, 2003).

Maynard, John, *Literary Intention, Literary Interpretation, and Readers* (Ontario: Broadview Press, 2009).

Merz, Annette, *Die fiktive Selbstauslegung des Paulus: Intertextuelle Studien zur Intention und Rezeption der Pastoralbriefe* (Göttingen: Vandenhoeck & Ruprecht, 2004).

Metzger, Bruce M., and Bart D. Ehrman, *The Text of the New Testament: Its Transmission, Corruption, and Restoration* (Oxford: Oxford University Press, 4th edn, 2005).

Metzger, Bruce M., *Manuscripts of the Greek Bible: An Introduction to Greek Palaeography* (New York: Oxford University Press, 1981).

—*The Canon of the New Testament: Its Origin, Development, and Significance* (Oxford: Clarendon Press, 1987).

—*A Textual Commentary on the Greek New Testament* (Stuttgart: Deutsche Bibelgesellschaft, 1994).

—*The New Testament, Its Background, Growth and Content* (Nashville, TN: Abingdon Press, 2003).

McDonald, Lee Martin, *The Biblical Canon: Its Origin, Transmission, and Authority* (Peabody, MA: Hendrickson Publishers, 2007).

—*The Origin of the Bible: A Guide for the Perplexed* (London: T. & T. Clark, 2011).

Millard, Alan, *Reading and Writing in the Time of Jesus* (London: T. & T. Clark, 2001).

Minear, Paul Sevier, *Christians and the New Creation: Genesis Motifs in the New Testament* (Louisville, KY: Westminster/John Knox Press, 1994).

Mitry, Jean, *The Aesthetics and Psychology of the Cinema* (trans. Christopher King; Bloomington, IN: Indiana University Press, 1997).

Moberly, R.W.L., *The Bible, Theology, and Faith: A Study of Abraham and Jesus* (Cambridge Studies in Christian Doctrine Series; Cambridge: Cambridge University Press, 2000).

Moule, C.F.D., *The Birth of the New Testament* (London: Continuum, 2000).

Moyise, Steve, *The Old Testament in the Book of Revelation* (Journal for the Study of the New Testament Supplement Series, 115; Sheffield: Sheffield Academic Press, 1995).

—*The Old Testament in the New* (London: T. & T. Clark, 2004).

—*Evoking Scripture: Seeing the Old Testament in the New* (London: T. & T. Clark, 2008).

Moyise, Steve (ed.), *The Old Testament in the New Testament: Essays in Honour of J.L. North* (Journal for the Study of the New Testament Supplement Series, 189; Sheffield: Sheffield Academic Press, 2000).

Neusner, Jacob (ed.), *The Talmud of Babylonia: An American Translation* (vol. 22A: Tractate Baba Batra Chapters 1-2; Atlanta, GA: Scholars Press, 1992).

Nicholson, E.W., *The Pentateuch in the Twentieth Century: The Legacy of Julius Wellhausen* (Oxford: Clarendon Press, 1998).

Nogalski, James, *Literary Precursors to the Book of the Twelve* (Beihefte zur Zeitschrift für die Alttestamentliche Wissenschaft, 217; Berlin: W. de Gruyter, 1993).

Nogalski, James, and Marvin A. Sweeney, *Reading and Hearing the Book of the Twelve* (Atlanta, GA: Society of Biblical Literature, 2000).

O'Gorman, Marcel, *Digital Media, Critical Theory, and the Humanities* (Toronto: University of Toronto, 2005).

Oliver, Kelly, *Reading Kristeva: Unraveling the Double-Bind* (Bloomington, IN: Indiana University Press, 1993).

Orr, Mary, *Intertextuality: Debates and Contexts* (Cambridge: Polity Press, 2003).

Parvis, Sara, and Paul Foster (eds.), *Justin Martyr and His Worlds* (Minneapolis, MN: Fortress Press, 2007).

Pasco, Allan H., *Allusion: A Literary Graft* (Toronto: University of Toronto Press, 1994).

Patzia, Arthur G., *The Making of the New Testament: Origin, Collection, Text and Canon* (Downers Grove, IL: InterVarsity Press, 2nd edn, 2011).

Pauck, Wilhelm, *Harnack and Troeltsch: Two Historical Theologians* (Oxford: Oxford University Press, 1968).

Porter, Stanley E. (ed.), *Hearing the Old Testament in the New Testament* (Grand Rapids, MI: Eerdmans, 2006).

Postman, Neil, *Technopoly: The Surrender of Culture to Technology* (New York: Vintage Books, 1993).

Powell, Mark A., *What is Narrative Criticism?* (Guides to Biblical Scholarship; Minneapolis, MN: Fortress Press, 1990).

Pramaggiore, Maria T., and Tom Wallis, *Film: A Critical Introduction* (Boston: Allyn & Bacon, 2011).

Pritchard, James B., *The Ancient Near East: An Anthology of Texts and Pictures* (Princeton, NJ: Princeton University Press, 2010).

Provan, Ian W., *1 and 2 Kings* (New International Biblical Commentary; Peabody, MA: Hendrickson, 1995).

Pucci, Joseph, *The Full-Knowing Reader: Allusion and the Power of the Reader in the Western Literary Tradition* (New Haven, CT: Yale University Press, 1998).

Rad, Gerhard von, *Deuteronomy* (The Old Testament Library; Philadelphia, PA: Westminster/John Knox Press, 1966).

Räisänen, Heikki, *Beyond New Testament Theology: A Story and a Programme* (London: SCM Press, 2nd edn, 2000).

Ramsay, William M., *The Letters to the Seven Churches of Asia and their Place in the Plan of the Apocalypse* (Peabody, MA: Hendrickson Publishers, 1994).

Redditt, Paul L., and Aaron Schart (eds.), *Thematic Threads in the Book of the Twelve* (Beihefte zur Zeitschrift für die Alttestamentliche Wissenschaft, 325; Berlin: W. de Gruyter, 2003).

Rendtorff, Rolf, *The Canonical Hebrew Bible: A Theology of the Old Testament* (trans. David E. Orton; Tools for Biblical Study Series, 7; Leiden: Deo Publishing, 2005).

Ricoeur, Paul, *Time and Narrative* (vol. 1; Chicago: University of Chicago Press, 1984).

Roberts, Colin H., and Theodore C. Skeat, *The Birth of the Codex* (Oxford: Oxford University Press, 1983).

Roberts, Colin H., *Manuscript, Society and Belief in Early Christian Egypt* (London: Oxford University Press, 1979).

Royse, James R., *Scribal Habits in Early Greek New Testament Papyri* (New Testament Tools, Studies and Documents Series, 36; Leiden: Brill, 2008).

Ruiz, J.P., *Ezekiel in the Apocalypse: The Transformation of Prophetic Language in Revelation 16:17–19:10* (Frankfurt am Main: Peter Lang, 1989).

Rumscheidt, Martin, *Adolf von Harnack: Liberal Theology at its Height* (San Francisco, CA: Harper & Row, 1989).

Sæbø, Magne, *On the Way to Canon: Creative Tradition History in the Old Testament* (Sheffield: Sheffield Academic Press, 1998).

Sailhamer, John H., *First and Second Chronicles* (Everyman's Bible Commentary; Chicago: Moody Press, 1983).

—*The Pentateuch as Narrative: A Biblical-Theological Commentary* (Grand Rapids, MI: Zondervan, 1992).

—*Introduction to Old Testament Theology: A Canonical Approach* (Grand Rapids, MI: Zondervan, 1995).

—*The Meaning of the Pentateuch: Revelation, Composition and Interpretation* (Downers Grove, IL: InterVarsity Press, 2009).

Scheetz, Jordan M., *The Concept of Canonical Intertextuality and the Book of Daniel* (Eugene, OR: Pickwick Publications, 2011).

Schechter, Solomon, and C. Taylor, *The Wisdom of Ben Sira: Portions of the Book of Ecclesiasticus from Hebrew Manuscripts in the Cairo Genizah Collection, Presented to the University of Cambridge by the Editors* (London: C.J. Clay & Sons, 1899).

Schniedewind, William M., *How the Bible Became a Book* (Cambridge: Cambridge University Press, 2004).

Schreiner, Thomas R., *New Testament Theology: Magnifying God in Christ* (Grand Rapids, MI: Baker, 2008).

Seitz, Christopher R., *Prophecy and Hermeneutics* (Studies in Theological Interpretation Series; Grand Rapids, MI: Baker, 2007).

—*The Goodly Fellowship of the Prophets: The Achievement of Association in Canon Formation* (Acadia Studies in Bible and Theology; Grand Rapids, MI: Baker, 2009).

—*The Character of Christian Scripture: The Significance of a Two-Testament Bible* (Studies in Theological Interpretation Series; Grand Rapids, MI: Baker, 2011).

Shepherd, Michael B., *The Twelve Prophets in the New Testament* (Studies in Biblical Literature, 140; New York: Peter Lang, 2011).

—*The Textual World of the Bible* (Studies in Biblical Literature, 156; New York: Peter Lang, 2013).

Sheppard, Gerald T., *Wisdom as a Hermeneutical Construct: A Study in the Sapientializing of the Old Testament* (Beiheft zur Zeitschrift für die Alttestamentliche Wissenschaft, 151; Berlin: W. de Gruyter, 1980).

Skeat, Theodore C., *The Collected Biblical Writings of T.C. Skeat* (ed. J.K. Elliott; Supplements to Novum Testamentum, 113; Leiden: Brill, 2004).

Slatoff, Walter J., *With Respect to Readers: Dimensions of Literary Response* (Ithaca, NY: Cornell University Press, 1970).

Smith, David E., *The Canonical Function of Acts: A Comparative Analysis* (Collegeville, MN: The Liturgical Press, 2002).

Staley, Jeff, *The Print's First Kiss: A Rhetorical Investigation of the Implied Reader in the Fourth Gospel* (Atlanta, GA: Scholars Press, 1988).

Steck, O.H., *Der Abschluss der Prophetie im Alten Testament: Ein Versuch zur Frage der Vorgeschichte des Kanons* (Biblisch-theologische Studien, 17; Neukirchen–Vluyn: Neukirchener Verlag, 1991).

Steinberg, Julius, *Die Ketuvim: Ihr Aufbau und ihre Botschaft* (Bonner Biblische Beiträge, 152; Hamburg: Philo, 2006).

Steins, Georg, *Die Chronik als kanonisches Abschlussphänomen: Studien zur Entstehung and Theologie von 1 / 2 Chronik* (Bonner Biblische Beiträge, 93; Beltz: Athenäum Verlag, 1995).

—*Die Bindung Isaaks im Kanon (Gen 22): Grundlagen und Programm einer Kanonisch-Intertextuellen Lektüre mit einer Spezialbibliographie zu Gen 22* (Herders Biblische Studien, 20; Frieburg: Herder, 1999).

Sternberg, Meir, *The Poetics of Biblical Narrative: Ideological Literature and the Drama of Reading* (Bloomington, IN: Indiana University Press, 1985).

Still, Judith, and Michael Worton (eds.), *Intertextuality: Theories and Practices* (Manchester: Manchester University Press, 1990).

Stowers, Stanley K., *Letter Writing in Greco-Roman Antiquity* (Philadelphia, PA: Westminster Press, 1986).

Stuhlhofer, Franz, *Der Gebrauch der Bibel von Jesus bis Euseb: Eine statistiche Untersuchung zur Kanonsgeschichte* (Wuppertal: R. Brockhaus, 1988).

Sundberg, Albert C., Jr, *The Old Testament of the Early Church* (Cambridge, MA: Harvard University Press, 1964).

Swain, Scott R., *Trinity, Revelation, and Reading: A Theological Introduction to the Bible and its Interpretation* (London: T. & T. Clark, 2011).

Swete, Henry B., *An Introduction to the Old Testament in Greek* (Cambridge: Cambridge University Press, 1902).

Tallis, Raymond, *Not Saussure: A Critique of Post-Saussurean Literary Theory* (London: MacMillan, 1995).

Tanner, Beth LaNeel, *The Book of Psalms through the Lens of Intertextuality* (Studies in Biblical Literature, 26; New York: Peter Lang, 2001).

Theissen, Gerd, *The New Testament: A Literary History* (trans. Linda M. Maloney; Minneapolis, MN: Fortress Press, 2012).

Thiselton, Anthony C., *New Horizons in Hermeneutics: The Theory and Practice of Transforming Biblical Reading* (Grand Rapids, MI: Zondervan, 1992).

—*1 & 2 Thessalonians Through the Centuries* (Blackwell Bible Commentaries; Malden, MA: Wiley-Blackwell, 2010).

Tischendorf, Constantin von, *Codex Ephraemi Syri Rescriptus sive Fragmenta Novi Testamenti* (Leipzig, 1843).

Toorn, Karel van der, *Scribal Culture and the Making of the Hebrew Bible* (Cambridge, MA: Harvard University Press, 2007).

Tov, Emanuel, *The Greek Minor Prophets Scroll from Nahal Hever (HevXIIgr) (The Seiyal Collection I)* (Discoveries in the Judean Desert, 8; Oxford: Clarendon Press, 1995).

—*Textual Criticism of the Hebrew Bible* (Minneapolis, MN: Fortress Press, 3rd edn, 2012).

Trail, Ronald L., *An Exegetical Summary of Revelation 1–11* (Dallas, TX: Summer Institute of Linguistics International, 2003).

Trobisch, David, *Die Entstehung der paulusbriefsammlung: Studien zu den Anfängen Christlicher Publizistik* (Freiburg/Schweiz; Universitätsverlag; Göttingen: Vandenhoeck & Ruprecht, 1989).

—*Paul's Letter Collection: Tracing the Origins* (Minneapolis, MN: Fortress Press, 1994).

—*The First Edition of the New Testament* (Oxford: Oxford University Press, 2000).

Trobisch, David, and Richard F. Ward, *Bringing the Word to Life: Engaging the New Testament through Performing It* (Grand Rapids, MI: Eerdmans, 2013).

Uspensky, Boris, *Poetics of Composition* (Berkeley, CA: University of California Press, 1973).

Vanderborg, Susan, *Paratextual Communities: American Avant-Garde Poetry Since 1950* (Carbondale, IL: Southern Illinois University Press, 2002).

VanderKam, James C., *The Dead Sea Scrolls and the Bible* (Grand Rapids, MI: Eerdmans, 2012).

Vanhoozer, Kevin J., *Is There a Meaning in this Text? The Bible, The Reader, and the Morality of Literary Knowledge* (Grand Rapids, MI: Zondervan, 1998).

—*The Drama of Doctrine: A Canonical-Linguistic Approach to Christian Theology* (Louisville, KY: Westminster/John Knox Press, 2005).

Vassar, John S., *Recalling a Story Once Told: An Intertextual Reading of the Psalter and the Pentateuch* (Macon, GA: Mercer University Press, 2007).

Venema, G.J., *Reading Scripture in the Old Testament: Deuteronomy 9–10, 31, 2 Kings 22–23, Jeremiah 36, Nehemiah 8* (trans. C.E. Smit; Leiden: Brill, 2004).

Wall, Robert K., *Revelation* (New International Biblical Commentary; Peabody, MA: Hendrickson Publishers, 1991).

Waltke, Bruce K., *The Book of Proverbs: Chapters 15–31* (The New International Commentary on the Old Testament; Grand Rapids, MI: Eerdmans, 2005).

Ward, Timothy, *Word and Supplement: Speech Acts, Biblical Texts, and the Sufficiency of Scripture* (Oxford: Oxford University Press, 2002).

—*Words of Life: Scripture as the Living and Active Word of God* (Downers Grove, IL: InterVarsity Press, 2009).

Webster, John, *Holy Scripture: A Dogmatic Sketch* (Cambridge: Cambridge University Press, 2003).

—*Word and Church: Essays in Christian Dogmatics* (Edinburgh: T. & T. Clark, 2001).

Wegner, Paul D., *The Journey from Texts to Translations: The Origin and Development of the Bible* (Grand Rapids, MI: Baker, 1999).

Wenham, Gordon J., *Genesis 1–15* (Word Biblical Commentary; Nashville, TN: Thomas Nelson Publishers, 1987).

Westfall, Cynthia Long, *A Discourse Analysis of the Letter to the Hebrews: The Relationship Between Form and Meaning* (Library of New Testament Studies; London: T. & T. Clark, 2005).

Whybray, R.N., *The Making of the Pentateuch: A Methodological Study* (Journal for the Study of the Old Testament Supplement Series, 53; Sheffield: Journal for the Study of the Old Testament Press, 1987).

Widdowson, Peter, *Literature* (The New Critical Idiom Series; London and New York: Routledge, 1999).

Wuthnow, Robert, *Communities of Discourse: Ideology and Social Structure in Reformation, the Enlightenment, and European Socialism* (Cambridge, MA: Harvard University Press, 1989).

Young, Robert, *Untying the Text: A Post-Structuralist Reader* (London: Routledge & Kegan Paul, 1981).

Zahn, Theodor, *Forschungen zur Geschichte des Neutestamentlichen Kanons und der Altkirchlichen Literatur* (10 vol.; Leipzig: A. Deichert, 1881–1929).

—*Grundriss der Geschichte des Neutestamentlichen Kanons: Eine Ergänzung zu der Einleitung in das Neue Testament* (Leipzig: A. Deichert, 1904).

Zenger, E., *Das Erste Testament: Die Jüdische Bibel und die Christen* (Düsseldorf: Patmos, 1991).

Articles and Essays

Aichele, George, 'Canon as Intertext: Restraint or Liberation?', in *Reading the Bible Intertextually* (ed. Stefan Alkier, Leory A. Huizenga, and Richard Hays; Waco, TX: Baylor University Press, 2009), pp. 139-56.

Aland, Barbara, 'Marcion: Versuch einer neuen Interpretation', *Zeitschrift Theologie und Kirche* 70 (1973), pp. 420-47.

—'The Significance of the Chester Beatty Papyri in Early Church History', in *The Earliest Gospels: The Origins and Transmission of the Earliest Christian Gospels—The Contribution of the Chester Beatty Gospel Codex P45* (ed. Charles Horton; Journal for the Study of the New Testament Supplement Series, 258; London: T. & T. Clark, 2004), pp. 108-21.

Alexander, Loveday, 'Ancient Book Production and the Circulation of the Gospels', in *The Gospels for All Christians: Rethinking the Gospel Audiences* (ed. Richard Bauckham; Grand Rapids, MI: Eerdmans, 1998), pp. 71-111.

—'What is a Gospel?', in *The Cambridge Companion to the Gospels* (ed. Stephen C. Barton; Cambridge: Cambridge University Press, 2006), pp. 13-33.

Alkier, Stefan, 'From Text to Intertext: Intertextuality as a Paradigm for Reading Matthew', *Hermvormde Teologiese Studies* 61 (2005), pp. 1-18.

—'Intertextuality and the Semiotics of Biblical Texts', in Stefan Alkier and Richard Hays (eds.), *Reading the Bible Intertextually* (Waco, TX: Baylor University Press, 2009), pp. 3-22.

—'New Testament Studies on the Basis of Categorical Semiotics', in Stefan Alkier and Richard Hays (eds.), *Reading the Bible Intertextually* (Waco, TX: Baylor University Press, 2009), pp. 223-48.

Arzt-Grabner, Peter, '"I Was Intending To Visit You, But..." Clauses Explaining Delayed Visits and their Importance in Papyrus Letters and in Paul', in *Jewish and Christian Scripture as Artifact and Canon* (ed. Craig A. Evans and H. Daniel Zacharias; Library of Second Temple Studies; London: T. & T. Clark, 2009), pp. 220-31.

Aune, David E., 'The Form and Function of the Proclamations to the Seven Churches (Revelation 2–3)', *New Testament Studies* 36 (1990), pp. 182-204.

Balás, David, 'Marcion Revisited: A "Post-Harnack" Perspective', in *Texts and Testaments: Critical Essays on the Bible and Early Church Fathers* (ed. W. Eugene March; San Antonio, TX: Trinity University Press, 1980), pp. 95-108.

Balla, Peter, 'Evidence for an Early Christian Canon (Second and Third Century)', in *The Canon Debate* (ed. Lee M. McDonald and James A. Sanders; Peabody, MA: Hendrickson, 2002), pp. 372-85.

Barr, David L., 'The Apocalypse as a Symbolic Transformation of the World: A Literary Analysis', *Interpretation* 38 (1984), pp. 39-50.

—'The Story John Told: Reading Revelation for its Plot', in *Reading the Book of Revelation* (ed. David L. Barr; Atlanta, GA: Society of Biblical Literature, 2003), pp. 11-24.

Barrera, Julio C.T., 'Origins of a Tripartite Canon', in *The Canon Debate* (ed. Lee M. McDonald and James A. Sanders; Peabody, MA: Hendrickson, 2002), pp. 128-45.

Barthes, Roland, 'From Work to Text', in *Image–Music–Text* (trans. Stephen Heath; London: Fontana, 1977), pp. 155-64.

—'The Death of the Author', in *Image–Music–Text* (trans. Stephen Heath; London: Fontana, 1977), pp. 142-48.

—'Theory of the Text', in *Untying the Text: A Post-Structuralist Reader* (ed. Robert Young; London and New York: Routledge and Kegan Paul, 1981), pp. 31-47.

Barton, John, 'What is a Book? Modern Exegesis and the Literary Conventions of Ancient Israel', in *Intertextuality in Ugarit and Israel: Papers Read at the Tenth Joint Meeting of the Society for Old Testament Study & Het Oudtestamentisch Werkgezelschap in Nederland & België, Held at Oxford, 1997* (ed. Johannes C. de Moor; Leiden: Brill, 1998), pp. 1-14.

—'Marcion Revisited', in *The Canon Debate* (ed. Lee M. McDonald and James A. Sanders; Peabody, MA: Hendrickson, 2002), pp. 341-54.

—'Canonical Approaches Ancient and Modern', in *The Biblical Canons* (ed. J.M. Auwers and H.J. de Jonge; Leuven: Leuven University Press, 2003), pp. 199-209.

Bauckham, Richard, 'For Whom Were the Gospels Written?', in *The Gospels for All Christians: Rethinking the Gospel Audiences* (ed. Richard Bauckham; Grand Rapids, MI: Eerdmans, 1998), pp. 9-48.

—'John for Readers of Mark', in *The Gospels for All Christians: Rethinking the Gospel Audiences* (ed. Richard Bauckham; Grand Rapids, MI: Eerdmans, 1998), pp. 147-71.

Bauer, D.R., 'Son of David', in *Dictionary of Jesus and the Gospels* (ed. Joel B. Green and Scott McKnight; Downers Grove, IL: InterVarsity Press, 1992), pp. 766-69.

Beale, G.K., 'Did Jesus and His Followers Preach the Right Doctrine from the Wrong Texts?', *Themelios* 14 (1989), pp. 89-96.

Beale, G.K., and Sean M. McDonough, 'Revelation', in *Commentary on the New Testament Use of the Old Testament* (ed. G.K. Beale and D.A. Carson; Grand Rapids, MI: Baker, 2007), pp. 1081-1162.

Beardsley, Monroe C., 'Textual Meaning and Authorial Meaning', *Genre* 1 (1968), pp.169-81.

—'Intentions and Interpretations: A Fallacy Revived', in *The Aesthetic Point of View: Selected Essays* (ed. Michael J. Wreen and Donald M. Callen; Ithaca, NY: Cornell University Press, 1982), pp. 188-207.

—'The Authority of the Text', in *Intention and Interpretation* (ed. Gary Iseminger; Philadelphia, PA: Temple University Press, 1992), pp. 24-40.

Ben-Porat, Ziva, 'The Poetics of Literary Allusion', *PTL: A Journal for Descriptive Poetics and Theory of Literature* 1 (1978), pp. 105-28.

Best, Ernest, 'Scripture, Tradition, and the Canon of the New Testament', *Bulletin of the John Rylands Library* 61 (1979), pp. 258-89.

Beyer, Hermann Wolfgang, 'Κανών', in *Theological Dictionary of the New Testament* (ed. Gerhard Kittel and Geoffrey W. Bromiley; trans. Geoffrey W. Bromiley; 10 vol.; Grand Rapids, MI: Eerdmans, 1965), III, pp. 96-602.

Biddle, Mark E., 'Obadiah-Jonah-Micah in Canonical Context: The Nature of Prophetic Literature and Hermeneutics', *Interpretation* 61 (2007), pp. 154-66.

Bleich, David, 'Epistemological Assumptions in the Study of Response', in *Reader-Response Criticism: From Formalism to Post-Structuralism* (ed. Jane P. Tompkins; Baltimore, MD: The Johns Hopkins University Press, 1980), pp. 134-63.

Blowers, Paul M., 'The *Regula Fidei* and the Narrative Character of Early Christian Faith', *Pro Ecclesia* 6 (1997), pp. 199-228.

Bockmuehl, Markus, 'Reason, Wisdom and the Implied Disciple of Scripture', in *Reading Texts, Seeking Wisdom: Scripture and Theology* (ed. David F. Ford and Graham N. Stanton; London: SCM Press, 2003), pp. 53-68.

—'Why Not Let Acts Be Acts? In Conversation with C. Kavin Rowe', *JSNT* 28 (2005), pp. 163-66.

Brakke, David, 'Canon Formation and Social Conflict in Fourth-Century Egypt: Athanasius of Alexandria's Thirty-Ninth *Festal Letter*', *Harvard Theological Review* 87 (1994), pp. 395-419.

—'A New Fragment of Athanasius's Thirty-Ninth *Festal Letter*: Heresy, Apocrypha, and the Canon', *Harvard Theological Review* 103 (2010), pp. 47-66.

Brawley, R.L., 'Canonical Coherence in Reading Israel's Scriptures with a Sequel', in *The Biblical Canons* (ed. J.M. Auwers and H.J. de Jonge; Leuven: Leuven University Press, 2003), pp. 627-34.

Bray, Gerald, 'Biblical Theology and From Where it Came', *Southwestern Journal of Theology* 55 (2013), pp. 193-208.

Breck, John, 'John 21: Appendix, Epilogue, or Conclusion?', *St. Vladimir's Theological Quarterly* 36 (1992), pp. 27-49.

Brodie, Thomas L., Dennis R. MacDonald and Stanley E. Porter, 'Introduction: Tracing the Development of the Epistles—The Potential and the Problem', in *The Intertextuality of the Epistles: Exploration of Theory and Practice* (ed. Thomas L. Brodie, Dennis R. MacDonald and Stanley E. Porter; New Testament Monographs, 16; Sheffield: Sheffield Phoenix Press, 2006), pp. 1-9.

Brown, Jeannine K., 'Direct Engagement of the Reader in Matthew's Discourses: Rhetorical Techniques and Scholarly Consensus', *New Testament Studies* 51 (2005), pp. 19-35.

Bruce, F.F., 'Some Thoughts on the Beginning of the New Testament Canon', *Bulletin of the John Rylands University Library* 65 (1982–83), pp. 37-60.

—'Harnack, Adolf', in *New Dictionary of Theology* (ed. Sinclair Ferguson and David Wright; Downers Grove, IL: InterVarsity Press, 1988), pp. 286-87.

Budde, A., 'Der Abschluß des Alttestamentlichen Kanons und seine Bedeutung für die Kanonische Schriftauslegung', *Biblische Notizen* 87 (1997), pp. 39-55.

Chapman, Stephen B., 'Reclaiming Inspiration for the Bible', in *Canon and Biblical Interpretation* (ed. Craig G. Bartholomew, Scott Hahn, Robin Parry, Christopher Seitz and Al Wolters; Scripture and Hermeneutics Series, 7; Grand Rapids, MI: Zondervan, 2006), pp. 167-206.

—'What Are We Reading? Canonicity and the Old Testament', *Word and World* 29 (2009), pp. 334-47.

—'The Canon Debate: What It Is and Why It Matters', *Journal of Theological Interpretation* 4 (2010), pp. 273-94.

Charlesworth, James H., 'Writings Ostensibly Outside the Canon', in *Exploring the Origins of the Bible: Canon Formation in Historical, Literary, and Theological Perspective* (ed. Craig A. Evans and Emanuel Tov; Grand Rapids, MI: Baker, 2008), pp. 57-86.

Charlesworth, Scott, 'T.C. Skeat, P⁶⁴⁺⁶⁷ and P⁴, and the Problem of Fibre Orientation in Codicological Reconstruction', *New Testament Studies* 53 (2007), pp. 582-604.

—'Public and Private—Second- and Third-Century Gospel Manuscripts', in *Jewish and Christian Scripture as Artifact and Canon* (ed. Craig A. Evans and H. Daniel Zacharias; London: T. & T. Clark, 2009), pp. 148-75.

—'Indicators of "Catholicity" in Early Gospel Manuscripts', in *The Early Text of the New Testament* (ed. Charles E. Hill and Michael J. Kruger; Oxford: Oxford University Press, 2012), pp. 37-48.

Childs, Brevard S., 'Reflections on the Modern Study of the Psalms', in *Magnalia Dei: The Mighty Acts of God. Essays on Bible and Archaeology in Memory of G.E. Wright* (ed. Frank Moore Cross, Werner E. Lemke and Patrick D. Miller, Jr; New York: Doubleday, 1976), pp. 377-88.

—'The Exegetical Significance of Canon for the Study of the Old Testament', *Vestus Testamentum Supplements* 29 (1977), pp. 66-80.

—'Retrospective Reading of the Old Testament Prophets', *Zeitschrift für die Alttestamentliche Wissenschaft* 108 (1996), pp. 362-77.

—'The Nature of the Christian Bible: One Book, Two Testaments', in *The Rule of Faith: Scripture, Canon, and Creed in a Critical Age* (ed. Ephraim Radner and George Sumner; Harrisburg, PA: Morehouse Publishers, 1998), pp. 115-25.

—'The One Gospel in Four Witnesses', in *The Rule of Faith: Scripture, Canon, and Creed in a Critical Age* (ed. Ephraim Radner and George Sumner; Harrisburg, PA: Morehouse Publishers, 1998), pp. 51-62.

—'Critique of Recent Intertextual Canonical Interpretation', *Zeitschriftfürdie Alttestamentliche Wissenschaft* 115 (2003), pp. 173-84.

—'The Canon in Recent Biblical Studies: Reflections on an Era', in *Canon and Biblical Interpretation* (ed. Craig G. Bartholomew, Scott Hahn, Robin Parry, Christopher Seitz and Al Wolters; Scripture and Hermeneutics Series, 7; Grand Rapids, MI: Zondervan, 2006), pp. 33-57.

Clarke, Kent D., 'Canonical Criticism: An Integrated Reading of Biblical Texts for the Community of Faith', in *Approaches to New Testament Study* (ed. Stanley E. Porter and David Tombs; Journal for the Study of the New Testament Supplement Series, 120; Sheffield: Sheffield Academic Press, 1995), pp. 170-221.

Collini, Stefan, 'Introduction: Interpretation Terminable and Interminable', in *Interpretation and Overinterpretation* (ed. Stefan Collini; Cambridge: Cambridge University Press, 1992), pp. 1-22.

Comfort, Philip W., 'Exploring the Common Identification of Three New Testament Manuscripts: P[4], P[64], P[67]', *Tyndale Bulletin* 46 (1995), pp. 43-54.

—'New Reconstructions and Identifications of New Testament Papyri', *Novum Testamentum* 41 (1999), pp. 214-30.

Culler, Jonathan, 'Literary Competence', in *Reader-Response Criticism: From Formalism to Post-Structuralism* (ed. Jane P. Tompkins; Baltimore, MD: The Johns Hopkins University Press, 1980), pp. 101-17.

Dahl, Nils A., 'The Particularity of the Pauline Epistles as a Problem in the Ancient Church', in *Neotestamentica et Patristica* (ed. A.N. Wilder, *et al.*; Leiden: Brill, 1962), pp. 261-71.

Dempster, Stephen G., 'Canon and Old Testament Interpretation', in *Hearing The Old Testament: Listening for God's Address* (ed. Craig G. Bartholomew and David J.H. Beldman; Grand Rapids, MI: Eerdmans, 2012), pp. 154-79.

—'An "Extraordinary Fact": Torah and Temple and the Contours of the Hebrew Canon, Part 1', *Tyndale Bulletin* 48 (1997), pp. 23-56.

—'An "Extraordinary Fact": Torah and Temple and the Contours of the Hebrew Canon, Part 2', *Tyndale Bulletin* 48 (1997), pp. 191-218.

—'From Many Texts to One: The Formation of the Hebrew Bible', in *The World of the Aramaeans. I. Biblical Studies in Honour of Paul-Eugène Dion* (ed. P.M. Michèle Daviau, John W. Wevers and Michael Weigl; Sheffield: Sheffield Academic Press, 2001), pp. 19-56.

—'Geography and Genealogy, Dominion and Dynasty: A Theology of the Hebrew Bible', in *Biblical Theology: Retrospect and Prospect* (ed. Scott J. Hafemann; Downers Grove, IL: InterVarsity Press, 2002), pp. 66-82.

—'The Place of Nehemiah in the Canon of Scripture: Wise Builder', *Southern Baptist Journal of Theology* 9 (2005), pp. 38-50.

—'The Prophets, the Canon and a Canonical Approach: No Empty Word', in *Canon and Biblical Interpretation* (ed. Craig G. Bartholomew, Scott Hahn, Robin Parry, Christopher Seitz and Al Wolters;. Scripture and Hermeneutics Series, 7; Grand Rapids, MI: Zondervan, 2006), pp. 293-329.

—'Torah, Torah, Torah: The Emergence of the Tripartite Canon', in *Exploring the Origins of the Bible: Canon Formation in Historical, Literary, and Theological*

Perspective (ed. Craig Evans and Emanuel Tov; Grand Rapids, MI: Baker, 2008), pp. 87-128.

—'Canons on the Right and Canons on the Left: Finding a Resolution in the Canon Debate', *Journal of the Evangelical Theological Society* 52 (2009), pp. 47-77.

Dickie, George, and W. Kent Wilson, 'The Intentional Fallacy: Defending Beardsley', *The Journal of Aesthetics and Art Criticism* 53 (1995), pp. 233-50.

Diebner, Bernd Jørg, 'Zur Funktion der Kanonischen Textsammlung im Judentum der vor-christlichen Zeit: Gedanken zu einer Kanon-Hermeneutik', *Dielheimer Blätter zum Alten Testament* 22 (1985–1986), pp. 58-73.

Donne, John, 'Meditation XVII', in *The Works of John Donne, D. D., Dean of Saint Paul's 1621–1631. With a Memoir of His Life* (ed. Henry Alford; London: John W. Parker, 1839), pp. 574-75.

Driver, Daniel R., 'Later Childs', *Princeton Theological Review* 38 (2008), pp. 117-29.

—Review of *Der Bibelkanon in der Bibelauslegung: Methodenreflexionen und Beispiel-exegesen* (ed. Egbert Ballhorn and Georg Steins; Stuttgart: Kohlhammer, 2007), in *Review of Biblical Literature* (2008), http://www.bookreviews.org/pdf/6401_6893. pdf.

Dungan, David L., 'The New Testament Canon in Recent Study', *Interpretation* 29 (1975), pp. 339-51.

Dunn, James D.G., 'Has the Canon a Continuing Function?', in *The Canon Debate* (ed. Lee M. McDonald and James A. Sanders; Peabody, MA: Hendrickson Publishers, 2002), pp. 558-79.

—'How the New Testament Began', in *From Biblical Criticism to Biblical Faith* (ed. William H. Brackney and Craig A. Evans; Macon, GA: Mercer University Press, 2007), pp. 122-37.

Dworkin, Craig, 'Textual Prostheses', *Comparative Literature* 57 (2005), pp. 1-24.

Eco, Umberto, '*Intentio Lectoris:* The State of the Art', in *The Limits of Interpretation* (Bloomington, IN: Indiana University Press, 1994), pp. 44-63.

—'Intertextual Irony and Levels of Reading', in *Umberto Eco on Literature* (Orlando, FL: Harcourt, 2004), pp. 212-35.

Edwards, Sarah Alexander, 'P75 Under the Magnifying Glass', *Novum Testamentum* 18 (1976), pp. 190-212.

Eisenstein, Sergei, 'Methods of Montage', in *Film Form: Essays in Film Theory* (ed. and trans. Jay Leyda; San Diego, CA: Harcourt, 1969), pp. 72-83.

Elliott, J.K., 'Manuscripts, the Codex and the Canon', *JSNT* 63 (1996), pp. 105-23.

—'Singular Readings in the Gospel Text of P⁴⁵', in *The Earliest Gospels: The Origins and Transmission of the Earliest Christian Gospels—The Contribution of the Chester Beatty Gospel Codex P45* (ed. Charles Horton; Journal for the Study of the New Testament Supplement Series, 258; London: T. & T. Clark, 2004), pp. 122-31.

Eslinger, Lyle M., 'Inner-Biblical Exegesis and Inner-Biblical Allusion: The Question of Category', *Vetus Testamentum* 42 (1992), pp. 47-58.

Ewald, Helen Rothschild, 'The Implied Reader in Persuasive Discourse', *Journal of Advanced Composition* 8 (1988), pp. 167-78.

Farkasfalvy, Denis, 'The Apostolic Gospels in the Early Church: The Concept of Canon and the Formation of the Four-Gospel Canon', in *Canon and Biblical Interpretation* (ed. Craig G. Bartholomew, Scott Hahn, Robin Parry, Christopher Seitz and Al Wolters; Scripture and Hermeneutics Series, 7; Grand Rapids, MI: Zondervan, 2006), pp. 111-22.

Fekkes, Jan, '"His Bride Has Prepared Herself": Revelation 19–21 and Isaian Nuptial Imagery', *Journal of Biblical Literature* 109 (1990), pp. 269-87.

Fensham, F.C., 'Common Trends in Curses of the Near Eastern Treaties and Kudurru-Inscriptions Compared with Maledictions of Amos and Isaiah', *Zeitschrift für die Alttestamentliche Wissenschaft* 75 (1963), pp. 155-75.

Ferguson, Everret, 'Canon Muratori: Date and Provenance', *Studia Patristica 17* (ed. Elizabeth Livingstone; Elmsford, NY: Pergamon, 1982), pp. 677-83.

—'Factors Leading to the Selection and Closure of the New Testament Canon: A Survey of Some Recent Studies', in *The Canon Debate* (ed. Lee M. McDonald and James A. Sanders; Peabody, MA: Hendrickson Publishers, 2002), pp. 295-320.

Fiddes, Paul, 'The Canon as Space and Place', in *Die Einheit der Schrift und die Vielfalt des Kanons: The Unity of Scripture and the Diversity of the Canon* (ed. John Barton and Michael Wolter; Berlin: W. de Gruyter, 2003), pp. 127-50.

Fish, Stanley, 'Literature in the Reader: Affective Stylistics', in *Reader-Response Criticism: From Formalism to Post-Structuralism* (ed. Jane P. Tompkins; Baltimore, MD: The Johns Hopkins University Press, 1980), pp. 70-100.

—'Why No One's Afraid of Wolfgang Iser', in *Doing What Comes Naturally: Change, Rhetoric, and the Practice of Theory in Literary and Legal Studies* (Oxford: Clarendon Press, 1989), pp. 68-86.

Fishbane, Michael, 'Revelation and Tradition: Aspects of Inner-Biblical Exegesis', *Journal of Biblical Literature* 99 (1980), pp. 343-61.

—'Inner Biblical Exegesis: Types and Strategies of Interpretation in Ancient Israel', in *The Garments of Torah: Essays in Biblical Hermeneutics* (ed. Michael Fishbane; Bloomington, IN: Indiana University Press, 1992), pp. 3-18.

—'The Hebrew Bible and Exegetical Tradition', in *Intertextuality in Ugarit and Israel: Papers Read at the Tenth Joint Meeting of the Society for Old Testament Study & Het Oudtestamentisch Werkgezelschap in Nederland & België, Held at Oxford, 1997* (ed. Johannes C. de Moor; Leiden: Brill, 1998), pp. 15-30.

Fernflores, Rachael, 'Beyond the Intentional Fallacy', *Literature and Aesthetics* 20 (2010), pp. 56-73.

Fox, Douglas E., 'Ben Sira on OT Canon Again: The Date of Daniel', *Westminster Theological Journal* 49 (1987), pp. 335-50.

Friedman, Susanne, 'Weavings: Intertextuality and the (Re)Birth of the Author', in *Influence and Intertextuality in Literary History* (ed. J. Clayton and E. Rothstein; Madison, WI: University of Wisconsin Press, 1991), pp. 146-80.

Friedrich, Gerhard, 'Εὐαγγέλιον', in *Theological Dictionary of the New Testament* (10 vols.; ed. Gerhard Kittel; trans. and ed. Geoffrey W. Bromiley; Grand Rapids, MI: Eerdmans, 1965), II, pp. 715-35.

Funk, Robert W., 'The Once and Future New Testament', in *The Canon Debate* (ed. Lee M. McDonald and James A. Sanders; Peabody, MA: Hendrickson Publishers, 2002), pp. 541-57.

Gamble, Harry Y., 'The Redaction of the Pauline Letters and the Formation of the Pauline Corpus', *Journal of Biblical Literature* 94 (1975), pp. 403-18.

—'The New Testament Canon: Recent Research and the *Status Quaestionis*', in *The Canon Debate* (ed. Lee M. McDonald and James A. Sanders; Peabody, MA: Hendrickson Publishers, 2002), pp. 267-94.

—'Book Trade in the Roman Empire', in *The Early Text of the New Testament* (ed. Charles E. Hill and Michael J. Kruger; Oxford: Oxford University Press, 2012), pp. 23-36.

Geitner, Ursula, 'Allographie: Autorschaft und Paratext—im Fall der *Portugiesischen Briefe*', in *Paratexte in Literatur, Film, Fernsehen* (ed. Klaus Kreimeier and Georg Stanitzek; Berlin: Akademie Verlag, 2004), pp. 55-99.

Genette, Gérard, 'The Proustian Paratexte', *SubStance: A Review of Theory and Literary Criticism* 17 (1988), pp. 63-77.

—'Introduction to the Paratext', trans. Marie Maclean, *New Literary History* 22 (1991), pp. 261-72.

Gibson, Walker, 'Authors, Speakers, Readers, and Mock Readers', *College English* 11 (1950), pp. 263-69.

Gillmayr-Bucher, Susanne, 'The Psalm Headings: A Canonical Reflecture of the Psalms', in *The Biblical Canons* (ed. J.M. Auwers and H.J. de Jonge; Leuven: Leuven University Press, 2003), pp. 247-54.

—'Intertextuality: Between Literary Theory and Text Analysis', in *The Intertextuality of the Epistles: Explorations of Theory and Practice* (ed. Thomas L. Brodie, Dennis R. MacDonald and Stanley E. Porter; New Testament Monographs, 16; Sheffield: Sheffield Academic Press, 2006), pp. 13-23.

Glueck, J.J., 'Some Remarks on the Introductory Notes of the Psalms', in *Studies of the Psalms* (Potchefstroom: Pro Rege, 1963), pp. 30-39.

Goshen-Gottstein, Alon, 'Ben Sira's Praise of the Fathers: A Canon-Conscious Reading', in *Ben Sira's God: Proceedings of the International Ben Sira Conference* (ed. Renate Egger-Wenzel; Berlin: W. de Gruyter, 2002), pp. 235-67.

Goswell, Greg, 'The Order of Books in the Greek Old Testament', *Journal of the Evangelical Theological Society* 52 (2009), pp. 449-66.

—'The Order of Books in the Hebrew Bible', *Journal of the Evangelical Theological Society* 51 (2008), pp. 673-88.

—'The Order of the Books of the New Testament', *Journal of the Evangelical Theological Society* 53 (2010), pp. 225-41.

Grant, Robert M., 'Literary Criticism and the New Testament Canon', *Journal for the Study of the New Testament* 16 (1982), pp. 24-44.

Green, Joel B., 'Discourse Analysis and New Testament Interpretation', in *Hearing the New Testament* (ed. Joel B. Green; Grand Rapids, MI: Eerdmans, 1995), pp. 175-96.

—'Practicing The Gospel in a Post-Critical World: The Promise of Theological Exegesis', *Journal of the Evangelical Theological Society* 47 (2004), pp. 387-97.

—'Context', in *Dictionary for Theological Interpretation of the Bible* (ed. Kevin J. Vanhoozer; Grand Rapids, MI: Baker, 2005), pp. 330-33.

Green-McCreight, Kathryn, 'Rule of Faith', in *Dictionary for Theological Interpretation of the Bible* (ed. Kevin J. Vanhoozer; Grand Rapids, MI: Baker, 2005), pp. 703-704.

Gregory, Andrew F., '*1 Clement* and the Writings that Later Formed the New Testament', in *The Reception of the New Testament in the Apostolic Fathers* (ed. Andrew Gregory and Christopher Tuckett; Oxford: Oxford University Press, 2005), pp. 129-57.

Hahneman, Geoffrey Mark, 'The Muratorian Fragment and the Origins of the New Testament Canon', in *The Canon Debate* (ed. Lee M. McDonald and James A. Sanders; Peabody, MA: Hendrickson Publishers, 2002), pp. 405-15.

Hamilton, James M., 'Still Sola Scriptura: An Evangelical View of Scripture', in *The Sacred Text: Excavating the Texts, Exploring the Interpretations, and Engaging the Theologies of the Christian Scriptures* (ed. Michael Bird and Michael Pahl; Piscataway, NJ: Gorgias Press, 2010), pp. 215-40.

Harris, R. Laird., 'Chronicles and the Canon in New Testament Times', *Journal of the Evangelical Theological Society* 33 (1990), pp. 75-85.

Hatch, William H.P., 'The Position of Hebrews in the Canon of the New Testament', *The Harvard Theological Review* 29 (1936), pp. 133-51.

Hays, Richard B., 'On the Rebound: A Response to Critiques of *Echoes of Scripture in the Letters of Paul*', in *Paul and the Scriptures of Israel* (ed. Craig A. Evans and James A. Sanders; Journal for the Study of the New Testament Supplement Series, 83; Sheffield: Sheffield Academic Press, 1993), pp. 70-96.

—'Can the Gospels Teach Us How to Read the Old Testament?', *Pro Ecclesia* 11 (2002), pp. 402-18.

—'The Liberation of Israel in Luke–Acts: Intertextual Narration as Countercultural Practice', in *Reading the Bible Intertextually* (ed. Stefan Alkier, Leroy A. Huizenga, and Richard Hays; Waco, TX: Baylor University Press, 2009), pp. 101-17.

Head, Peter M., 'Is P⁴, P⁶⁴ and P⁶⁷ the Oldest Manuscript of the Four Gospels? A Response to T.C. Skeat', *New Testament Studies* 51 (2005), pp. 450-57.

—'Graham Stanton and the Four-Gospel Codex: Reconsidering the Manuscript Evidence', in *Jesus, Matthew's Gospel and Early Christianity: Studies in Memory of Graham N. Stanton* (ed. Daniel M. Gurtner, Joel Willitts and Richard A. Burridge; Library of New Testament Studies; London: T. & T. Clark, 2011), pp. 93-101.

Hengel, Martin, 'The Four Gospels and the One Gospel of Jesus Christ', in *The Earliest Gospels: The Origins and Transmission of the Earliest Christian Gospels—The Contribution of the Chester Beatty Gospel Codex P45* (ed. Charles Horton; Journal for the Study of the New Testament Supplement Series, 258; London: T. & T. Clark, 2004), pp. 13-26.

Henry, Carl F.H., 'Canonical Theology: An Evangelical Appraisal', *The Scottish Bulletin of Evangelical Theology* 8 (1990), pp. 76-108.

Heard, Richard, 'The ΑΠΟΜΝΗΜΟΝΕΥΜΑΤΑ in Papias, Justin, and Irenaeus', *New Testament Studies* 1 (1954), pp. 122-33.

Hernández, Jr, Juan, 'The Early Text of Luke', in *The Early Text of the New Testament* (ed. Charles E. Hill and Michael J. Kruger; Oxford: Oxford University Press, 2012), pp. 121-39.

Hertzberg, H.W., 'Die Nachgeschichte Alttestamentlicher Texte Innerhalb des Alten Testaments', *Beihefte Zur Zeitschrift Fur Die Alttestamentliche Wissenschaft* 66 (1936), pp. 110-21.

Hieke, Thomas, 'Biblos Geneseos—Mt 1,1 vom Buch Genesis her gelesen', in *The Biblical Canons* (ed. J.M. Auwers and H.J. de Jonge; Leuven: Leuven University Press, 2003), pp. 635-50.

—'Biblische Texte als Texte der Bibel auslegen—Dargestellt am Beispiel von Offb 22, 6-21 und anderen kanonrelevanten Texten', in *Der Bibelkanon in der Bibelauslegung: Methodenreflexionen und Beispielexegesen* (ed. Egbert Ballhorn and Georg Steins; Stuttgart: Kohlhammer, 2007), pp. 331-45.

Hill, Charles E., 'The Debate Over the Muratorian Fragment and the Development of the Canon', *Westminster Journal of Theology* 57 (1995), pp. 437-52.

—'Justin and the New Testament Writings', *Studia Patristica* 30 (1997), pp. 42-48.

—'What Papias Said About John (and Luke): A New Papias Fragment', *Journal of Theological Studies* 49 (1998), pp. 582-629.

—'Was John's Gospel Among Justin's Apostolic Memoirs?', in *Justin Martyr and His Worlds* (ed. Sara Parvis and Paul Foster; Minneapolis, MN: Fortress Press, 2007), pp. 88-94.

—'God's Speech in These Last Days: The New Testament Canon as an Eschatological Phenomenon', in *Resurrection and Eschatology. Theology in Service of the Church. Essays in Honor of Richard B. Gaffin Jr* (ed. Lane G. Tipton and Jeffrey C. Waddington; Phillipsburg, NJ: P & R, 2008), pp. 203-54.

—'The New Testament Canon: Deconstructio Ad Absurdum?', *Journal of the Evangelical Theological Society* 52 (2009), pp. 101-19.

—'Skeat's Thesis, Not Dead Yet? On the Making of P⁴, P⁶⁴, and P⁶⁷', paper presented at the 2010 meeting of the Society of Biblical Literature, Atalanta, GA.

—'Intersections of Jewish and Christian Scribal Culture: The Original Codex Containing P⁴, P⁶⁴, and P⁶⁷, and its Implications', in *Among Jews, Gentiles, and Christians in Antiquity and the Middle Ages* (ed. R. Hvalvik and J. Kaufman; Trondheim: Tapir Academic Press, 2011), pp. 75-91.

—'"In These Very Words": Methods and Standards of Literary Borrowing in the Second Century', in *The Early Text of the New Testament* (ed. Charles E. Hill and Michael J. Kruger; Oxford: Oxford University Press, 2012), pp. 261-81.

Hill, Robert C., 'St John Chrysostom: Preacher on the Old Testament', *Greek Orthodox Theological Review* 46 (2001), pp. 267-86.

Hirsch, E.D., Jr, 'Objective Interpretation', *Publications of the Modern Language Association of America* 75 (1960), pp. 463-79.

—'Current Issues in Theory of Interpretation', *Journal of Religion* 55 (1975), pp. 298-312.

—'Meaning and Significance Reinterpreted', *Critical Inquiry* 11 (1984), pp. 202-25.

—'Transhistorical Intentions and the Persistence of Allegory', *New Literary History* 25 (1994), pp. 549-67.

Höffken, Peter, 'Zum Kanonbewusstsein des Josephus Flavius in *Contra Apionem* und in den *Antiquitates*', *Journal for the Study of Judaism in the Persian, Hellenistic and Roman Periods* 32 (2001), pp. 159-77.

Holmes, Michael W., 'The Biblical Canon', in *The Oxford Handbook of Early Christian Studies* (ed. Susan Ashbrook Harvey and David G. Hunter; Oxford: Oxford University Press, 2008), pp. 406-26.

Hurtado, Larry W., 'Review of *Die Endredaktion des Neuen Testaments: Eine Untersuchung zur Entstehung der Christlichen Bibel* (Göttingen: Vandenhoeck & Ruprecht, 1996), by David Trobisch', *Journal of Theological Studies* 50 (1999), pp. 288-91.

—'The Earliest Evidence of an Emerging Christian Material and Visual Culture: The Codex, the *Nomina Sacra* and the Staurogram', in *Text and Artifact in the Religions of Mediterranean Antiquity: Essays in Honour of Peter Richardson* (ed. Stephen G. Wilson and Michel Desjardins; Waterloo, Ontario: Wilfrid Laurier University Press, 2000), pp. 271-88.

—'P⁴⁵ and the Textual History of the Gospel of Mark', in *The Earliest Gospels: The Origins and Transmission of the Earliest Christian Gospels—The Contribution of the Chester Beatty Gospel Codex P45* (ed. Charles Horton; Journal for the Study of the New Testament Supplement Series, 258; London: T. & T. Clark, 2004), pp. 132-48.

—'The New Testament in the Second Century: Text, Collections and Canon', in *Transmission and Reception: New Testament Text-Critical and Exegetical Studies* (ed. J.W. Childers and D.C. Parker; Piscataway, NJ: Gorgias Press, 2006), pp. 3-27.

—'The "Meta-Data" of Earliest Christian Manuscripts', in *Identity and Interaction in the Ancient Mediterranean. Jews, Christians and Others: Essays in Honour of Stephen G. Wilson* (ed. Zeba A. Crook and Philip A. Harland; Sheffield: Sheffield Phoenix Press, 2007), pp. 149-63.

—'Manuscripts and the Sociology of Early Christian Reading', in *The Early Text of the New Testament* (ed. Charles E. Hill and Michael J. Kruger; Oxford: Oxford University Press, 2012), pp. 49-62.

Iser, Wolfgang, 'Indeterminacy and the Reader's Response in Prose Fiction', in *Aspects of Narrative: Selected Papers from the English Institute* (ed. J. Hillis Miller; New York: Columbia University Press, 1971), pp. 1-45.

—'The Reading Process: A Phenomenological Approach', in *Reader-Response Criticism: From Formalism to Post-Structuralism* (ed. Jane P. Tompkins; Baltimore, MD: The Johns Hopkins University Press, 1980), pp. 50-69.

—'Talk Like Whales: A Reply to Stanly Fish', *Diacritics* 11 (1981), pp. 82-87.

Jenny, Laurent, 'The Strategy of Forms', in *French Literary Theory Today: A Reader* (ed. T. Todorov; Cambridge: Cambridge University Press, 1982), pp. 34-63.

Kalin, Everett R., 'Early Traditions About Mark's Gospel: Canonical Status Emerges as the Story Grows', *Currents in Theology and Mission* 2 (1975), pp. 332-41.

—'Re-Examining New Testament Canon History, 1: The Canon of Origen', *Currents in Theology and Mission* 17 (1990), pp. 274-82.

—'The New Testament Canon of Eusebius', in *The Canon Debate* (ed. Lee M. McDonald and James A. Sanders; Peabody, MA: Hendrickson Publishers, 2002), pp. 386-404.

Karrer, Von Martin, 'Septuagint Deutsch—eine theologische Herausforderung', *Kerygma und Dogma* 55 (2009), pp. 276-95.

Kingsbury, Jack D., 'The Title "Son of David" in Matthew's Gospel', *Journal of Biblical Literature* 95 (1976), pp. 591-602.

—'The Gospel in Four Editions', *Interpretation* 33 (1979), pp. 363-75.

Knowles, Michael P., 'Scripture, History, Messiah: Scriptural Fulfillment and the Fullness of Time in Matthew's Gospel', in *Hearing the Old Testament in the New Testament* (ed. Stanley E. Porter; Grand Rapids, MI: Eerdmans, 2006), pp. 59-82.

Köhlmoos, Melanie, 'Kanon und Methode: Zu einer Zwischenbilanz der "Kanonischen Auslegung"', *Theologische Rundschau* 74 (2009), pp. 135-46.

Koorevaar, Hendrik J., 'Die Chronik als intendierter Abschluß des alttestamentlichen Kanons', *Jahrbuch für Evangelikale Theologie* 11 (1997), pp. 42-76.

—'The Torah Model as Original Macrostructure of the Hebrew Canon: A Critical Evaluation', *Zeitschrift für die alttestamentliche Wissenschaft* 122 (2010), pp. 65-80.

Koptak, Paul E., 'Intertextuality', in *Dictionary for Theological Interpretation of the Bible* (ed. Kevin J. Vanhoozer; Grand Rapids, MI: Baker, 2005), pp. 332-34.

Köstenberger, Andreas, 'The Present and Future of Biblical Theology', *Themelios* 37 (2012), pp. 445-64.

Kraft, Heinrich, 'Das besondere Selbstbewußtsein der Verfasser der Neutestamentlichen Schriften', in *Moderne Exegese und historische Wissenschaft* (ed. J.M. Hollenbach and Hugo Staudinger; Trier: Spee-Verlag, 1972), pp. 77-93.

Kraft, Robert A., 'The Codex and Canon Consciousness', in *The Canon Debate* (ed. Lee M. McDonald and James A. Sanders; Peabody, MA: Hendrickson Publishers, 2002), pp. 229-33.

—'Para-mania: Beside, Before and Beyond Bible Studies', *Journal of Biblical Literature* 126 (2007), pp. 5-27.

Krieg, Carola, 'Javne und der Kanon. Klärungen', in *Kanonisierung—die Hebräische Bibel im Werden* (ed. Georg Steins and Johannes Taschner; Biblisch-Theologische Studien, 110; Göttingen: Neukirchener Theologie, 2010), pp. 133-52.

Kristeva, Julia, 'Word, Dialogue, and Novel', in *The Kristeva Reader* (ed. Toril Moi;

trans. Leon S. Roudiez and Sean Hand; New York: Columbia University Press, 1986), pp. 34-61.

Kruger, Michael J., 'Deconstructing Canon: Recent Challenges to the Origins and Authority of the New Testament Writings', in *Did God Really Say? Affirming the Truthfulness and Trustworthiness of Scripture* (ed. David B. Garner; Phillipsburg, NJ: P&R Publishing, 2012), pp. 49-70.

—'Early Christian Attitudes Toward the Reproduction of Texts', in *The Early Text of the New Testament* (ed. Charles E. Hill and Michael J. Kruger; Oxford: Oxford University Press, 2012), pp. 63-80.

—'The Definition of the Term "Canon": Exclusive or Multi-Dimensional?', *Tyndale Bulletin* 63 (2012), pp. 1-20.

Kuppers, Petra, 'Dialectic and Dialectical Montage', in *Critical Dictionary of Film and Television Theory* (ed. Roberta E. Pearson and Philip Simpson; London and New York: Routledge, 2001), pp. 130-33.

Leschert, Dale, 'A Change of Meaning, Not a Change of Mind: The Clarification of a Suspected Defection in the Hermeneutical Theory of E.D. Hirsch, Jr.', *Journal of the Evangelical Society* 35 (1992), 183-87.

Leonard, Jeffery M., 'Identifying Inner-Biblical Allusions: Psalm 78 as a Test Case', *Journal of Biblical Literature* 127 (2008), pp. 241-65.

Lewis, Jack P., 'What Do We Mean by Jabneh?', *Journal of Bible and Religion* 32 (1964), pp. 125-32.

—'Jamnia Revisited', in *The Canon Debate* (ed. Lee M. McDonald and James A. Sanders; Peabody, MA: Hendrickson Publishers, 2002), pp. 146-62.

Lim, Bo H., 'Which Version of the Twelve Prophets Should Christians Read? A Case for Reading the LXX Twelve Prophets', *Journal of Theological Interpretation* 7 (2013), pp. 21-36.

Lindemann, Andreas, 'Die Sammlung der Paulusbriefe im 1. Und 2. Jahrhundert', in *The Biblical Canons* (ed. J.M. Auwers and H.J. de Jonge; Leuven: Leuven University Press, 2003), pp. 321-52.

Lindong, Zhang, '"The Intentional Fallacy" Reconsidered', *Canadian Social Science* 8 (2012), pp. 34-39.

Logan, Marie-Rose, '"Ut Figura Poiesis": The Work of Gérard Genette', in Gérard Genette, *Figures of Literary Discourse* (trans. Alan Sheridan; New York: Columbia University Press, 1982), pp. vii-xix.

Longman, Tremper, 'Merism', in *Dictionary of the Old Testament: Wisdom, Poetry, and Writings* (ed. Tremper Longman and Peter Enns; Downers Grove, IL: InterVarsity Press, 2008), pp. 464-66.

Lust, Johan, 'Septuagint and Canon', in *The Biblical Canons* (ed. J.M. Auwers and H.J. de Jonge; Leuven: Leuven University Press, 2003), pp. 39-55.

Luther, Martin, 'The Sermon the Risen Christ Preached to his Disciples', in *The Complete Sermons of Martin Luther* (ed. John Nicholas Lenker; trans. John Nicholas Lenker, *et al.*; Grand Rapids, MI: Baker, 2000), II/1, pp. 292-300.

May, Jordan D., 'The Four Pillars: The Fourfold Gospel Before the Time of Irenaeus', *Trinity Journal* 30 (2009), pp. 67-79.

McClean, Adrienne L., 'Kuleshov Effect', in *Critical Dictionary of Film and Television Theory* (ed. Roberta E. Pearson and Philip Simpson; London and New York: Routledge, 2001), pp. 254-55.

Maclean, Marie, 'Pretexts and Paratexts: The Art of the Peripheral', *New Literary History* 22 (1991), pp. 273-79.

McDonald, Lee Martin, and James A. Sanders, 'Introduction', in *The Canon Debate* (ed. Lee M. McDonald and James A. Sanders; Peabody, MA: Hendrickson Publishers, 2002), pp. 3-17.

McDonald, Lee Martin, 'The First Testament: Its Origin, Adaptability, and Stability', in *From Tradition to Interpretation: Studies in Biblical Intertextuality in Honor of James A. Sanders* (ed. C.A. Evans and S. Talmon; Biblical Interpretation Series, 18; Leiden: Brill, 1997), pp. 287-326.

—'Appendix A: Primary Sources for the Study of the Old Testament/Hebrew Bible Canon', in *The Canon Debate* (ed. Lee M. McDonald and James A. Sanders; Peabody, MA: Hendrickson Publishers, 2002), pp. 580-82.

—'Appendix B: Primary Sources for the Study of the New Testament Canon', in *The Canon Debate* (ed. Lee M. McDonald and James A. Sanders; Peabody, MA: Hendrickson Publishers, 2002), pp. 583-84.

—'Appendix C: Lists and Catalogues of Old Testament Collections', in *The Canon Debate* (ed. Lee M. McDonald and James A. Sanders; Peabody, MA: Hendrickson Publishers, 2002), pp. 585-90.

—'Appendix D: Lists and Catalogues of New Testament Collections', in *The Canon Debate* (ed. Lee M. McDonald and James A. Sanders; Peabody, MA: Hendrickson Publishers, 2002), pp. 591-98.

—'Identifying Scripture and Canon in the Early Church: The Criteria Question', in *The Canon Debate* (ed. Lee M. McDonald and James A. Sanders; Peabody, MA: Hendrickson Publishers, 2002), pp. 416-39.

—'The Gospels in Early Christianity: Their Origin, Use, and Authority', in *Reading the Gospels Today* (ed. Stanley E. Porter; Grand Rapids, MI: Eerdmans, 2004), pp. 150-78.

—'Canon', in *The Oxford Handbook of Biblical Studies* (ed. J.W. Rogerson and J.M. Lieu; Oxford: Oxford University Press, 2006), pp. 777-809.

—'Wherein Lies Authority? A Discussion of Books, Texts, and Translations', in *Exploring the Origins of the Bible: Canon Formation in Historical, Literary, and Theological Perspective* (ed. Craig A. Evans and Emanuel Tov; Grand Rapids, MI: Baker, 2008), pp. 203-240.

McLoughlin, Kate, and Carl Gardner, 'When is Authorial Intention Not Authorial Intention?', *European Journal of English Studies* 11 (2007), pp. 93-105.

McKechnie, Paul, 'The Career of Joshua Ben Sira', *Journal of Theological Studies* 51 (2000), pp. 3-26.

Mead, Richard T., 'A Dissenting Opinion about Respect for Context in Old Testament Quotations', *New Testament Studies* 10 (1964), pp. 279-89.

Meade, David G., 'Ancient Near Eastern Apocalypticism and the Origins of the New Testament Canon of Scripture', in *The Bible as a Human Witness to Divine Revelation: Hearing the Word of God Through Historically Dissimilar Traditions* (ed. Randall Heskett and Brian Irwin; Library of Biblical Studies; London: T. & T. Clark, 2010), pp. 302-21.

Meier, John P., 'The Inspiration of Scripture: But What Counts as Scripture?', *MidStream* 38 (1999), pp. 71-78.

Merz, Annette, 'The Fictitious Self-Exposition of Paul: How Might Intertextual Theory Suggest a Reformulation of the Hermeneutics of Pseudepigraphy?', in *The Intertextuality of the Epistles: Explorations of Theory and Practice* (ed. Thomas L. Brodie, Dennis R. MacDonald and Stanley E. Porter; New Testament Monographs, 16; Sheffield: Sheffield Phoenix Press, 2006), pp. 113-32.

Metzger, Bruce M., 'Canon of the New Testament', in *Dictionary of the Bible* (ed. F.C. Grant and H.H. Rowley; Edinburgh: T. & T. Clark, 1963), pp. 123-27.

Michels, James, 'Roland Barthes: Against Language', *ETC: A Review of General Semantics* 52 (1995), pp. 155-73.

Moloney, Francis J., 'Who is "The Reader" In/Of The Fourth Gospel?', *Australian Biblical Review* 40 (1992), pp. 20-33.

Moore, Stephen D., 'A Modest Manifesto for New Testament Literary Criticism: How to Interface with a Literary Studies Field that is Post-Literary, Post-Theoretical, and Post-Methodological', *Biblical Interpretation* 15 (2007), pp. 1-25.

Morgan, Thaïs E., 'Is There an Intertext in this Text? Literary and Interdisciplinary Approaches to Intertextuality', *American Journal of Semiotics* 3 (1985), pp. 1-40.

Moyise, Steve, 'Intertextuality and the Study of the Old Testament in the New Testament', in *The Old Testament in the New Testament: Essays in Honour of J.L. North* (ed. Steve Moyise; Journal for the Study of the New Testament Supplement Series, 189; London: T. & T. Clark, 2000), pp. 14-41.

—'Intertextuality and Biblical Studies: A Review', *Verbum et Ecclesia* 23 (2002), pp. 418-31.

—'Intertextuality and Historical Approaches to the Use of Scripture in the New Testament', in *Reading the Bible Intertextually* (ed. Stefan Alkier, Leroy A. Huizenga and Richard Hays; Waco, TX: Baylor University Press, 2009), pp. 23-32.

–'Models for Intertextual Interpretation of Revelation', in *Revelation and the Politics of Apocalyptic Interpretation* (ed. Richard B. Hays and Stefan Alkier; Waco, TX: Baylor University Press, 2012), pp. 31-45.

Neale, Stephen, 'Paul Grice and the Philosophy of Language', *Linguistics and Philosophy* 15 (1992), pp. 509-59.

Nelles, William, 'Historical and Implied Authors and Readers', *Comparative Literature* 45 (1993), pp. 22-46.

Nickelsburg, George W.E., 'Tobit, Genesis, and the Odyssey: A Complex Web of Intertextuality', in *Mimesis and Intertextuality in Antiquity and Christianity* (ed. Dennis R. MacDonald; Harrisburg, PA: Trinity Press International, 2001), pp. 41-55.

Nicklas, Tobias, '"The Words of the Prophecy of this Book": Playing with Scriptural Authority in the Book of Revelation', in *Authoritative Scriptures in Ancient Judaism* (ed. M. Popović; Leiden and Boston: Brill, 2010), pp. 309-26.

—'The Apocalypse in the Framework of the Canon', in *Revelation and the Politics of Apocalyptic Interpretation* (ed. Richard B. Hays and Stefan Alkier; Waco, TX: Baylor University Press, 2012), pp. 143-53.

O'Neil, Linda, 'Hermeneutic Haunting: E.D. Hirsch, Jr and the Ghost of Interpretive Validity', *Educational Studies* 47 (2011), pp. 451-68.

Orlinsky, Harry M., 'Some Terms in the Prologue to Ben Sira and the Hebrew Canon', *Journal of Biblical Literature* 110 (1991), pp. 483-90.

Oxman, Elena, 'Sensing the Image: Roland Barthes and the Affect of the Visual', *Substance: A Review of Theory & Literary Criticism* 39 (2010), pp. 71-90.

Paul, Ian, 'The Use of the Old Testament in Revelation 12', in *The Old Testament in the New Testament: Essays in Honour of J.L. North* (ed. Steve Moyise; Journal for the Study of the New Testament Supplement Series, 189; Sheffield: Sheffield Academic Press, 2000), pp. 256-76.

Paulien, Jon, 'Elusive Allusions: The Problematic Use of the Old Testament in Revelation', *Biblical Research* 22 (1988), pp. 37-53.

—'Criteria and Assessment of Allusions to the Old Testament in the Book of Revelation', in *Studies in the Book of Revelation* (ed. Steve Moyise; Edinburgh: T. & T. Clark, 2001), pp. 113-29.

—'Elusive Allusions in the Apocalypse: Two Decades of Research into John's Use of the Old Testament', in *The Intertextuality of the Epistles: Explorations of Theory and Practice* (ed. Thomas L. Brodie, Dennis R. MacDonald and Stanley E. Porter; New Testament Monographs, 16; Sheffield: Sheffield Phoenix Press, 2006), pp. 61-68.

Payne, Phillip Barton, 'The Fallacy of Equating Meaning with the Human Author's Intention', *Journal of the Evangelical Theological Society* 20 (1977), pp. 243-53.

Peckham, John C., 'The Canon and Biblical Authority: A Critical Comparison of Two Models of Canonicity', *Trinity Journal* 28 (2007), pp. 229-49.

—'Intrinsic Canonicity and the Inadequacy of the Community Approach to Canon-Determination', *Themelios* 36 (2011), pp. 203-15.

Peels, H.G.L., 'The Blood "from Abel to Zechariah" (Matthew 23,35; Luke 11, 50f.) and the Canon of the Old Testament', *Zeitschrift für die alttestamentliche Wissenschaft* 113 (2001), pp. 583-601.

Pfister, Manfred, 'Konzepte der Intertextualität', in *Intertextualität: Formen, Funktionen, Anglistische Fallstudien* (ed. Ulrich Broich and Manfred Pfister; Sprach- und Literaturwissenschaft, 35; Tübingen: Niemeyer, 1985), pp. 1-30.

Phillips, Peter, 'Biblical Studies and Intertextuality: Should the Work of Genette and Eco Broaden our Horizons?', in *The Intertextuality of the Epistles: Explorations of Theory and Practice* (ed. Thomas L. Brodie, Dennis R. MacDonald and Stanley E. Porter; New Testament Monographs, 16; Sheffield: Sheffield Phoenix Press, 2006), pp. 35-45.

Pickup, Martin, 'New Testament Interpretation of the Old Testament: The Theological Rationale of Midrashic Exegesis', *Journal of the Evangelical Theological Society* 51 (2008), pp. 253-82.

Pippin, Tina, 'Jezebel Re-Vamped', in *A Feminist Companion to Samuel and Kings* (ed. Athalya Brenner; Sheffield: Sheffield Academic Press, 1994), pp. 196-206.

Porter, Stanley E., 'Why Hasn't Reader-Response Criticism Caught On in New Testament Studies?', *Literature and Theology* 4 (1990), pp. 278-92.

—'Allusions and Echoes', in *As it is Written: Studying Paul's Use of Scripture* (ed. Stanley E. Porter and Christopher D. Stanley; Atlanta, GA: Society of Biblical Literature, 2008), pp. 29-40.

—'Reader-Response Criticism and New Testament Study: A Response to A.C. Thiselton's *New Horizons in Hermeneutics*', *Literature and Theology* 8 (1994), pp. 94-102.

—'Literary Approaches to the New Testament: From Formalism to Deconstruction and Back', in *Approaches to New Testament Study* (ed. Stanley E. Porter and David Tombs; Journal for the Study of the New Testament Supplement Series, 120; Sheffield: Sheffield Academic Press, 1995), pp. 77-128.

—'The Use of the Old Testament in the New Testament: A Brief Comment on Method and Terminology', in *Early Christian Interpretation of the Scriptures of Israel: Investigations and Proposals* (ed. Craig A. Evans and James A. Sanders; Journal for the Study of the New Testament Supplement Series, 14; Sheffield: Sheffield Academic Press, 1997), pp. 79-96.

—'When and How was the Pauline Canon Compiled? An Assessment of Theories', in *The Pauline Canon* (ed. Stanley E. Porter; Pauline Studies Series, 1; Leiden: Brill, 2004), pp. 95-128.

—'Further Comments on the Use of the Old Testament in the New Testament', in *The Intertextuality of the Epistles: Explorations of Theory and Practice* (ed. Thomas L. Brodie, Dennis R. MacDonald and Stanley E. Porter; New Testament Monographs, 16; Sheffield: Sheffield Phoenix Press, 2006), pp. 98-110.

—'Paul and the Process of Canonization', in *Exploring the Origins of the Bible: Canon Formation in Historical, Literary, and Theological Perspective* (ed. Craig A. Evans and Emanuel Tov; Grand Rapids, MI: Baker, 2008), pp. 173-202.

Provan, Ian, 'Canons to the Left of Him: Brevard Childs, His Critics, and the Future of Old Testament Theology', *Scottish Journal of Theology* 50 (1997), pp. 1-38.

Riffaterre, Michael, 'La Trace de l'intertexte', *La Pensée* 215 (1980), pp. 4-18.

—'Compulsory Reader Response: The Intertextual Drive', in *Intertextuality: Theories and Practices* (ed. Michael Worton and Judith Still; Manchester: Manchester University Press, 1990), pp. 56-78.

Rosebury, B., 'Irrecoverable Intentions and Literary Interpretation', *British Journal of Aesthetics* 37 (1997), pp. 15-30.

Rossman, Jae, 'Reading Outside the Lines: Paratextual Analysis and Artists' Books', *Journal of Arts and Books* 23 (2008), pp. 30-41.

Rowe, C. Kavin, 'Biblical Pressure and Trinitarian Hermeneutics', *Pro Ecclesia* 11 (2002), pp. 295-312.

—'History, Hermeneutics and the Unity of Luke–Acts', *JSNT* 28 (2005), pp. 131-57.

—'Literary Unity and Reception History: Reading Luke–Acts as Luke and Acts', *JSNT* 29 (2007), pp. 449-57.

Royse, James R., 'The Early Text of Paul (and Hebrews)', in *The Early Text of the New Testament* (ed. Charles E. Hill and Michael J. Kruger; Oxford: Oxford University Press, 2012), pp. 175-203.

Rüger, Hans Peter, 'The Extent of the Old Testament Canon', *The Bible Translator* 40 (1989), pp. 301-308.

Sæbø, Magne, 'Vom "Zusammen-Denken" zum Kanon. Aspekte der traditions-geschichtlichen Endstadien des Alten Testaments', in *Zum Problem des Biblischen Kanons* (ed. Ingo Baldermann; Neukirchen–Vluyn: Neukirchener Verlag, 1988), pp. 115-33.

Sailhamer, John H., 'The Messiah and the Hebrew Bible', *Journal of the Evangelical Theological Society* 44 (2001), pp. 5-23.

—'Biblical Theology and the Composition of the Hebrew Bible', in *Biblical Theology: Retrospect and Prospect* (ed. Scott J. Hafemann; Downers Grove, IL: InterVarsity Press, 2002), pp. 25-37.

Sanders, James A., 'Adaptable for Life: The Nature and Function of Canon', in *Magnalia Dei: The Mighty Acts of God. Essays on Bible and Archaeology in Memory of G.E. Wright* (ed. Frank Moore Cross, Werner E. Lemke, and Patrick D. Miller, Jr; New York: Doubleday, 1976), pp. 531-60.

—'Canon: Hebrew Bible', in *The Anchor Bible Dictionary* (ed. David Noel Freedman; 6 vol.; New Haven, CT: Yale University Press, 1992), I, pp. 837-52.

—'The Issue of Closure in the Canonical Process', in *The Canon Debate* (ed. Lee M. McDonald and James A. Sanders; Peabody, MA: Hendrickson Publishers, 2002), pp. 252-63.

Sarna, Nahum M., 'The Order of the Books', in *Studies in Honor of I. Edward Kiev* (ed. Charles Berlin; New York: Ktav Publishing House, 1971), pp. 407-13.

Schmidt, Daryl D., 'The Greek New Testament as a Codex', in *The Canon Debate* (ed. Lee M. McDonald and James A. Sanders; Peabody, MA: Hendrickson Publishers, 2002), pp. 469-84.

Schneemelcher, Wilhelm, 'Bibel III. Die Entstehung des Kanons des Neuen Testaments und der christlichen Bibel', in *Theologische Realenzyklopädie* (ed. G. Krause and G. Müller; 36 vol.; Berlin: W. de Gruyter, 1980), VI, pp. 22-48.

—'General Introduction', in *New Testament Apocrypha* (ed. Wilhelm Schneemelcher; 2 vol.; Louisville, KY: Westminster/John Knox Press, 1991), I, pp. 9-76.

Schröter, J., 'Die Apostelgeschichte und die Entstehung des neutestamentlichen Kanons. Beobachtungen zur Kanonisierung der Apostelgeschichte und ihrer Bedeutung als kanonischer Schrift', in *The Biblical Canons* (ed. J.M. Auwers and H.J. de Jonge; Leuven: Leuven University Press, 2003), pp. 395-430.

Schwáb, Zoltán, 'Mind the Gap: The Impact of Wolfgang Iser's Reader-Response Criticism on Biblical Studies—A Critical Assessment', *Literature and Theology* 17 (2003), pp. 170-81.

Schwering, Gregor, '"Achtung vor dem Paratext!" Gérard Genettes Konzeption und H.C. Artmanns Dialektidichtung', in *Paratexte in Literatur, Film, Fernsehen* (ed. Klaus Kreimeier and Georg Stanitzek; Berlin: Akademie Verlag, 2004), pp. 165-78.

Scobie, Charles H., 'A Canonical Approach to Interpreting Luke: The Journey Motif as a Hermeneutical Key', in *Reading Luke: Interpretation, Reflection, Formation* (ed. Craig G. Bartholomew, Joel B. Green and Anthony Thiselton; Scripture and Hermeneutics Series, 6; Grand Rapids, MI: Zondervan, 2005), pp. 327-49.

Seeligmann, Isaac L., 'Voraussetzungen der Midraschexegese', *Supplements to Vetus Testamentum* 1 (1953), pp. 150-81.

Seitz, Christopher R., 'Two Testaments and the Failure of One Tradition History', in *Figured Out: Typology and Providence in Christian Scripture* (ed. Christopher R. Seitz; Louisville, KY: Westminster/John Knox Press, 2001), pp. 35-47.

—'Canonical Approach', in *Dictionary for Theological Interpretation of the Bible* (ed. Kevin J. Vanhoozer; Grand Rapids, MI: Baker, 2005), pp. 100-102.

—'The Canonical Approach and Theological Interpretation', in *Canon and Biblical Interpretation* (ed. Craig G. Bartholomew, Scott Hahn, Robin Parry, Christopher Seitz and Al Wolters; Scripture and Hermeneutics Series, 7; Grand Rapids, MI: Zondervan, 2006), pp. 58-110.

Shepherd, Michael B., 'Compositional Analysis of the Twelve', *Zeitschrift für die alttestamentliche Wissenschaft* 120 (2008), pp. 184-93.

Sheppard, Gerald T., 'Canon Criticism: The Proposal of Brevard Childs and an Assessment for Evangelical Hermeneutics', *Studia Biblica et Theologica* 4 (1974), pp. 3-17.

—'The Epilogue to Qoheleth as Theological Commentary', *Catholic Biblical Quarterly* 39 (1977), pp. 182-89.

—'Canonization: Hearing the Voice of the Same God through Historically Dissimilar Traditions', *Ex Auditu* 1 (1985), pp. 106-14.

—'Canon', in *Encyclopedia of Religion* (ed. Mircea Eliade; New York: Macmillan Publishing Company, 1987), III, pp. 62-69.

—'Theology and the Book of the Psalms', *Interpretation* 46 (1992), pp. 143-55.

Skeat, Theodore C., 'Early Christian Book-Production: Papyri and Manuscripts', in *The Cambridge History of the Bible* (ed. Peter R. Ackroyd and C.F Evans; Cambridge: Cambridge University Press, 1969), II, pp. 54-79.

—'The Length of the Standard Papyrus Roll and the Cost-Advantage of the Codex', *Zeitschrift für Papyrologie und Epigraphik* 45 (1982), pp. 169-76.

—'Irenaeus and the Four-Gospel Canon', *Novum Testamentum* 34 (1992), pp. 194-99.

—'A Codicological Analysis of the Chester Beatty Papyrus Codex of the Gospels and Acts (P⁴⁵)', *Hermathena* 155 (1993), pp. 27-43.

—'The Origin of the Christian Codex', *Zeitschrift für Papyrologie und Epigraphik* 102 (1994), pp. 263-68.

—'The Oldest Manuscript of the Four Gospels?', *New Testament Studies* 43 (1997), pp. 1-34.

Smith, D. Moody, 'John, the Synoptics, and the Canonical Approach to Exegesis', in *Tradition and Interpretation in the New Testament* (ed. Gerald F. Hawthorne and Otto Betz; Grand Rapids, MI: Eerdmans, 1987), pp. 166-80.

—'When Did the Gospels Become Scripture?', *Journal of Biblical Literature* 119 (2000), pp. 3-20.

Smith, Greg M., 'Moving Explosions: Metaphors of Emotion in Sergei Eisenstein's Writings', *Quarterly Review of Film and Video* 21 (2004), pp. 303-15.

Smith, Jonathan Z., 'Sacred Persistence: Toward a Redescription of Canon', in *Imagining Religion: From Babylon to Jonestown* (Chicago: Chicago University Press, 1982), pp. 36-52.

—'Canons, Catalogues and Classics', in *Canonization and Decanonization* (ed. A. van der Kooij and K. van der Toorn; Studies in the History of Religions, 82; Leiden: Brill, 1998), pp. 295-311.

Söding, Thomas, 'Inmitten der Theologie des Neuen Testaments: Zu den Voraussetungen Und Zielen Neutestamentlicher Exegese', *New Testament Studies* 42 (1996), pp. 161-84.

—'Der Kanon des alten und neuen Testaments. Zur Frage nach seinem theologischen Anspruch', in *The Biblical Canons* (ed. J.M. Auwers and H.J. de Jonge; Leuven: Leuven University Press, 2003), pp. xlvii-lxxxvii.

Somner, Benjamin D., 'Allusions and Illusions: The Unity of the Book of Isaiah in Light of Deutero-Isaiah's Use of Prophetic Tradition', in *New Visions of Isaiah* (ed. Roy F. Melugin and Marvin A. Sweeney; Journal for the Study of the Old Testament Supplements Series, 214; Sheffield: Sheffield Academic Press, 1996), pp. 156-86.

Spellman, Ched, 'The Canon after Google: Implications of a Digitized and Destabilized Codex', in *Princeton Theological Review* 16 (2010), pp. 39-42.

Stanitzek, Georg, 'Texte, Paratexte, in Medien: Einleitung', in *Paratexte in Literatur, Film, Fernsehen* (ed. Klaus Kreimeier and Georg Stanitzek; Berlin: Akademie Verlag, 2004), pp. 3-20.

—'Texts and Paratexts in Media', trans. Ellen Klein, *Critical Inquiry* 32 (2005), pp. 27-42.

Stanton, Graham N., 'The Fourfold Gospel', *New Testament Studies* 43 (1997), pp. 317-46.

—'Jesus Traditions and Gospels in Justin Martyr and Irenaeus', in *The Biblical Canons* (ed. J.M. Auwers and H.J. de Jonge; Leuven: Leuven University Press, 2003), pp. 353-70.

Steck, O.H., 'Der Kanon des Hebräischen Alten Testament', in *Vernuft und Glauben* (ed. J. Rohls; Göttingen: Vandenhoeck & Ruprecht, 1988), pp. 231-52.

Steins, Georg, 'Der Bibelkanon als Denkmal und Text: Zu einigen methodologischen Aspekten kanonischer Schriftauslegung', in *The Biblical Canons* (ed. J.M. Auwers and H.J. de Jonge; Leuven: Leuven University Press, 2003), pp. 177-98.

—'Der Kanon ist der erste Kontext: Oder, Zurück an den Anfang!', *Bibel und Kirche* 62 (2007), pp. 116-21.

—'Kanon und Anamnese: Auf dem Weg zu einer Neuen Biblischen Theologie', in *Der Bibelkanon in der Bibelauslegung: Methodenreflexien und Beispielexegesen* (ed. Egbert Ballhorn and Georg Steins; Stuttgart: Kohlhammer, 2007), pp. 110-29.

—'Kanonisch-Intertextuelle Bibellektüre—My Way', in *Intertextualität: Perspektiven auf ein interdisziplinäres Arbeitsfeld* (ed. Karin Herrmann and Sandra Hübenthal; Aachen: Shaker, 2007), pp. 55-68.

—'Zwei Konzepte—ein Kanon. Neue Theorien zur Entstehung und Eigenart der Hebräischen Bibel', in *Kanonisierung—die Hebräische Bibel im Werden* (ed. Georg Steins and Johannes Taschner; Biblisch-Theologische Studien, 110; Göttingen: Neukirchener Theologie, 2010), pp. 8-45.

Stendahl, Krister, 'The Apocalypse of John and the Epistles of Paul in the Muratorian Fragment', in *Current Issues in New Testament Interpretation* (ed. William Klassen; New York: Harper & Brothers, 1962), pp. 239-45.

Stone, Timothy J., 'The Biblical Canon According to Lee McDonald: An Evaluation', *European Journal of Theology* 18 (2009), pp. 55-64.

Stout, Jeffrey, 'What is the Meaning of a Text?', *New Literary History* 14 (1982), pp. 1-12.

Suh, Robert H., 'The Use of Ezekiel 37 in Ephesians 2', *Journal of the Evangelical Theological Society* 50 (2007), pp. 715-33.

Sundberg, A.C., 'The "Old Testament": A Christian Canon', *Catholic Biblical Quarterly* 30 (1968), pp. 143-55.

—'Towards a Revised History of the New Testament Canon', in *Studia Evangelica 4* (ed. F.L. Cross; Berlin: Akademie Verlag, 1968), pp. 452-61.

—'The Making of the New Testament Canon', in *The Interpreter's One-Volume Commentary on the Bible* (ed. George A. Buttrick and Charles M. Laymon; Nashville, TN: Abingdon Press, 1971), pp. 1216-24.

—'Canon Muratori: A Fourth Century List', *Harvard Theological Review* 66 (1973), pp. 1-41.

Tannen, Deborah, 'What is a Frame? Surface Evidence for Underlying Expectations', in *Framing in Discourse* (ed. Deborah Tannen; Oxford: Oxford University Press, 1993), pp. 14-56.

Taschner, Johannes, 'Das Deuteronomium als Abschluss der Tora', in *Kanonisierung—die Hebräische Bibel im Werden* (ed. Georg Steins and Johannes Taschner; Göttingen: Neukirchener Theologie, 2010), pp. 46-63.

—'"Fügt nichts zu dem hinzu, was ich euch gebiete, und streicht nichts heraus!" Die Kanonformel in Deuteronomium 4,2 als hermeneutischer Schlüssel der Tora', in *Kanonisierung—die Hebräische Bibel im Werden* (ed. Georg Steins and Johannes Tascher; Göttingen: Neukirchener Theologie, 2010), pp. 64-92.

Thiemann, Ronald, 'Radiance and Obscurity in Biblical Narrative', in *Scriptural Authority and Narrative Interpretation* (ed. Garrett Green; Philadelphia, PA: Fortress Press, 1987), pp. 21-41.

Thompson, Michael B., 'The Holy Internet: Communication Between Churches in the First Christian Generation', in *The Gospels for All Christians: Rethinking the Gospel Audiences* (ed. Richard Bauckham; Grand Rapids, MI: Eerdmans, 1998), pp. 49-70.

Thompson, Richard P., 'Scripture, Christian Canon, and Community: Rethinking Theological Interpretation Canonically', *Journal of Theological Interpretation* 4 (2010), pp. 253-72.

Thurén, Lauri, 'John Chrysostom as a Rhetorical Critic: The Hermeneutics of an Early Father', *Biblical Interpretation* 9 (2001), pp. 180-218.

Tolhurst, William, 'On What a Text Is And How It Means', *The British Journal of Aesthetics* 19 (1979), pp. 3-14.

Tompkins, Jane P., 'The Reader in History: The Changing Shape of Literary Response', in *Reader-Response Criticism: From Formalism to Post-Structuralism* (ed. Jane P. Tompkins; Baltimore, MD: The Johns Hopkins University Press, 1980), pp. 201-32.

Tov, Emanuel, 'Scribal Practices and Physical Aspects of the Dead Sea Scrolls', in *The Bible as a Book* (ed. J.L. Sharpe and K. van Kampen; London: Oak Knoll, 1998), pp. 45-60.

—'Scribal Practices Reflected in the Texts from the Judean Desert', in *The Dead Sea Scrolls after Fifty Years: A Comprehensive Assessment* (ed. Peter W. Flint and J.C. VanderKam; Leiden: Brill, 1998), I, pp. 403-29.

Trobisch, David, 'The Book of Acts as a Narrative Commentary on the Letters of the New Testament: A Programmatic Essay', in *Rethinking the Unity and Reception of Luke and Acts* (ed. Andrew F. Gregory and C. Kavin Rowe; Columbia, SC: University of South Carolina Press, 2010), pp. 119-27.

Tuckett, Christopher, 'Forty Other Gospels', in *The Written Gospel* (ed. Markus Bockmuehl and Donald A. Hagner; Cambridge: Cambridge University Press, 2005), pp. 238-53.

Ulrich, Eugene, 'The Notion and Definition of Canon', in *The Canon Debate* (ed. Lee M. McDonald and James A. Sanders; Peabody, MA: Hendrickson Publishers, 2002), pp. 21-35.

—'The Non-Attestation of a Tripartite Canon in 4QMMT', *Catholic Biblical Quarterly* 65 (2003), pp. 202-14.

Vanhoozer, Kevin J., 'From Speech Acts to Scripture Acts: The Covenant of Discourse and the Discourse of the Covenant', in *First Theology: God, Scripture & Hermeneutics* (Downers Grove, IL: InterVarsity Press, 2002), pp. 159-203.

—'Intention/Intentional Fallacy', in *Dictionary for Theological Interpretation of the Bible* (ed. Kevin J. Vanhoozer; Grand Rapids, MI: Baker, 2005), pp. 327-30.

—'Preface to the Anniversary Edition', in *Is There a Meaning in this Text? The Bible, The Reader, and the Morality of Literary Knowledge* (Landmarks in Christian Scholarship; Grand Rapids, MI: Zondervan, 2009), pp. 1-8.

Verheyden, Joseph, 'The Canon Muratori: A Matter of Dispute', in *The Biblical Canons* (ed. J.M. Auwers and H.J. de Jonge; Leuven: Leuven University Press, 2003), pp. 487-556.

—'Justin's Text of the Gospels: Another Look at the Citations in 1 Apol. 15.1-8', in *The Early Text of the New Testament* (ed. Charles E. Hill and Michael J. Kruger; Oxford: Oxford University Press, 2012), pp. 313-35.

Wagner, J. Ross, 'The Septuagint and the "Search for the Christian Bible"', in *Scripture's Doctrine and Theology's Bible: How the New Testament Shapes Christian Dogmatics* (ed. Markus Bockmuehl and Alan J. Torrance; Grand Rapids, MI: Baker, 2008), pp. 17-28.

Waltke, Bruce K., 'A Canonical Process Approach to the Psalms', in *Tradition and Testament: Essays in Honor of Charles Lee Feinberg* (ed. John S. Feinberg and Paul D. Feinberg; Chicago: Moody Press, 1981), pp. 3-18.

Wall, Robert W., 'The Acts of the Apostles in Canonical Context', in *The New Testament as Canon: A Reader in Canonical Criticism* (ed. Robert W. Wall and E. Eugene Lemcio; Journal for the Study of the New Testament Supplement Series, 76; Sheffield: Sheffield Academic, 1992), pp. 110-32.

—'The Apocalypse of the New Testament in Canonical Context', in *The New Testament as Canon: A Reader in Canonical Criticism* (ed. Robert W. Wall and E. Eugene Lemcio; Journal for the Study of the New Testament Supplement Series, 76; Sheffield: Sheffield Academic, 1992), pp. 274-98.

—'The Problem of the Multiple Letter Canon of the New Testament', in *The New Testament as Canon: A Reader in Canonical Criticism* (ed. Robert W. Wall and E. Eugene Lemcio; Journal for the Study of the New Testament Supplement Series, 76; Sheffield: Sheffield Academic, 1992), pp. 161-83.

—'Reading the New Testament in Canonical Context', in *Hearing the New Testament* (ed. Joel B. Green; Grand Rapids, MI: Eerdmans, 1995), pp. 370-93.

—'The Significance of a Canonical Perspective of the Church's Scripture', in *The Canon Debate* (ed. Lee M. McDonald and James A. Sanders; Peabody, MA: Hendrickson Publishers, 2002), pp. 528-40.

—'The Function of the Pastoral Letters Within the Pauline Canon of the New Testament: A Canonical Approach', in *The Pauline Canon* (ed. Stanley E. Porter; Pauline Studies Series, 1; Leiden: Brill, 2004), pp. 27-44.

Wasserman, Tommy, 'A Comparative Textual Analysis of P⁴ and P⁶⁴⁺⁶⁷', *Textual Criticism* 15 (2010), pp. 1-26. Online at http://rosetta.reltech.org/TC/v15/Wasserman 2010.pdf

—'The Early Text of Matthew', in *The Early Text of the New Testament* (ed. Charles E. Hill and Michael J. Kruger; Oxford: Oxford University Press, 2012), pp. 83-107.

Watkins, Evan, 'Criticism and Method: Hirsch, Frye, Barthes', *Soundings* 58 (1975), pp. 257-80.

Webster, John B., 'A Great and Meritorious Act of the Church? The Dogmatic Location of the Canon', in *Die Einheit der Schrift und die Vielfalt des Kanons: The Unity of Scripture and the Diversity of the Canon* (ed. John Barton and Michael Wolter; Berlin: W. de Gruyter, 2003), pp. 95-126.

—'Canon', in *Dictionary for Theological Interpretation of the Bible* (ed. Kevin J. Vanhoozer; Grand Rapids, MI: Baker, 2005), pp. 97-100.

—'Scripture, The Authority of', in *Dictionary for Theological Interpretation of the Bible* (ed. Kevin J. Vanhoozer; Grand Rapids, MI: Baker, 2005), pp. 724-27.

Wenham, Gordon J., 'Sanctuary Symbolism in the Garden of Eden Story', in *I Studied Inscriptions from Before the Flood: Ancient Near Eastern, Literary and Linguistic Approaches to Genesis 1-11* (ed. Richard S. Hess and David T. Tsumura; Winona Lake, IN: Eisenbrauns, 1994), pp. 399-404.

Wiles, Maurice F., 'Origen as Biblical Scholar', in *The Cambridge History of the Bible: From the Beginnings to Jerome* (ed. Peter R. Ackroyd and C.F. Evans; Cambridge: Cambridge University Press, 1993), pp. 454-89.

Williams, Peter J., 'The Bible, The Septuagint, and The Apocrypha: A Consideration of Their Singularity', in *Studies on the Text and Versions of the Hebrew Bible in Honour of Robert Gordon* (ed. Geoffrey Khan and Diana Lipton; Supplements to Vetus Testamentum, 149; Leiden: Brill, 2012), pp. 169-80.

—'"Where Two or Three Are Gathered Together": The Witness of the Early Versions', in *The Early Text of the New Testament* (ed. Charles E. Hill and Michael J. Kruger; Oxford: Oxford University Press, 2012), pp. 37-48.

Wilson, Gerald H., 'Psalms and Psalter', in *Biblical Theology: Retrospect and Prospect* (ed. Scott J. Hafemann; Downers Grove, IL: InterVarsity Press, 2002), pp. 100-10.

Wilson, Daniel W., 'Readers in Texts', *Publications of the Modern Language Association of America* 96 (1981), pp. 848-63.

Wimsatt, William K., 'Genesis: A Fallacy Revisited', in *On Literary Intention: Critical Essays Selected and Introduced* (ed. David Newton-de-Molina; Edinburgh: Edinburgh University Press, 1976), pp. 116-38.

Wimsatt, William K., and Monroe Beardsley, 'Intention', in *Dictionary of World Literature* (ed. Joseph T. Shipley; New York: Philosophical Library, 1953), pp. 229-32.

—'The Intentional Fallacy', in *On Literary Intention: Critical Essays Selected and Introduced* (ed. David Newton-de-Molina; Edinburgh: Edinburgh University Press, 1976), pp. 1-13.

Windisch, H., 'Der Apokalyptiker Johannes als Begründer des Neutestamentlichen Kanons', *Zeitschrift für die Neutestamentliche Wissenschaft* 10 (1909), pp. 148-74.

Wolters, Albert, 'Metanarrative', in *Dictionary for Theological Interpretation of the Bible* (ed. Kevin J. Vanhoozer; Grand Rapids, MI: Baker, 2005), pp. 506-507.

—'Worldview', in *Dictionary for Theological Interpretation of the Bible* (ed. Kevin J. Vanhoozer; Grand Rapids, MI: Baker, 2005), pp. 854-56.

Wrede, William, 'The Task and Methods of "New Testament Theology"', in *The Nature of New Testament Theology: The Contribution of William Wrede and Adolf Schlatter* (ed. and trans. Robert Morgan; London: SCM Press, 1973), pp. 68-116.

Wright, Benjamin G., III, 'Why a Prologue? Ben Sira's Grandson and his Greek Translation', in *Emanuel: Studies in Hebrew Bible, Septuagint, and Dead Sea Scrolls in Honor of Emanuel Tov* (ed. Weston W. Fields, Robert Kraft, Shalom M. Paul, and Lawrence H. Schiffman; Leiden: Brill, 2003), pp. 633-44.

Yarbrough, Robert W., 'The Embattled Bible: Four More Books', *Themelios* 34 (2009), pp. 6-25.

—'God's Word in Human Words: Form-Critical Reflections', in *Do Historical Matters Matter to Faith? A Critical Appraisal of Modern and Postmodern Approaches to Scripture* (ed. James K. Hoffmeier and Dennis R. Magary; Wheaton, IL: Crossway, 2012), pp. 327-44.

Yeago, David S., 'The Bible', in *Knowing the Triune God: The Work of the Spirit in the Practices of the Church* (ed. James J. Buckley and David S. Yeago; Grand Rapids, MI: Eerdmans, 2001), pp. 49-94.

Zahn, Theodor, 'The Permanent Value of the New Testament Canon for the Church', trans. Ernst P.H. Pfatteicher, *The Lutheran Church Review* 19 (1900), pp. 3-36.

—'Canon of Scripture', in *New Schaff-Herzog Encyclopedia of Religious Knowledge* (ed. S.M. Jackson; New York: Funk and Wagnalls, 1908), II, pp. 398-400.

Zenger, Erich, 'Der Psalter im Horizont von Tora und Prophetie. Kanonsgeschichtliche und kanonhermeneutische Perspecktiven', in *The Biblical Canons* (ed. J.M. Auwers and H.J. de Jonge; Leuven: Leuven University Press, 2003), pp. 111-34.

INDEXES

INDEX OF REFERENCES

OLD TESTAMENT

NEW TESTAMENT

OTHER ANCIENT REFERENCES